24362
U.S. AIR FORCE
71508
AIR FORCE
1508

The Republic F-105 Thunderchief

Wing and Squadron Histories

THE REPUBLIC
F-105 THUNDERCHIEF
WING AND SQUADRON HISTORIES

James Geer

Schiffer Military History
Atglen, PA

Dedication
This book is dedicated to those brave men who piloted Thuds into wartime skies over Southeast Asia.

Book design by Robert Biondi.

Library of Congress Catalog Number: 2002108283.

Printed in China.
ISBN: 0-7643-1668-0

We are always looking for people to write books on new and related subjects. If you have an idea for a book, please contact us at the address below.

Published by Schiffer Publishing Ltd.
4880 Lower Valley Road
Atglen, PA 19310
Phone: (610) 593-1777
FAX: (610) 593-2002
E-mail: Schifferbk@aol.com.
Visit our web site at: www.schifferbooks.com
Please write for a free catalog.
This book may be purchased from the publisher.
Please include $3.95 postage.
Try your bookstore first.

In Europe, Schiffer books are distributed by:
Bushwood Books
6 Marksbury Ave.
Kew Gardens
Surrey TW9 4JF
England
Phone: 44 (0)208 392-8585
FAX: 44 (0)208 392-9876
E-mail: Bushwd@aol.com.
Free postage in the UK. Europe: air mail at cost.
Try your bookstore first.

Contents

Introduction

Designed as a nuclear strike fighter, the Republic F-105 Thunderchief became operational with the USAF in 1959. Although its early career was troublesome, the Thud was deployed worldwide to units in Europe and the Far East during the early 1960s. More than 800 F-105s were built, and the aircraft equipped seven operational wings during its peak years as the prime tactical fighter of the USAF. The Thud gained legendary status when it was called into action as a carrier of conventional weapons during the Vietnam War. It flew more strikes against North Vietnam than any other aircraft and was employed as a suppresser of enemy air defenses in the Wild Weasel role. Operating against the heavily defended targets in the North was costly. By the time the war ended, a total of over 350 Thuds had been lost in combat.

This book is not a study on the development, testing, and technical aspects of the F-105; that story has been told. Instead, this work provides brief histories for all wings and squadrons that flew the Thud. The idea to detail unit histories came about from my own desire to understand the aircraft's unique story, especially its role in the initial phases of the war in Southeast Asia. Accurate information on early squadron deployments and operations was not readily available; hence, I began gathering every scrap of information about the F-105 and its crews I could find in an effort to piece the story together. Inevitably, the discoveries from more than ten years of research led to the thought of writing a book.

A project like this cannot be completed without the help of many people. I give special thanks to my father, Jerry Geer, who offered unrelenting encouragement and support. This book would not have been possible without his photographs, files, library, and contacts. I am also especially indebted to Robert Robinson, who spent endless hours preparing the color artwork for this volume. Any study about the F-105 must include input from the men who flew this superb airplane. Thanks go the Rex Dull, John Schaub, Willie Secker, Vic Vizcarra, Don Ware, and George Weeks for taking time to answer questions from a previously unknown stranger. Each spoke with fondness in recollecting their experience with the Thud, and their firsthand accounts and records have made this book complete.

Other contributors of information and photographs include Joe Bruch, John Davis, Robert F. Dorr, Yukio Enomoto, Stewart Hurd, Marty Isham, JEM Aviation Slides, Kansas Air Museum, Jack Keefer, Richard Kierbow, Don Kutyna, Don Logan, Terry Love, Frank MacSorley, Toyokazu Matsuzaki, David Menard, Kirk Minert, Paul Minert, Merle Olmstead, Doug Olson, Fred Retter, Matsuro Shimozato, Hiroshi Suzuki, Yasuhiko Takahashi, and Norm Taylor. Every effort was made to credit the original photographers of the images contained in this coverage of the F-105. Any oversights will be corrected in subsequent printings. Alec Fushi, Randy Troutman, and Rick Versteeg provided the unit patches for this book.

Finally, to my wife Amy and my children Ethan and Kylie, my thanks for your support and understanding of the time necessary to complete this book.

CHAPTER ONE

4th Tactical Fighter Wing

The 4th Tactical Fighter Wing (TFW) history dates back to the Second World War in England as the 4th Fighter Group, part of the Eighth Air Force. Formed on 12 September 1942, the unit operated Spitfires, P-47s, and P-51s in succession. Upon conclusion of the war, the group returned to the U.S. and was inactivated during November 1945.

The unit was activated again on 9 September 1947 at Selfridge Field, Michigan as the 4th Fighter Group flying the F-80. Moving several times over the next three years, it was redesignated the 4th Fighter Interceptor Group and converted to the F-86A. Now associated with the 4th Fighter Interceptor Wing, the group relocated to the Far East when it deployed to Johnson AB, Japan in December 1950; to Suwon AB, Korea in March 1951; and then to Kimpo AB, Korea in August 1951. The group served valiantly in the Korean War and built an impressive combat record. During the war, the unit successfully transitioned to the F-86E and later the F-86F. Following the Korean armistice, the group moved to Chitose AB, Japan.

On 8 December 1958, the 4th returned to the U.S. when it took over the assets and mission of the 83rd Fighter Day Wing at Seymour Johnson AFB, North Carolina. At the time of the 4th's arrival, the 83rd was in the process of re-equipping from the F-86H to the F-100C. The transition process continued, and by mid-1958, the 4th was designated a Tactical Fighter Wing and its four squadrons–the 333rd, 334th, 335th, and 336th–had a full compliment of Super Sabres. Concurrently, the wing was chosen to be the first unit to receive Republic's new F-105B Thunderchief.

The wing entered F-105 operations by participating in a joint contractor-USAF effort to speed the aircraft from test to operational use. To accomplish this, a portion of the wing's 335th squadron temporarily relocated to Eglin AFB, Florida in May 1958 to participate in pre-operational flight tests. The 4th continued to train as a combat-ready wing with F-100Cs (and a small number of F-100Fs) while the Thunderchief was readied for service at Eglin, and it was not until 19 June 1959 that it officially accepted TAC's first F-105B at Seymour Johnson.

To punctuate the arrival of the F-105 and its entrance into operational service, the wing set out to break the world speed record for the 100-kilometer closed course during late 1959. The effort was carried out at Edwards AFB, California under Project Fast Wind. A new record was set when an F-105B flown by Brig. Gen. Joseph H. Moore, commander of the 4th TFW, attained an average speed of 1,216.48 mph on 11 December 1959.

Because of Republic's continual production problems, the wing's transition to the new aircraft was slow, forcing it to carry out its mission in both the F-100C and F-105B over an extended period of time. Throughout the long transition process, the 4th TFW maintained an excellent safety record. This resulted in the wing being awarded the Ninth Air Force Flying Safety Award in October 1958 and again in February 1959. In addition, the 4th won the USAF Flying Safety Award for operations over the period July to December 1959.

The wing had 56 F-105Bs at the end of 1959, although none of the aircraft were operationally ready until April 1960. With this limited number of aircraft available, only the 334th, 335th, and 336th TFS were equipped with the Thunderchief. The wing's early experience with the F-105B was troublesome as the reliability of the aircraft remained low during the first few years of operations due to engineering shortcomings, shortages of spare parts, and lack of maintenance skills amongst the ground crews. Temporary groundings were frequent during this time, and a program dubbed Project Optimize was initiated to correct many of the problems.

The F-105D arrived in the fall of 1960, with the first group of aircraft being dispatched to Eglin for operational tests with the 335th

TFS. Soon thereafter, deliveries to the 333rd TFS began; however, the 334th and 336th TFS did not transition to this variant until early 1964. Like the F-105B, the early production D-models suffered from many operational difficulties due to engineering deficiencies. To correct the problems, as well as improve the aircraft's conventional weapons capabilities, the USAF launched a repair and modification program known as Operation Look-Alike in mid-1962.

As a result of the presence of Russian offensive missiles in Cuba, the 4th TFW was alerted for war on 18 October 1962. Three days later, the wing deployed the 334th, 335th, and 336th TFS to McCoy AFB, Florida for anticipated strikes against the missile sites. Because many of the wing's aircraft were cycling through the Look-Alike program, the mobilization included about twenty F-105s and their aircrews from the 4520th Combat Crew Training Wing (CCTW) at Nellis AFB, Nevada. The three squadrons were placed on one-hour alert status at 4:00 am on 22 October, later to be placed on 15-minute alert that afternoon. Bombing missions never took place. Instead, the squadrons flew combat air patrol off the coast of Florida. This duty proved uneventful as they never encountered threats from opposing aircraft. Six weeks after the crisis began, Russia agreed to remove the missiles from Cuba. This allowed the squadrons to return to Seymour Johnson on 29 November 1962.

Significant events for the 4th TFW during 1963-64 included the deployment of squadrons worldwide and the acceptance of the first F-105F for front-line operational service. The overseas tours began in the spring of 1963 and involved rotational duty in Europe to support NATO defense requirements. The first F-105F was received on 23 December 1963, and this delivery gave the wing the distinction of introducing all major production variants of the Thud to combat-ready operations.

By 1965, the wing was sending squadrons to the Far East and Southeast Asia as a result of the Vietnam War. Both the 334th and 335th TFS served on temporary duty (TDY) in the region, and the demands of the war and the associated requirement to establish permanently based combat units in Southeast Asia saw the 4th TFW lose one of its squadrons in December 1965. Lost was the 333rd TFS, which was reassigned to the 355th TFW at Takhli Royal Thai Air Force Base (RTAFB), Thailand.

The mission of the 4th TFW changed to that of training F-105 replacement pilots during the spring of 1966. Around that same time, steps to re-equip the wing with the F-4D Phantom II were developed due to the need to send its F-105s to Southeast Asia as replacement aircraft. Due to the planned conversion, the wing's training function was carried out on a reduced scale. The 336th TFS gave up its Thuds in March 1966 and assumed a non-operational status until the arrival of the Phantoms. About six months later, the wing's remaining two squadrons began relinquishing their F-105s, and the last aircraft departed Seymour Johnson on 22 November 1966.

Nine different individuals led the 4th TFW during its association with the F-105. First to command was Col. Timothy F. O'Keefe (5 January 1958), followed by Brig. Gen. Joseph H. Moore (28 February 1959), Col. Albert L. Evans, Jr. (18 October 1961), Brig. Gen. Gordon M. Graham (15 July 1962), Col. John R. Murphy (16 October 1963), Col. William E. Bryan, Jr. (4 January 1965), Col. Homer C. Boles (27 January 1966), Col. William R. Eichelberger (30 May 1966), and Col. Robert V. Spencer (1 July 1966).

Shown taking off from Seymour Johnson in 1960, this specially marked F-105B (57-5782) was flown by Brig. Gen. Joseph H. Moore during his tenure as commander of the 4th TFW. (USAF via Paul Minert)

An F-105B (57-5836) of the 4th TFW cruises over the Florida landscape while participating in bombing trials out of Eglin AFB. This aircraft carries an experimental load of 500-pound Mk-82 Navy bombs. (Republic via Paul Minert)

The 4th TFW carried out two overseas deployments during the summer of 1961 to demonstrate the firepower of the F-105 for units expecting to convert to the new fighter. This F-105B (57-5821) is seen at Ramstein AB, Germany during one such operation named Thundereast. (David Menard)

Three squadrons of the 4th TFW are seen on alert during the Cuban Missile Crises in this view of the flightline at McCoy AFB, Florida on 23 October 1962. (USAF via James Geer)

This F-105D (61-0144) carried special markings while representing the 4th TFW at TAC's Fighter Weapons Meet at Nellis AFB, Nevada in September 1962. (Walter Jefferies via David Menard)

Seen here at Andrews AFB, Maryland in 1964, this F-105F (62-4423) of the 4th TFW displays the aluminized lacquer finish and standard TAC markings brought into widespread use following Operation Look-Alike. (Roger Besecker via Norm Taylor)

These "buttoned-up" 4th TFW Thuds line the ramp on a rare quiet day at Seymour Johnson in 1964. (David Menard Collection)

Two squadrons of the 4th TFW are seen on rotational combat duty in Southeast Asia in this view of the flightline at Takhli RTAFB, Thailand in early December 1965. The Thuds with blue tail bands in the near row belonged to the 334th TFS, while the aircraft in the far row with green tail bands were assigned to the 335th TFS. (USAF via James Geer)

A camouflaged F-105F (63-8321) of the 4th TFW makes a low-level pass over Wilmington, North Carolina during a training mission in September 1966. (Jim Sullivan via Jerry Geer)

333rd Tactical Fighter Squadron

The 333rd Tactical Fighter Squadron was the last component of the 4th TFW to convert to the F-105. The unit relinquished its F-100C Super Sabres in mid-1960, but unlike its sister squadrons, was not equipped with the B-model variant of the Thunderchief. Rather, the 333rd transitioned directly to the new D-model, although six months passed before the squadron received its first aircraft after giving up its Super Sabres.

During the fall of 1963, the 333rd participated in the largest transoceanic Army-USAF deployment ever made by air during a demonstration of strategic mobility for reinforcement of NATO forces. The operation was named Exercise Big Lift and involved transporting 16,000 soldiers and airmen to U.S. bases in Germany and France between 22-25 October. Altogether, 116 TAC and 240 MATS aircraft were involved in the deployment. On arrival, the services participated in a week-long field training exercise, during which time the 333rd performed low-level, close air support missions out of Chaumont AB, France.

The squadron was detached from the 4th TFW when it moved to Eglin AFB, Florida on 10 March 1964 for duty with the 4485th Composite Wing, part of the recently established USAF Tactical Air Warfare Center (TAWC). The 333rd's role at Eglin was to assist in the formation of the TAWC's function of introducing newly developed weapons into operational service with the F-105. The special nature of this assignment saw only the squadron's more experienced pilots assigned to Eglin, and those left behind were

The roar of the mighty Pratt & Whitney J-75 engine is about to fill the air as four 333rd TFS F-105Ds are seconds from beginning their take-off roll at Seymour Johnson in May 1963. (Republic via Paul Minert)

absorbed by other constituents of the 4th TFW. On or about 15 March 1965, the 333rd TFS reformed at Seymour Johnson and assumed combat-ready operations.

The escalation of the air war in Southeast Asia brought forth a new assignment for the 333rd TFS on 4 December 1965. On that day, the unit arrived without aircraft at Takhli RTAFB, Thailand on a permanent change of station (PCS) basis to serve as an element of the 355th TFW. The squadron's deployment coincided with the departure of its former sister unit, the 335th TFS, which had been serving on TDY in the region for five months. Accordingly, the 333rd gained operational control of the 335th's aircraft during a brief transition period.

Seven F-105Ds of the 333rd TFS fly in formation over Seymour Johnson in May 1963. The bare metal finish on the aircraft indicates they have yet to cycle through the Look-Alike modification program. (Republic via Paul Minert)

A 333rd TFS F-105D (62-4277) maneuvers on one of the many hardstands at Chaumont AB, France on 30 October 1963 while participating in Exercise Big Lift. (USAF via James Geer)

During the 333rd's special duty with the 4485th Composite Wing at Eglin AFB, the squadron assisted the USAF TAWC in adapting new weapons systems for operational use. This F-105D (62-4226) is about to fire a test round of 2.75-inch Mighty Mouse rockets at the Eglin Air Proving Ground in 1964. (P. Albrecht via David Menard via Jerry Geer)

334th Tactical Fighter Squadron

The 334th Tactical Fighter Squadron began transitioning to the F-105B from the F-100C Super Sabre during the summer of 1959. The switch commenced when a flight of four Thunderchiefs arrived at Seymour Johnson for service with the squadron on 16 June. Up to full strength by the fall, the unit was essentially TAC's first operational F-105 unit as the 335th TFS was serving in a test and evaluation capacity.

In July 1960, the squadron deployed to Williams AFB, Arizona to augment the 335th TFS for Category III flight testing of the F-105B's conventional armament system. These tests concentrated on the aircraft's newly modified MA-8 fire control system. Testing ended on 15 August 1960, after severe spare parts shortages greatly delayed the evaluation process. Shortly after completing Category III tests, the 334th was sent to Eglin AFB, Florida for training and qualification in the delivery of nuclear weapons. This tour was completed on 15 December 1960.

In mid-1961, the 334th TFS was tasked to support two 4th TFW overseas deployments to demonstrate the firepower of the F-105 for United States Air Forces in Europe (USAFE) and Pacific Air Forces (PACAF) units expecting to convert to the aircraft. The first mobilization involved a trip to Ramstein AB, Germany in July under Operation Thundereast. The second took place in August and saw personnel deploy to Kadena AB, Okinawa under the appropriate name Operation Thunderwest. In both instances, crews dropped a wide range of conventional ordnance while participating in local gunnery exercises.

Over the next year, the 334th carried out routine training operations to maintain combat-readiness. The squadron's ability to respond was tested in the fall of 1962 when it was alerted for war after Soviet missile sites were discovered in Cuba. Along with the 335th and 336th TFS, the unit deployed to McCoy AFB, Florida in anticipation of strikes against the missile sites. Bombing never took place, but the squadron was tasked to fly patrol missions off the coast of Florida. After tensions eased, the 334th TFS returned to Seymour Johnson on 29 November 1962.

Six F-105Bs of the 334th TFS fly a beautiful step-down formation in the North Carolina sky on 13 November 1959. (Republic via Paul Minert)

This F-105B (57-5821) is seen taxiing out for a training mission during the 334th's visit to Eglin AFB, Florida to qualify in the delivery of nuclear weapons during the fall of 1960. (G. Sommerich via Norm Taylor)

On 1 April 1963, the 334th deployed eighteen F-105Bs to Moron AB, Spain under Operation Fox Able 147. This temporary overseas assignment represented the first instance in which a TAC Thunderchief unit was tasked with rotational alert duty in support NATO commitments. At Moron, the squadron served as an element of the USAFE General War Deterrent Forces while attached to the 65th Air Division (AD). The 334th TFS concluded this deployment upon return to Seymour Johnson on 13 August 1963.

After converting to F-105D/Fs in 1964, the 334th spent nearly eight months of the next year overseas on two separate deployments. The first took place from 15 February to 29 May 1965 and saw the squadron deploy to the eastern part of the Mediterranean for another rotational tour in support of NATO defense requirements. The unit operated out of Incirlik AB, Turkey for the duration of this trip while under the control of the Seventeenth Air Force.

The second major overseas tour in 1965 involved rotational combat duty in Southeast Asia. This deployment was carried out under Operation Two Buck 18 and began when the 334th launched eighteen F-105Ds out of Homestead AFB, Florida on 28 August 1965 enroute to Takhli RTAFB, Thailand. The squadron was at Homestead to train in the tactics of pop-up weapons delivery, a bombing method that was widely used in the Vietnam War. The 334th TFS arrived in Thailand on 2 September and was immediately attached to the provisional 6235th TFW. Pilots conducted area check-out flights for four days before flying the unit's first combat sorties.

The 334th's primary role at Takhli was to support the Rolling Thunder campaign against North Vietnam, with a secondary requirement to augment Barrel Roll and Steel Tiger operations in Laos. Missions in the North during the month of September included attacks on lines of communications, army barracks, ammunition depots, and surface-to-air missile (SAM) sites. In October, the squadron carried out numerous strikes along northeast supply routes between Hanoi and China. The squadron suffered two losses on strikes in North Vietnam during its first two months of combat. The first took place on 20 September when Capt. Willis E. Forby was taken Prisoner of War (POW) after his F-105D was shot down by antiaircraft artillery (AAA) fire while attacking a bridge near Ha Tinh. Ten days later, Squadron Commander Lt. Col. Melvin J. Killian was killed when his Thud was hit by a SAM near Hanoi.

On 8 November 1965, the squadron was placed under the control of the newly arrived 355th TFW. The change had no impact on operations as the 334th continued to support the war effort by bombing Communist targets. Three additional aircraft were shot down over the North prior to the 24 December 1965 announcement of a suspension of the bombing in that region. The first of these happened on 28 November and saw Capt. Jon A. Reynolds imprisoned after his aircraft was downed by AAA fire during an armed reconnaissance mission. Three days later, Capt. Thomas E. Reitmann was killed after his Thud fell victim to intense flak during a major strike against the Cao Nung Railroad Bridge. The third shoot down occurred on a 15 December attack on the Uong Bi Thermal Power Plant, but the pilot ejected and was recovered.

From the start of the bombing pause until the end of its combat tour on 5 February 1966, the 334th TFS mainly hit transportation and supply oriented targets in Laos as the bombing of North Vietnam did not resume until 31 January 1966. During their final month of combat, the unit lost one additional aircraft while conducting an 11 January strike against a major infiltration route along the Ho Chi Minh Trail. For a second time, the setback was eased with the rescue of the pilot. When the 334th departed Takhli in early February, the squadron's role and aircraft were passed on to the newly arrived 357th TFS. During their duty in Thailand, the 334th TFS completed 2,231 combat sorties and logged nearly 5,500 combat flying hours. Weapons delivered totaled 9,920 tons of bombs, 17,031 2.75-inch rockets, and 351,547 rounds of ammunition. For its outstanding record during this deployment, the squadron received the Air Force Outstanding Unit Award with Combat "V" Device.

Two months after returning stateside, the 334th ended its operational mission and followed the 4th TFW's new directive to train F-105 pilots. For the its performance in Southeast Asia, as well as for the execution of the Replacement Training Unit (RTU) mission, the squadron was awarded the Presidential Unit Citation for the period 1 January to 10 October 1966. The 334th TFS gave up its Thuds in the late fall of 1966 and began operating the F-4D Phantom II in early 1967.

A 334th TFS F-105B (57-5834) returns to its parking spot at Ramstein AB, Germany after completing a mission during Operation Thundereast in July 1961. (David Menard)

Seen at Kadena AB, Okinawa during Operation Thunderwest, this F-105B (57-5807) of the 334th TFS carries a load of fire bombs and rocket pods for a firepower demonstration flight on 17 August 1961. (USAF via James Geer)

An F-105B (57-5837) of the 334th TFS formates with a KC-135 tanker on a cross-country hop in the early 1960s. (USAF via Paul Minert)

The markings used by the 334th TFS during their Two Buck 18 combat deployment consisted of a blue tail band with superimposed white dots as seen on this F-105D (59-1717) climbing out of Yokota AB, Japan enroute to Thailand on 25 October 1965. (Yasuhiko Takahashi)

Ground support personnel scramble around this 334th F-105D (62-4347) upon arrival at Yokota on 16 November 1965. Note the impressive number of combat mission tallies just below the intake. (Yasuhiko Takahashi)

A 334th TFS F-105D (59-1723) taxis in at Yokota after a long transit flight from Takhli RTAFB, Thailand in December 1965. (Yukio Enomoto)

This F-105D (61-0080) of the 334th TFS is about to take on fuel from a KC-135 tanker before proceeding on a Rolling Thunder mission against North Vietnam in December 1965. (USAF via Robert F. Dorr)

Two 334th Thuds (61-0127 and 62-4367) hit the tanker over Laos while enroute to North Vietnam in December 1965. (USAF via Jerry Geer)

After the U.S. suspended bombing operations against North Vietnam on Christmas Eve 1965, the 334th was relegated to striking enemy positions in Laos. Here, a flight of 334th Thuds refuels prior to hitting targets along the Ho Chi Minh Trail in January 1966 with a less than ideal load of three M117 750-pound bombs and rocket pods. (USAF via Paul Minert)

A good number of 334th TFS aircraft had been camouflaged by the time the unit entered its final month of combat duty in Southeast Asia. Seen landing at Yokota on 21 January 1966, this F-105D (62-4234) wears the new battle dress, but retains the squadron's trademark blue tail band. (Toyokazu Matsuzaki)

335th Tactical Fighter Squadron

Under the command of Lt. Col. Robert R. Scott, the F-100C-equipped 335th Fighter Day Squadron established Detachment 1 at Eglin AFB, Florida on 1 May 1958 to participate in a joint contractor-USAF effort to conduct pre-operational F-105B flight tests. With the formation of the detachment, the 335th assumed operations as a split unit as it continued to fly the Super Sabre in dwindling numbers over the next two years at Seymour Johnson.

At Eglin, Detachment 1 was teamed with members of the Weapons Systems Project Office, Air Materiel Command, Air Force Flight Test Center, Air Proving Ground Command, Air Research and Development Command, and Republic to conduct Category II flight tests for the F-105B. Although the USAF accepted the first production F-105B on 27 May 1958 at Republic's Farmingdale plant in Long Island, New York, it was not until August of that year that the aircraft was accepted by the 335th to commence operational tests at Eglin. Fittingly, one month prior to receiving their first Thunderchief, the 335th was redesignated a Tactical Fighter Squadron.

This early production F-105B (54-0111) was the first aircraft to be delivered to Detachment 1, 335th TFS and carried special publicity markings that saw the unit's Indian head motif positioned over a narrow green tail band. (Republic via Paul Minert)

Seen at Eglin AFB, Florida in 1959, these F-105Bs from Detachment 1, 335th TFS display the unit's standard markings: broad green tail band, green nose band, and Indian head motif on the forward fuselage. (Republic via Paul Minert)

The Category II evaluation program was plague by a series of problems from the outset. Issues such as poor program management and difficulties in overcoming advanced technological shortcomings greatly delayed the process. After special tests were conducted on the unproven components of the weapons system, the results often called for the incorporation of modifications, causing constant delays in the program. Compounding the problem was Republic's production slippages, which slowed the 335th's build-up of a complete squadron of eighteen F-105Bs until mid-1959.

Although originally scheduled to end by 30 November 1959, Category II tests were not completed until 30 March 1960. Four additional tests, properly part of Category II, were carried out over the next two months under an amended directive. Around the same time, the 335th TFS closed out F-100 operations at Seymour Johnson. Consequently, the squadron was detached from the 4th TFW on 1 May 1960 and placed under the control of Headquarters TAC. This action ended the split nature of the unit's operations, and Detachment 1 was discontinued.

In late July 1960, the 335th TFS deployed to Nellis AFB, Nevada to carry out Category III tests on the F-105B's weapons system. Focusing of the aircraft's newly modified fire-control system, the Category III tests were completed on 15 August after being severely hampered by a lack of spare parts. Prior to finishing this round of tests, the squadron embarked on a project to demonstrate the Thud's automatic control capability. Lt. Col. Scott and Capt. Albert A. Funk, 335th navigation officer, successfully flew two F-105Bs on a 1,600-mile hop from Eglin to George AFB, California and back under "automatic control", except for routine pilot con-

Carrying 750-pound bombs on the inboard pylons, this F-105B (57-5782) of Detachment 1, 335th TFS is ready for a test mission out of Nellis AFB, Nevada on 15 April 1959. (Doug Olson)

trol during take-off and landing. These flights were made on 6-8 August 1960 and gave the aircraft some much-needed positive press.

The 335th's vast experience in testing the F-105B made it a logical choice to conduct advanced flight tests for Republic's new Thunderchief variant, the F-105D. Hence, the squadron began Category II tests of the all-weather D-model at Eglin on 26 December 1960, about seven months later than originally planned. The F-105D's airframe and engine had undergone evaluation either on the F-105B or during the D-model's Category I tests; thus, the 335th TFS carried out an abbreviated program that focused on the unproven components of the aircraft, such as the instrument display, fire-control system, and the navigation system. For the most part, the F-105D Category II program proceeded on schedule as most of the support problems encountered during the F-105B tests were eliminated.

Highlighting the Category II program was a 10 July 1961 test flight flown by the 335th's new commander, Lt. Col. Paul Hoza. On that day, Hoza flew a non-stop 1,520-mile, blind-navigation mission at altitudes ranging from 500 to 1,000 feet. The mission was flown from Eglin to Nellis and included a simulated nuclear bomb delivery enroute. After this milestone flight, nearly four months passed before the Category II program was completed on 31 October 1961.

On 22 November 1961, the 335th was placed back under 4th TFW control when it returned to Seymour Johnson to begin Category III flight tests for the F-105D. After successfully completing

This F-105B (57-5776) of Detachment 1, 335th TFS was marked for the commander of the 4th TFW, Col. Timothy F. O'Keefe, when photographed at Nellis on 15 April 1959. It carried the 4th TFW insignia on a broad white tail band trimmed with the wing's four squadron colors. (Doug Olson)

An F-105B (57-5793) of the 335th TFS stands ready for a mission at Seymour Johnson in late 1959. (R.C. Seely via David Menard)

these advanced weapons tests in early 1962, the squadron ended its long-term test and evaluation role and reverted back to training as a combat-ready unit. The 335th's first operational challenge came later that year when it was alerted for war during the Cuban Missile Crisis. For the six-week period 21 October to 29 November 1962, the squadron successfully served on high alert with its sister units, the 334th and 336th TFS, at McCoy AFB, Florida.

Between 30 April and 20 May 1963, the squadron refined its conventional weapons delivery skills by deploying to Fairchild AFB, Washington for Exercise Coulee Crest. The exercise, held at the Yakima Firing Range, was a free-play, two-sided training event that involved more than 43,000 Army and USAF troops maneuvering over one million acres. During the course of the simulated war exercise, which included live-fire drills, the squadron gained proficiency in close air support operations.

In late 1964, the squadron embarked on its first overseas European deployment. Departing Seymour Johnson on 16 November, the squadron flew eighteen F-105Ds to Incirlik AB, Turkey for a rotational tour in support of NATO defense requirements. After spending three months on nuclear alert duty while attached to the Seventeenth Air Force, the 335th returned home on 21 February 1965.

Led by their commander, Lt.Col. Fred H. Henderson, the squadron deployed to Yokota AB, Japan on 3 July 1965 under Operation Two Buck 13. Over the next four months, the 335th was attached to the 6441st TFW while backing up resident Thud squadrons that were rotating one at a time to Takhli RTAFB, Thailand for combat duty. During this time, the 335th assumed a significant portion of the 41st AD's Single Integrated Operational Plan (SIOP) at both Yokota and Osan AB, Korea.

On 3 November 1965, the 335th TFS relocated from Yokota to Takhli for combat duty. The squadron was placed under the control of the provisional 6235th TFW for several days before being attached to the 355th TFW, which was established as the new parent wing at Takhli on 8 November 1965. For nearly five weeks, the 335th struck military, transportation system, and air defense targets in North Vietnam and Laos without losing any pilots or aircraft. On 5 December 1965, the 333rd TFS arrived PCS at Takhli and relieved the 335th from combat duty over a one-week transition period. The 335th returned to Seymour Johnson without aircraft on 15 December and was placed back under 4th TFW control.

The 335th TFS assumed a replacement training function during March 1966. Eight months later, the squadron gave up its last Thunderchiefs as the 4th TFW was slated to convert to the F-4D Phantom II. The majority of the squadron's F-105s were sent to the Southeast Asia as replacement aircraft.

The broad green tail band that was used on the 335th's F-105Bs was applied to only a portion of its D-models as seen in this three-ship formation photograph taken on 20 February 1961. (Republic via Paul Minert)

A clean F-105D (59-1719) of the 335th TFS banks left while on a local flight out of Eglin during 1961. (Republic via Robert Robinson)

As indicated by the exercise bands, the 335th TFS operated as part of the "Red" force while taking part in the Coulee Crest training maneuver. Carrying 2.75-inch rockets and 750-pound bombs, this F-105D (62-4259) is seen taxiing out for a mission at Fairchild AFB, Washington in May 1963 during the live-fire portion of the exercise. (USAF via James Geer)

The markings used by the 335th TFS during their Two Buck 13 combat deployment are illustrated by this F-105D (62-4327) on final approach at Yokota AB, Japan. The tail markings consisted of a green band with a white "V" and a dot in the form of a silhouetted Chief's head. (Toyokazu Matsuzaki)

Armed with a typical load of six M117 750-pound bombs, an F-105D (62-4370) of the 335th TFS cruises high above a solid layer of clouds while enroute to North Vietnam on 22 November 1965. (USAF via James Geer)

Wearing a newly applied reverse camouflage scheme, this 335th TFS F-105D (61-0085) is seen on a Rolling Thunder mission from Takhli RTAFB, Thailand on 25 November 1965. (USAF via James Geer)

Larger warheads were introduced in Southeast Asia as the war escalated in the second half of 1965. This 335th TFS F-105D (62-4318) is preparing to hit a target in the North with Mk-84 2,000-pound bombs in late November 1965. (Fred Retter via Merle Olmstead via Jerry Geer)

335th Thud (62-4379) heads for North Vietnam during the squadron's final week of combat duty in early December 1965. (USAF via Jerry Geer)

336th Tactical Fighter Squadron

The 336th Tactical Fighter Squadron was the third unit within the 4th TFW to transition from the F-100C Super Sabre to the F-105B. The squadron began the conversion process during the summer of 1959 and received its final Thunderchief during December of that same year. The unit spent the next several years training as a combat-ready unit, and its readiness posture was given a test when it was deployed to McCoy AFB, Florida between 21 October and 29 November 1962 during the Cuban Missile Crisis.

The squadron successfully deployed eighteen F-105Bs to Moron AB, Spain for rotational nuclear alert duty while under the control of the 65th AD from 12 August 1963 to 7 January 1964. After this tour, the 336th replaced its F-105Bs with F-105D/Fs. One year later, the unit returned overseas when it deployed to Incirlik AB, Turkey in The U.S. Logistics Group (TUSLOG) with the Seventeenth Air Force from 25 May to 30 August 1965. This was the squadron's last overseas tour while flying the F-105 as it never participated in a rotational tour to Southeast Asia.

Unlike the 334th and 335th TFS, the 336th TFS did not convert to an F-105 RTU function. Instead, it began to drawdown Thud operations in March 1966 and assumed a non-operational status on 1 April. The squadron remained in this state until 8 February 1967, when it was equipped with the F-4D Phantom II.

The sleek aerodynamic lines of the Thunderchief are evident in this look at a 336th F-105B (57-5825) on the flightline at Congree AB, South Carolina in 1960. (J. Finley via Norm Taylor)

CHAPTER TWO

8th Tactical Fighter Wing

With an origin that dates back to before the Second World War, the 8th Fighter Wing has a long and illustrious history. Activated on 1 April 1932, the 8th Pursuit Group operated the PB-2, P-6, P-12, P-36, P-39, and the P-40 during the 1930s. The unit served in the Pacific region during the war as the 8th Fighter Group equipped with the P-39, P-40, and P-38. After the war ended, the group was stationed in Japan and operated the P-51 for several years before converting to the F-80 in 1949.

The early 1950s found the unit involved in the Korean War. As the 8th Fighter Bomber Wing, the unit flew combat missions in F-80s (and for a brief period F-51s) from a variety of bases from 1950 to 1952. While based at Suwon AB, Korea in 1953, the wing converted to the F-86F. After building an impressive combat record during four years of war, the 8th returned to Japan at Itazuke AB in late 1954. Two years later, the unit started its conversion to F-100D/Fs, although it should be noted that a good number of F-100Cs were also flown during the transition process. The 8th became a Tactical Fighter Wing in mid-1958 and continued to operate the Super Sabre with its three squadrons–the 35th, 36th, and 80th–until the spring of 1963. At that time, the wing became the second PACAF unit to receive the F-105D Thunderchief.

Commanded by Col. William E. Buck, Jr. at the time of its conversion to the Thud, the 8th TFW was charged with the primary mission of providing air defense in Japan and Korea, along with the maintenance of a quick strike reaction force. With this task, the wing employed the F-105 in the nuclear role and assigned squadrons rotated assets and crews to Osan AB, Korea for alert duty. For its successful transition to the F-105 and adaptation of the aircraft to its assigned mission, the wing won the Air Force Outstanding Unit Award for the period 12 May 1963 to 21 March 1964.

The 8th TFW's association with the F-105 was short lived. With the decision to close Itazuke AB, the wing's three squadrons were detached on 13 May 1964, and subsequently, on 18 June, all remaining wing components except headquarters were inactivated. The unit's former squadrons, still flying the F-105D/F, moved to Yokota AB, Japan and were reassigned to the 41st AD. On 10 July 1964, the 8th moved without personnel or equipment to George AFB, California and absorbed the resources of the 32nd TFW. Upon relocation, the wing began flying the F-4C Phantom II.

With current regulations restricting the use of individual unit markings, the 8th TFW Thuds carried only a PACAF badge on the tail as seen on this F-105D (62-4362) of the 80th TFS visiting Misawa AB, Japan in September 1963. (David Menard)

An 8th TFW pilot boards his airplane for a flight out of Itazuke in October 1963. (USAF via Jerry Geer)

Three 80th TFS F-105Ds enter the pattern at Itazuke on 31 October 1963. Each aircraft carries a practice bomb dispenser and two 450-gallon fuel tanks. (USAF via James Geer)

A ground crewman directs an F-105D (62-4313) of the 35th TFS into its parking spot at Itazuke on 31 October 1963. (USAF via James Geer)

Two F-105Ds of the 8th TFW take-off from Itazuke enroute to the Mito Gunnery Range on 23 November 1963. The lead aircraft (62-4287) was assigned to the 35th TFS, while the second (62-4350) belonged to the 80th TFS. (Matsuro Shimozato)

Another mixed flight of 8th TFW Thuds, comprised of 36th (62-4380 and 62-4375) and 80th (62-4355) aircraft, climbs out of Itazuke on a routine training mission on 23 November 1963. (Matsuro Shimozato)

By early 1964, distinctive unit markings appeared in the form of an arrow on the intake painted in the squadron colors. Making final checks before entering the runway at Itazuke, this pair of F-105Ds (62-4352 and 62-4348) wears the yellow arrow markings of the 80th TFS. (M. Lotti via Jerry Geer)

This early 1964 photograph records the first air refueling operation of Itazuke Thuds by KC-135 versus KB-50 tankers. This aircraft has red ailerons and intake arrows to denote its assignment to the 36th TFS. (Vic Vizcara)

This F-105D (62-4361) of the 80th TFS was photographed at an NAS Atsugi open house on 10 May 1964, just three days before the Itazuke Thuds were detached from the 8th TFW and relocated to Yokota AB, Japan. (Toyokazu Matsuzaki)

CHAPTER THREE

18th Tactical Fighter Wing

The 18th Tactical Fighter Wing traces its lineage back to 21 January 1927, when the War Department organized a Provisional Pursuit Group at Wheeler Field, Hawaii. Quickly redesignated the 18th Pursuit Group, the unit spent the years from 1927 to 1941 taking part in maneuvers, exercises, and training as part of the air defenses of Hawaii. Aircraft flown during that time included DH-4s, PW-9s, P-12s, P-26s, and P-40s.

Redesignated the 18th Fighter Group, the unit relocated to the South Pacific in 1943. Here, the unit joined the war effort and flew P-38s and P-39s. At the end of the war, the group moved to Clark AB, Philippines and flew P-47s and F-51s. In April 1948, the group became a subordinate unit of the newly activated 18th Fighter Wing. After converting to F-80s in 1949, the next year saw both units become the 18th Fighter Bomber Group and Wing respectively.

With the start of hostilities in Korea during June 1950, two of the group's three squadrons, the 12th and 67th, deployed to the combat zone and re-equipped with F-51s. The remaining squadron at Clark AB, the 44th, retained F-80s. During early 1953, the Korean-based squadrons converted to the F-86F. When the armistice was signed in July 1953, the two combat squadrons were located at Osan AB, Korea. In November 1954, the group and its 12th and 67th squadrons moved to Kadena AB, Okinawa. The long-detached 44th squadron rejoined the group at Kadena in July 1955.

The F-86F served with the 18th until being replaced by F-100D/F Super Sabres in 1957. That year, the 18th Fighter Bomber Group was inactivated and its squadrons and lineage were passed on to the 18th Fighter Bomber Wing. One year later, in July 1958, the 18th became a Tactical Fighter Wing. The wing added a fourth flying component in March 1960 with the attachment of the RF-101C-equipped 15th Tactical Reconnaissance Squadron (TRS). Operational control of this squadron was maintained throughout the 1960s, and the unit played a significant role in the reconnaissance of North Vietnamese forces in the early phases of the war in Southeast Asia.

During the fall of 1962, the 18th TFW started it conversion to F-105Ds, thus becoming the first Thunderchief unit in PACAF. The transition took place under the command of Col. George B. Simler and was successfully completed by the spring of 1963. With the new fighter, the wing continued its primary mission of maintaining assigned aircraft, crews, and support personnel in a high state of readiness for tactical air requirements of the 313th AD, Fifth Air Force, and PACAF. Specific tasks called for the defense of Japan and Korea, as well as nuclear alert duty at Osan AB, Korea. The wing excelled at adapting the F-105 to its mission, resulting in the receipt of the Air Force Outstanding Unit Award for the period 1 September 1962 to 31 August 1963.

The 18th TFW helped introduce the Thud to combat during December 1964, and over the next year, its fighter squadrons served successive tours of duty in Southeast Asia. The rotational tours ended in late 1965, but the wing continued to support the war over the next several years by deploying pilots to Thailand on an individual TDY basis. The wing received two additional Air Force Outstanding Unit Awards for the individual periods 1 August 1964 to 5 June 1965 and 6 June 1965 to 31 December 1966, and the earlier cited the wing for its contributions in the initial stages of the air war in Vietnam.

On 15 May 1966, the wing was involved in the organization of a new F-105 squadron to be assigned PCS to Korat RTAFB, Thailand. The unit, designated the 13th TFS, was primarily formed from the assets of the wing's 44th TFS. Upon activation, the new squadron was assigned to the 18th TFW but was detached to the 388th TFW. This action essentially left the wing with two operational Thud squadrons as the 44th TFS was maintained with minimal assets and personnel until it assumed a "paper unit" status in December 1966.

The year 1967 saw the 18th TFW lose three assigned squadrons. First to leave was the 44th TFS, which was transferred to the 388th TFW in April for combat duty. The 13th TFS closed out its distant association with the 18th TFW in November when it ended F-105 operations at Korat with the 388th TFW and was reassigned to the 432nd Tactical Reconnaissance Wing (TRW) at Udorn RTAFB, Thailand as an F-4 squadron. Finally, the constant drain on the wing's Thuds to Southeast Asia as replacement aircraft saw the 67th TFS cease operations in December. Subsequently, the 67th was reassigned to the 475th TFW at Misawa AB, Japan and assumed F-4 operations.

The multitude of squadron transfers left the 12th TFS as the last fighter unit assigned to the 18th TFW, although the 15th TRS, now equipped with the RF-4C, also remained with the wing. Both squadrons maintained combat-ready operations over the next three years, and each supported the war by deploying personnel to Southeast Asia as required. In 1971, the 44th and 67th TFS returned to the wing and were equipped with the F-4C. The wing's association with the F-105 ended when the 12th TFS ceased operations in May 1972.

Following Col. Simler, F-105 wing commanders included Col. Jones E. Bolt (16 May 1964), Col. Robert L. Cardenas (19 July 1964), Col. Neil J. Graham (28 June 1966), Col. Clarence E. Anderson, Jr. (17 June 1967), Col. Monroe S. Sams (22 December 1967), Col. Philip V. Howell, Jr. (24 June 1970), and Brig. Gen. Robert F. Titus (19 May 1971).

The Thunderchief was deployed to PACAF to equip two fighter wings under Project Flying Fish. Seen at Kadena AB, Okinawa on 30 October 1962, these F-105s are displayed for base personnel and families after the official acceptance ceremony of the first group of aircraft for the 18th TFW. (USAF via James Geer)

This F-105D (62-4269) of the 18th TFW carried no distinctive unit markings when photographed at Kadena in early 1963. (M. Lotti via Jerry Geer)

By late 1963, the 18th TFW had adopted simple markings consisting of a nose band in the squadron color painted behind the radome. Here, red-trimmed jets (61-0185 and 61-0188) of the 67th TFS and a yellow-trimmed ship (62-4339) of the 12th TFS are seen in tight formation during a practice mission from Kadena circa 1964. (F. Street via David Menard via Jerry Geer)

The blue nose band on this 18th TFW F-105D (62-4233) identifies it as an aircraft of the 44th TFS. (F. Street via David Menard via Jerry Geer)

The 18th TFW helped introduce the F-105 to combat when it committed resources to Southeast Asia in December 1964. The wing established Detachment 2 at Da Nang AB, South Vietnam, where these aircraft are seen supporting early operations against Communist forces in the region under the Barrel Roll campaign. (USAF via James Geer)

The 18th TFW was left with two operational fighter squadrons when the assets of the 44th TFS were used to form the 13th TFS at Korat RTAFB, Thailand in 1966. The wing's remaining two squadrons are represented in this 1967 view of a mixed flight of 12th and 67th TFS Thuds refueling over the Pacific Ocean. (USAF via Joe Bruch)

The demands of the war effort reduced the 18th TFW to only one assigned squadron, the 12th, by the end of 1967. Seen at Yokota AB, Japan on 22 February 1970, these two ZA-coded F-105Ds (62-4299 and 62-4328) of the 12th TFS are about to take-off in formation for a flight back to Kadena. (Toyokazu Matsuzaki)

The 18th TFW was the last PACAF operator of the F-105D after this variant was withdrawn from service in Southeast Asia during the fall of 1970. This 12th TFS D-model (62-4248) was photographed on 28 October 1971 while on static display at Kowaki AB. (Jerry Geer Collection)

12th Tactical Fighter Squadron

The 12th Tactical Fighter Squadron was the last unit of the 18th TFW to give up their F-100D/Fs and re-equip with the Thunderchief. Pilots underwent transition training to the F-105D starting in late 1962 at Nellis AFB, Nevada. After completing the course, they ferried their new aircraft from Brookley AFB, Alabama to Okinawa and commenced training to achieve a combat-ready rating. For successfully transitioning to the Thud and performing well during its first year of operations in the aircraft, the squadron was awarded the Air Force Outstanding Unit Award for the period 1 September 1962 to 31 August 1963.

As early as January 1965, the squadron deployed a small number of crews and aircraft to Da Nang AB, South Vietnam for combat duty in Southeast Asia with Detachment 2, 18th TFW. Early operations saw the 12th TFS participate in escort duty for Yankee Team reconnaissance operations over Laos, plus conduct strikes in support of the newly authorized Barrel Roll campaign. Carried out under rigid political restrictions, the Barrel Roll effort aimed at interrupting Communist infiltration routes in Laos. On 1 February 1965, the remainder of the squadron at Kadena was sent to Da Nang, resulting in the squadron's temporary attachment to the 2nd AD. One week later, a portion of the squadron moved to Korat RTAFB, Thailand, with the balance of the unit following on 20 February.

The 12th TFS sent eighteen pilots on the first USAF Rolling Thunder combat mission on 2 March 1965. The raid, augmented by the 67th TFS, involved a large strike force of Thuds fragged to destroy the ammunition storage facility at Xom Bang. The mission inflicted heavy damage on the depot, but three F-105s from the 67th were lost in the process. The squadron returned to Kadena on 15 March after flying 279 combat sorties without any pilot or aircraft losses. For its contribution to the early air war in Vietnam and operations connected to its peacetime mission, the 12th TFS received the Air Force Outstanding Award for the period 1 August 1964 to 5 June 1965.

The squadron returned to Korat for a two-month combat tour on 15 June 1965. Upon arrival, the 12th replaced their sister unit, the 44th TFS, and was attached to the provisional 6234th TFW. A good number of missions were carried out in Laos under the Barrel Roll and Steel Tiger campaigns, but strikes against military and transportation targets in the central region of North Vietnam were the primary focus. The squadron suffered its first loss when Capt. Don Williamson was listed Missing in Action (MIA) after his aircraft was downed by automatic weapons fire on a 6 July strike over the North.

On 27 July 1965, the 12th TFS was tasked to participate in the first SAM site attacks of the war. The mission involved a strike force of 46 Thuds from both Korat and Takhli hitting two separate SA-2 missile sites 30 miles northwest of Hanoi. The sites were hit as planned, but no less than six F-105s were lost that day. Two of the aircraft were from the 12th TFS, and both fell victim to AAA fire. The pilots safely ejected, but only one could be rescued. Lost and taken POW was Capt. Robert Purcell.

Two F-105Ds (61-0217 and 62-4227) of the 12th TFS show their yellow nose band markings as they pass over the Ryukyu Islands near the end of a transit flight back to Kadena circa 1964. (F. Street via David Menard via Jerry Geer)

During the two weeks following the historic SAM raid, the unit had two more aircraft downed by hostile action in the North. One loss occurred on 2 August and saw Capt. Robert Daughtrey taken POW after his Thud was hit by anti-aircraft fire on a strike against the Thanh Hoa Bridge. The other shoot down took place on 10 August, but the pilot was recovered after ejecting over Laos. The 12th returned to Kadena on 25 August 1965 after being replaced by the 67th TFS. For completing 1,520 combat missions over the two-month period 25 June to 25 August 1965, the unit earned the Presidential Unit Citation.

After concluding its second combat deployment, the 12th TFS resumed its peacetime mission, but continued to support the war effort by periodically rotating pilots to Southeast Asia on an individual TDY basis to augment Thud units at Korat and Takhli. In 1967, the squadron's operational record over the period 6 June 1965 to 31 December 1966 was recognized with the receipt of a third Air Force Outstanding Unit Award.

On 23 January 1968, the squadron deployed to Osan AB, Korea under Operation Coronet Wasp following the seizing of the American intelligence ship USS *Pueblo* by North Korea. At Osan, the 12th TFS operated alongside EF-105Fs from the 4537th Fighter Weapons Squadron (FWS), 4525th Fighter Weapons Wing (FWW), which was deployed from Nellis AFB, Nevada. Around May 1968, tensions between the two countries subsided, and preparations were

This 12th TFS F-105D (62-4228) is seen alongside a 44th TFS aircraft (62-4233) during a routine training mission in the mid-1960s. (F. Street via David Menard via Jerry Geer)

made to return the bulk of the squadron to Kadena. At that time, the 12th added its first Wild Weasel crews and EF-105F aircraft, some of which were reassigned from the 4537th FWS. The squadron's deployment concluded on 13 June 1968, but the unit's presence in Korea did not end at that point. Over the next few years, the 12th periodically rotated a small number of aircraft to Korea to serve as part of a contingent force ready to respond to the possibility of renewed hostilities in the region.

The squadron's Weasels were tasked to augment the 44th TFS, 388th TFW at Korat in the summer of 1968. During several months of supporting the 44th, the Weasel pilots recorded over 1,500 combat flight hours. This contribution to the war, as well as the unit's ongoing rotation of pilots to Southeast Asia on an individual TDY basis, was recognized when the 12th received the Republic of Vietnam Gallantry Cross with Palm for operations during the period 1 April 1966 to 30 June 1970.

In the fall of 1970, the squadron was again tasked with supporting Weasel operations out of Korat by augmenting the establishment of Detachment 1, 12th TFS. The unit was formed on 24 September 1970 due to the pending end of F-105 operations at Takhli and the corresponding need to retain a Weasel presence in Southeast Asia. Detachment 1 was placed under the control of the 388th TFW and was initially equipped with six Weasel Thuds. Within a month of its formation, the unit doubled in size as additional aircraft were received from the inactivating 355th TFW. This growth saw the detachment redesignated the 6010th Wild Weasel Squadron (WWS) on 1 November 1970. Despite the change in designation, the 12th's Weasels maintained close ties to the squadron by rotating crews for combat duty through December 1971.

The 12th Weasel crews returned to Korat for another tour in early 1972 to supplement the 17th WWS (formerly the 6010th WWS). They accumulated more than 1,400 combat flight hours before heading back to Kadena during April 1972 to prepare for the

A 12th TFS pilot steps into the cockpit of his F-105D (61-0209) at the start of an early Barrel Roll mission against hostile communication lines in Laos. This photograph was taken at Da Nang AB, South Vietnam in late January 1965, when a portion of the 12th was operating as part of Detachment 2, 18th TFW. (USAF via James Geer)

squadron's inactivation. Orders called for the transfer of the unit's F-105D/Fs to the Reserve Air Forces, while the Weasel team was to be absorbed by the 17th WWS. Before winding down operations, the squadron put an exclamation point on the Thud's exit by taking first in the Fifth Air Force Weapons Meet.

On 16 May 1972, the squadron assumed a non-operational status after its pilots had ferried the last of its Thuds to the U.S. for service with the Air Force Reserves' 465th TFS, 507th Tactical Fighter Group (TFG) at Tinker AFB, Oklahoma. The 12th TFS remained dormant until it received the F-4D Phantom II in December 1975.

With no weapons pylons showing, this F-105D (62-4287) of the 12th TFS may have been returning from a local check-out flight when photographed during the squadron's first rotation to Korat RTAFB, Thailand. (Paul Paulsen via Jerry Geer)

At rest on the Korat ramp in early 1965, this 12th TFS Thud (62-4271) carries 2.75-inch rocket pods on the outboard pylons. These rockets were used to destroy soft targets along enemy infiltration routes that carried troops and supplies to the South. (Paul Paulsen via Jerry Geer)

Armed with a full load of M117 750-pound bombs, this F-105D (61-0217) of the 12th TFS is ready for an early Rolling Thunder mission out of Korat. (Paul Paulsen via Jerry Geer)

Seen on a visit to Tengah, Singapore on 25 September 1965, this 12th TFS F-105D (61-0212) wears the yellow "wing" tail band adopted by the 18th TFW earlier that year. In these markings, the sole indicator of the aircraft's squadron assignment was the color of the name block on the lower frame on each side of the canopy. (H. Buchanan via Paul Minert)

Having only recently been assigned to the 12th TFS when photographed at Yokota AB, Japan on 16 May 1968, this EF-105F (63-8296) retains the black and yellow checkered tail band from its previous service with the 4537th FWS. This aircraft was part of the Weasel force deployed to Korea by the 4537th following the Pueblo Incident. (Toyokazu Matsuzaki)

The ZA tail code was applied to the 12th TFS Thuds in early 1968. This F-105D (62-4320) displays the new unit identification marking while taxiing out for take-off at Yokota on 22 June 1968. (Jerry Geer Collection)

This 12th TFS EF-105F (62-4416) had the famous Barney Google and Snuffy cartoon characters painted below the left intake when seen at Yokota in July 1968. (S. Okano via Jerry Geer)

An early F-105G (62-4436) of the 12th TFS gets airborne from Yokota AB on 18 February 1970. The prominent ALQ-105 (QRC-380) ECM fairings on the lower fuselage sides were not added to the G-models until 1971. (Toyokazu Matsuzaki)

As seen on this F-105D (62-4244) lining up for departure at Yokota, the 12th TFS had supplanted the yellow nose band for a tail band of the same color by the time this photograph was taken on 6 March 1971. (Katsuhiko Tokunaga via Jerry Geer)

This 12th TFS Thud (62-4372) is about to take-off on a dreary day at Yokota in December 1971. Note the addition of the squadron insignia on the forward fuselage. (Katsuhiko Tokunaga via Jerry Geer)

44th Tactical Fighter Squadron

The 44th Tactical Fighter Squadron was the second constituent of the 18th TFW to relinquish its F-100D/F Super Sabres for the Thunderchief. Its transition started in November 1962, and the unit was declared combat-ready in its F-105Ds by the summer of the following year. Together with other squadrons within the 18th TFW, the squadron won the Air Force Outstanding Unit Award for the period 1 September 1962 to 1 August 1963 for its successful conversion to the Thud.

Early training requirements gave the 44th the distinction of sending the first F-105s to Thailand when it participated in a multinational peacetime exercise named Air Boon Choo at Korat RTAFB between 20-30 April 1964. Fittingly, the squadron became the first unit within the 18th TFW to deploy to Southeast Asia for combat duty. The 44th's first combat tour began on 18 December 1964. Placed under 2nd AD control, the squadron sent aircraft and crews to both Da Nang AB, South Vietnam and Korat for early contingency operations against Communist forces in the region.

At Da Nang, six F-105s were deployed to establish Detachment 2, 18th TFW. This detachment was primarily organized to provide constant fighter-bomber resources capable of support strikes on enemy supply lines in Laos under the newly authorized Barrel Roll campaign. The unit's first mission under this campaign was flown on 25 December 1964. It involved a flight of four F-105s striking military barracks at Tchepone and was led by Lt. Col. William B. Craig, commander of the 44th TFS. The operation went well, but the dive-bombing technique employed against the barracks proved inaccurate.

Another early Barrel Roll mission involved bombing the Ban Ken Bridge in Laos for the first time on 13 January 1965. Heavily surrounded by anti-aircraft guns, the bridge was viewed as one of the more critical checkpoints in Laos. The force consisted of an RF-101 as pathfinder and another for bomb damage assessment, eight F-100s for flak suppression, and sixteen F-105s from the 44th and 67th squadrons as strike aircraft. The mission was successful in cutting the bridge, but one aircraft from the 44th was downed by AAA fire. The loss of this aircraft was historically significant in that it represented the first F-105 to be shot down in combat. The aircraft's pilot, Capt. Al Vollmer, was subsequently recovered.

At Korat, the balance of the 44th TFS flew Yankee Team escort missions and sat on alert for rapid response as needed for rescue combat air patrol (ResCAP) duty. For the time being, Barrel

High over the Pacific during 1963, this F-105D (61-0181) displays the early blue nose band markings of the 44th TFS. (James Geer Collection)

In company with two 67th TFS aircraft, this 44th TFS F-105D (61-0204) is about to hook up with a drogue from a KC-135 tanker over the Philippine Islands in the spring of 1965. (Ron McNeil via Paul Minert)

Roll missions were not flown out of Thailand due to the Geneva Convention guidelines that required strikes in Laos be launched from South Vietnam. Later Barrel Roll missions were flown out of Thailand under a veil of secrecy. By mid-January 1965, the portion of the 44th located at Da Nang moved to Korat, where the entire squadron remained until returning to Kadena on or about 25 February 1965.

As a unit, the 44th TFS returned to Korat for a second tour on 21 April 1965. Placed under the control of the provisional 6234th TFW, the squadron's primary duty was to support the Rolling Thunder bombing campaign against North Vietnam, although Barrel Roll and Steel Tiger missions were also flown against Communist positions in Laos. For the most part, the strikes in the North were flown in the central and southern panhandle region and focused on key links in the enemy's supply and transportation system, and military storage areas and barracks. Some of the critical targets hit included the Thien Linh supply depot an 30 April and the Vinh Airfield on 8-9 May.

The 44th lost two aircraft to the growing North Vietnamese air defense system during this deployment. One of the losses occurred on 14 June 1965. On that day, the squadron was scheduled to lead a dual strike over the North. One target was to be the control center near the Thanh Hoa Bridge, and the second was the large army supply depot at Son La. Bad weather in the Thanh Hoa area scrubbed that part of the mission, and the Thuds set to fly against the control center were diverted to Son La. While approaching to the target area, the strike force encountered heavy anti-aircraft fire. Hit and forced to eject was Maj. Larry Guarino. He was captured by the North Vietnamese and held as a POW for nearly eight years before being released in 1973.

Around 15 June 1965, the 44th was relieved from combat duty by its sister squadron, the 12th TFS. After a one-week transition period, the squadron returned to Kadena on or about 23 June 1965. The 44th TFS performed exceptionally well during its second combat tour, resulting in the receipt of the coveted Presidential Unit Citation for the period 22 April to 23 June 1965. In addition to winning that honor, the 44th received another Air Force Outstanding Unit Award for combat and peacetime operations from 1 August 1964 to 5 June 1965.

Throughout the second half of 1965, the 44th TFS continued to contribute to the war effort by augmenting combat operations at Korat. During the short period of 10-29 October 1965, the entire squadron was at Korat to support a campaign against major bridges along northeast supply routes from Hanoi to China. Bridges hit along this line included the Bac Can on 17 October and the Choi Moi on 20 October. For its role on a series of strikes over a seven-day period beginning on 22 October, the 44th TFS received its second Presidential Unit Citation. No pilots or aircraft were lost during this brief deployment, which saw the squadron temporarily attached to the provisional 6234th TFW from 19-29 October.

Many of the 44th TFS aircraft retained their blue nose bands when the yellow "wing" tail band was adopted in mid-1965. The mix of old and new markings is illustrated by this F-105D (62-4335) taking off for a Rolling Thunder mission out of Korat RTAFB, Thailand. (USAF via James Geer)

At the close of 1965, the 44th had logged more than 1,100 combat sorties and dropped more than 3,000 tons of ordnance. The unit's support of the air war continued into 1966 with aircraft and pilots rotating to Southeast Asia on an individual TDY basis. In line with the decision to establish a new PCS squadron at Korat with the 388th TFW, the bulk of the 44th's personnel and resources were used to form the 13th TFS on 15 May 1966. The decision to not relocate the 44th designator to Korat was a political move to conceal the fact that a combat unit had been moved out of Okinawa to Southeast Asia.

The 44th TFS remained active at Kadena on a reduced scale until 31 December 1966. On that day, the unit was formally relegated to "paper unit" status. Subsequently, the squadron received its third Air Force Outstanding Unit Award for its support of the air war and maintenance of its standard PACAF mission over the period 6 June 1965 to 31 December 1966. The squadron remained dormant until it was reassigned to the 388th TFW on 25 April 1967, when it absorbed the personnel and resources of the wing's 421st TFS.

A crew chief guides his 44th TFS Thud out of its parking spot at Korat for a strike against North Vietnam in 1965. (USAF via James Geer)

This F-105F (63-8285) of the 44th TFS was photographed on final approach for landing at Yokota AB, Japan on 17 December 1965. (Toyokazu Matsuzaki)

Camouflaged rapidly replaced the silver lacquer finish on all Thuds beginning in late 1965. Seen turning finals at Yokota on 26 January 1966, this freshly painted F-105F (63-8288) has no distinctive markings to signify that it was assigned to the 44th TFS. (Toyokazu Matsuzaki)

67th Tactical Fighter Squadron

The 67th Tactical Fighter Squadron was the first unit in PACAF to receive the Thunderchief. Its first three F-105Ds arrived at Kadena on 30 October 1962, and over the next several months, the squadron phased-out its F-100D/F Super Sabres on receipt of a full complement of Thuds. The 67th received the Air Force Outstanding Unit Award for the period 1 September 1962 to 31 August 1963 for successfully incorporating the Thud to its assigned mission as a component of the 18th TFW.

The squadron's experience in Southeast Asia began in January 1965 with the deployment of seven aircraft and crews to Da Nang AB, South Vietnam. Here, they operated as part of Detachment 2, 18th TFW while flying Yankee Team escort missions and conducting strikes against hostile communication lines in Laos under the Barrel Roll campaign. Highlighting the 67th's action at Da Nang was its participation in a 13 January mission against the Ban Ken Bridge. The strike saw sixteen Thuds from the 44th and 67th TFS successfully cut the bridge with 750-pound bombs.

As a unit, the 67th TFS deployed to Korat RTAFB, Thailand on 18 February 1965 for combat duty while under the control of the 2nd AD. During its first two weeks on station, the 67th flew a number of missions in Laos, but it was not until the start of the Rolling Thunder campaign on 2 March 1965 that valued targets in North Vietnam came under attack. The unit's first mission under this campaign saw it teamed with its sister unit, the 12th TFS, on a raid against the ammunition depot at Xom Bang. The force successfully destroyed the target, but three Thuds from the 67th were downed by enemy ground fire. All three pilots ejected and were subsequently rescued.

Missions against military and transportation targets in the North increased throughout March as the war slowly escalated. Early strikes were carried out on the Hon Gio military barracks on Tiger Island, the Phu Qui ammo depot, the Phu Van supply depot, and numerous radar warning sites. On 22 March, the unit lost its fourth aircraft when Lt. Col. Robinson Risner, commander of the 67th TFS, was downed by small arms fire while striking the Vinh Son radar site in North Vietnam. Risner bailed out and was recovered.

On 3-4 April 1965, Lt. Col. Risner led two maximum effort attacks against the massive Thanh Hoa Railroad and Highway Bridge. The heavily defended bridge was the most important target hit to date in the war, requiring meticulous planning and coordination of the large force of Thuds involved in the strikes. The missions were executed as planned, and the structure was damaged; but the weapons employed proved ineffective in cutting the bridge. In addition, the enemy shot down three F-105s during the second day of strikes against the bridge. One of aircraft lost was from the 67th TFS, and the pilot, Capt. Smitty Harris, was taken POW. Despite the shortcomings, the raids were significant, and Risner received the Air Force Flying Cross for his tremendous leadership and efforts on the Thanh Hoa missions.

Operational control of the 67th TFS shifted to the newly established provisional 6234th TFW on 5 April 1965. This change had no impact on operations as the unit continued to support the air war in Laos and North Vietnam until it concluded its deployment on or about 26 April 1965. Losses during this tour totaled five aircraft and one pilot. For its performance in combat, as well as for exceptional peacetime operations, the 67th TFS earn the Air Force Out-

Destined for service with the 67th TFS, this F-105D (61-0163) is seen taking off from Hickam AB, Hawaii after being serviced during a ferry flight to Kadena AB, Okinawa on 23 October 1962. This aircraft was a member of the first element of four Thuds to be delivered to the 18th TFW. (USAF via James Geer)

A 67th TFS pilot boards his F-105D (61-0194) at Kadena for a mission during Exercise Sky Soldier IV. Held in October 1963, this operation was designed to train Chinese and American soldiers in the defense of Taiwan. (USAF via James Geer)

Taken in 1964, this nice in-flight shot of a 67th TFS F-105D (62-4235) provides a good look at the squadron's early red nose band markings. (F. Street via David Menard via Jerry Geer)

standing Unit Award for the period 1 August 1964 to 5 June 1965.

During the summer of 1965, a number of pilots from the 67th TFS were resident at Korat to augment combat units flying in support of the Rolling Thunder campaign. As a unit, the squadron returned to Korat on 16 August 1965 for another combat tour in Southeast Asia. The 67th's deployment coincided with the departure of its sister unit, the 12th TFS. Placed under the control of the provisional 6234th TFW, the squadron immediately entered combat by flying missions in North Vietnam against vital military and transportation system targets. Other action saw the unit support the air campaign in Laos by conducting Barrel Roll strikes in the north and Steel Tiger interdiction missions in the panhandle region.

Like its previous tour at Korat, the 67th's second combat deployment was marked by a high number of losses. Three aircraft were shot down over the North within two weeks of the squadron's arrival. The first loss occurred on 28 August when an F-105F flown by Capt. Wesley Schierman was downed by small arms fire. Schierman ejected and was subsequently captured by the enemy. The second loss took place on 29 August and saw Capt. Ronald Byrne, Jr. taken POW after his Thud was downed by AAA fire. The third aircraft fell on 31 August, but the pilot safely ejected and was rescued.

In September, the 67th had five more aircraft shot down as pilots averaged nearly one sortie a day over North Vietnam. One aircraft was lost on 6 September, but for a second time the pilot was recovered. The next two losses occurred on a 16 September mission against a North Vietnamese headquarters and ammunition storage area. Shot down and taken POW were Lt. Col. Risner and Maj. Raymond Merritt. In captivity, Risner became a key leader in the American prisoner's resistance against the enemy. The remaining two losses that month saw 1st Lt. Dean Klenda and Capt. Edgar Hawkins killed when their aircraft were hit on 17 and 20 September respectively.

The 67th TFS continued to bomb enemy targets in North Vietnam until it returned to Kadena on 23 October 1965. For its contribution to the air war over the period 14 April to 21 October 1965, the unit was awarded the Presidential Unit Citation. The squadron's contributions to the war effort in the Thud did not end at that point as pilots returned to Thailand on an individual TDY basis over the next two years. An indication of the unit's operational excellence came in 1967 when it received another Air Force Outstanding Unit Award for the period 6 June 1965 until 31 December 1966.

The squadron phased-out the Thud during late 1967 and on 1 December was declared non-operational. Fifteen days later, the unit designator was transferred to the 475th TFW at Misawa AB, Japan. Upon relocation, the 67th TFS received the F-4C Phantom II.

First Strikes on the Thanh Hoa Bridge

The first strikes on the Thanh Hoa Railroad and Highway Bridge were a direct result of the March 1965 decision to interdict North Vietnamese lines of communication and specifically, to destroy the southern portion of the rail system. The bridge, known to the Vietnamese as the Ham Rong (the Dragon's Jaw), was located 70 miles south of Hanoi and spanned the Son Ma River, making it a critical link in the movement of men and materials into South Vietnam.

The bridge was built with the assistance of Chinese technicians during the late 1950s and early 1960s. It was 540 feet long and 56 feet wide and included a single railway dividing two 22-

A 67th TFS F-105D (61-0184) leads a section of 15th TRS RF-101Cs during a 1964 training operation involving Kadena's fighter and recce air assets. (F. Street via David Menard via Jerry Geer)

Three 67th TFS Thuds pass in formation over Iruma AB, Japan during an open house on 3 November 1964. (Toyokazu Matsuzaki)

foot highways. Two steel through-truss spans rested on a massive reinforced concrete center pier and on two concrete abutments on each end. Grossly over engineered, this bridge would prove to be one of the most difficult targets to destroy throughout the entire war.

The 67th TFS was tasked with planning and coordinating the first strikes on the Thanh Hoa Bridge. The first raid on the bridge involved 79 aircraft and was carried out on 3 April 1965 under Rolling Thunder Mission 9-Alpha. A force of 46 F-105s was supported by F-100s for MiG combat air patrol (MiGCAP) and flak suppression duties, RF-101s for pre and post strike reconnaissance, and KC-135s for refueling. Of the 46 Thuds involved in the mission, sixteen were loaded with a pair of 250-pound AGM-12A Bullpup missiles, and the remaining 30 aircraft carried eight M117 750-pound bombs. The Thuds were tasked with both strike and flak suppression duties.

Lt. Col. Risner served as overall mission coordinator and developed the plan of attack. In intervals only several minutes apart, the F-105s were to hit the bridge in flights of four. The aircraft carrying Bullpups were to be the first on target. They were to launch their missiles at 12,000 feet in two passes since the Bullpups had to be released and guided to the target one at a time. The bomb carriers were to follow and drop their ordnance around 7,000 feet.

The aircraft departed their Thai bases in the early afternoon and after refueling cycled through the target area as planned. Risner's flight was the first to press the attack. His flight and the following three scored multiple direct hits with their missiles, but they failed to damage the bridge. The 250-pound missile warheads proved to be no match for the strong steel and concrete structure. The bomb carrying Thuds faired somewhat better, but also fell short of dropping any spans. Intense AAA fire claimed one F-100 and one RF-101 on the first strike. No F-105s were lost; however, Risner's aircraft sustained damage from the AAA fire, but he was able to safely land his aircraft at Da Nang.

Because the Thanh Hoa Bridge had suffered little damage, a second strike was ordered the following day. Again, Risner was designated mission coordinator and charged with leading the restrike. Changes were made in force size, weapons, and tactics. On

This line-up at Korat RTAFB, Thailand in early 1965 is lead by F-105s with the red nose band of the 67th TFS, while beyond are yellow-marked aircraft of the 12th TFS. (Paul Paulsen via James Geer)

This flight of 67th TFS F-105Ds is on a bridge busting mission over North Vietnam in October 1965. The nearest aircraft has a typical load of six M117 750-pound bombs, while those behind carry AGM-12B Bullpup missiles. (USAF via James Geer)

this raid, a strike force of 48 F-105s loaded with eight 750-pound bombs were joined by F-100s for MiGCAP, ResCAP, and weather reconnaissance support.

As before, Risner was the first pilot over the target, followed by fellow 67th pilot Capt. Smitty Harris. After dropping his ordnance, the aft fuselage of Harris' Thud was struck by 37-mm AAA fire. He ejected from his severely damaged aircraft and spent the next seven years as a POW. Two other F-105s from the 354th TFS were shot down by MiG-17s prior to reaching the target. This marked the first time MiGs had attacked American aircraft in the war. Despite the heavy AAA fire and MiG attacks, the strike proceeded as planned.

A vast majority of the bombs scored hits on the bridge and caused severe damage, but again, no spans were dropped. The highway was heavily cratered, and the rail line had multiple holes, making it inoperable without major repairs. Two secondary targets, a local thermal power plant and a train trapped south of the bridge, were also destroyed during the second raid. With the strongest weapons available at that time, the 67th TFS and supporting Thud units inflicted the maximum destruction possible against the formidable Thanh Hoa Bridge. For his leadership and extraordinary heroism during the Thanh Hoa raids, Risner was awarded the Air Force Cross.

The mission tally markings just below the cockpit of this F-105D (62-4264) of the 67th TFS leave little doubt that it spent considerable time in Southeast Asia during 1965. (H. Buchanan via Robert Robinson)

A 67th TFS F-105F (63-8364) approaches the runway at Yokota AB, Japan on 17 December 1965. The yellow "wing" tail band used during this period was abandoned as aircraft received the new camouflage finish in early 1966. (Toyokazu Matsuzaki)

Although difficult to discern, this camouflaged 67th TFS F-105F (63-8268) carried a red nose band when photographed landing at Yokota on 21 October 1966. (Toyokazu Matsuzaki)

CHAPTER FOUR

23rd Tactical Fighter Wing

The 23rd Tactical Fighter Wing history dates back to the early stages of the Second World War when the 23rd Fighter Group activated on 4 July 1942 at Kunming, China. The unit had the unique distinction of replacing Chennault's legendary American Volunteer Group, which were civilian mercenaries flying P-40s hired to protect the Burma Road for China. Over the next three years, the group operated P-40s (and later P-51s) against the Japanese in China, French-Indo China, and Burma. Upon conclusion of the war, the unit was inactivated.

The group was reactivated on 10 October 1946 at Northwest Field, Guam and equipped with P-47s. In April 1948, the 23rd Fighter Wing was activated with the 23rd Fighter Group subordinate to it. One year later, the 23rd relocated to Howard AFB, Canal Zone, Panama with plans to enter the jet age with factory fresh F-84Es a few months later. Prior to the delivery of the new aircraft, the unit flew RF-80s, T-6s, and C-47s. Plans to equip the wing with F-84s abruptly changed in August of that same year as it was decided to deactivate the unit instead.

The 23rd Fighter Wing reactivated again on 12 January 1951 at Presque Isle AFB, Maine. Initially operating a few T-33s and a single C-47, the unit was slated to receive F-86Es during mid-year. The resource demands of the Korean War, coupled with inadequate facilities and supply, eventually led to the inactivation of the unit on 6 February 1952. Although the 23rd Fighter Wing would not activate again until twelve years later, the 23rd Fighter Group was active between 1955 and 1959. During this period, the group operated out of Presque Isle with F-89Ds and was subordinate to the 4711th Air Defense Wing.

On 8 February 1964, the unit was reactivated as the 23rd Tactical Fighter Wing at McConnell AFB, Kansas and replaced the 388th TFW. The 23rd inherited the 388th's resources and the F-105D-equipped 560th, 561st, 562nd, and 563rd TFS. The wing's mission was to maintain proficiency in tactical fighter operations, being combat-ready in the event of any hostilities. This would soon be the case as the 23rd's squadrons began rotational deployments to Southeast Asia in March 1965. During the wing's action in Southeast Asia, three pilots were killed and another four were listed as Missing in Action (MIA).

On 1 January 1966, the 23rd TFW's mission changed to that of training F-105 replacement pilots. Two years later, the wing reorganized its training program and activated a new unit, the 4519th Combat Crew Training Squadron (CCTS). This new squadron was added as a result of the end of F-105 training operations at Nellis AFB, Nevada. Six months after the reorganization, the 560th TFS ceased operations and was later transferred to another wing.

By late 1970, the Thud's high attrition rate during five years of war over Southeast Asia forced the USAF to begin shifting the F-105D/Fs from front-line service to duty with the Reserve Air Forces. Consequently, the 23rd TFW ceased the RTU function in November 1970, but the 419th TFTS (which replaced the 4519th CCTS one year earlier) immediately assumed the mission to train ANG pilots to fly the F-105. The ANG training program was passed on to the Kansas Air Guard during the fall of 1971, resulting in the inactivation of the 419th TFTS.

The wing received the Air Force Outstanding Unit Award for exceptionally meritorious service from 1 June 1970 to 15 June 1971. During this period, the wing successfully executed the dual mission of reconstituting from a RTU wing to an operational wing, and training and equipping ANG units in conversion to the F-105. The 23rd's change in mission brought the arrival of the F-105G with the 561st TFS and the F-105D Thunderstick II with the 563rd TFS. The wing maintained a combat-ready posture over the next few years and successfully deployed a portion of the 561st TFS to Southeast Asia for combat duty in April 1972.

For a short time after being reactivated, the 23rd TFW carried sharkmouths on their aircraft in reference to the unit's heritage as the P-40-equipped "Flying Tigers" of the 23rd Fighter Group during World War II. This F-105D (61-0163) of the 562nd TFS bears its teeth on a live-fire training mission during a war exercise in 1964. (Harrison Rued via Robert F. Dorr)

On 1 July 1972, the F-105 era of the 23rd TFW ended when the wing moved without personnel and equipment to England AFB, Louisiana, where it was tasked with the new mission of providing close air support, search and rescue support, and interdiction in the A-7D Corsair II. The wing's former F-105 squadrons at McConnell were subsequently reassigned to the 832nd AD, although the 562nd and 563rd TFS were phasing down operations in preparation for their inactivation at the close of July 1972. The 561st TFS soldiered on with its Weasel Thuds for another year at McConnell before relocating to George AFB, California to join the 35th TFW.

During its eight years of flying the Thunderchief, the wing was commanded by Col. Olin E. Gilbert (1964), Col. Edmund B. Edwards (8 February 1964), Col. Edmund B. Edwards (17 August 1964), Col. Deward E. Bower (12 July 1965), Col. Max T. Beall (9 October 1967), Col. James V. Hartlinger (28 August 1968), Col. Walter D. Dreun, Jr. (15 June 1970), Col. Garry A. Willard, Jr. (21 October 1971), and Col. Harry W. Schurr (28 April 1972).

This 23rd TFW F-105F (63-8332) carried olive drab bands on the fuselage and wings while operating out of Whiteman AFB, Missouri for Exercise Goldfire I. This maneuver was held in the Fort Leonard Wood area from 20 October to 11 November 1964 and tested newly developed tactical air support techniques against conventional tactics. (USAF via James Geer)

In 1965, three squadrons of the 23rd TFW deployed overseas on a TDY basis to support the war in Southeast Asia. This 561st TFS F-105D (61-0161) was photographed on 4 May 1965 while serving on back-up duty at Yokota AB, Japan for resident Thud units that had rotated to Thailand. (Toyokazu Matsuzaki)

A pair of F-105Ds (62-4398 and 61-0127) of the 563rd TFS, 23rd TFW heads back to base after a strike against Viet Cong positions in South Vietnam during the squadron's 1965 combat tour. (Paul Minert Collection)

A view of the flightline at McConnell AFB, Kansas in the fall of 1966. By this time, the 23rd TFW was operating in the RTU mission and nearly all aircraft had received the new camouflage finish. (USAF via James Geer)

With distinctive unit markings being non-existent at the time this photograph was taken at McConnell on 11 November 1967, this 23rd TFW F-105F (62-4418) relies on a reverse camouflage scheme to differentiate itself from its sister ships. (Jerry Geer)

The 23rd TFW augmented its large fleet of F-105D/Fs with a number of F-105Bs while functioning in the training role. These B-models are seen at McConnell on 11 November 1967. (Jerry Geer)

Due to the end of F-105 pilot training at Nellis AFB, Nevada in early 1968, the 23rd TFW increased the size of its training program with the addition of the 4519th CCTS. This F-105D (60-0500) wears the MG tail code used by the new squadron when photographed at McConnell in April 1969. (Jerry Geer)

The 23rd TFW reorganized its ongoing training mission in October 1969 by replacing the 4519th CCTS with the 419th TFTS. As seen on this F-105D (59-1733) at McConnell in November 1970, the new unit retained the MG tail code of its predecessor. (Jerry Geer)

When the 23rd TFW resumed combat-ready operations, the 561st TFS began functioning in the Wild Weasel mission with newly modified F-105Gs such as this MD-coded aircraft (63-8345) seen at McConnell in November 1970. (Jerry Geer)

Another change to the 23rd's makeup during late 1970 saw the 563rd TFS re-equip with Thunderstick II modified F-105Ds. Seen at McConnell in April 1971, this MF-coded aircraft (61-0044) shows the enlarged dorsal fairing associated with this variant. (Jerry Geer)

The 562nd TFS was the only unit within the 23rd TFW to retain standard F-105Ds when it returned to combat-ready operations. This example (61-0183) displays the unit's ME tail code when photographed at McConnell in April 1972. (Jerry Geer)

419th Tactical Fighter Training Squadron

The 419th Tactical Fighter Training Squadron replaced the 4519th CCTS on 15 October 1969 and assumed the training mission of the former squadron. The unit primarily flew the F-105D/F, although a few F-105Bs and a single F-105D Thunderstick II were also flown for a short period of time. Beginning in November 1970, the 419th was tasked with training ANG pilots in the conversion to the Thunderchief. The squadron ceased operations on 8 May 1971 following the transfer of the training program to the Kansas Air Guard's 127th TFTS, 184th TFTG. Formal inactivation followed on 1 October 1971. During its existence, the 419th TFTS earned the Air Force Outstanding Unit Award for operations over the period 1 June 1970 to 8 May 1971.

BELOW: In addition to the MG tail code, the 419th TFTS markings included a green tail band bordered in white and the squadron insignia on the left side of the forward fuselage as seen on this F-105D (61-0108) at McConnell in June 1970. (Jerry Geer)

BOTTOM: The 419th TFTS operated this F-105D Thunderstick II (61-0047) during 1970 to assist in the development of a training syllabus for the new Thud variant after it had been successfully tested for operational use by the TAWC under Operation Combat Thunder at Eglin AFB, Florida. (Jerry Geer)

This storeless F-105F (63-8274) of the 419th TFTS is seen parked on the McConnell ramp in June 1970. (Jerry Geer)

A 419th TFTS F-105D (60-0527) passes over the threshold at McConnell on return from a training mission over the Smokey Hill Gunnery Range in August 1970. (Jerry Geer)

A nice side view of an F-105F (62-4440) of the 419th TFTS sitting idle at McConnell. This shot was taken in April 1971, less than one month before the squadron was inactivated. (Jerry Geer)

At the time this F-105F (62-4433) was photographed in November 1970, the 419th TFTS was the last flying unit within the 23rd TFW dedicated to the training mission as its sister squadrons had returned to combat-ready operations. (Jerry Geer)

560th Tactical Fighter Squadron

The 560th Tactical Fighter Squadron was reassigned from the 388th TFW to the 23rd TFW on 8 February 1964. The squadron began its transition from F-100Ds to F-105Ds in late 1963 and was nearing completion of the upgrade at the time of its reassignment. The unit maintained a combat-ready posture over the next few years, but unlike its sister squadrons, the 560th never deployed to Southeast Asia to support the air campaign against North Vietnam.

On 1 January 1966, the 560th's mission changed as a result of the 23rd's new directive to train F-105 replacement pilots. While functioning in the RTU role, the squadron supplemented its F-105D/Fs with a few F-105Bs. The training mission was carried out until 19 June 1968, when the 560th TFS ceased operations. The unit was reassigned to the 4531st TFW at Homestead AFB, Florida on 25 September 1968 and began flying the F-4D Phantom II.

BELOW: The introduction of camouflage made unit identification difficult prior to the adaptation of two-letter squadron identification tail codes in 1968. The black nose gear radar reflector with "560" painted in white is all that identifies this F-105B (57-5813) as belonging to the 560th TFS when photographed at McConnell on 11 November 1967. (Jerry Geer)

This 560th TFS F-105D (62-4257) was photographed at Wright-Patterson AFB, Ohio on 15 May 1965, shortly before it was ferried to Southeast Asia as a replacement aircraft for the unit's sister squadron, the 563rd TFS. It was subsequently shot down over North Vietnam during the first SAM site raid of the war on 27 July 1965. (Clyde Gerdes via Norm Taylor)

This F-105D (61-0084) of the 560th TFS carried the squadron's legend on the nose gear doors when it visited Forbes AFB, Kansas for an open house in October 1967. (Jerry Geer)

561st Tactical Fighter Squadron

The 561st Tactical Fighter Squadron was reassigned from the 388th TFW to the 23rd TFW on 8 February 1964. The squadron began operating F-105Ds in the second half of 1963 and had achieved Initial Operating Capability (IOC) prior to its reassignment. It trained as a combat-ready squadron over the next year before becoming the first unit of the 23rd TFW to deploy overseas in support of the war in Southeast Asia.

On 27 February 1965, the first support aircraft departed McConnell on the 561st TFS One Buck Nine deployment to provide personnel and aircraft to fulfill Far East theater requirements. At the last minute, a change in destination was made from Takhli RTAFB, Thailand to Yokota AB, Japan. Four days later, fifteen F-105Ds and three F-105Fs with 33 officers and 334 airmen from the 561st followed. They arrived at Yokota on 6-7 March, and once settled in, plans for the squadron to assume a share of the 41st AD's SIOP were put into action. The squadron had assumed six SIOP targets at Osan AB, Korea and seven follow-on targets at Yokota by 10 March.

On 6 April, the first contingent of six 561st Thuds rotated to Takhli from Yokota for combat duty. Initial plans called for the entire squadron to deploy to Southeast Asia, but that decision was rescinded. Instead, only one third of the squadron went to Takhli while the balance of the unit maintained SIOP duties at Osan and Yokota. Although this was the case, most 561st pilots flew combat missions during the squadron's role of providing logistical support and ferrying service to units at Takhli. In total, the squadron recorded 42 combat support, five Rolling Thunder, seventeen ResCAP, six Yankee Team, and two MiGCAP missions without losing any pilots or aircraft. The 561st returned to McConnell from its One Buck Nine deployment on 10 July 1965.

The aircraft of the 561st TFS sported black and yellow checkered tail markings when they arrived at Yokota AB, Japan on their One Buck Nine deployment. The handsome appearance of these markings is evident in this view of an F-105D (62-4405) landing at Yokota on 4 May 1965. (Toyokazu Matsuzaki)

A 561st TFS F-105D (61-0120) recovers at Yokota on 5 May 1965. The practice bomb dispenser on the centerline station indicates the aircraft probably carried out a training mission over the Mito Gunnery Range. (Toyokazu Matsuzaki)

Three F-105Fs were among the eighteen aircraft deployed overseas by the 561st under Operation One Buck Nine. This example (63-8351) is seen in formation with a D-model (61-0161) upon return to Yokota from a 4 May 1965 training mission over Japan. (Toyokazu Matsuzaki)

In line with the 23rd TFW's new mission to train F-105 replacement pilots for combat units in Southeast Asia, the 561st TFS began operating in the RTU function beginning in January 1966. While serving in this role over the next five years, the unit supplemented its F-105D/Fs with several F-105Bs.

Upon conclusion of its training mission in the fall of 1970, the 561st was selected to transition to the F-105G and become the only operational, combat-ready Wild Weasel squadron in TAC. Assigned crewmembers cycled through the Weasel training program at Nellis AFB, Nevada while the unit gradually received F-105Gs that were fresh from being modified from standard F-105F or Weasel EF-105F configuration. During the transition period, the 561st operated a few Combat Martin F-105Fs, which were also converted to G-model standard by about mid-1971. Together with other squadrons of the 23rd TFW, the 561st TFS earned the Air Force Outstanding Unit Award for its transition from a training role to combat-ready operations during the period 1 June 1970 to 15 June 1971.

On 6 April 1972, the 561st split into Advance and Rear echelons, both under the squadron commander, with each having a designated commander. This organizational action came after the unit was ordered to Southeast Asia in response to President Richard M. Nixon's call for the renewed bombing of North Vietnam following the Communist's Easter offensive. Under Operation Constant Guard I, the Advance element immediately moved to Korat RTAFB, Thailand with twelve F-105Gs and nearly 200 personnel in the form of Detachment 1, 561st TFS. The unit arrived at Korat

For the 561st TFS crews unfamiliar with the flying conditions in Japan and Korea, the two-seat F-105Fs proved valuable for theater indoctrination flights. This aircraft (63-8348) is making its final approach for landing at Yokota on 5 May 1965. (Toyokazu Matsuzaki)

on 10-12 April and commenced combat operations while under the control of the 388th TFW.

The 561st TFS was reassigned to the 832nd AD when the 23rd TFW ended F-105 operations and moved to England AFB, Louisiana on 1 July 1972 to commence flying the A-7D Corsair II. Unlike the 562nd and 563rd TFS, which were inactivated one month after the 23rd TFW departed, the 561st TFS retained its operational status due to the critical nature of the Weasel mission and its commitment in Southeast Asia.

Nearly all 561st pilots saw combat in Southeast Asia when they rotated to Takhli RTAFB, Thailand during the squadron's role of providing logistical support for Thud units deployed to the base. This F-105D (62-4408) carried an AIM-9B Sidewinder on the outboard pylon when caught visiting Da Nang AB, South Vietnam in May 1965. (David Menard)

The 561st had only recently applied the MD tail code to its aircraft when this F-105D (60-0526) was photographed on 20 August 1968. (Norm Taylor Collection)

Like all squadrons of the 23rd TFW, the 561st TFS flew several F-105Bs during the time it was tasked with the RTU mission. Seen at NAS Miramar in August 1968, this B-model (57-5808) sports a reverse camouflage scheme. (Warren Bodie via Norm Taylor)

A 561st TFS F-105D (60-0521) is serviced on the ramp at McConnell in April 1969. Note the aircraft markings have been enhanced with the addition of the squadron insignia on the left side of the forward fuselage. (Jerry Geer)

The 835th AD badge on the forward fuselage of this 561st TFS F-105D (60-0526) means that it was assigned to the upper echelon's commander when photographed at McConnell in April 1969. (Jerry Geer)

Seen pulling into its parking spot on the McConnell ramp in April 1969, this EF-105F Wild Weasel (63-8359) was oddly serving as a general trainer with the 561st as the squadron was still functioning in the RTU mission at that time. (Jerry Geer)

The yellow tail band displayed by this F-105D (60-0493) was a standard marking on all 561st TFS aircraft by the time this photograph was taken in June 1970. (Jerry Geer)

Although the 561st carried out the RTU function through the fall of 1970, the initial stages of the unit's transition to the Wild Weasel mission with F-105Gs started some time earlier. Seen at McConnell in June 1970, this G-model (63-8300) was one of the first assigned to the squadron. (Jerry Geer)

When this early F-105G (63-8342) of the 561st TFS was photographed at McConnell in November 1970, the squadron had yet to receive a combat-ready rating with their new aircraft. (Jerry Geer)

The newly modified F-105Gs arrived for service with the 561st TFS in pristine condition as illustrated by this example (63-8332) on the McConnell apron in November 1970. (Jerry Geer)

Several Combat Martin F-105Fs were assigned to the 561st TFS when they returned from Thailand following the inactivation of the 355th TFW. This Martin (62-4432) was converted to F-105G standard shortly after being photographed at McConnell in April 1971. (Jerry Geer)

This F-105G (62-4439) of the 561st TFS was one of the first of the unit to have the distinctive ALQ-105 (QRC-380) ECM blisters added to the lower fuselage below each wing. This view was taken in May 1971 while the aircraft was conducting trials on the newly installed equipment at Eglin AFB, Florida. (Jerry Geer)

Ground crews ready this 561st TFS F-105G (63-8303) for a mock SAM suppression mission at McConnell in March 1972. One month later, the squadron was ordered to Southeast Asia as part of the Constant Guard series of deployments following the North Vietnamese Easter offensive. (Jim Rotramel via James Geer)

The 561st ramp at McConnell was nearly empty after twelve F-105Gs from the unit deployed to Korat RTAFB, Thailand in early April 1972. Photographed just weeks after their departure, this F-105F (63-8309) was one of several left behind as an element of the squadron's Rear echelon. (Jerry Geer)

Seen in April 1972, this 561st TFS F-105G (63-8328) remained at McConnell subsequent to the Constant Guard I deployment. (Jerry Geer)

562nd Tactical Fighter Squadron

The 562nd Tactical Fighter Squadron was reassigned from the 388th TFW to the 23rd TFW on 8 February 1964. The squadron started operations in the F-105D in the second half of 1963 and was training to achieve a combat-ready rating at the time of its reassignment. The 562nd's first major test took place in the spring of 1964, when a portion of the unit deployed to Hickam AFB, Hawaii to partake in a joint Army-USAF project named Tropic Lighting. Ten F-105Ds and two F-105Fs took part in the exercise that saw crews train in tactical and close air support operations with the Army. After returning from Hickam, the 562nd spent the next year in an intensive training schedule that included participating in additional readiness exercises.

In August 1965, the 562nd TFS deployed to Takhli RTAFB, Thailand for combat duty under Operation Two Buck Nine. The deployment entailed the replacement of its sister squadron, the 563rd TFS, which had been on temporary assignment at Takhli since April 1965. Rather than ferry their aircraft from McConnell, the 562nd gradually assumed control of the 563rd's aircraft during a one-week transition period. The transfer commenced on 6 August, when an advanced contingent of nine aircrews from the 562nd arrived at Takhli to fly alongside the 563rd TFS. Twelve more pilots arrived on 12-13 August, and operational control was passed to the commander of the 562nd. This action saw the squadron attached to provisional 6235th TFW. By the end of August, the squadron had 24 pilots on station and had recorded 358 sorties.

The 562nd flew 533 combat sorties during the month of September, averaging 23 sorties and 54 hours per pilot. Three F-105s

These sharkmouthed 562nd TFS F-105s were mobilized for participation in Operation Desert Strike in May 1964. The grounding of the Thunderchief fleet due to the crash of a Thunderbird F-105B greatly curtailed the squadron's role in this simulated war exercise. (Jerry Geer Collection)

The 562nd TFS deployed to Thailand in August 1965 under Operation Two Buck Nine to take over the mission and aircraft of the 563rd TFS. The 562nd removed the gaudy aircraft markings of the former unit and adopted a simple blue-white-blue tail band as seen on this F-105D (61-0116) visiting Yokota AB, Japan. (Yukio Enomoto)

A flight of four 562nd TFS F-105Ds takes on fuel over Laos before striking a target in North Vietnam during the fall of 1965. (USAF via James Geer)

from the unit were lost in Southeast Asia that month, but in each case the pilot ejected and was recovered. Two crashes were due to mechanical problems and the third was shot down while striking a target in Laos. The high sortie rate continued during October with 420 sorties flown, averaging around 18 sorties and 41 hours per pilot. That month, the 562nd lost another F-105 on a 13 October strike in North Vietnam near Dien Bien Phu, but again the pilot ejected and was rescued. Altogether, from August to October, the squadron had dropped 3,375 tons of ordnance and had amassed 1,740 sorties including 926 Rolling Thunder, 126 Barrel Roll, 33 Steel Tiger, and sixteen Whip Lash missions.

Of all the missions flown during the 562nd's first three months of combat, a 5 October strike against the heavily defended Lang Met Bridge proved to be the most difficult. Located 50 miles northeast of Hanoi, the bridge spanned the Rong River and was critical to the flow of supplies from China to North Vietnam. For the mission, the 562nd TFS joined the 36th TFS to send 24 F-105s on the attack. Carrying two Mk-118 3,000-pound bombs each, the Thuds knocked the north end down and rendered the bridge unserviceable, but a high price was paid. Two F-105s from the 36th TFS were shot down on the mission and another twelve landed at airfields other than Takhli due to extensive battle damage. Three of the damaged aircraft were from the 562nd. For their efforts on the raid, two of the squadron's pilots received the Distinguished Flying Cross.

The squadron processed through a shift in operational control to the 355th TFW on 8 November 1965. The change had no impact on the unit's mission, and the high operational tempo continued in support of the Rolling Thunder campaign. The 562nd suffered two more setbacks in November. The first loss saw Capt. Dwight P. Bowles killed while he was on a 3 November mission to cut a bridge along the northeast railroad line way up north close to the Chinese border with Mk-118 3,000-pound bombs. While dropping his ordnance, one Mk-118 failed to release, and the resulting heavy asymmetrical load of the hung bomb put his Thud into an uncontrollable roll that caused him to crash into the target. The second loss occurred on 12 November, when Capt. William "Nasty" Ned Miller was killed when his plane exploded without warning or indication of trouble while enroute to a target in North Vietnam.

The 562nd concluded its combat tour when it departed Takhli on 4 December 1965. Its aircraft were passed on to the newly arrived 354th TFS, which was assigned PCS at Takhli. The squadron received the Air Force Outstanding Unit Award with Combat "V" Device for its performance in Southeast Asia from 13 August to 1 December 1965. During this period, the unit was credited with destroying 73 bridges, eleven radar sites, 58 naval craft, four SAM sites, five military storage areas, and numerous secondary military targets. The 562nd also played a large part in the successful rescue of nine downed pilots by providing ResCAP operations behind enemy lines.

In January 1966, the 562nd began operating in the F-105 replacement training role. While carrying out this mission over the next five years, the unit augmented its complement of F-105D/Fs with several B-models. After completing its last training course in August 1970, the 562nd TFS aimed all their effort at returning to operational status and successfully earned a combat-ready rating within a 90-day period. This accomplishment gave the unit the distinction of becoming the first Thud squadron within TAC to attain this status since 1965. Appropriately, the 562nd received the Air Force Outstanding Unit Award for operations over the period 1 June 1970 to 15 June 1971.

One year after gaining operational proficiency, the 562nd TFS was informed of the planned transfer of its F-105D/Fs to the Reserve Air Forces and its impending inactivation. During its last several months of operations, the squadron carried out transitional pilot training for Reserve pilots destined to fly the F-105. Conducted under two six-week courses, the 562nd trained sixteen pilots from Tinker AFB, Oklahoma, where the 465th TFS, 507th TFG was earmarked to receive the Thud. During the training program, the 562nd maintained its operational mission requirements.

On 1 July 1972, the 562nd TFS was reassigned to the 832nd AD after the 23rd TFW moved without personnel and equipment to England AFB, Louisiana to begin operations in the A-7D Corsair II. The squadron rapidly phased down Thud operations over the next month and was inactivated on 31 July 1972. A few years later, the 562nd resurfaced within the 35th TFW at George AFB, California as an F-105G Wild Weasel squadron.

ABOVE: Seen on the tanker, four 562nd TFS F-105Ds join forces with two 335th TFS aircraft for a Rolling Thunder mission in November 1965. The mixing of squadrons within a strike package was common on the larger raids against the North. (USAF via Jerry Geer)

OPPOSITE

TOP: As illustrated by this F-105D (60-0493), the 562nd TFS flew camouflaged aircraft without any distinctive markings during the 1966-67 time period. (Jerry Geer Collection)

CENTER: This F-105D (60-0535) of the 562nd TFS carried the unit's recently adopted ME tail code when it visited Richards Gebaur AFB, Missouri for an open house in October 1968. (Jerry Geer)

BOTTOM: This F-105F (63-8278) had previously been modified to perform night, all-weather radar bombing missions in Southeast Asia under the code name Commando Nail. It is seen here at McConnell in April 1969 after being returned to its original configuration for duty as a trainer with the 562nd TFS. (Jerry Geer)

0493
00493

ME
AF
60 535

ME
278

This 562nd TFS F-105D (61-0041) carries the early version of the squadron insignia on the forward fuselage when seen at McConnell in June 1969. (James Geer Collection)

Col. Edward McNeff flew this specially marked 562nd TFS F-105D (60-0535) during 1970 while serving as commander of the 835th AD. (Jerry Geer)

A 562nd TFS F-105F (63-8331) taxis off the transient ramp at Andrews AFB, Maryland on 16 September 1970. (Paul Minert Collection)

This November 1970 view catches a 562nd TFS F-105D (62-4411) with a serial number presentation that suggests that it had recently returned from being overhauled at the Sacramento Air Material Area at McClellan AFB, California. (Jerry Geer)

This line-up of 562nd Thuds stands ready for a heavy day of flying during the squadron's all-out effort to achieve a combat-ready rating in the fall of 1970. (Jerry Geer)

The ground crews of these 562nd TFS F-105Fs have prepared their aircraft for a morning launch in November 1970. (Jerry Geer)

This F-105D of the 562nd TFS (61-0199) had its bomb bay fuel tank lowered for servicing when photographed in April 1972. (Jerry Geer)

A 562nd TFS F-105F (63-8263) awaits its next training sortie at McConnell in April 1972. Note this aircraft carries the late version of the squadron insignia on the forward fuselage. (Jerry Geer)

This 562nd Thud (61-0056) is seen returning from a training mission during the squadron's final days of service at McConnell. At the time this photograph was taken on 10 July 1972, the unit was operating under the control of the 832nd AD as the 23rd TFW had moved to England AFB, Louisiana ten days earlier. (Bob Pickett via Kansas Air Museum)

An F-105D (62-4311) of the 562nd TFS at rest on the McConnell ramp shortly before the squadron was inactivated on 31 July 1972. (Bob Pickett via Kansas Air Museum)

This unique photograph shows the tail section of a 563rd TFS Thud serving as the only entrance to the Officer's Club during the 562nd TFS inactivation party. (Barry Miller)

563rd Tactical Fighter Squadron

The 563rd Tactical Fighter Squadron was reassigned from the 388th TFW to the 23rd TFW on 8 February 1964. Like the 561st and 562nd TFS, the squadron began operations in the F-105D in the second half of 1963. The squadron maintained combat readiness upon reassignment to the 23rd and was well prepared for war when it was alerted for deployment to Southeast Asia in support of Operation Two Buck Charlie on 6 April 1965. One day after receiving the notification, Squadron Commander Maj. Jack Brown took eighteen F-105s out of McConnell enroute to Takhli RTAFB, Thailand.

Upon arrival at Takhli, 563rd personnel received a series of briefing to familiarize them with operating requirements and procedures in Southeast Asia. On 14 April, the squadron commenced flying combat missions against targets in Laos and North Vietnam while under the control of the provisional 6235th TFW. The 563rd suffered its first casualty on 17 April, when Capt. Samuel A. Woodworth was killed on a rocket pass over North Vietnam. By the end of April, the 563rd TFS had logged a total of 177 combat missions. Major achievements included the destruction of six major highway bridges in North Vietnam. Among those hit were the Ly Hahn on 22 April, Vinh on 24 April, and the Ly Buc Thon on 26 April.

Also noteworthy during the month of April was the 563rd's participation in Operation Fact Sheet, a psychological warfare program calling for the dropping of some four million leaflets over North Vietnam. The squadron flew its first Fact Sheet mission on 19 April, when it dropped 1,200,000 leaflets on Bai Thung, Ha Trung, Thanh Hoa, Phu Qui, Phu Dien Chau, Vinh, and Bai Tinh. The leaflets warned civilians to stay away from military installa-

Devoid of unit markings, this 563rd TFS F-105F (62-4435) was on display at an open house at Davis-Monthan AFB, Arizona in February 1965. (Norm Taylor Collection)

Seen at Da Nang AB, South Vietnam in May 1965, this worn 563rd TFS F-105D (61-0169) shows the red and white tail markings used by the squadron during their Two Buck Charlie combat deployment. The unit's "Ace of Spades" device is centered on the tail band. (David Menard)

This F-105D (61-0158) of the 563rd TFS is seen landing at Yokota AB, Japan on 17 May 1965. Note the aircraft lacks the standard TAC shield and lightning bolt on the tail. (Toyokazu Matsuzaki)

tions, compared life in the south with life in the north, and explained the reason for the strikes against North Vietnam.

In May, the squadron's sortie rate increased considerably. The most important targets attacked that month were the ammo storage areas at Xon Run, Phu Ban, and the Hoai An, and the army barracks at Xon Thung and Phuc Que. Also attacked was the most heavily defended target in North Vietnam at that time, the Thanh Hoa Railroad and Highway Bridge. Additionally, the 563rd flew many Barrel Roll, Steel Tiger, Queen Bee, and ResCAP missions. While flying 408 combat sorties during the month, the squadron lost two aircraft and their pilots. Listed as MIA were Captains Robert C. Wistrand and David L. Hrdlicka.

The squadron flew 345 combat missions during June. Major targets hit in North Vietnam included the Hoai An ammo storage area, the Ben Quang barracks area, the Phu Qui ammo depot, the Vinh army depot, the Son La army barracks and storage area, and the Ban Nuock Chieu ammo storage area. Outside of these Rolling Thunder strikes, the unit flew a considerable number of the missions against key choke points along the Ho Chi Minh Trail in Laos. It was also during June that the 563rd participated in a combat "first"

Taken over South Vietnam in June 1965, this historic photograph records the 563rd TFS flying the F-105 with its maximum ordnance load of sixteen 750-pound bombs on a strike against Viet Cong targets. This was first time the Thud had used this load in combat. (Norm Taylor Collection)

for the F-105. Deploying six aircraft from Takhli to Tan Son Nhut AB, South Vietnam on 25 June, the unit bombed Viet Cong targets while flying the Thud with its maximum ordnance load of sixteen 750-pound iron bombs. A total of 232 bombs were dropped in seventeen sorties over two days.

The 563rd recorded 447 combat sorties while flying 20-28 sorties a day in July. The squadron inflicted damage on Dien Bien Phu, Son La, Yen Dey marshalling yards and ammo depot, and the entire Red River railroad complex from Hanoi to the border of Red China. In addition, the Thanh Hoa barracks and two major bridges near Dien Bien Phu were also hit. The highlight that month took place when the squadron was directed to participate in a maximum effort raid on two SA-2 SAM sites near Hanoi. The mission was conducted on 27 July and eleven 563rd Thuds successfully struck the one of the sites, but two aircraft were shot down while coming off the target. The two officers shot down, Captains Kile Berg and Walt Kosko, were listed as MIA. For their participation in the mission, Berg and Kosko received the Silver Star, and all eleven 563rd pilots were awarded the Distinguished Flying Cross.

The first part of August saw the 563rd continue to operate over North Vietnam, with most missions directed toward route and area armed recce duty. The sortie rate slowed when the 563rd began preparations to end its combat tour and pass its aircraft and mission to the 562nd TFS. The one-week transition process began on 7 August, when nine pilots from the 562nd arrived to fly with the 563rd for acclimation to combat operations in Southeast Asia. On 13 August, operational control was shifted to its sister squadron following the arrival of twelve more pilots. Two days later, the 563rd TFS returned to McConnell. Prior to their departure, pilots of the 563rd recorded 131 combat missions during August.

As of 15 August 1965, the 563rd was the most experienced combat fighter squadron in the USAF. In addition, it was the first unit to have served a continuous four-month combat tour since the Korean conflict. During the deployment, the 563rd TFS flew 1,508 sorties, including 744 Rolling Thunder, 337 Barrel Roll, and 75 Steel Tiger missions. The unit received two Air Force Outstanding Unit Awards with Combat "V" Device for military operations in Southeast Asia, one for action from 8 April to 8 June 1965 and one from 29 June to 15 August 1965.

On 1 January 1966, the 563rd's mission shifted to training pilots to the fly the F-105 with a proficiency that would enable them to proceed directly to Southeast Asia. This mission was carried out for the next five years, although it should be noted that the unit was relegated to a non-operational status from 15 August to 2 November 1966 due to aircraft and pilot shortages caused by the war. During the time it served in the training role, the 563rd TFS supplemented its F-105D/Fs with several F-105Bs.

In mid-1970, the squadron received word that it would revert back to combat-ready operations later that year. Rather than retain its standard F-105Ds upon completion of its training role, the 563rd was chosen to be the sole USAF front-line unit to transition to the Thunderstick II modified F-105D. The Thunderstick II modification focused around the installation of the AN/ARN-92 Long Range Aid to Navigation (LORAN) system, giving the aircraft significant improvements in both blind bombing capability and existing weapons delivery modes. The first Thunderstick II aircraft arrived for indoctrination training with the 563rd TFS during the summer of 1970.

After graduating its last F-105 training class in September 1970, squadron personnel began carrying out intensive ground and flight

The 563rd TFS turned their aircraft over to the 562nd TFS when they completed their combat tour in mid-August 1965. This F-105D (61-0116) was under the domain of the its new owner when photographed at Yokota on 1 September 1965, but is included here to provide a further illustration of the 563rd's markings. (Yasuhiko Takahashi)

The MF tail code was assigned to the 563rd TFS when this unit identification standard was adopted by TAC in mid-1968. This F-105D (61-0183) displays the new marking in this view taken in September 1968. (Jerry Geer)

By the spring of 1969, all of the 563rd TFS aircraft carried the unit's insignia on the left side of the forward fuselage. This marking can be seen on this F-105D (60-0496) just to the right of the boarding ladder. (Jerry Geer)

A 563rd TFS F-105D (61-0065) on the McConnell ramp in April 1969 carries six 750-pound bombs for its next training mission. (Jerry Geer)

training programs in the Thunderstick II aircraft. Deliveries of the retrofitted F-105Ds continued at a steady pace throughout the second half of 1970 and into 1971, with the last of 30 arriving for service with the 563rd on 4 April 1971. To begin training in the use of LORAN and to initially qualify its pilots in the LORAN blind bombing mode, the 563rd deployed 35 pilots and 290 support personnel to Eglin AFB, Florida between 22 April and 3 June 1971. After returning to McConnell, the squadron was declared mission-ready. Its successful return to operational status saw the unit earn the Air Force Outstanding Unit Award for the period 1 June 1970 to 15 June 1971.

In line with the 23rd TFW's pending relocation to England AFB, Louisiana and the corresponding end of Thud operations for the 563rd TFS, the unit joined the 562nd TFS in transition training Reserve pilots to the F-105 beginning in April 1972. The squadron trained crews from Carswell AFB, Texas, where its F-105D Thunderstick II aircraft were scheduled to be delivered to the newly activated 457th TFS, 506th TFG. Following the 23rd TFW's departure on 1 July 1972, the 563rd was reassigned to the 832nd AD and spent the next several weeks phasing down operations in preparation for its inactivation on 31 July 1972. The 563rd emerged again three years later within the 35th TFW at George AFB, California as an F-105G and F-4C Wild Weasel RTU squadron.

Several F-105Bs served with the 563rd TFS while the unit was tasked with the RTU mission. This example (57-5820) was photographed at McConnell in April 1969. (Jerry Geer)

The later style markings used the 563rd TFS included a red tail band as seen on this F-105D (61-0145) at McConnell in November 1970. (Jerry Geer)

The commander of the 23rdTFW, Col. Walter D. Dreun, Jr., was assigned this 563rdTFS F-105D (58-1155) during the fall of 1970. Note the wing insignia on the forward fuselage. (Jerry Geer)

After completing its last training course in the fall of 1970, the 563rd TFS retained its standard F-105Ds pending delivery of a sufficient number of the new Thunderstick II modified variant. This D-model (61-0061) was photographed at McConnell in November 1970. (Jerry Geer)

With three external fuel tanks fitted, this 563rd TFS F-105F (63-8357) is ready for a cross-country flight when photographed at McConnell in April 1971. (Jerry Geer)

A Thunderstick II modified F-105D (60-0458) of the 563rd TFS at McConnell in April 1971. The enlarged saddleback area accommodated an advanced weapon delivery and navigation system that significantly improved the aircraft's blind bombing capability and existing weapons delivery modes. (Jerry Geer)

A 563rd TFS crew chief and his assistant check out the arresting hook on this F-105D Thunderstick II (60-0455) while preparing the aircraft for an April 1971 training mission at McConnell. (Jerry Geer)

The 563rd TFS took its Thunderstick II aircraft to Eglin AFB, Florida in late April 1971 to qualify its pilots in the use of the LORAN blind bombing system. These aircraft are seen at McConnell shortly before the deployment. (Jerry Geer)

The badge on the forward fuselage of this F-105D Thunderstick II (61-0075) of the 563rd TFS indicates that it was assigned to the commander of the 835th AD. This marking was short-lived as the division was inactivated less than three months after this photograph was taken in April 1971. (Jerry Geer)

A 563rd TFS F-105F (63-8309) basks in the Florida sun while visiting Eglin AFB in August 1971. (Bill Malerba via James Geer)

This F-105D Thunderstick II (61-0074) at McConnell in April 1972 lacks the TAC badge typically carried on the tail of all 563rd TFS aircraft. (Jerry Geer)

A 563rd TFS Thud (60-5375) sits idle on the McConnell ramp during the squadron's rapid phase-down of operations subsequent to the 23rd TFW's departure. After the unit was inactivated on 31 July 1972, the Thunderstick II aircraft were given to the Reserve Air Forces' 457th TFS, 506th TFG at Carswell AFB, Texas. (Bob Pickett via Kansas Air Museum)

4519th Combat Crew Training Squadron

The 4519th Combat Crew Training Squadron was activated within the 23rd TFW on 1 August 1967 in anticipation of the end of F-105 pilot training at Nellis AFB, Nevada and the subsequent transfer of their aircraft and function to McConnell in early 1968. The squadron was declared operational on 21 January 1968 and carried out its RTU mission with F-105D/Fs and several F-105Bs during its existence. The squadron was inactivated on 16 October 1969 after being replaced one day earlier by the 419th TFTS.

BELOW: An F-105D (61-0202) of the 4519th CCTS displays the squadron's newly applied MG tail code as it pulls out of its parking spot at McConnell for a training mission in June 1968. (James Geer Collection)

A typical busy day at McConnell in August 1968 finds this 4519th CCTS Thud (61-0056) waiting for its pilot to complete his mission briefing for a late morning launch. (Jerry Geer)

A 4519th CCTS pilot completes his preflight inspection with the crew chief of this F-105D (61-0111) prior to a 9 August 1968 mission out of McConnell. (Jerry Geer)

An F-105F (63-8288) taxis back to the 4519th CCTS flightline after completing a training sortie on 9 August 1968. (Jerry Geer)

This F-105D (61-0146) of the 4519th CCTS is seen arriving at Forbes AFB, Kansas for an October 1968 open house. (Jerry Geer)

The opened access door on the nose of this 4519th CCTS F-105B (57-5826) indicates that the aircraft's air turbine motor was being serviced when photographed at McConnell in April 1969. (Jerry Geer)

A single EF-105F Wild Weasel was operated by the 4519th CCTS as a general trainer for a limited period during 1969. The aircraft (63-8360) is seen here with the squadron insignia on the forward fuselage. (Jerry Geer)

This 4519th CCTS F-105B (57-5816) was photographed at McClellan AFB, California on 3 May 1969 while processing through the Sacramento Air Material Area for overhaul. (Doug Olson)

A few F-105Fs modified to fly Commando Nail strikes against North Vietnam were assigned to the 4519th CCTS when they returned from Southeast Asia in early 1969. This example (63-8276) is seen on 24 May 1969 during a visit to the Sacramento Air Material Area for reconfiguration back to its original form as a standard trainer. (Doug Olson via Jerry Geer)

An F-105F (63-8315) of the 4519th CCTS sits quietly on the McConnell ramp on 7 June 1969. (James Geer Collection)

Although this F-105B (57-5835) carries the MG tail code of the 4519th CCTS, the "Flying Tiger" insignia on the fuselage denotes that it was the personal mount of the commander of the 23rd TFW, Col. James V. Hartlinger. This photograph was taken at an open house at Richards Gebaur AFB, Missouri in September 1969. (Jerry Geer)

Replacement Training at McConnell

By late 1965, it became clear that the Thud's role in the air war over North Vietnam was going to continue for some time. Consequently, the USAF began the process of establishing two permanently stationed F-105 wings in Thailand and needed to develop the ability to replace pilots that had been lost in combat or had completed their 100-mission tour of duty. Thus, the replacement training program was established at McConnell to develop a pipeline of well-trained pilots able to proceed directly from training to the combat zone.

Student pilots came from bombers, tankers, interceptors, transports, and other tactical fighters. Upon arrival at McConnell, the students entered a four-month training program that involved comprehensive instruction on the F-105 aircraft and its weapons systems. The first phase of the course placed heavy emphasis on academics and simulator training. Two cockpit simulators and one air-to-ground missile simulator were used by the 23rd TFW. Students were required to spend at least eighteen hours in the cockpit simulator and mock fire 120 missiles before the progressing to the flying portion of the program.

Early in the course, pilots received flight time in McConnell's training support aircraft. Pilots who had been flying non-fighter aircraft spent a brief period refreshing themselves in single-engined jet aircraft by conducting training flights in AT-33s. This modified version of the T-Bird had two .50-caliber machine guns, a practice bomb dispenser, and basic rocket launching capabilities. The second training support aircraft used by McConnell was the T-39 Sabreliner. This aircraft was equipped with three radar consoles identical to those found in the F-105. This allowed for supervised training of students in the use of the Thunderchief's radar mapping and targeting systems.

Air-to-ground weapons training was conducted at the Smoky Hill Air Force Gunnery Range in central Kansas, located just 90 miles northwest of McConnell. The process to gain mastery in weapons delivery in the F-105 was based on a staged approach. Accordingly, Smoky Hill was divided into three separate target complexes– a conventional range, a tactical range, and a radar range. The pilots had to attain proficiency on one range before they were able to advance to the next.

On the conventional range, the first for the new pilots, the training consisted of skip bombing, dive bombing, strafing, rockets, napalm, and cluster bombing. On this range, the pilot focused solely on hitting targets and pulling out of the dive. Once the pilot passed the conventional range, they advanced to the more challenging tactical range. Here, pilots developed the ability to operate in a search and destroy mode, aiming for targets such as a pontoon bridge, a simulated SAM site, cars, trucks, or complete convoys. The final step was the radar range, where pilots practiced delivery of conventional bombs using the radar toss-bomb system.

During the 23rd TFW's peak training years, Thuds could be found operating over the Smoky Hill range almost constantly. On any given day, the first training flights bound for the weapons range took off from McConnell at daybreak and were followed by additional flights about every thirty minutes. On a typical mission, the students would spend about 25 minutes on the range, making approximately twelve passes while firing on targets.

Although there were four training squadrons assigned to the 23rd TFW, only two squadrons were generally using the weapons range at a time. One squadron usually could be found at George AFB, California. Here, a class of students that had graduated from the Smoky Hill range spent three weeks in air-to-air and air-to-ground gunnery training, which included firing live missiles. Another squadron was typically preparing to complete its training or would be working on aerobatics and formation flying.

During the fall of 1970, the last Thuds operating in the strike role over Southeast Asia returned to the U.S. This allowed three of the 23rd TFW's squadrons to return to combat-ready operations. Over its five-year tenure of replacement training, the wing graduated over 600 new Thud pilots and retrained more than 150. Nearly all of the students that graduated from McConnell served one or more tours of duty in Southeast Asia, and many distinguished themselves by extraordinary heroism. Up to five pilots went on to down MiGs in air-to-air combat.

This F-105D (61-0183) of the 563rd TFS, seen at McConnell in April 1969, shows a common training mission configuration consisting of a practice bomb dispenser on the centerline and rocket pods on the outboard pylons. (Jerry Geer)

A true sense of bombing targets in North Vietnam was experienced when students hit mock targets on the Smokey Hill Gunnery Range with inert 750-pound bombs. This 563rd TFS Thud (61-0065) was prepared for such a mission when photographed at McConnell in April 1969. (Jerry Geer)

This 4519th CCTS F-105D (60-0519) at McConnell in April 1969 carries a captive AIM-9B Sidewinder missile on the outboard pylon for an air-to-air training mission. (Jerry Geer)

After ending their RTU mission in the fall of 1970, the squadrons of the 23rd TFW continued to frequent the Smokey Hill Gunnery Range as part of their training program to maintain combat-readiness. Here, a flight of 561st TFS F-105Gs return to McConnell after making the rounds on the range in the spring of 1972. (Don Kutyna)

The ammunition drum of this 562nd TFS F-105D (61-0199) has been exposed for servicing during a deployment to George AFB, California in May 1970. (Lars Soldeus via James Geer)

A 563rd TFS F-105B (57-5823) carries a dart gunnery target for advanced air-to-air training out of George in July 1969. The B-models were strictly flown by instructor pilots due to the significant differences in the aircraft's weapons system to the F-105D. (J. Duny via Paul Minert)

CHAPTER FIVE

35th Tactical Fighter Wing

The 35th Tactical Fighter Wing traces its lineage to the activation of the 35th Pursuit Group at Moffett Field, California on 1 February 1940. The unit trained pilots in P-35s, P-36s, and P-39s before moving to Australia in May 1942 and becoming the 35th Fighter Group. During the next several years, the group served in many World War II air campaigns while operating from a variety of bases in the South Pacific.

After the war, the group found its way to Japan where it operated F-51s (and later F-61s and F-82s) in the air defense mission. On 18 August 1948, the 35th Fighter Wing was activated, with the 35th Fighter Group subordinate to it. After converting to F-80s in early 1950, both units respectively became the 35th Fighter Bomber Group and Wing. Over the next seven years, the group relocated to various bases in Japan and Korea and operated the RF-51, RF-80, RC-45, RT-7, F-82, F-86, and F-94 aircraft before inactivating with its parent wing in October 1957.

On 1 April 1966, the unit replaced the 7572nd TFW when it reactivated as the 35th Tactical Fighter Wing, flying combat missions in F-4Cs, B-57s, and F-102s out of Da Nang AB, South Vietnam. The wing replaced the 366th TFW when it relocated to Phan Rang AB, South Vietnam during October 1966. With the transfer, the 35th became the parent organization at Phan Rang and began operating F-100s alongside B-57s, which followed the wing to its new base. The 35th added the A-37 in 1970 before inactivating the following year on 31 July 1971.

The 35th TFW was tasked with training F-4 flight crews when it was activated again on 1 October 1971 at George AFB, California, replacing the 479th TFW. Initially, the assigned flying components were the 434th TFS, 4435th TFRS, 4535th CCTS, and the 4452nd CCTS. In late 1972, the 20th and 21st TFTS replaced the 4452nd and 4535th CCTS respectively. Beginning in 1973, the wing's mission expanded when a staged process to consolidate TAC F-105G and F-4C Wild Weasel assets at George was put into action.

The first step in the consolidation program took place during July 1973, when the F-105G-equipped 561st TFS relocated from McConnell AFB, Kansas to George. A second F-105G component was added when the 17th WWS returned from Southeast Asia and arrived at George as the 562nd TFS during October 1974. Finally, the end of Weasel operations at Nellis AFB, Nevada during July 1975 brought the F-105G and F-4C Weasel training programs to George in the form of the 563rd TFTS. These actions gave the 35th TFW the mission of not only training F-4 crews, but also the responsibility of training Weasel crews while providing combat-ready squadrons in the F-105G.

To maintain combat proficiency, the Weasel squadrons trained extensively in electronic warfare and ground attack operations. Electronic warfare encompassed nearly 60 percent of the total flying time and primarily involved training at the Caliente Range at Nellis. The ground attack program was carried out at the Cuddleback and Leach Lake Ranges, both located in the California desert. To test their readiness, the 561st and 562nd TFS regularly participated in tactical exercises and made several deployments to Europe for training in overseas environments. For its exceptional peacetime operations in standing combat-ready in the F-105G and providing aircrews for deployment to Wild Weasel and F-4 operational units, the 35th TFW received the USAF Outstanding Unit Award for the period 2 February 1976 to 31 March 1977.

The makeup of the 35th TFW went through additional changes in the second half of the 1970s. The first involved the F-4 training program and saw the 431st TFTS replace the 4435th TRTS in early 1976. A year and a half later, the 35th TFW reorganized its Weasel training function and replaced the 563rd TFTS with the 39th TFTS. The wing started receiving the new F-4G advanced Wild Weasel in the spring of 1978 and shortly thereafter, began to gradually phase-out its F-105Gs. The last of the Thuds departed George on 27 July 1980 for the Military Aircraft Storage and Disposition Center (MASDC) at Davis-Monthan AFB, Arizona.

Wing commanders during the 35th TFW's period of operating the Thunderchief were Col. William J. Holton (20 July 1972), Col. Charles R. Beaver (24 August 1973), Col. Richard A. Haggren (11 July 1975), Brig. Gen. Robert W. Clement (2 February 1976), Brig. Gen. Cecil D. Crabb (9 August 1976), Col. Dudley J. Foster (21 October 1977), Col. Roland W. Moore, Jr. (22 December 1978), and Col. James D. Terry (17 January 1980).

The first Weasel outfit to join the 35th TFW was the 561st TFS in July 1973. This F-105G (63-8306) bears the wing's standard GA tail code when seen one month after the squadron arrived at George AFB, California. (J.P. Loomis via Jerry Geer)

Although originally unique to the 561st TFS, the yellow tail band was applied to all of the 35th's Thuds while the wing followed the centralized maintenance concept during the 1974-75 time period. This F-105G (62-4416) displays these standardized markings when photographed at George in August 1975. (Jerry Geer)

Three F-105Gs of the 35th TFW are seen over California in October 1975 with their four petal speed brakes wide open. (Bill Malerba via Paul Minert)

The 35th TFW discontinued using the standard yellow tail band during the fall of 1975 and started allowing squadrons to use different colored tail bands to designate their aircraft. The 562nd TFS used a dark green tail band trimmed in white as illustrated by this F-105G (63-8345) at George in October 1975. (Bill Malerba via James Geer)

Despite their age, the combat veteran F-105Gs of the 35th TFW performed well during their final years of service as TAC's primary Weasel platform. This 561st TFS machine (62-4439) is seen at George on 17 July 1977. (Bob Pickett via Kansas Air Museum)

The 35th TFW reorganized its Weasel RTU program in mid-1977 and replaced the 563rd TFTS with the 39th TFTS. Seen at George on 2 August 1977, this F-105G (62-4427) was one of about twelve that operated alongside a similar number of F-4Cs with the new squadron. (Peter Bergagnini via James Geer)

An F-105G (63-8355) of the 562nd TFS at George in June 1979 displays the WW tail code brought into use during the aircraft's final year of service with the 35th TFW. (Peter Mancus via Jerry Geer)

The 562nd TFS was the last squadron of the 35th TFW to give up its Weasel Thuds. As the F-105G neared retirement from active duty service, the squadron painted sharkmouths on its aircraft as seen in this photograph taken at Nellis AFB, Nevada in April 1980. (Paul Minert Collection)

39th Tactical Fighter Training Squadron

The 39th Tactical Fighter Training Squadron replaced the 563rd TFTS on 1 July 1977 as part of a training reorganization within the 35th TFW. The squadron assumed the Wild Weasel RTU mission of the former unit for both the Thud and Phantom programs. Accordingly, the unit inherited an equal number of F-105Gs and F-4Cs, the latter being a mix of standard and Weasel variants. The 39th TFTS trained F-105G crews until the fall of 1978, when it phased-out the program and began transitioning Thud crews to the Phantom in anticipation of the arrival of the F-4G advanced Wild Weasel.

BELOW: This view of an F-105G (62-4428) of the 39th TFTS was taken just seventeen days after the squadron replaced the 563rd TFTS as the Weasel RTU at George on 1 July 1977. The 39th retained the red tail band markings of its forerunner, but removed the superimposed "Ace of Spades" device in time. (Bob Pickett via Kansas Air Museum)

BOTTOM: A 39th TFTS F-105G (62-4427) taxis to the George runway after completing its "last chance" inspection for a training sortie on 17 July 1977. (Bob Pickett via Kansas Air Museum)

561st Tactical Fighter Squadron

The 561st Tactical Fighter Squadron was reassigned from the 832nd AD to the 35th TFW on 15 July 1973, although operational control was gained two weeks earlier when the unit moved from McConnell to George. The squadron first began operating the Thud back in 1963, when it was equipped with F-105Ds within the 388th TFW at McConnell. It was reassigned to the 23rd TFW in early 1964 and operated as a combat-ready unit before commencing an RTU function in 1966. The 561st returned to operational status in late 1970 after transitioning to F-105Gs. In the spring of 1972, the squadron became a split unit when it deployed twelve F-105Gs as Detachment 1, 561st TFS to Korat RTAFB, Thailand for combat duty. After the 23rd TFW ended Thud operations in mid-1972, the portion of the 561st still at McConnell was reassigned to the 832nd AD.

The 561st TFS remained divided after joining the 35th TFW until 10 September 1973, when Detachment 1 returned from Thailand under Operation Coronet Bolo IV. For the next seven years, the 561st trained as a combat-ready unit with the F-105G. Like all flying components of the 35th TFW, the squadron was given the Air Force Outstanding Unit Award for operations over the period 2 February 1976 to 31 March 1977. The conversion to the F-4G started when the first of the new advanced Wild Weasels arrived on 28 April 1978. Through an extended transition period, the 561st TFS continued to operate the F-105G alongside a growing number of F-4Gs. Beginning in the early fall of 1978, the unit began sending its Thuds to the Georgia Air Guard's 128th TFS, 116th TFW or MASDC at Davis-Monthan AFB, Arizona. The last F-105G had departed by the beginning of 1980, ending the unit's seventeen-year association with the Thunderchief.

An F-105G (62-4428) of the 561st TFS on the George flightline in December 1973. By this time, the squadron's long-term split unit status had ended as Detachment 1 had returned from Southeast Asia three months earlier. (Peter Mancus via Jerry Geer)

Carrying an inert Standard ARM on the inboard pylon, a 561st TFS F-105G (62-4442) heads for the Caliente Range at Nellis AFB, Nevada to engage some simulated air defense sites on 8 January 1975. (Jim Rotramel via Jerry Geer)

This F-105G (62-4425) of the 561st TFS is seen parked on the crowded George ramp in August 1975. The yellow tail band that was once exclusive to the 561st was adopted by the 35th TFW as a standard marking on all its Thuds for about one year beginning in the fall of 1974. (Jerry Geer)

Sporting a fresh paint job, this 561st TFS F-105G (63-8304) waits for its next mission on a typical sunny day at George in August 1975. (Jerry Geer)

A 561st TFS F-105G (63-8266) is about to slide into position for refueling from a KC-135 tanker during a training flight in 1976. (Leroy Nielsen via Paul Minert)

This 561st TFS Thud (63-8276) was photographed while the squadron was deployed to Spangdahlem AB, Germany in September 1976 for training in the NATO operational environment. Note the specially painted fuel tank fins and nose gear radar reflector commemorating the American bicentennial. (James Geer Collection)

Another training sortie comes to an end as this 561st TFS F-105G (63-8285) makes its final approach for landing at George in January 1977. (Peter Mancus via Norm Taylor)

Nestled amongst the 561st TFS Weasels at George on 17 July 1977 was this standard F-105F (63-8263) trainer. Note the addition of the squadron's "Black Knights" device to the yellow tail band. (Bob Pickett via Kansas Air Museum)

This 561st F-105G (63-8320) claimed three MiG kills during the war in Southeast Asia, although only a downing on 19 December 1967 was officially credited. This photograph was taken at George on 17 July 1977. (Bob Pickett via Kansas Air Museum)

562nd Tactical Fighter Squadron

The 562nd Tactical Fighter Squadron was activated on 31 October 1974 as the second F-105G-equipped unit within the 35th TFW. The squadron's history with the Thud began in 1963 with the 388th TFW at McConnell. In early 1964, it was reassigned to the 23rd TFW and flew F-105D/Fs until being inactivated in the summer of 1972. Upon being reactivated at George, the 562nd was formed from the personnel and resources of the 17th WWS, 388th TFW, which redeployed from Korat RTAFB, Thailand during the last week of October 1974 under Operation Coronet Exxon.

Through the second half of the 1970s, the 562nd TFS trained as a combat-ready unit with its F-105Gs. The transition to the F-4G began during 1979; however, the squadron retained its Thuds in dwindling numbers for another year. As the last F-105 unit in TAC, the 562nd brought an end to the aircraft's active duty career when it flew its last Thunderchief training sortie on 12 July 1980. During the squadron's time with the F-105G, it received the Air Force Outstanding Unit Award for operations over the period 2 February 1976 to 31 March 1977.

BELOW: During its first year at George, the 562nd TFS aircraft carried a yellow tail band in common with all of the 35th TFW Thuds. This F-105G (63-8350) was photographed at George in August 1975. (Jerry Geer)

A dark green tail band trimmed in white formed the 562nd's distinctive markings when this F-105G (63-8307) was caught at George on 17 July 1977. (Bob Pickett via Kansas Air Museum)

Visiting McConnell AFB, Kansas during a cross-country hop on 30 June 1978, an F-105F (63-8343) of the 562nd TFS evokes memories of a bygone era at the base when it was under TAC jurisdiction and supported active duty Thud operations. (Chuck Stewart via James Geer)

A 562nd TFS F-105G (63-8278) taxis off the transient ramp at Davis-Monthan AFB, Arizona on 24 May 1979. (Ben Knowles via Paul Minert)

Seen at George in June 1979, this famous triple MiG killer F-105G (63-8320) closed out its career with the 562nd TFS. Carried just below the windscreen in a white box is the name Hanoi Hustler with three red stars representing the aerial victories. (Peter Mancus via Norm Taylor)

An F-105G (63-8305) of the 562nd TFS displays the squadron's newly adopted WW tail code when seen at Davis-Monthan in the fall of 1979. (Brian Rogers via Jerry Geer)

Taken on 30 March 1980, this 562nd TFS F-105G (63-8278) at Nellis AFB, Nevada for Red Flag displays newly applied black tail codes and serial numbers. (Brian Rogers via Jerry Geer)

The 562nd TFS was the last remaining unit of the 35th TFW still flying the Thud by the time this F-105G (63-8285) was photographed at George in January 1980. (Paul Minert Collection)

This F-105G of the 562nd TFS (63-8296) is seen landing at Nellis after a Red Flag mission in early April 1980. (Paul Minert Collection)

The 562nd TFS started adding sharkmouths to its Thuds during the early spring of 1980. This F-105G (62-4434) carried the new marking when photographed at Nellis in April 1980 during the squadron's Red Flag deployment. (Paul Minert Collection)

A 562nd TFS F-105G (63-8285) taxis back to the George ramp after completing a routine training mission on 29 April 1980. (James Geer Collection)

An F-105G (63-8303) recovers at George during its latter days of service with 562nd TFS. The squadron withdrew the last Thuds from active duty status just over two weeks after flying its final training sortie in the aircraft on 12 July 1980. (Paul Minert Collection)

563rd Tactical Fighter Training Squadron

The 563rd Tactical Fighter Training Squadron was activated within the 35th TFW on 31 July 1975. The squadron's history with the F-105 began in 1963 while assigned to the 388th TFW at McConnell. After being reassigned to the 23rd TFW in early 1964, the unit operated Thuds for eight years before being inactivated. Upon being reactivated at George, the 563rd was tasked with the F-105G and F-4C Wild Weasel RTU mission. Its personnel and resources came from the 66th FWS, 57th FWW, which previously carried out the Weasel training program at Nellis AFB, Nevada.

The squadron served in its training role until 1 July 1977, when it was replaced by the 39th TFTS. For the diligent execution of its mission over the period 2 February 1976 to 31 March 1977, the 563rd received the Air Force Outstanding Unit Award. After being replaced, the squadron maintained a non-operational status until 1981. At that time, it began functioning as a combat-ready unit in the F-4G with the 37th TFW at George.

The 563rd TFTS was using a red tail band as its distinctive unit identifier when this F-105G (63-8274) was photographed at George in 1976. The band was bordered in white and had the unit's "Ace of Spades" device at its center. (James Geer Collection)

BELOW: The 563rd TFTS (63-8300) was formed when the Weasel RTU function and associated assets were transferred from Nellis AFB, Nevada to George in July 1975. Pictured less than one month after the move, this 563rd F-105G displays the standard GA code and yellow tail band carried by all 35th TFW Thuds at that time. (Jerry Geer)

This F-105F (63-8263) at George in August 1975 was also a former Nellis-based Thud that relocated to George to serve with the 563rd TFTS. (Jerry Geer)

CHAPTER SIX

36th Tactical Fighter Wing

The 36th Tactical Fighter Wing history began when it was activated as the 36th Pursuit Group on 1 February 1940 at Langley Field, Virginia. The group was equipped with P-36s and carried out extensive training for about one year before moving to Puerto Rico. In 1942, the unit was assigned to the Defense Command and became the 36th Fighter Group with P-39s and P-40s. Change continued in early 1943 as the group moved to Charleston, South Carolina and was re-equipped with P-47s. The unit took its Thunderbolts to England and joined war effort with the Eighth Air Force in April 1944. It relocated to France four months later and remained in Europe for the next two years before returning to the U.S.

The group was located at Howard Field, Canal Zone flying F-80s when it became a subordinate unit of the newly activated 36th Fighter Wing in July 1948. One month later, the 36th moved to Furstenfeldbruck AB, Germany to become a component of USAFE. A respective change in designation to the 36th Fighter Bomber Group and Wing took place in January 1950, followed by a transition to F-84Es later that year. Located at Bitburg AB, Germany from December 1952, the 36th flirted with F-84Gs before re-equipping with F-86Fs in mid-1954. This action saw the units become the 36th Fighter Day Group and Wing.

During the spring of 1956, F-100Cs began replacing the F-86Fs. Organizational change followed in December 1957, when the 36th Fighter Day Group was inactivated and its squadrons and lineage were passed on to its parent unit. In July 1958, the 36th became a Tactical Fighter Wing. At one point during its Super Sabre era, the wing directly controlled up to five squadrons. Although this was the case, only the 22nd, 23rd, and 53rd TFS were assigned when it became the first overseas wing to receive the F-105D Thunderchief during 1961.

As with all units converting to the Thud in the early 1960s, pilots were sent to Nellis AFB, Nevada for transition training with the 4520th CCTW. The wing's first class started in March 1961 and was made-up of pilots from the 22nd TFS. Upon conclusion of the two-month course, the newly trained pilots ferried aircraft from the Mobile Air Material Area (MOAMA) at Brookley AFB, Alabama to Germany. The first ferry operation concluded on 12 May 1961, when Lt. Gary Retterbush and his wingman landed two Thuds at Bitburg. Three weeks later, on 3 June 1961, the new aircraft was officially accepted into USAFE service at the Paris Air Show by General Frederic H. Smith, USAFE commander, and Brig. Gen. Robert L. Delashaw, 36th TFW commander.

22nd TFS

23rd TFS

53rd TFS

The early markings applied to the 36th TFW F-105s consisted of three broad diagonal tail bands painted in the squadron color, trimmed in white or black. Seen in 1961, the red bands on this F-105D (60-0438) signal that it was an aircraft of the 22nd TFS. (Norman Powell via Jerry Geer)

The switch to the F-105 occurred at a steady pace during 1961, with the 22nd TFS becoming fully equipped by July, followed by the 23rd TFS in August, and the 53rd TFS in October. With the new aircraft, the 36th TFW continued its established Cold War mission of tactical nuclear weapons delivery in support of the NATO alliance. To attain IOC, the wing deployed to Wheelus AB, Libya, where the vast El Uotia Bombing Range allowed for training in nuclear strike techniques. By the end of 1961, the wing had established a permanent detachment at Wheelus. This extension utilized about ten percent of the wing's aircraft and half of its total flying time.

During the fall of 1962, the 36th TFW entered the F-105D modification program known as Operation Look-Alike. The modifications, aimed at upgrading the wing's -10RE configured aircraft with conventional warfare capabilities, were completed over a twelve-month period. During this time, the wing successfully maintained a combat-ready rating even though many of its aircraft were continually rotating through the program.

As a result of the extensive use of the Thud in the air war against North Vietnam and the corresponding need for replacement aircraft, the 36th TFW was earmarked for conversion to the F-4D Phantom II during late 1965. By the time the first F-4s arrived in March 1966, the wing had already returned about half of its F-105s to the U.S. for overhaul. After upgrading, the aircraft were either delivered to the 23rd TFW at McConnell AFB, Kansas or were dispatched to Southeast Asia.

A 22nd TFS F-105D (60-0430) sits on the soggy ramp at Hahn AB, Germany in 1961. (David Menard via Norm Taylor)

Following Brig. Gen. Delashaw, those who commanded the wing during its Thunderchief era were Col. John H. Buckner (11 June 1963), Brig. Gen. Gordon F. Blood (11 July 1963), Col. James F. Hackler, Jr. (22 August 1964), and Col. Benjamin B. Cassiday, Jr. (6 August 1966).

Weapons Training at Wheelus

Wheelus AB, Libya served as the principal weapons training site for USAFE fighter units during the 1950s and 1960s. Serving as the USAFE Weapons Center, the primary mission of the base was to provide gunnery, bombing, and rocket-firing training to pilots assigned to fighter units in Europe. Air-to-ground weapons training was conducted at the nearby El Uotia Bombing Range, while nearly all air-to-air training took place over the Mediterranean.

Simultaneous with the Thunderchief's arrival, planners at Wheelus were challenged to restructure the training program to follow the new flexible response policy that was introduced by the Kennedy administration. The new program emphasized conventional weapons capability and eventually led to the reorganization and redesignation of the resident 7272nd Air Base Wing to the 7272nd Flying Training Wing. Under the new structure, the wing was responsible for the planning, execution, and evaluation for all units deployed at Wheelus.

The training facilities at Wheelus eased the 36th TFW's transition to the F-105, although the introduction of the technologically advanced aircraft placed great strain on day-to-day operations at the base. Advanced plans to integrate the Thud into the training program began some two years before the arrival of the first aircraft. To provide some measure of combat readiness during the wing's transition period, the initial phase of training concentrated on nuclear weapons delivery techniques. Only limited conventional weapons training took place, which mainly comprised of air-to-ground training in the use of the aircraft's Vulcan cannon.

The first group of Thunderchiefs to deploy to the Libyan base was from the wing's 22nd TFS. The unit arrived at Wheelus with twelve aircraft on 16 July 1961. Two days later, the 22nd flew its first training sorties and within a short period of time was averaging eighteen sorties a day. Although this was the case, early training operations proved to be troublesome for the F-105. The advanced electronic components were the main source of the problem. Spare parts were in short supply and maintenance personnel often lacked the experience needed to perform the necessary fixes.

This line-up of 23rd TFS Thuds displays the unit's blue tail bands in the late afternoon sun at Wheelus AB, Libya in late 1961. (R. Griffin via Jerry Geer)

An F-105D (60-0500) visiting Hahn in 1961 carries the yellow and black tail band markings of the 53rd TFS. (David Menard via Jerry Geer)

These difficulties limited the number of aircraft available to between six and ten on any given day. To overcome the deficiencies and achieve combat capability in the shortest time possible, the squadron flew some aircraft up to four times during one day until the problems were resolved.

After the 22nd's pilots had achieved a qualified rating in the delivery of nuclear weapons, the wing's 23rd and 53rd TFS successfully cycled through the first phase of the training program. To become fully combat qualified in the Thud, the wing's pilots returned to Wheelus for subsequent training that focused on conventional bombing techniques and advanced nuclear weapons delivery.

Training at Wheelus did not end after pilots achieved an initial combat-ready rating. To stay proficient at using the aircraft's weapons systems, aircrews returned to Libya on a rotational basis at the frequency of about once every two months for two to four-week training sessions. This ongoing use of the Wheelus facilities was essential to sustaining operational readiness as the weather and terrain in Germany restricted training to such areas as formation, navigation, and instrument flying.

Two 53rd TFS F-105Ds (60-0527 and 60-0506) cruise high over the Atlantic during a 1961 transit flight. (James Geer Collection)

A line-up of 36th TFW Thuds prepares to launch out of Wheelus for conventional weapons training on the El Uotia Bombing Range. Nearest the camera is an F-105D of the 22nd TFS, while behind are aircraft from the 53rd and 23rd TFS. (Jerry Geer Collection)

A change in USAFE marking policy in 1962 required the 36th TFW to revise its tail band design to include all three squadron colors. This F-105D (61-0155) sported the new look when it was photographed on 22 September 1962 while participating in the biennial weapons competition at Nellis AFB, Nevada. (Doug Olson)

A small blue triangle painted below the cockpit on the left side identifies these F-105Ds (60-0441 and 61-0124) as belonging to the 23rd TFS. This method of denoting squadron assignment was used after the adoption of the tri-colored "wing" tail band. (USAF via Jerry Geer)

This 23rd TFS F-105D (60-0474) was part of the static display at an open house at Sculthorpe, England in the early 1960s. (Paul Minert Collection)

These 36th TFW Thuds are seen in formation over Germany circa 1964. (USAF via Jerry Geer)

Each squadron of the 36th TFW was assigned at least two F-105Fs for training purposes. This example (63-8319) was photographed at Soelingen AB, Germany in November 1964. (Norm Taylor Collection)

The aluminized lacquer finish on this 36th TFW F-105D (60-0436) at Soelingen in February 1965 is starting to show signs of wear from being exposed to the constant inclement weather conditions in Germany. (Norm Taylor Collection)

This view shows 36th TFW F-105Ds and French Super Mystere B-2s flying in formation near Cambrai AB during a NATO exchange operation that saw the units train together at their respective home bases for a ten-day period in April 1965. (USAF via James Geer)

The three external fuel tanks carried by this 36th TFW F-105D (61-0136) at Wheelus in 1965 suggests that it is scheduled for a return flight back to Bitburg. (USAF via Kansas Air Museum)

In early 1965, some USAFE Thuds received experimental camouflage finishes prior to the introduction of this paint scheme in Southeast Asia. This F-105D (60-5376) at Bitburg in May 1965 was one of several 36th TFW aircraft to carry the new battle dress. (Paul Minert Collection)

A 23rd TFS F-105F (63-8327) stands ready for its next training sortie at Bitburg in September 1965. (Stephen Peltz via Norm Taylor)

This F-105D (60-0481) of the 53rd TFS was photographed during an open house at Beauvechain, Belgium in May 1966. Note the buzz numbers have been removed from the forward fuselage. (Jerry Geer Collection)

CHAPTER SEVEN

41st Air Division/6441st Tactical Fighter Wing

The 41st Air Division history dates back to the 1950s, when it was formed as a subordinate unit of the Fifth Air Force. Initially located at Johnson AB, Japan, the division moved to Yokota AB on 1 July 1962. Two years later, it assumed operations in the Thunderchief as a result of the decision to close Itazuke AB, Japan and relocate the three fighter squadrons and supporting elements formerly assigned to the 8th TFW to Yokota.

The 35th, 36th, and 80th TFS were reassigned to the 41st AD on 18 June 1964, although operational control of the units was gained upon their arrival at Yokota one month earlier. With the F-105D/F, the 41st was tasked with the primary mission of maintaining an around-the-clock readiness for tactical air requirements of the Fifth Air Force and Pacific Air Forces. Specific operational tasks included supplying fighter squadrons to Osan AB, Korea for nuclear alert duty.

The 41st AD introduced the Thud to combat when it began sending its squadrons on rotational tours to Southeast Asia in August 1964. The deployments continued into 1965, but organizational changes at Yokota saw the 35th, 36th, and 80th TFS reassigned to a new parent unit, the provisional 6441st TFW. This wing was formed at Yokota as an interim host unit for the F-105 squadrons pending USAF approval of a new permanent wing designation and insignia. The 6441st was activated on 1 April 1965 and was subordinate to the 41st AD. Its establishment had no impact on mission status or rotational combat duty for its assigned squadrons. The wing's diligence in performing its mission over the period 4 May to 8 June 1965 saw it earn the Air Force Outstanding Unit Award.

Yokota's Thud squadrons continued to maintain their alert commitment at Osan during the time they supported the air war in Southeast Asia. Initially, TAC squadrons on temporary assignment in Japan were on hand to augment the alert requirement. However, backup units were not available by 1966 since all other F-105 units were either flying combat or training replacement crews. This caused the pilots at Yokota to rotate to Osan more frequently than ever before. Prior to the war, pilots rotated to Osan one week out of every month. During 1965, they found themselves returning to Osan every third week and by 1966, as often as every other week.

Rotational tours to Southeast Asia ended in late 1965, but the wing's involvement in the war did not end at that point. Over the next few years, pilots were sent to Thailand on an individual TDY basis to augment combat units at Takhli or Korat. In addition, the 41st AD organized a new Thud squadron to be sent PCS to Korat in May 1966. Designated the 34th TFS, the new unit was made-up from the assets of the 36th TFS, although pilots were drawn from all of Yokota's squadrons. Upon activation, the 34th was assigned to the 41st AD but attached to the 388th TFW. The formation of the 34th TFS left Yokota with two operational Thud squadrons, reducing the need for the provisional 6441st TFW. Consequently, the wing was discontinued on 15 November 1966, and the two remaining F-105 squadrons were reassigned to the 41st AD. Active flying components assigned to the 41st at that time included not only the 35th and 80th TFS, but also the 6091st RS, which operated EB-57Es and RC-130Bs.

The wing's contribution to the war was significant but the price was high. Between August 1964 and January 1968, 27 pilots from Yokota had been shot down. Of these, nine were killed or listed MIA, eight were taken POW, and ten were rescued. All the while, the wing's Thuds were gradually depleted. Twelve aircraft were lost while squadrons served on rotational duty in Thailand. Of this total, ten were combat losses and two were operational. The formation of the 34th TFS saw 21 F-105Ds deploy to Southeast Asia, and numerous other aircraft were sent to the war zone as attrition replacements.

This drain on the wing's complement of F-105s forced the 35th TFS to cease operations in the early summer of 1967, leaving the 80th TFS as the sole Thud operator at Yokota. Plans to re-equip the 35th, 36th, and 80th TFS with the F-4C Phantom II were put into action during late 1967. At that time, the 35th and 36th TFS regained operational status with the new aircraft; however, the 80th TFS retained its Thuds into 1968. On 15 January 1968, the 41st AD was inactivated and replaced by a new host unit at Yokota, the 347th TFW. Accordingly, all units previously assigned to the 41st were reassigned to the 347th.

Commanders during the 41st AD's association with the F-105 included Col. Maurice L. Martin (27 July 1963) and Col. Paul P. Douglas, Jr. (26 July 1965). Commanders of the provisional 6441st TFW were Col. Chester "John Black" L. Van Etten (1 April 1965) and Col. Allen K. McDonald (by 1 September 1966).

When the Itazuke Thuds were reassigned to the 41st AD at Yokota, they retained their distinctive unit markings consisting of an arrow on the intake painted in the individual squadron colors. This F-105D (62-4344) landing at Yokota on 26 May 1964 displays the yellow arrow markings of the 80th TFS. (Toyokazu Matsuzaki)

Two 41st AD Thuds are seen against Mount Fuji in Japan circa mid-1964. The lead aircraft is an F-105F (63-8280) bearing the red arrow markings of the 36th TFS, while the second is an F-105D (62-4355) with the yellow arrows of the 80th TFS. (Paul Minert Collection)

Final days of peace: F-105s of the 41st AD line the ramp at Yokota on a "down day" in July 1964. One month later, the division started rotating squadrons to Thailand in response to the outbreak of hostilities in Southeast Asia. (Yukio Enomoto)

This view catches two 41st AD Thuds on a section approach to one of Yokota's runways in September 1964. The closest aircraft is a 36th TFS F-105D (62-4377), while behind is an 80th TFS F-105F (62-8283). (Yukio Enomoto)

In April 1965, the provisional 6441st TFW assumed control of Yokota's Thud squadrons when it was formed as a subordinate unit of the 41st AD. Here, a mixed flight of 6441st Thuds prepares to launch out of Yokota on 15 June 1965, comprising F-105Fs of the 35th (63-8279), 80th (63-8291), and 36th TFS (63-8271). (Toyokazu Matsuzaki)

This 35th TFS F-105F (63-8274) in the pattern at Yokota displays the tri-colored "wing" tail band adopted by the 6441st TFW in mid-1965. (Toyokazu Matsuzaki)

A diamond formation of three 6441st TFW F-105Fs and a TAC F-105D makes a low pass over Yokota on 3 October 1965. (Toyokazu Matsuzaki)

Silver Thuds became increasingly rare during 1966 as orders required all aircraft to be camouflaged as they processed through overhaul facilities. Seen on 8 June 1966, this F-105F (63-8359) of the 6441st TFW was one of the last of Yokota's Thuds to give up its aluminized lacquer finish. (Toyokazu Matsuzaki)

The 6441st TFW lost one of its squadrons in mid-1966, when the 36th TFS was reorganized as the 34th TFS and sent to Korat on a PCS basis to join the 388th TFW. This F-105D (62-4372) was only days away from deploying to Thailand as an element of the 34th when photographed at Yokota on 8 June 1966. (Toyokazu Matsuzaki)

The 41st AD resumed control of Yokota's Thud squadrons after the provisional 6441st TFW was inactivated in November 1966. Here, an F-105D (62-4301) assigned to the division's 80th TFS taxis in after completing a training mission in April 1967. (Jerry Geer Collection)

The continual draw of Yokota's Thuds to Southeast Asia as replacement aircraft left the base with only one Thud squadron, the 80th, by mid-1967. Seen on 5 January 1968, these GR-coded F-105Ds (60-0453 and 62-4375) of the 80th TFS, 41st AD are undergoing final checks prior to heading out to the active runway at Yokota. (Katsuhiko Tokunaga via Jerry Geer)

35th Tactical Fighter Squadron

The 35th Tactical Fighter Squadron was detached from the 8th TFW and placed under the control of the 41st AD when it moved from Itazuke to Yokota on 13 May 1964. The squadron was formally reassigned to the 41st on 18 June 1964. Originally equipped with F-105Ds within the 8th TFW in 1963, the unit's reassignment saw it continue to maintain combat readiness in the Thud.

In the fall of 1964, the 35th TFS became the second unit at Yokota to deploy to Southeast Asia in support of early contingency operations in the region. The first crews arrived at Korat RTAFB, Thailand on 24 September to gradually replace the 36th TFS. The balance of the 35th had rotated to Korat by 5 October, allowing its sister unit to return home. Placed under the control of the 2nd AD, the squadron's primary responsibility was to be ready to assist in the recovery of downed aircrews in Laos. Pilots pulled cockpit alert for 30-minute intervals and several launches took place, but most calls for air support turned out to be false alarms. During their time at Korat, the squadron did not fly any strike missions. The 35th concluded its first combat deployment on 20 November 1964.

The 35th TFS was reassigned from the 41st AD to the provisional 6441st TFW on 1 April 1965. The establishment of this temporary wing at Yokota did not change the squadron's mission within PACAF. A major aspect of their mission was to provide aircraft and crews for nuclear alert duty at Osan AB, Korea. In a three-squadron rotation, the 35th would typically spend one week at Osan, return to Yokota for two weeks, and then go back to Osan for one week, repeating the pattern again and again.

The squadron returned to Thailand on or about 4 May 1965 for combat duty at Takhli RTAFB while attached to the provisional 6235th TFW. For nearly two months, the 35th TFS bombed military installations and lines of communication in the southern panhandle region of North Vietnam under the Rolling Thunder campaign. Targets attacked included ammo and supply depots, barracks, port facilities, airfields, radar sites, and bridges. Highlighting the unit's action in the North was its participation in a massive strike against the Thanh Hoa Bridge on 7 May. In Laos, the 35th TFS conducted Barrel Roll strikes in the north and Steel Tiger interdiction missions against Communist supply routes in the panhandle region. Also flown were a number of Yankee Team missions that consisted of armed escort of reconnaissance aircraft.

On 26 June 1965, the 35th concluded its combat tour when it returned to Yokota after being replaced by the 80th TFS. The squadron did not lose any pilots or aircraft to enemy action during its TDY at Takhli, but one aircraft crashed due to operational causes. For its performance in Southeast Asia from 4 May to 8 June 1965, the unit received the Air Force Outstanding Unit Award with Combat "V" Device. In addition, together with all squadrons assigned to the 6441st TFW, the 35th TFS received an Outstanding Unit Award for operations over the period 1 April to 30 June 1965.

The 35th TFS returned to Southeast Asia for a third time during the fall of 1965. The deployment began on or about 19 October, when the bulk of the squadron rotated to Takhli to replace the 36th TFS. Attached to the provisional 6235th TFW, the 35th flew alongside its sister unit for about one week to refamiliarize itself with theater operating requirements. During this transition period, the 35th TFS participated in a costly mission against a SAM site in central North Vietnam. Flown on 22 October, the strike involved sixteen Thuds crewed by pilots from both the 35th and 36th TFS.

An F-105D (62-4306) of the 35th TFS, 41st AD glides down to the Yokota runway in September 1964. The markings consisted of blue intake arrows trimmed in white, blue tail codes, and a squadron insignia with flash on both sides of the forward fuselage. (Yukio Enomoto)

Heavy flak pummeled the strike force as they approached the target at low-level, downing one Thud and damaging the remaining fifteen aircraft. Shot down and taken POW was 35th pilot Maj. Fred Cherry.

Unlike its previous combat deployments, the 35th's third stay in Thailand was brief. During the first week of November, the 335th TFS, 4th TFW from Seymour Johnson AFB, North Carolina moved to Takhli after spending about four months on back-up duty at Yokota. This move allowed the 35th TFS to return home over the one-week period 8-15 November 1965. The squadron's contribution to the war did not end at that point. For the next year and a half, the unit sent pilots to Southeast Asia on an individual TDY basis to augment combat units in Thailand.

The deactivation of the 6441st TFW saw the squadron reassigned to the 41st AD on 15 November 1966. The 35th operated the F-105 until the late spring of 1967, when it ceased operations due to aircraft unavailability. The unit remained dormant until being equipped with the F-4C Phantom II in the fall of 1967. On 15 January 1968, the squadron was reassigned to the 347th TFW.

Two 35th TFS, 41st AD Thuds (62-4330 and 63-8274) are seen making a paired approach to Yokota in September 1964. Operational tempo was high that month as the squadron geared up for its first deployment to Southeast Asia while meeting its peacetime mission requirements. (Yukio Enomoto)

Off to war: an F-105D (62-4366) of the 35th TFS, 41st AD climbs out of Yokota in full afterburner on 2 October 1964 bound for Korat RTAFB, Thailand. This aircraft was assigned to the squadron commander and carried tri-colored ailerons and intake arrow markings. (Toyokazu Matsuzaki)

Seen at Yokota on 12 October 1964, this F-105F (63-8279) was one of several 35th TFS aircraft that did not make the trip to Korat for the unit's first combat tour in Southeast Asia. Note the F-models used a numeric tail code versus the alpha characters worn by the D-models. (Toyokazu Matsuzaki)

With its drag chute streaming behind, an F-105F (63-8279) of the 35th TFS, 41st AD pulls off the Yokota runway after completing a training mission in late 1964. Note the squadron insignia with flash and tail code markings were deleted by this time. (Yukio Enomoto)

This 35th TFS Thud (63-8274) was a rare sort at Yokota when photographed on 4 May 1965, as the majority of the squadron had just deployed to Takhli RTAFB, Thailand for a second combat tour. (Toyokazu Matsuzaki)

Seen at Yokota in July 1965, this F-105D (62-4330) displays the experimental blue tail markings applied to a few of the 35th TFS Thuds while the unit served on TDY at Takhli. When the squadron returned home, the markings were quickly removed and replaced with the new tri-colored "wing" tail band adopted by the 6441st TFW. (Yukio Enomoto)

A 35th TFS F-105F (63-8279) taxiing in at Yokota shows the blue-yellow-red tail band that became standard on all 6441st TFW Thuds in mid-1965. (Yukio Enomoto)

This pre-strike refueling scene finds F-105Ds of the 35th (62-4312) and 36th TFS (62-4379) partnered for a Rolling Thunder mission out of Takhli RTAFB, Thailand in the fall of 1965. (Paul Minert Collection)

This F-105F (63-8274) of the 35th TFS, 6441st TFW is seen on final approach to Yokota at the end of a routine training sortie on 26 January 1966. (Toyokazu Matsuzaki)

Two F-105Ds assigned to the 35th (62-4329) and 80th TFS (61-0175) display diverse finishes when photographed inbound to Yokota on 4 February 1966. (Toyokazu Matsuzaki)

The 35th TFS was back under the control of the 41st AD when this F-105D (62-4299) was caught landing at Yokota on 3 January 1967. The only hint of the aircraft's squadron assignment was the "Black Panther" device on the practice bomb dispenser. (Toyokazu Matsuzaki)

36th Tactical Fighter Squadron

The 36th Tactical Fighter Squadron was detached from the 8th TFW on 13 May 1964 and placed under the control of the 41st AD. This action coincided with the squadron's move to Yokota due to the pending closure of Itazuke and planned transfer of the 8th TFW to TAC. About one month after its move, on 18 June, the squadron was reassigned to the 41st. Having received F-105Ds with its former wing one year earlier, the 80th maintained the mission of providing combat-ready crews and aircraft for the defense of Japan and Korea. About three months after moving to Yokota, a chain of events off the coast of Vietnam known as the Gulf of Tonkin Incident resulted in the 36th sending the first F-105s to combat in Southeast Asia.

The squadron's call to action was a direct result of two separate North Vietnamese torpedo boat attacks on the Navy destroyer *Maddox*, which had been sailing on international waters in the Gulf of Tonkin. The first attack took place on 2 August 1964, and a second, unconfirmed round of aggression followed two days later. On 8 August, Fifth Air Force sent word to Wing Commander Col. Chester "John Black" L. Van Etten to deploy eighteen Thuds to Clark AB and then on to Korat RTAFB, Thailand. Van Etten selected Lt. Col. Don McCance, commander of the 36th TFS, to supply the aircraft and pilots for the deployment. They left Yokota the following day and arrived at Korat on 12 August.

Placed under 2nd AD control, the squadron flew its first combat mission on 14 August 1964. The mission involved a flight of four F-105Ds sent on a ResCAP mission in the Laotian Plaine des Jarres, where the enemy had reportedly shot down an aircraft. Upon arrival, the F-105s were asked to suppress anti-aircraft guns that had been firing on an orbiting de Havilland from Air America. During a strafing pass, 1st Lt. David Graben's Thud was hit by 37-mm AAA fire, but he was able to get his stricken aircraft back to Korat. This incident marked the first official case of "battle damage" in Southeast Asia. The extensive damage to the aircraft proved too costly to repair, and the aircraft was later written off to become the first F-105 lost in the war.

After the abrupt start, the remainder of the 36th's time at Korat during the fall of 1964 was somewhat uneventful. The limited combat support role of maintaining a ground alert force for possible ResCAP duty for downed pilots in Laos continued, but no additional "hot" missions took place. During this tour, pilots of the 36th TFS kept proficient by flying low-level navigation missions in Thailand. On 5 October 1964, the squadron returned to Yokota after being replaced by its sister unit, the 35th TFS.

The 36th TFS returned to Southeast Asia when it deployed as a unit to Takhli RTAFB, Thailand on 6 March 1965. This was the first appearance of the Thud at Takhli, giving the squadron the unique distinction of opening both Korat and Takhli to F-105 combat operations. Initially, the 36th TFS was attached to the 2nd AD, but operational control was shifted to the provisional 6235th TFW on 10 April 1965. With the start of the Rolling Thunder campaign a few days before their arrival, the squadron's second combat tour proved quite different than its previous experience at Korat. The 36th flew strikes against targets in the southern region of North Vietnam, with many missions involving flights of four aircraft tasked to drop bridges along north-south road and rail routes. The squadron also participated in large-scale attacks against the Hon Gio military barracks, the Phu Van army supply depot, the Vu Con army

This look at an F-105F (63-8295) of the 36th TFS, 41st AD at Yokota on 23 July 1964 provides a good view of the revised markings used by the squadron shortly after it relocated from Itazuke. In addition to the holdover red intake arrows, the aircraft carried a tail code and squadron insignia with flash on the forward fuselage. (Yasuhiko Takahashi)

A 36th TFS F-105D (62-4382) is seen approaching the Yokota runway in early August 1964. Later that month, the squadron introduced the Thud to combat when it deployed eighteen aircraft to Southeast Asia to support contingency operations in the region following the Gulf of Tonkin Incident. (Jerry Geer Collection)

barracks, and the Thanh Hoa Railroad and Highway Bridge. In the air campaign over Laos, the 36th supported Yankee Team reconnaissance operations and conducted Barrel Roll interdiction strikes.

After nearly two months on station, the 36th TFS spent one week transitioning its role at Takhli to the 35th TFS before returning to Yokota on or around 4 May 1965. While the squadron was deployed at Takhli, organizational changes at Yokota dictated the establishment of the provisional 6441st TFW on 1 April 1965 to directly control the three F-105 squadrons permanently stationed at Yokota. The resulting change in assignment to the new provisional wing had no impact on mission status, and the 36th resumed fulfilling its standard PACAF responsibilities after returning from combat duty. Primary among the unit's peacetime role was the rotation of aircraft and crews to Osan AB, Korea for nuclear alert duty. For combat and peacetime operations over the period 1 April to 30 June 1965, the squadron earned the Air Force Outstanding Unit Award.

The 36th TFS was sent to Southeast Asia for a third time in the late summer of 1965 under Fifth Air Force Operations Order 141-65. Its return to Thailand entailed the replacement of the 80th TFS at Takhli, and the first crews from the 36th arrived to start the transfer process beginning on 17 August. The 36th TFS lost one aircraft during the transition period when Operations Officer Maj. Dean A. Progreba was shot down and rescued on a 22 August mission in central North Vietnam. The balance of the squadron had arrived by 26 August, and operational control was passed to Lt. Col. Howard F. Hendricks, commander of the 36th TFS. Four days later, on 30 August, an operational failure on takeoff saw Hendricks crash his F-105D off the end of the runway. Hendricks was able to exit the aircraft, but he sustained a back injury that kept him off flying status for the remainder of the squadron's stay at Takhli.

Flying under the operational control of the provisional 6235th TFW, the squadron was again tasked to support the Rolling Thunder campaign against North Vietnam, as well as Barrel Roll and Steel Tiger operations in Laos. The 36th's arrival coincided with a significant escalation in the bombing of targets in the North. In September, the unit participated in a series of strikes against major

Ground crews complete final checks on these 36th TFS, 41st AD Thuds (62-4388 and 63-8271) at Yokota's "last chance" area in September 1964. (Yukio Enomoto)

A pair of F-105Fs (63-8296 and 63-8271) of the 36th TFS, 41st AD lands in formation at Yokota in October 1964. (Yukio Enomoto)

ammo depots and military barracks located northwest of Hanoi. Beginning in October, the first attacks against bridges on the main supply routes between Hanoi and China were carried out in an effort to destroy the enemy's supply link to the South.

Two missions in October 1965 proved especially costly for the 36th TFS. The first involved a large strike against the heavily defended Lang Met Bridge on 5 October. The squadron lost two F-105s on the raid and another nine aircraft sustained damage. Shot down were Maj. Progreba and Capt. Bruce G. Seeber. Progreba was killed, while Seeber ejected and was taken POW. The second mission involved a flight of four Thuds on a Rolling Thunder strike in the North on 14 October. While locating the target just below a patchy overcast, Capt. Thomas A. Sima was hit by AAA fire and forced to eject. Capt. Robert H. Schuler, Jr. was subsequently lost to hostile action while flying ResCAP for his downed wingman. Sima was captured and held as a POW until 1973, while Schuler was listed MIA.

The 36th returned to Yokota on 28 October 1965 after flying 1,175 combat sorties during two months of combat. For its performance in Southeast Asia over the period 26 August to 28 October 1965, the squadron received the Presidential Unit Citation. Although this was their last combat deployment as a unit, the 36th continued to contribute to the war by sending pilots to Southeast Asia on an individual TDY basis to augment combat units in Thailand. The escalation of the Rolling Thunder campaign during the spring of 1966 brought the decision to send the 36th TFS to Korat on a PCS basis. To ease the political strains of moving a combat unit from Japan to Southeast Asia, the USAF concealed the move by using the assets and personnel of the 36th TFS to form the 34th TFS. Subsequent to the formation of the new squadron on 15 May 1966, the 36th remained at Yokota as a "paper unit" within the provisional 6441st TFW.

The 36th TFS was reassigned to the 41st AD on 15 November 1966 as a result of the deactivation of the provisional 6441st TFW. The squadron remained dormant until being equipped with the F-4C Phantom II in December 1967. On 15 January 1968, the 36th TFS was reassigned to the 347th TFW.

With its landing gears and flaps down, a 36th TFS F-105F (63-8295) hangs on the wing of an 80th TFS F-105F (63-8291) as it recovers at Yokota in October 1964. (Yukio Enomoto)

This view shows a 36th TFS F-105D (62-4388) being led by an 80th TFS F-105F (63-8281) on a section approach to Yokota on 9 December 1964. By this time, the squadron insignia with flash and tail code markings were no longer being used. (Toyokazu Matsuzaki)

Carrying three external fuel tanks, this 36th TFS F-105D (62-4389) makes its way to the Yokota runway at the close of a long transit flight on 17 May 1965. The aircraft may have been returning from Southeast Asia as the squadron had recently completed its second 60-day combat tour. (Toyokazu Matsuzaki)

This F-105D (62-4399) of the 36th TFS, 6441st TFW is seen parked on the NAS Atsugi flightline for an open house in May 1965. (Jerry Geer Collection)

A 36th TFS F-105F (63-8280) returns to the Yokota ramp after a training flight on 12 October 1965. The squadron's red intake arrows disappeared when the 6441st TFW adopted a standard blue-yellow-red tail band during mid-1965. (Yasuhiko Takahashi)

Thuds of the 36th TFS line the taxiway at Takhli RTAFB, Thailand prior to a mission over North Vietnam in the fall of 1965. Each aircraft is armed with AIM-9B Sidewinders on the outboard pylons and an incomplete bomb load of two M117 750-pound bombs on the centerline. (USAF via Stewart Hurd)

An F-105F (63-8280) of the 36th TFS, 6441st TFW lands at Yokota on 4 November 1965, having completed a practice bombing sortie over the Mito Gunnery Range. (Toyokazu Matsuzaki)

A clean 36th TFS F-105F (63-8296) taxis out at Yokota for a short hop in late 1965. (Paul Minert Collection)

This camouflaged F-105D (62-4380) of the 36th TFS, 6441st TFW was photographed at Yokota on 5 May 1966, just one month before the squadron was renumbered the 34th TFS and deployed on a PCS basis to Korat RTAFB, Thailand to serve as a component of the 388th TFW. (Toyokazu Matsuzaki)

80th Tactical Fighter Squadron

The 80th Tactical Fighter Squadron transferred from the 8th TFW at Itazuke to the 41st AD at Yokota in the same manner as its sister units, the 35th and 36th TFS. As an element of the 8th TFW, the squadron maintained combat-ready operations and transitioned from the F-100C to the F-105D in 1963. After reassignment to the 41st AD on 18 June 1964, the unit continued to meet PACAF peacetime operational requirements until November 1964, when it became the third unit from Yokota to take-up temporary station in Thailand.

Under the command of Maj. John P. Anderson, the 80th TFS deployed as a unit to Korat RTAFB, Thailand on 30 October 1964 for combat duty while attached to the 2nd AD. Outside of providing an alert contingent force, the 80th performed armed escort for Yankee Team reconnaissance flights over Laos. On these recce missions, rigid rules of engagement were placed on the Thud pilots as they could only attack the enemy once they were fired upon. The unit's first "hot" mission took place on 21 November 1964, when Capt. Chuck McClarren and his wingman, Capt. Neal Jones, were escorting an RF-101C that got shot down over Tchepone. They flew ResCAP for the downed pilot and were able to get an Air America chopper in to pick him up. For his action on this mission, McClarren became the first Thud pilot to receive the Distinguished Flying Cross.

On 14 December 1964, the 80th TFS was tasked to conduct the maiden mission of a newly authorized, very restricted bombing campaign on hostile communication lines in Laos. The program, code named Barrel Roll, was coordinated out of Washington and proved generally ineffective through time because combat commanders had little input on tactics and ordnance. The first mission, Barrel Roll-001, emphasized this fact.

For the mission, the 80th sent a flight of four F-105s to Da Nang AB, South Vietnam. There, the Thuds were joined by three RF-101Cs to serve as pathfinders and damage assessment aircraft and eight F-100s to fly top air cover. The fifteen-plane force was tasked to destroy a small bridge and conduct an armed recce sweep along a major infiltration route in northern Laos. The weapons load, dictated by higher headquarters, saw the F-105s loaded with 750-pound bombs, Bullpup missiles, and rocket pods. By all accounts, the mission was a disaster. The Thuds were able to drop the bridge, but as they proceeded to conduct the armed road recce at low altitude and slow speed, the pilots found themselves operating the F-105 completely out of its element. To keep the super heavy Thuds from stalling out, the crews had to move in and out of full throttle, which burned fuel at a rapid pace. As their fuel level became critical and with no refueling aircraft available, the pilots essentially dumped the ordnance so they could make it back to Da Nang.

The 80th participated in another early Barrel Roll mission on 21 December. This time, the Thuds escorted F-100s on a pre-planned strike on a major infiltration route near the Mu Gia Pass. This mission proved uneventful for the F-105s as they were relegated to circling high over the Super Sabres on their bomb runs. For a second time, the mission failed when the F-100s became disoriented after receiving heavy flak near the primary target. Low on fuel, the strike force returned to base after finding no secondary target. The 80th TFS was scheduled to end its TDY in Thailand a few days after this mission, but the deployment was extended for another week, and the unit did not return to Yokota until 29 December 1964.

On 1 April 1965, the 80th TFS was reassigned from the 41st AD to the provisional 6441st TFW. With no change in location or mission status, the shift to the new wing was little more than an administrative action. For the execution of its operational requirements as a component of the 6441st TFW, the 80th earned the Air

The original 80th TFS markings consisting of yellow ailerons and intake arrows were revised in mid-1964 with the addition of a tail code and squadron insignia with flash on the forward fuselage. Both the old and new variations are represented in this view of an F-105D (62-4362) landing with an F-105F (63-8283) at Yokota in August 1964. (Yasuhiko Takahashi)

An F-105F (63-8290) of the 80th TFS, 41st AD slips under a low overcast to recover at Yokota in September 1964. (Yukio Enomoto)

Force Outstanding Unit Award for the period 1 April to 30 June 1965. During this time, the squadron performed exceptionally well while meeting nuclear alert commitments at Korea and supporting the air war in Southeast Asia.

The 80th TFS returned to Southeast Asia for a second tour on or about 27 June 1965, when Maj. Anderson took the unit to Takhli RTAFB, Thailand to relieve the 35th TFS from combat duty. Upon arrival, the squadron was attached to the provisional 6235th TFW. For the most part, the 80th was tasked to destroy military and transport targets in North Vietnam in support of the Rolling Thunder campaign, but a number of Barrel Roll and Steel Tiger interdiction missions were also flown in Laos. Specific targets hit in North Vietnam included the army storage areas at Dien Ben Phu, Yen Bay, and Son La, the army barracks at Vinh, the railroad complex from Hanoi to the Chinese border, and the ferry crossing at Ron's Ferry.

The most significant mission of this deployment was the first air strike against a SAM site on 27 July 1965. The mission was a maximum effort by F-105 squadrons on TDY at Takhli and Korat, with each base supplying 24 aircraft to hit two separate sites about 30 miles northwest of Hanoi. Several aborts brought the total number of aircraft involved in the mission to 46. The SAM sites were only two miles apart and plans called for them to be hit simultaneously. Their close proximity required close coordination between the two strike forces. The Takhli group approached the target from the northwest coming down the Red River, and the Korat group attacked from the south. At an altitude of 50 to 100 feet, the aircraft flew through heavy ground fire to deliver cluster bomb units (CBUs) and napalm on the two SAM sites. Six F-105s were lost on the mission, although none were from 80th TFS. All pilots who flew on the strike received the Distinguished Flying Cross. It was later reported that one of the SAM sites was identified as a dummy, possible intended as a trap; the other site was unoccupied, but there was damage to revetments or associated structures.

After spending two months at Takhli, the squadron returned to Yokota on 26 August 1965. The 80th lost one F-105D during its second combat tour when Maj. William McClelland was shot down and rescued while on a 24 July ResCAP mission in Laos. Subsequent to its departure from Takhli, the unit lost its first pilot when Capt. Quincy Collins remained behind to fly with the 36th TFS. Collins was taken POW after he was shot down during a 2 September 1965 mission in North Vietnam. For the 80th's outstanding combat record over the period 27 June to 26 August 1965, it received another Air Force Outstanding Unit Award. Although this was the squadron's final combat deployment as a unit, it continued to play an important role in the war by sending pilots to Thailand on an individual TDY basis.

Between 4-17 October 1965, a portion of the 80th TFS participated in a tri-national mutual air defense training exercise involving the U.S., Australian, and New Zealand Air Forces when six Yokota Thuds deployed to RAAFB Williamtown, Australia for Pacific Concord I. During the exercise, the F-105s flew both as air defense interceptors and supersonic targets for Australian Mirage IIIs. In addition, a one-day live firepower demonstration saw the unit launch AGM-12 Bullpup missiles, drop M117 750-pound bombs, and carry out a low-level attack against a parked convey of trucks with CBU-2 fragmentation bomblets. At that time, the CBU-2s were new and their existence sensitive. The devastating effect of the weapon brought many questions from the Australian and New Zealand senior officials that could not be answered.

This 80th TFS F-105F (63-8291) and his wingman, a 36th TFS F-105D (62-3470), pass over Yokota on return from a 29 September 1964 training mission. (Toyokazu Matsuzaki)

In line with the deactivation of the provisional 6441st TFW, the 80th TFS was reassigned to the 41st AD for a second time on 15 November 1966. Within six months, the unit was only active F-105 squadron at Yokota as both the 35th and 36th TFS were dormant due to aircraft unavailability. The 80th TFS retained its Thuds into 1968 and was preparing to convert to the F-4C Phantom II when it was reassigned to the 347th TFW on 15 January 1968.

BELOW: This fall of 1964 view catches two F-105Fs belonging to the 80th TFS (63-8291) and 35th TFS (63-8284) as they are about to land in formation at Yokota. (Hiroshi Suzuki)

A cloud of black smoke kicks out of this 80th TFS F-105D (62-4356) on cartridge start at Korat RTAFB, Thailand circa November 1964. The ordnance configuration of 2.75-inch rocket pods on the outboard stations was typical of early missions into Laos. (Vic Vizcarra)

Capt. Vic Vizcarra of the 80th TFS seeks refuge from the hot Thailand sun in the shade of an umbrella while sitting cockpit alert at Korat circa November 1964. As indicated by the markings on the fuselage, his mount was one of several Thuds left behind by the previous TDY unit from Yokota, the 35th TFS. (Vic Vizcarra)

80th TFS pilot Capt. Neal Jones points to two gun kills after the 21 November 1964 escort mission in which an RF-101C got shot down over Tchepone. Jones received an Air Medal for his actions that day, while his flight leader, Capt. Chuck McClarren, became the first Thud pilot to receive the Distinguished Flying Cross. (Vic Vizcarra)

This F-105D (62-4362) of the 80th TFS, 6441st TFW is seen recovering at Yokota on 4 May 1965 with three external fuel tanks, suggesting that it may have been returning from a nuclear alert deployment to Osan AB, Korea. (Toyokazu Matsuzaki)

An 80th TFS F-105F (63-8291) works its way down the glide path for landing at Yokota on 4 May 1965. (Toyokazu Matsuzaki)

This view of the flightline at Yokota on 16 May 1965 shows a line-up of Thuds led by an F-105F (63-8294) of the 80th TFS, 6441st TFW. Just visible down the line are several tail fins marked with the black and yellow checkered design of the 561st TFS, which was deployed on a TDY basis from the 23rd TFW at McConnell AFB, Kansas. (Toyokazu Matsuzaki)

Taken on 17 May 1965, this photograph catches an 80th TFS F-105D (62-4360) with everything down and out at it crosses the threshold at Yokota. (Toyokazu Matsuzaki)

ABOVE: An 80th TFS F-105D (62-4356) roars down the runway in full afterburner as it departs on a Rolling Thunder mission out of Takhli RTAFB, Thailand during the unit's second combat tour in mid-1965. The tri-colored tail band of the 6441st TFW replaced the squadron's yellow intake arrow markings just prior this deployment. (M. Lotti via James Geer)

RIGHT: This raunchy nose art was found on an 80th TFS F-105D (62-4357) flown by Capt. Vic Vizcarra at Takhli in July 1965. Dubbed *Pussy Galore*, the aircraft had a nude painting strategically placed over the refueling receptacle as a humorous play on tanker boom operators. Vizcarra recreated this nose art on another Thud while assigned TDY to the 354th TFS at Takhli in 1966. (Vic Vizcarra)

This F-105F (63-8294) of the 80th TFS, 6441st TFW is seen taxiing back to the Yokota ramp after completing a training sortie in the fall of 1965. (Yukio Enomoto)

These 80th TFS Thuds were photographed on 2 October 1965 while tanking on the way to Guam for an intermediate stop enroute to RAAFB Williamtown, Australia for the tri-national training exercise named Pacific Concorde I. (Vic Vizcarra)

An 80th TFS F-105D (62-4367) descends on Yokota as it makes it final approach for landing on 28 November 1965. (Toyokazu Matsuzaki)

A newly camouflaged F-105F (63-8283) of the 80th TFS, 6441st TFW lands at Yokota on 21 January 1966. Making a mirrored approach in the background is a visiting F-105D (58-1153) of the 334th TFS, which was operating out of Takhli RTAFB, Thailand on a TDY basis from the 4th TFW at Seymour Johnson AFB, North Carolina. (Toyokazu Matsuzaki)

This gaggle of 80th TFS Thuds receives last minute checks before proceeding on an April 1967 training mission out of Yokota. (Jerry Geer Collection)

As seen on this F-105D (62-4360) landing at Yokota, the 80th TFS brought the GR tail code into use during late October 1967 after flying unmarked camouflaged Thuds for more than a year and a half. (Katsuhiko Tokunaga via Jerry Geer)

An F-105D (61-0093) of the 80th TFS, 41st AD is towed back to the Yokota ramp on 29 October 1967 following routine servicing at an auxiliary area. (Toyokazu Matsuzaki)

PLACE
STAMP
HERE

SCHIFFER PUBLISHING LTD
4880 LOWER VALLEY ROAD
ATGLEN, PA 19310-9717 USA

This 80th TFS F-105D (62-4320) is lined up to recover at Yokota at the end of a flight on 10 December 1967. (Toyokazu Matsuzaki)

With "last chance" checks completed and chocks pulled, this 80th TFS F-105F (63-8291) is ready to launch out of Yokota circa December 1967. (Katsuhiko Tokunaga via Jerry Geer)

An 80th Thud (60-0453) is about to close out another training sortie as it nears contact with the Yokota runway. Ten days after this photograph was taken on 5 January 1968, the squadron gained a new parent unit when the 41st AD was inactivated and replaced by the 347th TFW. (Yasuhiko Takahashi)

Operation Northscope

During the spring of 1967, Yokota played a key role in the development of a night, all-weather radar bombing capability for use in Southeast Asia. The idea to develop the capability was politically driven by competition between the USAF and Navy. PACAF chief General John D. Ryan did not like that the Navy was getting the upper hand with their new A-6 Intruder's all-weather capability and came up with the idea of using the F-105 to perform the mission for the USAF. Ryan's push to develop the capability saw Operation Northscope initiated at Yokota on 4 March 1967.

Under Northscope, a small group of EF-105F Wild Weasels (and later several standard F-105Fs) received unique modifications to pioneer the all-weather mission. The aircraft had their R-14A radars upgraded to expand target definition and their toss-bomb computers optimized to increase delivery accuracy. In addition, the two-seat Thuds had the pilot's weapons release switch rearranged to enable the rear seat to control bomb release. The object of the modifications was to give the aircraft the ability to carry out accurate night, all-weather radar strikes by dropping bombs from a level delivery at 500 to 2,000 feet. In Southeast Asia, the mission of bombing targets with self-contained radar became known as Commando Nail.

Concurrent with the Northscope modifications, a group of pilots were drawn from both the 35th and 80th TFS to train for the new mission. Due to the unique nature of the program, rated pilots were chosen to fill both seats of the cockpit. Instructor pilots were placed in the front seat, while newly trained pilots or those with previous navigator experience were selected to serve as bombardiers in the backseat. Early in the program, the crews received extensive ground instruction in the use of the R-14A radar and associated bombing techniques. Actual training flights and trials at Yokota started when the first set of modified aircraft became available in early April 1967.

The first set of four crews arrived at Korat RTAFB, Thailand on 24 April 1967 to begin night bombing operations with the 388th TFW. Here, the specialized aircraft and crews soon became known as "Ryan's Raiders" due to General Ryan's motion for the program. Over the next month, crew training continued at Yokota as additional aircraft were modified, and eight more dual-pilot crews were sent to Korat during May. Yokota's function in the program ended during the early summer of 1967, when crewmember requirements changed to call for the backseater to be Weasel qualified. Thereafter, the 4537th FWS, 4525th FWW at Nellis AFB, Nevada assumed the training function for the Commando Nail mission.

ABOVE: A Northscope modified EF-105F (63-8269) lands at Yokota after completing a low-level training mission on 21 April 1967, less than one week before deploying to Korat with the initial cadre of Raiders. This aircraft became the first casualty of the program when it was lost on a Commando Nail strike over North Vietnam on 12 May 1967. (Toyokazu Matsuzaki)

BELOW: These two EF-105Fs modified for the Commando Nail mission are seen taxiing out at Yokota for a training exercise in April 1967. The lead aircraft (62-4429) was shot down by AAA fire on a strike against the Kep railyards on 15 May 1967, while the second (63-8312) was downed by a SAM over the North on 29 February 1968. (Yukio Enomoto)

CHAPTER EIGHT

49th Tactical Fighter Wing

The history of the 49th Tactical Fighter Wing dates back to January 1941, when it was activated as the 49th Pursuit Group (Interceptor). The unit was initially equipped with P-35s and flew out of Selfridge Field, Michigan. In about a year, the group converted to P-40s and moved to Darwin, Australia for air defense duties. The unit moved again in September 1942 to Port Moresby, New Guinea. Here, it operated the P-40 for another two years, although the P-47 was also flown from November 1943.

A conversion to the P-38 preceded a move to the Philippines in October 1944. Redesignated the 49th Fighter Group, the unit earned honors in the South Pacific during World War II. After the war, the group conducted training exercises from Misawa AB with P-51s as a part of the occupational forces in Japan. In August 1948, the group was redesignated the 49th Fighter Wing and commenced transition to the F-80.

The unit was redesignated the 49th Fighter Bomber Wing in February 1950 and relocated to Taugu AB, Korea later that year to serve in the Korean War. Initially equipped with the F-51, the unit returned to operating the F-80 (making it the first jet operational unit in the war) before converting to the F-84 in June 1951. Following the Korean ceasefire in 1953, the 49th returned to Misawa and absorbed the resources of the 6016th Air Base Wing. It served in an administrative support role without aircraft until July 1954, when an air defense mission with F-86Fs was added.

On 10 December 1957, the 49th moved without personnel and equipment to USAFE and replaced the 388th Fighter Bomber Wing at Etain-Rouvres AB, France. Here, the 49th and its three squadrons–the 7th, 8th, and 9th–operated F-100D/Fs in support of the NATO alliance. On 8 July 1958, the unit was redesignated the 49th Tactical Fighter Wing and one year later moved to Spangdahlem AB, Germany with its Super Sabres.

The wing began preparing for the arrival of the F-105 for more than two years before the first aircraft was delivered in 1961. Its conversion began immediately after the 36th TFW received its full complement of Thunderchiefs. Col. Wilbur J. Grumbles, 49th TFW commander, landed the unit's first F-105D at Spangdahlem on 30 October 1961. All three squadrons of the wing had successfully converted to the Thud by the late spring of 1962.

The operations of the wing closely mirrored those of the 36th TFW, its sole counterpart F-105 wing in USAFE. Wheelus AB,

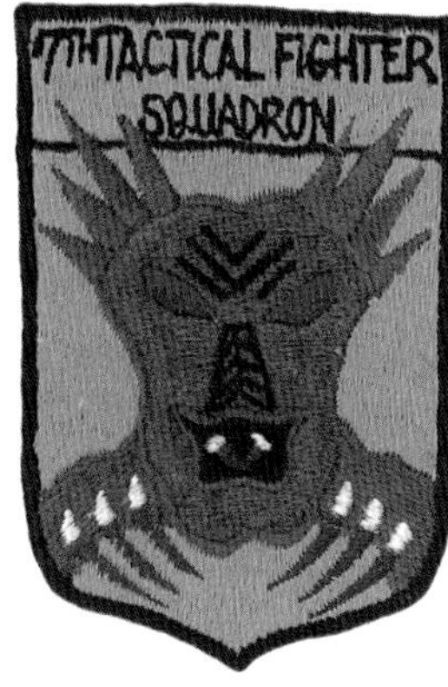

The commander of the 49th TFW, Col. Wilbur J. Grumbles, ushered in the Thud era at Spandahlem AB, Germany when he arrived with the wing's first F-105D on 30 October 1961. As seen here, Grumbles' aircraft (61-0041) was dubbed *KORDEL-EDEN*, which was derived from the names of a nearby city, Kordel, Germany, and his hometown, Eden, Texas. (USAF via James Geer)

Libya was the focal point for the wing's training spectrum. The first group of 49th TFW F-105s deployed to Wheelus during January 1962 for initial qualifications in nuclear weapons delivery and air-to-ground gunnery training. A permanent detachment was soon established for the continual rotation of crews for training. On average, pilots returned to Wheelus every two months for several weeks of intense training.

During its first several years of flying the Thunderchief, the 49th TFW successfully overcame a series of operational challenges. Among those was maintaining combat readiness while upgrading its aircraft under Operation Look-Alike. In time, the wing settled into a period of performing at an exceptionally high level. As a result, the unit earned the Air Force Outstanding Unit Award for the period 1 March 1964 to 28 February 1966.

The wing operated the F-105 until early 1967, when it began receiving the F-4D Phantom II. Similar to the 36th TFW, many of the wing's Thuds were sent to the 23rd TFW at McConnell AFB, Kansas or to Southeast Asia as replacement aircraft.

Following Col. Grumbles as commander of the 49th TFW during the Thunderchief era were Col. Thomas D. DeJarnette (15 June 1962), Col. William P. McBride (26 February 1963), Col. William S. Chairsell (17 August 1964), and Col. John C. Giraudo (21 June 1966).

Operation Look-Alike

As the F-105 entered operational service in USAFE during 1961, the Thunderchief wings struggled to maintain a high aircraft in-commission rate. This problem was brought about by many factors

The markings used by the 49th TFW during their first year of operating the Thud are illustrated in this nice shot of an F-105D (61-0077) on a High Flight ferry operation. On the tail was the wing's insignia with a red-yellow-blue flash, while painted on the nose was a similar tri-colored lighting bolt. (Ron McNeil via Paul Minert)

A 49th TFW F-105D (61-0046) cruises high over Libya during an early deployment to Wheelus AB for conventional weapons training. (USAF via Paul Minert)

including technical shortcomings in the early production variants of the F-105D and corrosion problems caused by the wet European climate. To resolve these problems, the USAF initiated a program to modify the early production D-models with appropriate fixes devised after the aircraft entered service.

The modification program, code named Operation Look-Alike, was not limited to correcting technical and corrosion problems. Simultaneous with the introduction of the Thud to Germany, USAF policy changes dictated a shift in focus from training in nuclear strike operations to the delivery of conventional weapons. In response to this directive, Look-Alike included upgrading the F-105D's conventional warfare capability. The changes incorporated under Look-Alike brought all Thuds up to -25RE configuration, the current production variant at that time.

Look-Alike posed serious operational challenges for the two Thud wings in Germany. To facilitate the goal of keeping enough aircraft in service to maintain deterrent capability, the program was undertaken in two phases. The first phase involved on-base modifications performed by Republic Company technicians, while the second phase involved sending aircraft to the MOAMA facility at Brookley AFB, Alabama for additional upgrades by USAF personnel.

The 49th TFW, equipped with a mix of -15RE and -20RE block F-105Ds, entered the first phase of the Look-Alike program during September 1962. In preparation for the modification work by Republic technicians, aircraft were stripped down by wing personnel. Initially, incorporation of the on-base technical changes took seven days, but as improvements and experience were gained, the time was reduced to four days. Once the modifications were complete, aircraft were handed over to the wing for acceptance flight tests. By the end of November 1962, all aircraft had completed this portion of the program.

For the major modification work to be performed under the second phase of Look-Alike, aircraft were ferried to the MOAMA facility under Project High Flight. With a shortage of qualified maintenance personnel, the flights caused added difficulty in maintaining operational capability. On average, each F-105 required between four and five days of preparation for the flight back. Aircraft were flown back in flights of four, although two additional aircraft were prepared as spares in case of any last minute aborts. The flight itself was a grueling 4,400-mile, non-stop journey that lasted more than ten hours and included three air refuelings.

At any given time over the next year, about ten of the 49th's Thuds were at the MOAMA facility. The majority of the modifications were directed towards the aircraft's avionics package and weapons carrying capability, although multitudes of structural improvements were also made. After resolving some early problems, aircraft modifications were completed in about one month.

The wing received its first modified aircraft back during March 1963, and by the end of the year, all aircraft had cycled through MOAMA. Aircraft arrived back at Spangdahlem with not only a greatly enhanced conventional warfare capability, but also with a new appearance. The Thuds carried a new aluminized lacquer external finish to eliminate the corrosion problems caused by water seepage encountered when the aircraft was previously unfinished.

Six F-105Ds of the 49th TFW practice formation flying near Tripoli in 1962. (USAF via Paul Minert)

ABOVE: This immaculate 49th TFW F-105D (61-0160) was photographed at Nellis AFB, Nevada while taking part in TAC's Fighter Weapons Meet in September 1962. Note the new aluminized lacquer finish and thin red nose band behind the radome denoting assignment to the wing's 9th TFS. (Doug Olson)

OPPOSITE

TOP: The 1962 Nellis Gunnery Meet saw participating units fly a variety of missions including nuclear, blind-bombing, and close air support. Here, a 49th TFW F-105D (61-0160) drops two fire bombs during a low-level run over the target area of the Indian Springs Gunnery Range. (USAF via James Geer)

CENTER: This F-105D (61-0044) of the 49th TFW is parked on dispersal at RAF Bentwaters, England in 1963. (Charles Snyder via Jerry Geer)

BOTTOM: A pair of 49th TFW Thuds lifts off from Wheelus for a training mission over the El Uotia Bombing Range. (USAF via Jerry Geer)

U.S. AIR FORCE
10160

U.S. AIR FORCE
FH-044
10044

10086
U.S. AIR FORCE

By late 1964, the 49th TFW Thuds had their nose gear doors painted in the appropriate color to denote squadron assignment. Seen on display at an open house in Germany, this F-105D (60-0517) has red doors to identify it as an aircraft of the 9th TFS. (David Menard Collection)

A 49th TFW F-105D (61-0076) with the blue nose gear doors of the 7th TFS makes its final approach for landing at Spangdahlem in 1965. (Jerry Geer Collection)

This F-105D (60-0100) of the 9th TFS, 49th TFW is seen on static display at a 1965 airshow in England. (Paul Minert Collection)

With the help of his crew chief, 1st Lt. David Carter of the 7th TFS, 49th TFW straps into his Thud for a mission out of Chamount AB, France during the 4th AIRCENT (Allied Air Forces, Central Europe) Tactical Weapons Meet in June 1965. This exercise tested the degree of training and operational readiness of strike units of the central region. (USAF via James Geer)

Seen during a rotation to Wheelus in September 1965, this F-105D (61-0050) of the 9th TFS, 49th TFW is being serviced for its next training sortie. (USAF via Robert Robinson)

A great air-to-air shot of a 49th TFW F-105F (63-8326) over the Atlantic enroute to Germany in December 1965. (Richard Kierbow via JEM Aviation Slides)

An F-105F (63-8311) of the 8th TFS, 49th TFW bears yellow main and nose gear doors at an open house at RAF Wethersfield, England in June 1966. Note the tri-colored lightning bolt on the forward fuselage had been removed by this time. (Jerry Geer Collection)

Another look at this 8th TFS F-105F (63-8311) at the 1966 Wethersfield open house reveals extensive touch-ups to the aluminized lacquer finish on the aft section of the aircraft. (D. Hughes via Norm Taylor)

CHAPTER NINE

57th Fighter Weapons Wing

The 57th Fighter Weapons Wing history began when the United States Army Air Force constituted the 57th Pursuit Group on 20 November 1940. The group was activated at Mitchell Field, New York on 15 January 1941 and received P-40s. In May 1942, the unit was redesignated the 57th Fighter Group and two months later, departed for North Africa for combat duty in World War II. The group converted to the P-47 in November 1943 and operated the Thunderbolt until it was inactivated in November 1945.

The unit was reactivated at Shemya Field, Alaska on 15 August 1946. Redesignated the 57th Fighter Interceptor Group in January 1947, the unit moved to Elmendorf Field, Alaska a few months later. On 15 March 1948, the USAF established the 57th Fighter Wing, which assumed control of the group. Operating out of Elmendorf, plus several satellite bases, the wing carried out the dual mission of air defense and intra-theater troop carrier and airlift support. The unit was redesignated the 57th Fighter Interceptor Wing in January 1950. One year later, the wing was inactivated and replaced by the 39th Air Depot Wing. During its tenure in Alaska, the wing operated a variety of aircraft including the F-51, F-80, F-94, C-47, C-54, and C-82.

The 57th remained dormant until 15 October 1969, when it was reactivated as the 57th Fighter Weapons Wing at Nellis AFB, Nevada. The wing replaced and absorbed the resources of the 4525th FWW. Squadron components of the 4525th FWW absorbed were the 4536th (F-100s), 4537th (F-105s), 4538th (F-4s), and the 4539th FWS (F-111s). These squadrons were redesignated the 65th, 66th, 414th, and 422nd FWS respectively. The wing was assigned to the USAF Tactical Fighter Weapons Center and assumed the 4525th's function of graduate-level training and development, testing, evaluation, and demonstration of tactical fighter weapons systems and tactics.

The 66th FWS inherited the F-105 "Wild Weasel College" role, which not only encompassed training aircrews in the SAM suppression mission, but also involved the development and evaluation of new Weasel tactics and weapons systems. Upon activation, the squadron gained control of about fourteen EF-105F and F-105G Weasel Thuds, as well as several F-105Ds, F-105Fs, and T-39F Wild Weasel trainers. Early operations saw the 66th FWS focus on refining the use of updated versions of the AGM-78 Standard ARM, which was entering service in the Vietnam War.

The 57th FWW was instrumental in advancing a number of major weapons systems during its first two years of existence. While the 66th FWS made significant improvements to the F-105 Weasel program, the 414th FWS successfully adapted the F-4C to the Weasel mission, and the 422nd FWS developed weapons tactics for the technologically advanced F-111. These achievements helped the wing and its squadrons earn the Air Force Outstanding Unit Award for the period 25 October 1969 to 25 September 1971.

During September 1971, the 57th FWW centralized its Weasel operations when it transferred the 414th squadron's Weasel development role and associated F-4Cs to the 66th FWS. The 66th proceeded to fly both the F-105 and F-4 until the summer of 1975. At that time, the USAF completed final steps to consolidate all TAC Wild Weasel operations at George AFB, California.

On 25 July 1975, the F-105s and F-4Cs of the 66th FWS departed Nellis for their new home at George to form the 563rd TFTS. The departure of the Weasel Thuds ended the F-105's fifteen-year presence at Nellis. In addition, this transfer marked the end of F-105D operations with the regular USAF as the 66th transferred its single-seat Thuds to the Reserve Air Forces. The 66th FWS was declared non-operational one day later, but the 57th FWW activated the unit again during October 1977 as an A-10 Warthog squadron.

Wing commanders for the 57th FWW during its association with the Thunderchief were Col. William B. Williamson, Sr. (15 October 1969), Col. Brian J. Lincoln (1 February 1970), Col. Freddie L. Poston (16 February 1971), Col. David D. Young (23 May 1972), Col. Wilford E. Deming III (5 July 1973), and Col. William L. Strand (3 March 1975).

The 66th FWS inherited several early F-105Gs from the 4537th FWS including this WC-coded aircraft (63-8303) shot at Nellis AFB, Nevada on 14 March 1970. Note the 66th applied a thin black and yellow checkered band on the tail versus the broad band used by its predecessor. (Doug Olson)

A handful of F-105Ds were flown by the 66th FWS on a wide range of duties in support of the squadron's weapons instruction and development programs. This D-model (60-0525) was photographed at Nellis on 14 March 1970. (Doug Olson)

Seen at Nellis in April 1970, this EF-105F (63-8333) of the 66th FWS was one of the first Weasel Thuds to be equipped with the AGM-78A (Mod 0) Standard ARM weapons package. (Duane Kasulka via Jerry Geer)

An early F-105G (62-4438) of the 66th FWS skirts a layer of cumulous clouds enroute to the Nellis weapons range during a practice bombing sortie in May 1970. (USAF via Kirk Minert)

Devoid of external stores, a 66th FWS EF-105F (63-8307) begins its gradual descent on Nellis as its completes the final leg of a short hop in the summer of 1970. (USAF via Kirk Minert)

The 66th FWS was instrumental in helping the 561st TFS, 23rd TFW transition from the mission of training new Thud pilots to that of combat-ready operations with newly modified F-105Gs in the fall of 1970. This G-model (62-4427) was shot in November 1970 during one of the squadron's recurring visits to McConnell in support of the 561st's conversion. (Jerry Geer)

The squadron-level tail code of WC was used by the 66th FWS until the 57th FWW adopted the WA code for all of its aircraft in the fall of 1971. This F-105G (63-8350) bears the new standardized tail letters when photograph during a 1972 Nellis open house. (Jerry Geer Collection)

Flanked by two D-models, an F-105F (63-8288) is prepared for the day's mission in this view of the 66th FWS flightline taken in December 1972. (Rich Alexander via James Geer)

The transfer of the F-105D from active duty combat wings to the Reserves in the early 1970s gave the 66th FWS the distinction of being the last regular USAF unit to operate this particular Thud variant. This D-model (61-0073) was photographed at Nellis on 13 March 1973. (Doug Olson)

This 66th FWS F-105G (62-4438) is seen on the transient ramp at Kelly AFB, Texas on 17 May 1973. (Norm Taylor via James Geer)

An F-105G (63-8318) of the 66th FWS awaits its crew for a training sortie at Nellis in August 1973. (J.P. Loomis via Jerry Geer)

A 66th FWS F-105F (63-8343) undergoes servicing on the Nellis flightline in August 1973. The squadron had at least three F-models on strength for training and proficiency purposes. (J.P. Loomis via James Geer)

With a practice Shrike missile installed, this 66th FWS F-105G (63-8274) at Nellis in March 1975 is ready for a mission against the simulated radar and SAM sites of the Caliente Range. (Arnold Swanberg via Jerry Geer)

This F-105G (63-8339) of the 66th FWS was caught during a break in the action at Nellis on 25 March 1975. The transfer of the "Wild Weasel College" role to George AFB, California four months later ended a fifteen-year run of Thud operations at Nellis. (James Geer Collection)

CHAPTER TEN

347th Tactical Fighter Wing

The history of the 347th Tactical Fighter Wing began on 3 October 1942, when it was activated as the 347th Fighter Group at New Caledonia. In January 1943, portions of the group were sent to Guadalcanal where they flew P-39s and P-40s in support of the Allied campaign to recover the central and northern Solomon Islands. During the next year, the 347th converted to the P-38 and continued to participate in the war effort from a variety of locations in the South Pacific. At the end of the war, the group returned to the U.S. where it was inactivated on 1 January 1946.

On 10 August 1948, the 347th Fighter Wing, All-Weather was activated in Japan. For the next few years, the wing provided air defense with F-51s, F-61s, and the F-82s. A slight change in designation to the 347th Fighter All-Weather Wing took place five months before the unit was inactivated on 24 June 1950.

The unit was reactivated as the 347th Tactical Fighter Wing on 21 December 1967 at Yokota AB, Japan. Upon formal organization on 15 January 1968, the wing assumed control of a variety of fighter and reconnaissance types that were previously assigned to the 41st AD. Components inherited were the 35th and 36th TFS (F-4Cs), the 80th TFS (F-105D/Fs), and the 6091st RS (EB-57Es and RC-130Bs). The 34th TFS was also assigned, but this squadron was detached to the 388th TFW and assigned PCS at Korat RTAFB, Thailand for combat operations.

The wing was a short-term operator of the Thunderchief. At the time of the wing's activation, a staged process to replace the F-105D/F at Yokota with the F-4C was well underway. The 35th and 36th TFS had just completed their conversion to the F-4C, and the 80th TFS had started relinquishing its F-105s in anticipation of receiving the Phantom. In the midst of the transition, a portion of the 80th TFS was ordered to deploy to Osan AB, Korea in response to the seizing of the American intelligence ship USS *Pueblo* by North Korea. The remaining Thuds left behind at Yokota continued to depart, and Col. Allen K. McDonald, commander of the 347th TFW, flew out the last F-105 on 30 January 1968. Upon the arrival of reinforcements at Osan during February, the 80th's remaining Thuds were given up, and the unit completed its transition to the F-4C.

The 347th TFW went through a rapid change in wing commanders during the short period it operated the Thunderchief. First to command the wing was Col. Paul P. Douglas (15 January 1968), followed by Col. Allen K. McDonald (23 January 1968), who was succeeded by Col. Thomas M. Carhart (29 January 1968).

As part of Operation Coronet Wasp, the 80th TFS, 347th TFW deployed a number of aircraft to Osan AB, Korea in response to the Pueblo Incident. Here, one of the unit's GR-coded F-105Ds is seen with a ZA-coded Thud of the 12th TFS, 18th TFW in the backdrop of this view of a military police guard patrolling the outskirts of the Osan ramp in late January 1968. (USAF via James Geer)

CHAPTER TEN

355th Tactical Fighter Wing

The 355th Tactical Fighter Wing flew the F-105 for eight years, of which five were spent in front-line combat operations in Southeast Asia. The wing originally was activated on 12 November 1942 as the 355th Fighter Group at Orlando Army Air Base, Florida. Equipped with P-47s, the 355th rapidly prepared for World War II combat. In July 1943, the group deployed to England, where it was assigned to the Eighth Air Force. The unit operated the Thunderbolt in combat until April 1944, when it converted to the P-51. The group continued combat operations until April 1945. Shortly thereafter, the 355th relocated to West Germany as part of the Army's occupational forces. After returning to the U.S. during November 1946, the group was inactivated.

Nearly nine years later, on 18 August 1955, the 355th Fighter Group (Air Defense) reactivated at McGhee-Tyson Airport, Tennessee. Comprised of three squadrons of F-86Ds, the group operated under Air Defense Command and was tasked with providing fighter defense for the southeastern region of the U.S. Operations continued until October 1957, when it began a phase-down of operations that culminated with the unit's inactivation on 8 January 1958.

On 13 April 1962, the unit reactivated at George AFB, California as the 355th Tactical Fighter Wing. Tasked with the mission of training as a combat-ready unit, the wing was slated to receive the F-105 during the fall of that same year. Formal organization took place on 8 July 1962, when it was placed under the control of the 831st AD. The 354th, 357th, 421st, and 469th TFS were assigned as the flying units.

The wing's first three F-105Ds arrived at George during September 1962. The aircraft were transferred from the 4th TFW and were flown in from Nellis AFB, Nevada, where the 4th had been competing in the USAF's Annual Gunnery Meet. Subsequent deliveries to the 355th TFW included a mix of early production and factory fresh aircraft, and it took almost two years to equip all of the wing's squadrons with the Thud. The 354th and 357th TFS were initially outfitted, followed by the 421st TFS in the spring of 1963, and the 469th TFS in the summer of 1964.

The 355th TFW entered a prolonged period of up-tempo operations and constant change during mid-1964. A realignment of TAC assets saw the wing move all personnel and resources to McConnell AFB, Kansas on 21 July 1964. Upon relocation, the wing was reassigned to the 835th AD. Just prior this move, the 355th started sending squadrons on extensive overseas deployments. The first tours involved rotational duty to Europe in support of NATO requirements. Later, the wing sent squadrons to the Far East and Southeast Asia as a result of the Vietnam War.

On 2 October 1965, the 355th TFW received news that it was to be assigned PCS to Takhli RTAFB, Thailand. The move commenced under Operation Ready Alpha later that month with assigned personnel and equipment beginning the long trip to Southeast Asia. For the time being, the flying squadrons stayed behind pending assignment to Thailand with either the 355th TFW at Takhli or the provisional 6234th TFW at Korat. On 8 November 1965, the move was complete, and the wing was attached to the 2nd AD. On that same day, the 355th TFW lost control of its four original Thud squadrons, but gained control of four units on TDY at Takhli. F-105 squadrons temporarily attached to the wing were the 334th, 335th, and 562nd TFS. The fourth squadron attached to the wing was the 41st TRS, an RB-66C (later designated EB-66C) unit providing electronic warfare and pathfinder capabilities in Southeast Asia.

The second phase of Operation Ready Alpha involved the permanent relocation of stateside Thunderchief squadrons to Takhli. Squadrons arrived for assignment to the 355th TFW as the Thud units on TDY at Takhli completed their rotational combat tours.

The standard TAC markings displayed by this 355th TFW F-105D (59-1721) at George AFB, California was carried by all of the wing's aircraft during the 1962-64 time period. (Duane Kasulka via Jerry Geer)

The 333rd and 354th TFS were assigned to the 355th by the end 1965, replacing the 335th and 562nd TFS respectively. By the last week of January 1966, the final piece was in place as the 357th TFS arrived to replace the 334th TFS. Also around this time, a small number of B-66B (later designated EB-66B) aircraft arrived from USAFE in the form of Detachment 1, 25th TRW. This unit was placed under the operational control of the 41st TRS.

The process of relocating squadrons permanently to Takhli occurred at an opportune time. On 24 December 1965, President Lyndon B. Johnson ordered a pause to the Rolling Thunder campaign, hoping to lure the North Vietnamese to the negotiating table. This not only gave the Thud squadrons proper time to conduct area check-out flights, but also allowed newly arrived pilots to gain combat experience in the less hostile environment of Laos. Here, missions were flown in support of the Barrel Roll and Steel Tiger campaigns against Communist supply positions and lines of communication.

With no visible signs of a reduction in North Vietnamese aggressiveness, bombing operations over North Vietnam resumed at an increased pace on 31 January 1966, ending the brief reprieve

Some of the Thud's weapons were placed on exhibit with this 355th TFW F-105D (59-1745) at a 1964 George open house. (Jerry Geer Collection)

Displayed at an airshow, this F-105F (63-8263) was one of several that were delivered to the 355th TFW in 1964. (Duane Kasulka via Jerry Geer)

This F-105D (62-4290) of the 355th TFW was photographed on the George ramp shortly before the wing relocated to McConnell AFB, Kansas in mid-1964. (Duane Kasulka via Jerry Geer)

Starting in 1964, the 355th TFW deployed squadrons overseas as required, primarily in response to the outbreak of war in Southeast Asia. This F-105D (59-1718) of the 357th TFS was photographed on 9 December 1964 at Yokota AB, Japan, where the unit was charged with backing up resident Thud squadrons that were serving on TDY in Thailand. (Toyokazu Matsuzaki)

from the difficult missions encountered over this region. The escalation of the Rolling Thunder campaign, as well as the intensifying air war in Laos and South Vietnam, saw the USAF rapidly build-up the number of aircraft in Southeast Asia during early 1966. As a result, the 355th TFW gained a new controlling organization on 1 April 1966, when the 2nd AD was redesignated the Seventh Air Force.

The resumption of air strikes in early 1966 brought a concentrated effort to destroy key infiltration routes into Laos and on the principal north-south rail, water, and highway lines of communication. Plagued by bad weather, the majority of strikes during February and March were carried out using a new synchronous radar bombing procedure with a B-66 pathfinder aircraft leading the fighters on their bomb runs. Using this method, the wing participated in daily strikes against the Barthelmy and Mu Gia passes along the North Vietnamese-Laotian border.

In May 1966, the 355th TFW started flying a limited number of missions in support of Operation Gate Guard. This new program was developed to slow down the flow of enemy supplies into Laos and South Vietnam by striking a group of interdiction points located in the far southern region of North Vietnam, just north of the demilitarized zone (DMZ). While participating in this campaign, the wing conducted Combat Skyspot radar bombing missions, a type not often undertaken by the F-105 force. The Skyspot concept utilized MSQ-77 ground radar sites to direct aircraft to a point in space for ordnance release.

Outside of interdiction operations, the 355th TFW also hit numerous military targets in North Vietnam during the first half of 1966. Among the key targets attacked was the vast Yen Bay military storage area. For this raid, all three of the wing's squadrons joined Korat-based Thuds to supply the majority of the aircraft for the 150-plane force involved in the mission. The strike was carried out on 31 May and met with good success. Some 72 warehouses were destroyed, another 40 were damaged, and roughly 25 AAA sites in the area were bombed.

One month after the Yen Bay raid, the 355th participated in a strike against the major petroleum, oil, and lubricant (POL) storage complex located just outside of Hanoi. The strike was a direct result of the June 1966 decision to attack targets of greater strategic significance in North Vietnam. Conducted on 29 June, the mission was one of the most successful in the Vietnam War. Bombing accuracy was exceptional and nearly 90 percent of the facility was destroyed. Of the 32 tanks in the facility, only two remained standing and all had burned out. The complex was never used again by the North Vietnamese during the war.

Mid-1966 saw the 355th TFW bolster its electronic warfare capabilities with the arrival of the EF-105F Wild Weasel and additional EB-66B Destroyer aircraft. The EF-105F was added in July, when the 354th TFS received a small group of the two-seat Thuds modified to detect, locate, and destroy enemy air defense systems. The aircraft were fitted with Radar Homing and Warning (RHAW) equipment and armed with AGM-45 Shrike ARMs. Initially, the 354th was the only squadron to operate the EF-105F, but each squadron had a flight of the Weasel Thuds to combat the growing SAM threat by the end of 1966. The additional Destroyer assets arrived in June, and these aircraft were joined with the existing aircraft of Detachment 1, 25th TRW to form a new squadron, the 6460th TRS. Both the 41st and 6460th TRS remained with the 355th TFW until September 1966.

In the fall of 1966, the 355th TFW continued to hit the enemy's POL system, as well as carry out strikes against important supply and transportation targets in the North. This period also saw the wing introduce the newly developed electronic countermeasures (ECM) pod for use against the sophisticated North Vietnamese air

Flying near a late afternoon thunderhead, this F-105D (61-0060) of the 354th TFS, 355th TFW is seen returning to base following the completion of a successful strike against North Vietnam during the squadron's 1965 combat tour. (D. Steigers via James Geer)

Bearing the multicolored tail band of the 355th TFW, these two Thuds were caught in November 1965 while staging through Yokota AB, Japan on transfer to Southeast Asia. These aircraft were bound for Korat RTAFB, Thailand to join the 421st and 469th TFS on their PCS assignment to serve as a component of the provisional 6234th TFW. (Yukio Enomoto)

defense network under Project Vampyrus. The successful development of the ECM pod, as well as the advancement of the Wild Weasel program, helped curb the loss rate towards the end of the year. Nonetheless, the wing lost about 55 Thuds to hostile action and another seven to operational incidents while accumulating 45,810 flying hours during 1966.

Major targets struck during the first half of 1967 included the steelworks, army supply depot, railway station, and power station at Thai Nguyen beginning on 10 March and the MiG airfield at Hoa Lac, first attacked on 23 April. Other key missions were flown against the Xuan Mai barracks, the Son Toy barracks, the Ha Dong barracks and supply depot, the Vinh Yen barracks, the Kep barracks and railroad yard, the Nguyen Khe storage area, the Yen Vien railroad yards, the Bac Le railroad yards, and the Bac Giang thermal power plant and railroad yard. Strikes were also conducted along the two main railroad supply lines from China into Hanoi. Among the vital targets struck on these routes were the Chieu Ung and Bac Giang railroad bridges.

As Rolling Thunder progressed during 1967, the F-105s of the 355th TFW faced a growing and more capable North Vietnamese air arm. As a result, pilots found themselves engaged in many air-to-air battles with MiGs. During the first Thai Nguyen raid on 10 March, Capt. Max C. Brestel of the 354th TFS became the first pilot to down two MiGs on the same mission. On 26 March, Col. Scott R. Scott, commander of the 355th TFW, downed a MiG-17 while flying a strike mission on the Son Toy army barracks near the Hoa Lac airfield. During a major strike against the Xuan Mai army barracks on 19 April, 355th TFW pilots downed four MiGs. Encounters continued, and by the end of 1967, the wing had destroyed nineteen MiGs in air-to-air combat.

The 355th TFW earned its first Air Force Outstanding Unit Award with Combat "V" Device for its performance over the period 12 October 1966 to 11 April 1967. At the individual level, pilots displayed extreme professionalism and courage to accomplish their missions in the hostile environment over North Vietnam, exemplified by two 355th TFW pilots earning the Medal of

Upon moving to Takhli RTAFB, Thailand on 8 November 1965, the 355th TFW gained control of several F-105 units serving on rotational combat duty at the base. Taken just after the wing's arrival, this view of the Takhli ramp shows Thuds with the blue and green tail bands of the 334th and 335th TFS respectively. Also visible is a single tri-colored tail band that identifies an aircraft of the 6441st TFW that was carrying out augmentation duty. (USAF via James Geer)

Squadrons arriving at Takhli on a PCS basis to serve with the 355th TFW assumed control of the F-105s left behind by departing TDY units, creating a confusing mix of aircraft markings for a brief period. Photographed while participating in training exercises at Yokota on 21 January 1966, this F-105D (58-1151) was assigned to the 354th TFS, but still wears the full markings of its former owner, the 562nd TFS. (Toyokazu Matsuzaki)

Honor. Both pilots earned the awards while flying Iron Hand missions–Capt. Merlyn H. Dethlefsen during the Thai Nguyen raid on 10 March and Maj. Leo K. Thorsness during the Xuan Mai army barracks attack on 19 April.

The second half of 1967 saw the bombing of North Vietnam continue, and the wing's sortie rate reached its highest level. Strikes against power and industrial plants, rolling stock and railyards, bridges and causeways, and military support targets and storage areas dominated the picture for the rest of the year. On 11 August, the 355th TFW led a large strike force in the first attack on the Paul Doumer Railroad and Highway Bridge, dropping two spans on the mission. The wing was also selected to lead a strike on the Phuc Yen airfield, the largest in North Vietnam, on 24 October. The airfield, which had been previously untouched prior to the raid, was rendered unserviceable. One day later, the wing led a second successful strike on the Doumer Bridge. Other noteworthy targets included the Kep airfield, the VNAF Headquarters at Bac Mai, the Trai Thon army barracks, the Vinh Yen railyards, and the Canal des Rapides Bridge.

During August 1967, the 355th TFW regained control of the redesignated 41st and 6460th Tactical Electronic Warfare Squadron (TEWS). Having previously served with the wing during 1965-66, these units were still equipped with a mix of EB-66 Destroyer variants and supported F-105 operations by jamming the search and acquisition radars of the North Vietnamese AAA guns and SAM sites. In January 1968, the 6460th was redesignated the 42nd TEWS. Concurrent with the return of the EB-66 aircraft, the 355th TFW added a small group of Combat Martin F-105Fs to its inventory. These modified F-105Fs had their rear ejection seat removed and replaced with the QRC-128 VHF jamming system that allowed them to block communication between MiGs and their ground-control intercept (GCI) centers.

Despite the advancements in tactics and capabilities, the 355th TFW's mission of flying daily into the heavy concentration of air defense systems in North Vietnam and Laos took a great toll for a second straight year. The wing lost 57 F-105s during 1967, 48 in combat and nine to operational causes.

The annual monsoon season greatly impeded bombing operations over the North during the first three months of 1968. Nonetheless, the 355th TFW continued to bomb critical targets in this region, including supply routes, military storage areas, bridges, and railyards. As before, the unit struck targets with radar bombing techniques to overcome the bad weather. Not only were Combat Skyspot missions flown, but also a new experimental ground control radar technique known as Commando Club was also used to hit targets in the far reaches of North Vietnam. Targets struck under radar guidance included the Hoa Lac and Yen Bai airfields.

The evolution of the EF-105F to a more capable Wild Weasel platform took a major step forward during March 1968. At that time, the wing's 357th TFS was involved in the first combat launches of the AGM-78A Standard ARM Mod by a USAF aircraft. Further upgrades of the EF-105F's RHAW system, as well as a new modification that allowed the Weasel Thuds to fire the improved AGM-78B, effectively converted the aircraft into an F-105G. The first actual G-models arrived at Takhli during early 1969.

On 17 March 1968, the 355th TFW became associated with the introduction of the F-111 Aardvark to combat operations in Southeast Asia. Under Operation Combat Lancer, six F-111As from the 474th TFW deployed to Takhli from Nellis AFB, Nevada to form Detachment 1, 428th TFS. Flying under the operational control of the 355th TFW, Detachment 1 encountered serious problems from the outset. Two F-111s were lost on strikes in North Vietnam before the end of March. Two replacement aircraft arrived on 5 April, but operations were suspended a few weeks later after the loss of a third aircraft. The F-111's combat debut ended on 22 November 1968, when Detachment 1 returned to Nellis after having completed only 55 missions.

In another effort to bring the North Vietnamese to peace talks, President Johnson announced the first of a series of bombing restrictions on 31 March 1968. Beginning on 1 April, the bombing of North Vietnam was limited to an area below the 20th parallel. A few days later, the bombing area was further reduced with strikes allowed only south of the 19th parallel. Accordingly, the southern panhandle of North Vietnam became the primary focal point for the wing's operations.

The 355th TFW surpassed the 100,000 combat flying hours milestone during April 1968 and fittingly, the wing eventually received its second Air Force Outstanding Unit Award with Combat "V" Device for the twelve-month period ending on 11 April 1968. In addition, the spring of 1968 also saw the wing honored with its first Presidential Unit Citation for its performance over the period 1 January to 10 October 1966. During that time, the 355th TFW flew 11,892 sorties, with strikes against key targets such as railroad and highway bridges, petroleum storage areas, airfields, radar sites, and other weapons storage and staging areas in North Vietnam. In addition, the wing also was credited with its first MiG kill, with another eight confirmed damaged.

The wing continued to interdict vital lines of communication in the southern region of North Vietnam through the fall of 1968, but a significant number of missions were also conducted in Laos. The enemy's air defense system was not as concentrated in these areas; nevertheless, additional Thuds were lost as the 355th attacked important military and transportation targets. As many as twelve aircraft were shot down during 1968 before the bombing of North Vietnam ended on 1 November 1968. Operational losses accounted for another five aircraft.

After the Rolling Thunder campaign ended, the 355th TFW primarily spent the next two years supporting the air campaign in Laos. Here, the wing flew Barrel Roll strikes against Communist positions in the north and Steel Tiger interdiction missions against the Ho Chi Minh Trail in the panhandle region. The wing also participated in a new program known as Commando Hunt. This operation was an intensified effort aimed at reducing the flow of enemy troops and supplies in the Steel Tiger operating area, and it relied

Rolling Thunder resumes: a flight of 355th TFW Thuds, comprised of F-105Ds from the 333rd and 354th TFS, refuels over Laos before striking targets in North Vietnam in February 1966. Note the second and fourth aircraft from the camera show traces of previous use by the 335th and 562nd TFS, respectively, on the vertical fins. (USAF via Jerry Geer)

An EB-66B Destroyer acts as a pathfinder and ECM aircraft for a flight of 355th TFW F-105Ds on a blind bombing mission against a highway segment along the North Vietnamese-Laotian border in March 1966. (USAF via Paul Minert)

Activity abounds on the packed flightline at Takhli as ground crews prepare the 355th's Thuds for a big raid over North Vietnam in the spring of 1966. Able to be seen in the distant background are resident EB-66 Destroyer and KC-135 tanker aircraft. (USAF via Jerry Geer)

An F-105D (62-4364) of the 355th TFW pulls out its parking space for a mission out of Takhli in 1966. This aircraft went on to become one of the first Thuds to reach 3,000 flying hours, passing the mark in October 1968. (Republic via Jerry Geer)

The summer of 1967 saw the 355th TFW sortie rate climb as the air war expanded and targets of more strategic significance were authorized for destruction. Pictured around that time, this F-105D (58-1163) of the wing's 357th TFS is seen undergoing preflight checks prior to launching out of Takhli on another strike against the enemy. (Paul Minert Collection)

heavily on communications from Igloo White sensor fields and relay aircraft. While supporting the war in Laos, the wing regularly hit the passes of Nape, Mu Gia, and Ban Karai, as well as targets in the northern regions at the Plaine des Jarres, Ban Ban, Kang Khai, and Muoug Soi. Combat operations in this arena became increasingly dangerous as the enemy had moved a high number of conventional anti-aircraft guns into the region after the bombing ended in North Vietnam. Between November 1968 and October 1970, the wing had at least nineteen Thuds shot down in Laos.

Beginning in June 1969, the 355th Weasels periodically conducted strikes on SAM and radar controlled AAA sites in North Vietnam that had fired at American aircraft flying reconnaissance missions over the region. Carried out under a concept described as "limited duration, protective reaction air strikes", the mission progressed to armed escort duty after the North Vietnamese successfully shot down several recce aircraft. The wing lost one F-105G over the course of contributing to the "protective reaction" effort.

The 355th TFW underwent two squadron component changes in October 1969. The first move saw a fourth Thud squadron added to the wing when the 44th TFS relocated from Korat to Takhli. This reassignment ended F-105 operations at Korat and left the 355th as the sole Thud-equipped wing in Southeast Asia. The second change brought a reduction in the EB-66 presence at Takhli with the inactivation of the 41st TEWS.

A second Presidential Unit Citation was awarded to the wing during January 1970 for its key role in the destruction of the Paul Doumer Bridge and Phuc Yen airfield over the periods 11-12 August and 24-28 October 1967. Around that same time, the wing received the Republic of Vietnam Gallantry Cross with Palm for its courage during combat operations over the period 22 April 1966 to 30 April 1969.

In the summer of 1970, the 355th TFW received a third Presidential Unit Citation for combat operations over the period 12 April 1968 to 30 April 1969. During this time, the wing flew more than 17,000 combat sorties and delivered 32,000 tons of bombs. This resulted in the destruction of 2,100 targets and severely disrupted and curtailed the enemy's war making potential. This honor made the 355th the only wing to be a three-time recipient of the Presidential Unit Citation for action in Southeast Asia.

Plans to remove the "strike" Thuds from the fighting in Southeast Asia began to take shape during the summer of 1970, although the first outward signs of the pending end of operations for the 355th TFW did not take place until September of that year. During that month, the EB-66-equipped 42nd TEWS was attached to the 388th TFW and subsequently relocated to Korat. At the same time, the wing's Weasel Thuds started moving to Korat to form Detachment 1, 12th TFS, a new unit that would grow in size to become the 6010th WWS on 1 November 1970.

Unlike the 388th TFW's approach of concentrating all of its EF-105Fs into one squadron, the 355th TFW organized its Wild Weasel aircraft into flights within each of its three squadrons. Here, a 357th TFS Weasel (63-8356) drops six Mk-82 500-pound bombs on a North Vietnam target during 1967. (USAF via James Geer)

The wing flew its last F-105 combat mission over Southeast Asia on 6 October 1970. On that day, word came down from Seventh Air Force that the wing was to be inactivated and that all non-Weasel Thuds were to be redeployed to the U.S. at McConnell. Conducted under Operation Coronet Big Horn I, the F-105s of the 355th TFW returned to the U.S. in three separate waves on three separate dates; the first group of fifteen aircraft arrived on 23 October 1970. Over the next two weeks, 39 additional Thuds arrived to complete the operation. After their return, the aircraft remained in open storage at McConnell before being transferred to ANG units during 1971. On 10 December 1970, the 355th TFW was inactivated at Takhli.

From the time of its arrival in Thailand during November 1965, the wing established a remarkable combat record as it amassed over 101,304 combat sorties, logged 263,650 flying hours, delivered 202,596 tons of bombs, and destroyed 12,675 targets. Assigned pilots were credited with twenty MiG kills, with an additional eight MiGs destroyed on the ground and another nine damaged. The price of war was high as the wing lost 136 aircrew members in Southeast Asia during that same period. After the wing's inactivation, a third Air Force Outstanding Unit with Combat "V" Device was received for operations from 1 July 1969 to 24 November 1970.

The 355th TFW was reactivated at Davis-Monthan AFB, Arizona on 1 July 1971, flying the A-7D Corsair II. Ironically, the wing returned to Southeast Asia when it sent aircrews and support personnel to augment an advanced echelon from the 354th TFW at Korat RTAFB, Thailand during 1973-74.

Wing commanders during the 355th TFW's period of operating the Thunderchief were Col. Olin E. Gilbert (12 July 1962), Col. Paul E. Adams (20 July 1963), Col. Edward A. McGouch III (3 September 1963), Col. William H. Holt (2 August 1965), Col. Robert R. Scott (4 August 1966), Col. John C. Giraudo (2 August 1967), Col. Michael C. Horgan (30 June 1968), Col. Heath Bottomly (27 June 1969) and Col. Clarence E. Anderson, Jr. (22 June 1970).

The introduction of tail codes in late 1967 eased unit identification as demonstrated in this view of a mixed flight of 355th TFW Thuds preparing to depart Takhli for a strike in the southern region of North Vietnam in mid-1968. Seen are aircraft from 354th (61-0060), 357th (59-1731 and 60-0522) and 333rd TFS (59-1772), recognized by the RM, RU, and RK codes respectively. (Republic via Paul Minert)

The Paul Doumer Bridge

The Paul Doumer Railroad and Highway Bridge, located on the northern outskirts of Hanoi, was an important military and symbolic target. Militarily, all supplies bound for Hanoi from China and Haiphong passed by rail over the bridge. Thus, its destruction would impede the flow of materials to Communist forces in South Vietnam. Symbolically, to the airmen flying over North Vietnam, the go-ahead to strike the bridge meant that U.S. leadership had the resolve to go after important strategic targets within and near Hanoi.

The steel bridge, named for the Governor General of French Indochina who built the 1,300-mile rail system, was constructed at the turn of the 20th century. Located near the Gia Lam airport, the bridge crossed the Red River with nineteen spans extending a total of 5,532 feet, making it the longest bridge in North Vietnam. The approach viaducts measured another 2,935 feet, making the total length of the structure 8,437 feet. The bridge's width measured 38 feet and included one rail line and two ten-foot highways.

After being on the restricted target list for over two years, the authorization to bomb the Paul Doumer Bridge came unexpectedly to Seventh Air Force at Tan Son Nhut AB, South Vietnam on the morning of 11 August 1967. Immediately, word was passed down to the units chosen to conduct the raid that the bridge would be bombed that afternoon. The 355th TFW was chosen to lead the strike force, while the 388th TFW at Korat and the 8th TFW at Ubon were tasked with important support roles.

The change in the day's frag order from a comparatively routine target to the Paul Doumer Bridge drove a flurry of activity on the Takhli flightline. The large structure called for the use of the 3,000-pound bombs, requiring Thuds that were already carrying the standard mix of six 750-pound bombs and two wing tanks to be reconfigured with two 3,000-pound bombs and one centerline fuel tank. To accelerate the changeover, every available man reported to the flightline and rules prohibiting the loading of fuel and weapons simultaneously were temporarily waived.

While maintenance and munitions personnel readied the aircraft, mission planning and coordination hastily took place. Col. John Giraudo, 355th TFW commander and newly arrived in-theater, designated Col. Bob White, deputy commander for operations, as force commander and mission leader. Because the target was well defended and adjacent to civilian areas that were not to be damaged under any circumstances, the wing's most experienced pilots were chosen to go on the raid. Briefings were thorough and complete, and by early afternoon, twenty Takhli Thuds (plus spares) and their crews were ready to strike the Paul Doumer Bridge.

The strike force that day consisted of one Wild Weasel flight (four EF-105Fs from the 388th TFW), one flak suppression flight (four EF-105Fs from the 355th TFW), three bomb flights (a mix of 36 F-105Ds and F-4C/Ds from the 355th, 388th, and 8th TFW), and three MIGCAP flights (twelve F-4C/Ds from the 8th TFW). Providing additional support were KC-135 tankers, EB-66 radar jammers, and RF-4C reconnaissance aircraft.

The afternoon launch went without a hitch, and all elements of the force proceeded toward Hanoi as planned. Trolling ahead of the strike force were the flak and Wild Weasel flights. Leading the flak flight was Col. White. His group of Thuds was loaded with CBUs to keep the anti-aircraft gunners at bay. Leading the Wild Weasel flight from the 13th TFS, 388th TFW was Squadron Commander Lt. Col. James McInerney and his EWO, Capt. Fred Shannon. On entering the target area, the Weasel flight immediately encountered heavy SAM activity and promptly destroyed two sites. Additional SAMS were engaged, and before the end of the mission, the Weasels suppressed another four missile sites while protecting the strike force.

The first wave of strike aircraft to hit the bridge was the F-105s of the 355th TFW. Despite intense enemy fire from hundreds of 37, 57, and 85-mm guns, the Thuds executed their dive-bomb runs and dropped their 3,000-pound bombs on target. The number two aircraft in the Takhli wave scored a direct hit that dropped the center span of the bridge. Led by Col. Robin Olds, the F-4s of the 8th TFW were next to bomb the bridge, followed by the F-105s from the 388th TFW under the leadership of their commander, Lt. Col. Harry Schurr. The second and third waves inflicted more damage to the bridge by scoring additional direct hits.

The Paul Doumer raid was a major success. Together, the wings dropped 94 tons of bombs that resulted in the destruction of one rail span and two highway spans. This stopped the movement of an average of 26 trains per day with an estimated capacity of over 5,000 tons of supplies. In spite of the heavy air defenses, no aircraft or pilots were lost. White, Olds, Schurr, McInerney, and Shannon all received the Air Force Cross for their actions that day.

Only weeks after the first raid on the bridge, the North Vietnamese had begun extensive repairs, and by early October, the Paul Doumer was back open to both vehicular and rail traffic. Immediately, the 355th TFW was charged with leading another attack on the bridge, but bad weather prevented the second strike from taking place until 25 October 1967. On that day, a strike force of 21 F-105s dropped 63 tons of 3,000-pound bombs, again rendering the bridge unserviceable by putting two spans down.

After the bridge was repaired for a second time, additional strikes were carried out on 14 and 18 December 1967. On these missions, 50 F-105s were successful in causing severe damage to the bridge. At least four spans were dropped, and others were damaged beyond repair. No further strikes were conducted on the Paul Doumer prior to the bombing halt of targets north of the 20th parallel, announced on 31 March 1968. It was not until the 1972 Linebacker campaign that the bridge was hit again.

After the bombing of the North ended on 31 October 1968, the 355th TFW's primary focus turned to supporting the air campaigns in Laos and South Vietnam. This bomb-laden 357th TFS F-105D (62-4318) was photographed on a 24 February 1969 mission against North Vietnamese forces in Laotian territory. (Stewart Hurd)

An F-105D (62-4384) of 333rd TFS, 355th TFW leads a strike flight from Takhli to the target area on 24 April 1969. Armament includes six M117 750-pounds on the centerline and rocket pods on the outboard pylons. (Stewart Hurd)

The arrival of the F-105G within the 355th TFW in 1969 provided the USAF with a much improved Weasel platform to combat the North Vietnamese SAM threat. At rest on the Takhli ramp, this early G-model (63-8352) of the wing's 357th TFS carries AGM-78 Standard ARMs on the inboards and AGM-45 Shrikes on the outboard pylons. (USAF via Paul Minert)

In October 1969, the 355th TFW added a fourth F-105 squadron when the 44th TFS arrived at Takhli on transfer from the 388th TFW at Korat RTAFB, Thailand. The 44th Thud (59-1759) seen here still wears the JE tail code from its previous assignment when photographed as a member of this flight returning to Takhli on 30 October 1969. The aircraft (60-0504) nearest the camera belonged to the 357th TFS and the jet (60-0490) breaking away was assigned to the 354th TFS. (Stewart Hurd)

With the close out of Thud operations at Korat in the fall of 1969, the 355th TFW was left as the sole F-105-equipped wing in Southeast Asia. This view shows two aircraft (61-0161 and 62-4242) from the newly assigned 44th TFS awaiting their turn for refueling as a 354th TFS ship (62-4387) hangs on the boom during a 12 November 1969 mission. (Stewart Hurd)

Flying long raids from their home base in Thailand required the F-105s of the 355th TFW to complete two air refuelings during each combat mission. Taken on 26 November 1969, this photograph catches a 354th TFS Thud (62-4230) as it tops-up from a KC-135 tanker while returning from a bombing strike over Laos. (Stewart Hurd)

These 355th TFW Thuds are seen hauling their loads of Mk-82 500-pound bombs to a target on 4 December 1969. The lead aircraft is a 44th TFS F-105D (61-0093), while the second is a 354th TFS EF-105F (62-4446). (Stewart Hurd)

An F-105D (60-0504) of the 357th TFS, 355th TFW taxis out for a 1970 mission from Takhli, carrying M118 3,000-pound bombs with "daisy cutter" fuse extenders. The aircraft carries the name *Memphis Belle II* in tribute to the famous B-17 bomber of World War II. (James Geer Collection)

Subsequent to the end of the Rolling Thunder campaign, the 355th TFW intermittently flew missions in support of reconnaissance and limited strike operations over North Vietnam under the "protective reaction" concept. This lethally armed 333rd TFS F-105G (63-8320) is seen prowling the skies over the North during one such mission in 1970. (Paul Hoynacki via Jerry Geer)

This historic photograph shows a flight of four 355th TFW Thuds performing a ceremonial flyby over Takhli after successfully completing the wing's final combat mission over Southeast Asia on 6 October 1970. (Don Kutyna)

44th Tactical Fighter Squadron

The 44th Tactical Fighter Squadron was reassigned from the 388th TFW to the 355th TFW on 15 October 1969. The squadron's history with the Thud goes back to its time as a component of the 18th TFW at Kadena AB, Okinawa. It was equipped with F-105Ds in late 1962 and was heavily involved in the early air war in Southeast Asia. At the end of 1966, the 44th was relegated to a "paper unit" status after its resources were used to form the 13th TFS earlier that year. The squadron was reassigned to the 388th TFW at Korat RTAFB, Thailand in the spring of 1967, absorbing the 421st TFS and its general strike mission.

In the fall of 1967, the 44th switched to the Wild Weasel mission and maintained this role until its reassignment to the 355th TFW. Unlike the 388th TFW's structure of centralizing its EF-105Fs in one squadron, the 355th TFW organized its Weasel force by flights within each of its squadrons. Consequently, the 44th TFS gave up many of its EF-105Fs for F-105Ds and assumed the dual-role mission of strike and Wild Weasel operations when it was transferred to the 355th at Takhli.

The unit's strike mission primarily consisted of flying close air support, interdiction, and armed reconnaissance missions in support of the Barrel Roll and Steel Tiger campaigns in Laos. In conjunction with this duty, the 44th frequently carried out attacks on key checkpoints and transportation targets in the Laotian panhandle under the Commando Hunt operation. Weasel missions included flying armed escort for RF-4Cs on reconnaissance flights over North Vietnam under the "protective reaction" effort. Other Weasel escort duty involved supporting Gunship operations against infiltration routes near the North Vietnamese-Laotian border. Strike operations in Laos were conducted without any losses, but the limited "protective reaction" duty cost the unit one F-105G and its crew on 28 January 1970. Shot down and killed were Captains Richard J. Mallon and Robert J. Panek, Sr.

In line with the planned end of Thud operations at Takhli and corresponding inactivation of the 355th TFW, the 44th TFS flew its last combat mission on 6 October 1970. Over the next three weeks, most of the unit's aircraft were ferried to the U.S. under Operation Coronet Big Horn I. Left behind were the squadron's Weasel Thuds, which relocated to Korat to augment the formation of Detachment 1, 12th TFS. During the 44th's time with the 355th TFW, it earned the Air Force Outstanding Unit Award with Combat "V" Device for operations over the period 15 October 1969 to 24 November 1970.

On 10 December 1970, the 44th TFS was reassigned to the Thirteenth Air Force in a non-operational status. After spending four years in Thailand, the squadron returned to its pre-war parent when it was reassigned to the 18th TFW at Kadena on 15 March 1971. Two months later, the 44th resumed operations with the F-4C Phantom II.

On transfer to Takhli, the 44th TFS was quickly integrated into 355th TFW operations with a dual strike and Weasel mission requirement. Still bearing the JE code from its previous assignment with the 388th TFW, this 44th aircraft (59-1759) is seen passing over the Mekong River with a pair of Thuds from the 357th (60-0504) and 354th TFS (60-0490) during the return leg of a 30 October 1969 mission. (Stewart Hurd)

These two F-105Ds of the 44th (62-4242) and 354th TFS (62-4387) are seen on an interdiction mission against the Ho Chi Minh Trail on 12 November 1969. (Stewart Hurd)

A 44th TFS F-105D (61-0161) heads home after completing a mission over Laos on 12 November 1969. (Stewart Hurd)

Emergency and ground support crews check-out this 44th Thud (61-0093) after it was involved in a landing accident that caused damage to both main gears. This photograph was taken at Takhli circa late 1969. (USAF via Stewart Hurd)

Sinister Vampire, an EF-105F (63-8319) of the 44th TFS, prepares to depart Takhli on a Weasel mission in early 1970. The aircraft name on the intake and crew names on the canopy rails were painted in silver on a black field. (John Coon via James Geer)

Seen on a bombing mission in May 1970, this 44th TFS F-105D (61-0086) named *Big Sal* carries six Mk-82 500-pound bombs on the centerline and rocket pods on the outboard pylons. (USAF via James Geer)

The heavy use and hard flying experienced by the Thuds in Southeast Asia often showed in the aircraft's appearance as exemplified by *Mt Ida Flash*, a well-worn 44th TFS EF-105F (63-8347) caught at rest between missions in this May 1970 photograph. (Barry Miller via James Geer)

ABOVE: An F-105D (60-0464) of the 44th TFS hauls a load of Mk-82s to a target in Laos or South Vietnam. (USAF via Jerry Geer)

OPPOSITE
ABOVE: Taken in mid-1970, this photograph shows a flight of Thuds from the 44th (61-0076 and 62-4361) and 357th TFS (59-1731) returning from a strike against Laotian enemy supply lines. (Republic via Jerry Geer)

BOTTOM: Named *Sweet Caroline*, this 44th TFS EF-105F (63-8327) is seen taxiing out for a bombing sortie from Takhli during the late summer of 1970. (Don Kutyna)

RU
731
RE
361
RE
076
RE
327

333rd Tactical Fighter Squadron

The 333rd Tactical Fighter Squadron was reassigned from the 4th TFW to the 355th TFW on 8 December 1965, making it the second PCS squadron at Takhli RTAFB, Thailand. The unit operated F-105D/Fs with the 4th TFW for about five years before it was transferred to PACAF. Arriving at Takhli on 5 December, the squadron's 24 pilots were introduced to the Southeast Asia theater of operations by the 335th TFS, which was set to return home after spending five months on TDY in Japan and Thailand. By mid-December, the unit had assumed control of the 335th's aircraft and proceeded to fly up to 300 missions before the end of the year.

During the temporary suspension of operations over North Vietnam from 25 December 1965 to 30 January 1966, the 333rd TFS conducted Barrel Roll and Steel Tiger missions against Communist supply positions and transportation routes in Laos. In February, the unit resumed operations in the southern panhandle of the North and destroyed communication lines, supply routes, and storage areas. Operations extended to the Hanoi region by April. That month, Lt. Col. James A. Young, commander of the 333rd TFS, led a large strike force on a successful raid on the Thai Nguyen railyards. POL facilities were added to the target list by mid-year, and the squadron played an important role in the Hanoi POL strike on 29 June 1966.

The squadron's mission in Southeast Asia had taken a great toll by August 1966 as no less than thirteen aircraft had been shot down, with two others lost to operational mishaps. On 21 September 1966, the 333rd struck back at the North Vietnamese Air Force (NVAF) by destroying a MiG in air-to-air combat. The kill took place when 1st Lt. Fred A. Wilson shot down a MiG-17 with his 20-mm cannon during a strike mission against the Dap Cau Bridge. This aerial victory gave the 355th TFW its first confirmed MiG kill of the war.

The fall of 1966 saw attacks against targets such as railyards, fuel storage areas, bridges, and air defense sites in North Vietnam continue. At this time, the 333rd TFS mission changed to include Wild Weasel operations with the receipt of about six EF-105Fs. The Weasels immediately saw heavy action over the North by supporting bombing missions in regions where SAMs and radar-controlled AAA sites were known to pose a high threat. Although the squadron was logging a growing number of sorties, only one aircraft was lost in combat during the final four months of the year.

During the spring of 1967, the 333rd played an important role in the first attacks on the railyards and industrial center at Thai Nguyen in March and the Hoa Lac airfield in April, providing strike and Weasel forces for both raids. Precipitating the attack on the Hoa Lac airfield was the growing size and increasing effectiveness of the NVAF MiG force. The squadron's first MiG kill of 1967 came on 26 March, when mission lead Col. Robert R. Scott, 355th TFW commander, and Lt. Col. Donald K. Salmon, 333rd TFS commander, were teamed in a flight of four Thuds tasked to strike the Son Toy army barracks, 20 miles west-northwest of Hanoi. After bombing the target, Col. Scott shot down a MiG-17 with his 20-mm Gatling gun when he encountered the enemy aircraft not far from Hoa Lac airfield.

Col. Scott's victory was the first of five MiG kills confirmed by the 333rd during a three-month period of heavy air-to-air fighting. Thomas C. Lesan gunned down a MiG-17 on the morning of 30 April while striking railyards northeast of Bac Giang. On 12 May, Capt. Jacques A. Suzanne scored another MiG kill with 20-mm fire while leading a flight of four Thuds on a flak suppression mission. The following day, 333rd pilots destroyed two additional MiGs-17s, this time with AIM-9 missiles. Comprising one-half of a flight of four Thuds attacking the Yen Vien railroad, Maj. Robert

Upon arrival at Takhli in December 1965, the 333rd TFS assumed control of about 21 Thuds that were already deployed at the base, mainly those left behind the departing 335th TFS. Soon to be allocated to the 333rd, these two F-105Ds (60-0440 and 61-0168) were photographed on 16 November 1965 while operating out of Yokota AB, Japan prior to their transfer to Thailand. (Yukio Takahashi)

This view of the Takhli ramp in the fall of 1966 shows F-105Ds of the 333rd TFS being serviced and loaded for their next combat mission. Note the squadron painted the nose gear radar reflector and crew names on the white canopy name block in red to distinguish their aircraft during this period. (USAF via James Geer)

G. Rilling and Maj. Carl D. Osborne downed the MiGs while leaving the target area.

The second half of 1967 saw the squadron participate in nearly all of the critical targets struck by the 355th TFW. Highlights include the initial and follow-up strikes on the Paul Doumer Bridge, as well as flying in the largest single air strike of the war to date against the Phuc Yen airfield. On 18 October, the squadron claimed another aerial victory when Maj. Donald M. Russell shot down a MiG-17 with his 20-mm cannon while flying a strike on the Dai Loi railroad bypass bridge. On a subsequent mission against the Dai Loi bypass on 19 December, an EF-105F crewed by Maj. William M. Dalton, pilot, and Maj. James L. Graham, EWO, gunned down a MiG-17 that had been previously damaged by an F-4D. This gave the crewmembers credit for a one-half kill. This aerial victory was the last for the 333rd during the war, leaving it with a total of 7 1/2 MiG kills. On the opposite side of the scorecard, the enemy air defense system also had success. Flying into the hostile forces of MiGs, SAMs, and AAA fire to destroy vital targets during 1967 cost the squadron at least eleven F-105Ds and two EF-105Fs, while operational accidents claimed another four F-105Ds.

Strikes against supply lines and military targets in the North, plus actions to combat the MiG threat, continued into 1968. Under the Combat Martin program, the squadron added several specially equipped F-105Fs that were capable of blocking communication between MiGs and their GCI centers. Of a more destruction blow to the MiG force was the 333rd's participation in attacks against the Hoa Lac and Yen Bai airfields during the first two months of the year. Bad weather over the north prevented visual strikes from taking place, so the MiG bases were attacked using radar bombing techniques.

Operations shifted southward in April 1968 after President Johnson restricted the bombing of North Vietnam to below the 19th parallel. From that point, military and transportation targets in the southern panhandle region became the primary focal point of 333rd operations. Good weather conditions brought the number of attack sorties to high levels during the summer months, and that trend generally continued through the announcement of a complete bombing halt of North Vietnam on 1 November 1968. The bombing restrictions that shifted operations away from the MiG and SAM "high threat" areas effectively reduced the combat losses for the 333rd TFS to only four F-105Ds and one EF-105F in 1968.

Awards received during 1968 include a Presidential Unit Citation for the squadron's contribution to the destruction of many key enemy supply, transportation, and military targets over the period 1 January to 10 October 1966. In addition, the 333rd TFS received its first Air Force Outstanding Unit Award with Combat "V" Device for operations over the period 12 October 1966 to 11 April 1967.

Throughout the course of 1969-70, the squadron performed directed missions to interdict the flow of enemy men and materials through Laos into South Vietnam. These missions were generally in the Steel Tiger operating area, where a new campaign against lines of communication was being carried out under the code name Commando Hunt. Other missions in Laos were in the form of strikes against enemy supply positions in the Barrel Roll operating area in the north. Outside of using general-purpose iron bombs to destroy their targets, the 333rd often utilized the moderately effective 3,000-pound AGM-12C Bullpup missile. This weapon was used against key links in the transportation network that required precise hits to be destroyed, such as bridges and tunnels. Although it could be delivered with pinpoint precision, the AGM-12C warhead often lacked the punch to destroy its targets. Meanwhile, the action for the 333rd Weasels was relatively low, albeit periodic "protective reaction" missions were flown in support of tactical recce aircraft flying over North Vietnam. During this two-year period, the squadron lost at least nine F-105Ds, of which four were due to operational causes.

The squadron received many additional awards for action over Southeast Asia. Two more Presidential Unit Citations were awarded, one for its role in the Paul Doumer Bridge and Phuc Yen airfield strikes during 11-12 August and 24-28 October 1967 and another for outstanding war contributions over the period 1 July 1969 to 15 October 1970. In addition, two other Air Force Outstanding Unit Awards with Combat "V" Device were given for operations over the periods 12 April 1967 to 11 April 1968 and 1 July 1969 to 24 November 1970. The 333rd TFS also earned the Republic of Vietnam Gallantry Cross with Palm for actions from 1 April 1966 to 15 October 1970.

The first phase in the drawdown of operations for the 333rd TFS came with the transfer of its Weasel aircraft and crews to Korat RTAFB, Thailand to help form Detachment 1, 12th TFS during the last week of September 1970. The squadron's last combat mis-

An EF-105F (63-8316) of the 333rd TFS cruises over the southern panhandle of North Vietnam during a SAM suppression mission in August 1968. The aircraft is carrying Mk-84 2,000-pound bombs with "daisy cutter" fuse extenders on the inboards and AGM-45 Shrikes on the outboard pylons. (Joe Caldwell via Jerry Geer)

The Thud squadrons of the 355th TFW continued the wartime tradition of applying nose art to their aircraft, although the nude pin-ups that were common during World War II and Korea rarely appeared. One exception was *Fat Fanny*, an EF-105F (62-4436) of the 333rd TFS, seen here in the Takhli arming area in 1968. (Republic via Paul Minert)

Displaying the squadron's recently applied RK tail code, a 333rd TFS F-105D (59-1772) taxis out for take-off at Takhli circa mid-1968. Visible below the windscreen are two MiG kill markings earned by 355th TFW Commander Col. Robert R. Scott on 26 March 1967 and 357th TFS pilot Maj. Harry E. Higgins on 28 April 1967. (Republic via Paul Minert)

This view from the boom operator's position in a KC-135 tanker shows a Combat Martin F-105F (63-8318) of the 333rd TFS moving into precontact position for refueling while enroute to North Vietnam on 26 August 1968. The aircraft's rear seat has been removed and replaced with the QRC-128 VHF jamming system, but notice it has yet to have the Martin's characteristic blade antenna installed on top of the fuselage. (USAF via Paul Minert)

A 333rd TFS F-105D (62-4353) sits in the revetments at Tan Son Nhut AB, South Vietnam during a visit in 1969. (Paul Minert Collection)

sion was flown on 6 October. Immediately afterwards, preparations began for the return of all "strike" aircraft and crews to the U.S. at McConnell. On 15 October 1970, the 333rd TFS was reassigned to the 23rd TFW in a non-operational status. One week later, on 23 October, fifteen F-105s from the squadron arrived at McConnell as the first element of Thuds to be returned under the Coronet Big Horn I redeployment operation.

The squadron remained at McConnell in a non-operational state until it was transferred to the 58th TFTW at Luke AFB, Arizona on 22 March 1971. A short time later, on 31 July 1971, the unit rejoined the 355th TFW at Davis-Monthan AFB, Arizona and began operations with the A-7D Corsair II.

Seen on 24 April 1969, this 333rd Thud (59-1729) is seen heading into action carrying M117 750-pound bombs on the centerline and rocket pods on the outboard pylons. (Stewart Hurd)

With its drag chute fully deployed, an early F-105G (63-8320) of the 333rd TFS recovers at Takhli following the completion of a sortie circa late 1969. (USAF via Steward Hurd)

Thuds of the 333rd (62-4344) and 354th TFS (62-4230) refuel on a 26 November 1969 mission, probably against hostile lines of communication in Laos. (Stewart Hurd)

A 333rd TFS F-105D (60-0445) opens it four petal speed brakes at high altitude while returning from a 29 November 1969 bombing strike. During a previous assignment with the 388th TFW, this aircraft scored a MiG-17 kill while being flown by 13th TFS pilot Maj. Ralph L. Kuster, Jr. on 3 June 1967. (Stewart Hurd)

Awaiting its next mission at Takhli in this February 1970 photograph is *Big Red*, a 333rd Thud (62-4384) loaded with eight Mk-82 500-pound bombs. (John Coon via James Geer)

This 333rd TFS F-105D (60-0451) is armed with AGM-12C Bullpup missiles for an attack on a precision target in Laos during 1970. (Paul Hoynacki via James Geer)

Flying a standard bombing mission in May 1970, an early F-105G (62-4428) of the 333rd TFS holds on the left wing of a KC-135 tanker as it waits for its turn on the boom for pre-strike refueling. (USAF via James Geer)

354th Tactical Fighter Squadron

The 354th Tactical Fighter Squadron was activated within the 355th TFW at George on 13 April 1962. Upon organization on 8 July 1962, assigned pilots entered the F-105 pilot training program at Nellis AFB, Nevada with the 4520th CCTW. After being equipped with a complement of 24 F-105Ds by early 1963, the 354th spent the next year conducting routine training operations to maintain combat proficiency.

Between 24 January and 14 February 1964, the 354th participated in a large-scale, joint-service training exercise code named Polar Siege. This maneuver was held in Alaska and involved 10,000 Army and 700 USAF personnel training as combat-ready in Arctic simulated war conditions. During the exercise, the squadron operated out of Eielsen AFB, Alaska and flew support for both "friendly" and "aggressor" forces.

The squadron deployed as a unit to Incirlik AB, Turkey for a planned 90-day rotational tour of duty on 2 May 1964. Upon arrival, it replaced the 356th TFS, an F-100D-equipped unit assigned to the 354th TFW at Myrtle Beach AFB, North Carolina. At Incirlik, the 354th TFS fell under the control of the Seventeenth Air Force while assuming an alert position in support of the USAFE General War Deterrent Forces. The squadron's stay in Turkey was extended by another 45 days after its scheduled replacement, the 357th TFS, was sent to the Far East as a result of the Gulf on Tonkin Incident. Its deployment ended on or about 20 September 1964, when it was replaced by the 421st TFS. The 354th TFS initially returned to George, but rejoined the balance of the 355th TFW at its new home at McConnell AFB, Kansas in mid-October 1964.

On 3 March 1965, the 354th TFS became the third unit of the 355th TFW to serve a TDY assignment in the Far East when it deployed without aircraft to Kadena AB, Okinawa under Operation One Buck 10. Upon arrival on 6 March, the squadron spent about one week transitioning into its PACAF role by assuming control of about eighteen TAC Thuds that had been previously operated by the departing 469th TFS. After assuming command on 13 March, a portion of the 354th TFS rotated to Korat RTFAB, Thailand to support early strikes against North Vietnam under the newly authorized Rolling Thunder campaign. The dual-role mission of supporting PACAF mission requirements at Kadena and flying combat missions out of Korat continued until early April. At that time, the 421st TFS arrived at Kadena for back-up duty, allowing the remainder of the 354th to move to Thailand.

Once fully in place at Korat, the 354th TFS was attached to the provisional 6234th TFW. Pilots of the 354th participated in many aspects of the air war, but Barrel Roll and Steel Tiger interdiction missions in Laos and Rolling Thunder strikes against military and transportation targets in the central and southern regions of North Vietnam took top priority. Credits include participation in the first strikes on the Thanh Hoa Bridge on 3-4 April. On the second day of attacks on the bridge, two 354th Thuds fell victim to enemy MiGs when they were jumped prior to reaching the target. Shot down and killed were Capt. James A. Magnusson, Jr. and Maj. Frank E. Bennett.

Outside of the two setbacks suffered on the Thanh Hoa raids, the 354th lost five additional aircraft to hostile action during the course of its combat tour. In all but one instance, the pilots were recovered. The sole crewman lost was 1st Lt. Robert D. Peel, who was taken POW after ejecting over North Vietnam on 31 May. The 354th TFS ended it combat tour on 12 June 1965 after passing on its aircraft and combat role to its sister unit, the 357th TFS. During its deployment, the squadron recorded 1,132 sorties, which included 637 Rolling Thunder and 102 Barrel Roll/Steel Tiger missions. For outstanding operations over the period 5 May to 17 June 1965, the 354th was awarded the Presidential Unit Citation.

This factory fresh F-105D (62-4307) of the 354th TFS is seen on static display at a 1963 airshow. (Duane Kasulka vi Jerry Geer)

Under Operation Ready Alpha, the 354th TFS was ordered PCS to Takhli RTAFB, Thailand, following its current parent organization to Southeast Asia for combat duty. The 355th TFW's relocation preceded the squadron's move by about three weeks. As a result, the 354th was temporarily assigned to the 835th AD during the period 8-27 November 1965 until it moved to Takhli. The squadron's relocation to Thailand corresponded with the close of a four-month combat tour for the 562nd TFS. Upon arriving on station, the unit assumed control of the 562nd's aircraft and operational mission. The squadron recorded over 400 combat missions before the end of 1966, with one F-105D shot down on a strike in North Vietnam against the Vu Chua Railroad Bridge on 20 December. This loss proved to be a prelude of things to come for the unit during 1966.

The first month of 1966 saw the squadron fly many armed recce missions over Laos due to the suspension of air operations against North Vietnam that began on Christmas Eve 1965. On a 16 January strike in Laos, Col. Don C. Wood became the unit's first casualty of the year when he was killed on a strike against the Ho Chi Minh Trail. After the bombing halt ended on 31 January 1966, the 354th TFS began flying missions against the enemy's transportation system in the southern panhandle of North Vietnam. In April 1966, the squadron started to hit bridges, storage areas, and other military targets closer to the immediate Hanoi area. When the decision to attack targets of a more strategic value took place in June 1966, the 354th was chosen to lead a raid on the Hanoi POL facility, the first target chosen in the new campaign.

The Hanoi POL strike took place on 29 June and was led by Maj. James H. Kasler, operations officer for the 354th TFS. For the mission, Kasler selected his most skilled and experienced pilots to take sixteen F-105s loaded with eight 750-pound bombs each into the heavy air defenses of Hanoi. Approaching the target from the

A fur-clad crew chief directs his 354th TFS F-105D (62-4316) out of its parking space at Eielsen AFB, Alaska for a mission during Operation Polar Siege in February 1964. (USAF via James Geer)

This shot, taken in April 1965, shows a 354th TFS F-105D (61-0143) heading northward on an early Rolling Thunder mission out of Korat RTAFB, Thailand during the squadron's One Buck 10 deployment. Unit markings during this time consisted of a blue and white striped tail band. (D. Steigers via James Geer)

north, Kasler's force evaded heavy AAA fire and successfully struck the large storage tanks of the complex, putting it out of business for the remainder of the war. One F-105 was lost to the flak and three others sustained hits but landed safely. A fourth aircraft received minor damage from a MiG attack but was credited with a probable kill in the ensuing aerial battle.

Following in the footsteps of the Wild Weasel program at Korat, the 354th helped introduce the EF-105F to combat when it received a small group of the modified two-seat aircraft on 4 July 1966. As the EF-105F program was in its infancy, the 354th Weasels maintained close ties to their counterpart Weasel squadron at Korat, the 13th TFS, to facilitate improvements in the aircraft and its mission. Suffering from a lack of well-trained crews and the temperamental behavior of the newly installed electronic equipment, the Weasels struggled during the first several months of operations. Within a one-month period, the fledging 354th Weasels were nearly wiped out. The squadron lost its first EF-105F on 23 July. On 7 August, two more aircraft were shot down with both teams of crewmembers lost. The program was decimated after a fourth aircraft and crew were lost on 17 August. Replacement aircraft arrived, and as training, equipment, and tactics progressed, the 354th Weasels gained success by destroying numerous SAM sites during the fall and winter of 1966.

The high loss rate of the 354th Weasel team also applied to the squadron's strike operations. During July and August 1966, as many as nine F-105Ds were shot down over North Vietnam. As the Weasel program increased in size and gained experience, the F-105 loss rate dropped considerably; notwithstanding, the 354th lost at least five F-105Ds over the North during the last four months of 1966. Some of the more difficult missions carried out during that time were attacks on the Viet Tri railroad yard and Yen Bay storage area. The squadron ended the year with a total of 23 F-105 combat losses, the highest combat attrition of any Thud squadron in Southeast Asia to date. Among the pilots lost was Maj. Kasler, who was shot down on 8 August and interned as a POW until March 1973.

Armed with AGM-12A Bullpup missiles, this F-105D of the 354th TFS takes on fuel before heading into North Vietnam for the historic first strike on the Thanh Hoa Bridge on 3 April 1965. (USAF via James Geer)

On 2 January 1967, the 354th TFS participated in Operation Bolo, an anti-MiG fighter sweep over North Vietnam. The operation involved F-4s from both the 8th and 366th TFW posing as F-105s on a bombing mission to lure the NVAF MiGs into combat. The EF-105Fs of the 354th TFS led the 355th TFW team that provided one-half of the force that was tasked to suppress the SAM threat for the F-4s. The second half of the force was from the 388th TFW, led by the 13th TFS Weasels. The operation was a success as seven North Vietnamese MiG-21s were shot down by the Phantoms.

The 354th TFS took over the aircraft of the departing 562nd TFS when it deployed on a PCS basis to rejoin the 355th TFW at Takhli RTAFB, Thailand in late November 1965. Hints of previous ownership by the 562nd are clearly visible on the vertical fins of these 354th Thuds (62-4239 and 58-1151) when photographed during gunnery practice at Yokota AB, Japan on 21 January 1966. (Toyokazu Matsuzaki)

A 354th TFS F-105D (59-1770) makes an approach to Yokota at the end of a training mission on 8 February 1966. As seen here, the 354th retained the blue-white-blue tail band used by the 562nd TFS since the two units shared the same squadron color. (Toyokazu Matsuzaki)

Caught while visiting a KC-135 tanker for pre-strike refueling, these 354th TFS Thuds carry Mk-84 2,000-pound bombs for a Rolling Thunder strike in February 1966. Note the bizarre appearance of the second aircraft from the camera wearing a silver lacquer finish with a camouflaged vertical fin. (Fred Retter via Merle Olmstead via Doug Olson via Jerry Geer)

Photographed during a visit to Yokota AB, Japan on 4 May 1966, this F-105D (59-1731) of the 354th TFS was one of the last Thuds in Southeast Asia to be repainted in camouflage. (Toyokazu Matsuzaki)

During March 1967, the 354th TFS supported the first attacks against the Thai Nguyen iron and steel works, about 50 miles north of Hanoi. Two significant individual accomplishments took place on 10 March, the first day of strikes against the steel works. First, while flying in the number three position in a flight of four tasked with suppressing flak in and around the target area, Capt. Max C. Brestel downed two MiG-17s with his 20-mm cannon. With these aerial victories, Capt. Brestel became the first double MiG killer of the war. Second, 354th Weasel pilot Capt. Merlyn H. Dethlefsen became the first airman to receive the Medal of Honor after he displayed unusual courage for pressing an attack on SAM sites that surrounded the Thai Nguyen steel works while facing extremely heavy anti-aircraft fire and MiG opposition.

Strikes in North Vietnam intensified from April 1967 as the weather improved considerably with the end of the northeast monsoon season. In particular, the squadron flew many missions aimed at destroying transportation and military targets, as well as providing SAM suppression support on many key raids. On 19 April, the squadron found itself engaged in heavy aerial combat while supporting attacks against the Xuan Mai army barracks. The 354th downed three MiG-17s that day. Pilots credited with kills were Maj. Jack W. Hunt, Maj. Frederick G. Tolman, and Capt. William E. Eskew, each getting their MiG with 20-mm gunfire.

Intense dogfights continued over the North during May as the enemy sent its MiG force up with more regularity in an attempt to protect the vital targets now under attack. On 13 May, the 354th destroyed two more MiG-17s while flying strikes against the Yen Vien railyard. Gunning down the MiGs were Lt. Col. Philip C. Gast and Capt. Charles W. Couch.

The squadron participated in the destruction of numerous key targets during the second half of 1967. Those hit include the Bac Giang and Chieu Ung bridges, the Phuc Yen railyard, the NVAF Headquarters at Bak Mai, the Duc Noi railyard, the Ty Nuyen railyard and industrial complex, and the Vinh airfield. In addition, the 354th played an important part in the first attacks on the Paul Doumer Bridge during August, as well as the follow-up strikes on the Doumer in October and December. On a mission against the Canal des Rapides Bridge on 27 October, Capt. Gene I. Basel downed a MiG-17 with 20-mm fire. This was the eighth and final aerial victory credited to the 354th TFS in the war; however, the squadron destroyed four additional MiGs on the ground while conducting strikes against Hoa Lac, Phuc Yen and Kep airfields in 1967.

Although the 354th was flying into North Vietnam against heavily defended targets on a daily basis during 1967, improved tactics and the growing effectiveness of the Wild Weasel mission cut the squadron's loss rate significantly as compared to the prior year. Combat losses for the year totaled eleven F-105Ds and two EF-105Fs. Another four F-105Ds were lost to operational accidents.

This view from the boom pod of a KC-135 shows a flight of 354th TFS F-105Ds taking on fuel before heading into North Vietnam to destroy a target with M118 3,000-pound bombs in the spring of 1966. (USAF via James Geer)

Weasel and bombing missions over the North continued during the first quarter of 1968, although bad weather curtailed operations in the Hanoi area. As a result of the announcement of a partial bombing halt of North Vietnam during the spring of 1968, the 354th shifted their effort to the southern panhandle region. Here, the Communist transportation system was the main focus up until the 1 November 1968 complete bombing halt of the North. During the final two months of the year, the squadron primarily supported the Barrel Roll and Steel Tiger campaigns in Laos. The 354th TFS lost four F-105Ds in combat during 1968.

Maj. James H. Kasler, operations officer of the 354th TFS, completes his preflight checks before a mission "up north" on 31 July 1966, just eight days before he was shot down and taken POW. Kasler was one of the most experienced fighter pilots to fly with the 355th TFW, and was responsible for leading the wing on the highly successful strike on the Hanoi POL facility. (USAF via James Geer)

Black smoke from the starter cartridge exhaust surrounds this 354th TFS F-105D (58-1168) preparing to depart Takhli for a strike against North Vietnam circa early 1967. Maj. Jack W. Hunt flew this aircraft on his MiG killing mission of 19 April 1967. (USAF via Paul Minert)

The 354th TFS was honored with two awards in 1968. First, the squadron received the Air Force Outstanding Unit Award with Combat "V" Device for its combat record over the period 12 October 1966 to 11 April 1967. Second, for contributing to the substantial damage to the enemy's supply, transportation, and air defense networks for the period 1 January and 10 October 1966, the squadron received the Presidential Unit Citation.

During 1969-70, the 354th's general-purpose strike mission consisted of supply interdiction, armed reconnaissance, and troop support duty in Laos. Anti-aircraft guns and small arms fire claimed at least six 354th Thuds during that time. Without the threat of SAMs in this theater, the highlight for the 354th Weasels was flying armed escort for Gunships operating near the North Vietnam border and conducting "protective reaction" missions in support of reconnaissance flights over North Vietnam. By mid-1969, the Weasel crews were using the more capable F-105G in this role.

The 354th received two additional Presidential Unit Citations during 1970, giving it a total of four for combat in Southeast Asia. One was for its role in the Paul Doumer Bridge and Phuc Yen airfield strikes during 11-12 August and 24-28 October 1967, and the second was for combat operations over the period 12 April 1968 to 30 April 1969. In addition, the wing earned two more Air Force Outstanding Unit Awards with Combat "V" Device for its operational record during the periods 12 April 1967 to 11 April 1968 and 1 July 1969 to 15 October 1970.

With the announcement of the planned inactivation of the 355th TFW, the 354th flew its last combat mission during early October 1970. As part of Coronet Big Horn I, all of the squadron's non-Weasel aircraft and crews returned to the U.S. at McConnell by the end of October. The remaining F-105Gs moved to Korat to add to the formation of a cadre of Weasels designated Detachment 1, 12th TFS.

On 14 December 1970, the 354th TFS assumed a "paper unit" status upon reassignment to the Thirteenth Air Force. One day later, the squadron moved to Davis-Monthan AFB, Arizona. On 1 April 1971, the 354th joined the 4453rd CCTW, but remained dormant. Three months later, on 1 July, the 354th TFS rejoined the 355th TFW and began flying the A-7D Corsair II. In 1973, the squadron served TDY in Southeast Asia with their new aircraft. Later that year, the unit received the Vietnam Gallantry Cross with Palm for its contributions to the war over the period 1 April 1966 to 28 January 1973.

Captain Merlyn H. Dethlefsen

On 10 March 1967, Capt. Merlyn H. Dethlefsen took off from Takhli on an Iron Hand (SAM suppression) mission against the air defenses around the Thai Nguyen steel works. This was his 78th combat mission, and he had the number three position in a flight of four Thuds made-up of two EF-105Fs and two F-105Ds operating as hunter-killer teams.

As the flight approached the target area, they encountered intense AAA fire. Amidst the bursting shells, Dethlefsen trailed the two lead aircraft by some 3,000 to 5,000 feet as the flight pressed the attack. The lead aircraft had identified a SAM site and launched a Shrike missile, but it missed. The enemy gunners were more accurate. The flight leader was shot down, and his wingman had suffered heavy damage and was forced to abandon the effort.

Taking command of the flight, Dethlefsen circled the target area and repositioned his aircraft for a second pass on the target. Just as he and his backseater, Capt. Kevin "Mike" Gilroy, located the SAM site, he spotted two MiG-21s taking aim behind his Thud. He fired a Shrike missile at the SAM site and dove into a mushroom of flak just as the one of the MiGs fired a missile at his aircraft. His evasive maneuver worked as the MiGs failed to follow him into the barrage of AAA fire.

Aircraft with the RM tail code of the 354th TFS, along with a single RU-marked 357th TFS Thud, take on fuel from a KC-135 tanker before proceeding on a mission over the southern panhandle of North Vietnam in July 1968. Nearest the camera is an EF-105F (63-8351) carrying Shrikes and 2,000-pound bombs, while beyond are two F-105Ds (62-4242 and 61-0212) carrying Bullpups. (M. Nelson via Jerry Geer)

Having just completed 100 combat missions over North Vietnam, the pilot of this 354th Thud (61-0150) follows the tradition of extending the refueling probe to mark the windup of a successful tour in Southeast Asia. This shot was taken at Takhli in July 1968. (Joe Caldwell via Jerry Geer)

Dethlefsen reversed his course to gain visual contact on the SAM site to see if he had successfully knocked it out. By this time, the first elements of the strike force were bombing the steel mills, creating a cloud of debris and smoke over the target area. Through the cloud, Dethlefsen was able to see enemy missiles streaking up toward the strike force just as he encountered two MiGs attempting to gain position behind his aircraft. After shaking the MiGs with a tight left break, Dethlefsen realized that he had sustained damage from the AAA fire on his second pass.

While the strike force was completing its attack, Dethlefsen pulled off his run and checked over his damaged Thud. Fortunately, the engine and flight control systems were all right, even though the 57-mm gunner had knocked a hole in the bottom of the fuselage. Knowing that he had missed the SAM site and that the steel complex was a critical target that would require additional bombing over the next few days, he decided to re-engage the missile defense system.

Maneuvering around the flak pattern, Dethlefsen spotted the SAM site directly in front of him. He fired his second Shrike missile, and the site went promptly off the air. With the cloud of debris and smoke still hanging over the target area, Dethlefsen dropped his Thud on the deck to put the finishing touches on the site. Finding the SAM's radar van, he dropped his bombs squarely on it and followed it with a strafing pass with his 20-mm cannon, effectively destroying the site.

For his conspicuous gallantry at the risk of his life above and beyond the call of duty, Capt. Dethlefsen was awarded the Medal of Honor. President Johnson made the presentation at the White House on 1 February 1968.

Flying in the lead position, this 354th TFS F-105D (60-0490) is seen on a strike mission against Communist positions along the Ho Chi Minh Trail on 30 October 1969. The aircraft is armed with Mk-84 2,000-pound bombs on the inboards and Mk-82 500-pound bombs on the outboard pylons, each fitted with "daisy cutter" fuse extenders. (Stewart Hurd)

ABOVE: An F-105D (61-0064) of the 354th TFS totes a pair of Mk-84s to a Laotian target on 6 November 1969. (Stewart Hurd)

OPPOSITE
TOP: Pictured above the jungle terrain of Southeast Asia on 12 November 1969, a 354th TFS Thud (62-4387) refuels from a KC-135 tanker on its way to the target area. (Stewart Hurd)

BOTTOM: *MOSTES*, an EF-105F (62-4446) of the 354th TFS, is seen on a mission over Laos on 4 December 1969. This aircraft had been previously modified to fly night, all-weather radar bombing missions over North Vietnam under the Commando Nail program. (Stewart Hurd)

RM
446

A 354th TFS F-105D (61-0188) taxis out for a mission from Takhli in early 1970 with a load of M118 3,000-pound bombs. (John Coon via James Geer)

ABOVE AND RIGHT: Appropriately named *SAM FIGHTER*, this early F-105G (63-8311) of the 354th TFS recovered at Da Nang AB, South Vietnam after completing a May 1970 "protective reaction" mission in support of U.S. aircraft operating near the North Vietnamese border. Note the five SAM site kill marks on the nose art scoreboard. (Barry Miller via Jerry Geer)

Known as *Honeypot II/HAVE GUN WILL TRAVEL*, this 354th TFS F-105D (61-0159) at Takhli in February 1970 was the first Thud to attain 4,000 flying hours after completing more than 600 combat missions. Capt. Jacques A. Suzanne of the 333rd TFS gunned down a MiG-17 in this aircraft on 12 May 1967. (John Coon via James Geer)

357th Tactical Fighter Squadron

The 357th Tactical Fighter Squadron was activated at George on 13 April 1962 as one of four units to be equipped with the F-105D under the 355th TFW. It was organized on 8 July 1962 and immediately began the initial work-up process in anticipation of accepting the wing's first Thuds in September 1962. After receiving a full complement of 24 aircraft, the squadron spent just under two years training as an operational squadron at George before moving with the 355th TFW to McConnell.

On 5 August 1964, the 357th was scheduled to depart McConnell for Incirlik AB, Turkey for rotational duty in support of NATO commitments. Eight hours prior to their departure, the squadron was redirected to deploy to the Far East. The change in destination was in response to the Gulf of Tonkin Incident, the single event that led to the first major air strikes against North Vietnam. After making enroute stops at Hickam AFB, Hawaii and Anderson AFB, Guam, the squadron flew to Yokota AB, Japan. Here, the 357th was tasked to replace resident Thud squadrons that had deployed to Thailand for combat duty. The first squadron backed-up by the unit was the 36th TFS, followed by the 35th TFS starting in late September, and the 80th TFS by November. Over the course of its four-month tour, the 357th rotated aircraft and pilots to Osan AB, Korea to support the 41st AD's nuclear alert commitment. During the first week of December, the 469th TFS arrived by military transport to replace the 357th and assume control of its aircraft and back-up role for PACAF. After a one-week transition period, the 357th returned to McConnell on or about 12 December 1964.

Pilots from the 357th TFS saw their baptism of fire when the unit deployed to Korat RTAFB, Thailand during the summer of 1965. Relieving the 354th TFS on 12 June, the squadron was attached to the provisional 6234th TFW and entered combat by taking part in Rolling Thunder. Early missions involved conducting strikes against key lines of communication and military targets in the central and southern regions of North Vietnam. Later, the squadron participated in attacks against bridges along the northeast railroad line from Hanoi to China.

The 357th lost its first aircraft on a 23 June strike mission over southwestern North Vietnam, but the pilot, Maj. Robert Wilson, was recovered in a daring rescue. On 27 July, the 357th TFS participated in the first SAM mission of the war. A force of 46 Thuds from both Korat and Takhli struck two SA-2 missile sites near Hanoi. Six aircraft were lost that day, two of which were from the 357th. Following the strike, Capt. William J. Barthelmas, Jr. and Maj. Jack G. Farr were killed in a mid-air collision near the Thai-Laotian border. Capt. Barthelmas' aircraft had received many hits, and while Maj. Farr was looking over the damaged Thud, the aircraft pitched-up violently and struck his airplane. Less than a week later, on 3 August, the 357th TFS suffered another loss when Maj. Joseph E. Bower was killed when his Thud was shot down on a mission over North Vietnam.

Around 20 August 1965, the 357th essentially assumed a split unit status when a significant portion of the squadron relocated to Kadena AB, Okinawa to assume a back-up role for PACAF by re-

Following the Gulf of Tonkin Incident, the 357th TFS was hastily sent to Japan to replace a squadron from Yokota AB that had been rotated to Thailand. The unit was serving on its fourth month of back-up duty when this F-105D (61-0057) was photographed while making an approach to Yokota on 19 November 1964. (Toyokazu Matsuzaki)

lieving the 421st TFS, which was scheduled to return to the U.S. after an extended Far East tour. This part of the 357th remained at Kadena until returning to McConnell around 8 November 1965. On that day, the 355th TFW completed its PCS move to Takhli RTAFB, Thailand, and although a portion of the 357th remained in Southeast Asia, the squadron was reassigned to the 835th AD and attached to the 23rd TFW for operational control.

The small cadre of the 357th TFS remaining at Korat from mid-August 1965 continued to conduct combat operations under the provisional 6234th TFW until the establishment of permanently based combat squadrons in mid-November 1965. The unit suffered one additional loss during this time when Squadron Commander Col. George C. McCleary was killed when his F-105 fell victim to a SAM while on a mission in North Vietnam on 5 November. The

The 357th TFS concluded its Far East tour when the 469th TFS arrived at Yokota during the first week of December 1964 to assume control of its aircraft and backup role for PACAF. This pair of F-105Ds (61-0143 and 61-0056) is seen landing at Yokota during the brief transition period when the 357th introduced its sister squadron to local operating procedures. (Toyokazu Matsuzaki)

357th TFS was awarded the Presidential Unit Citation for its outstanding operational record for the period 11 June to 21 November 1965.

Less than three months after returning from their overseas tour, on 29 January 1966, the 357th was sent to Thailand as a PCS squadron with assignment to the 355th TFW at Takhli. Their arrival coincided with the end of rotational combat duty for the 334th TFS, 4th TFW out of Seymour Johnson AFB, North Carolina. During a one-week transition period, the squadron conducted area check-out flights and took over the 334th's aircraft and combat role at Takhli.

Poor weather limited missions during the 357th's first two months on station, but the squadron was able to conduct some key strikes on the enemy's transportation system in both Laos and the southern region of North Vietnam. By early summer 1966, the unit was flying missions against causeways, ferry complexes, POL facilities, and military storage areas. Prize among these targets was the Yen Bay storage area and the Hanoi POL complex, attacked on 31 May and 29 June respectively. Towards the fall of 1966, the squadron supported the effort to shut down the flow of materials along the north-south road and rail routes that supplied Hanoi from China. By the end of the year, the 357th TFS had lost at least seven Thuds in combat and two to operational accidents.

The Wild Weasel mission was added to the 357th's responsibilities during late 1966. Difficult missions continued over North Vietnam in 1967, and the Weasel crews flew some of the most demanding of the war, none more evident than a 19 April mission flown by Maj. Leo K. Thorsness. While flying an Iron Hand mission in support of a strike on the Xuan Mai army barracks, Thorsness and his EWO, Capt. Harold E. Johnson, destroyed two SAM sites, flew ResCAP for a downed wingman, shot down one confirmed and one probable MiG, and aided a lost Thud pilot. For his courageous and heroic efforts on this mission, Thorsness was awarded the Medal of Honor.

Eleven days after Thorsness got his MiG, the 357th bagged two more MiG-17s on a 28 April strike against the Han Phong causeway, twelve miles west of Hanoi. Getting the kills with the Thud's 20-mm cannon were Maj. Harry E. Higgins and Lt. Col. Arthur F. Dennis. Two days later, on 30 April, the NVAF struck back at the 357th when a MiG downed an EF-105F crewed by Thorsness and Johnson. The loss took place on a strike on the Hanoi thermal power plant, and the Medal of Honor winner and his backseater were captured and held as POWs until their release in March 1973. The downing of Thorsness and Johnson was just one in a string of combat losses during the spring-summer period that totaled as many as

After being restricted to a back-up role at Yokota during 1964, the 357th TFS was sent into combat when mobilized the following year for a second tour in support of the Vietnam War. Here, a flight on 357th Thuds refuels before striking Communist positions at low-level with Mk-82 500-pound Snakeye bombs on 11 November 1965. (USAF via James Geer)

Having spent a portion of 1965 on rotational combat duty in Southeast Asia, the 357th TFS rejoined the war effort in late January 1966, when it deployed on a PCS basis to Takhli RTAFB, Thailand to resume its association with the 355th TFW. This 357th machine (61-0042) was photographed at Da Nang AB, South Vietnam in September 1966. (Terry Love via Jerry Geer)

Taking a break from combat operations, a well-weathered F-105D (59-1728) of the 357th TFS lands at Yokota AB, Japan circa early 1967. (Jerry Geer Collection)

The high loss rate suffered by most Thud squadrons in Southeast Asia required a constant flow of replacement aircraft from other units. Taken on 7 April 1967, this view shows a former USAFE F-105D (60-0415) staging through Yokota on its way to Takhli to serve with the 357th TFS. (Toyokazu Matsuzaki)

Named *OLE MISS*, this 357th TFS F-105D (58-1163) is seen in the Takhli arming area having its safety pins removed before taking off on a mission in the spring of 1967. (Paul Minert Collection)

seventeen Thuds by the end of August. July was especially difficult for the squadron as no less than seven F-105s were shot down on strikes against North Vietnam that month.

Despite the heavy losses, the unit continued to press the attack against the enemy by playing an important role in the effort to destroy vital targets in the North during the second half of 1967. The squadron participated in the key raids on the Paul Doumer Bridge, Bac Giang Bridge, Canal des Rapides Bridge, Phuc Yen airfield, Kep railyard, Viet Tri railyard, Tien Cuong railyard, and the Dai Loi Railroad Bridge. Conducted on 19 December, the Dai Loi raid saw the 357th get its fourth aerial victory of the war when an EF-105F crewed by Capt. Philip M. Drew, pilot, and Maj. William H. Wheeler, EWO, gunned down a MiG-17 while on SAM suppression duty for the strike force.

During the last four months of 1967, the 357th lost five more aircraft, with all but one being classified as combat losses. This brought the total number of Thuds downed by the enemy's air defense system to at least 21 Thuds for the year. To stem the losses, new measures to counter the North Vietnamese air defense capabilities continued to be developed. As part of the effort to counter the MiG threat, the squadron received several Combat Martin F-105F radar jammers. At the same time, to develop the EF-105F into a more effective SAM suppression platform, additional modifications to a small number of Weasel Thuds took place to enable them to launch the AGM-78A (Mod 0) Standard ARM.

The Standard ARM modification program took place during the second half 1967, with the first group of aircraft assigned to the 357th TFS. After the modifications were complete and the missile

These two newly modified EF-105Fs are seen over Thailand towards the end of a delivery flight in May 1967. The nearest aircraft (63-8267) was destined for Takhli to join the 357th TFS, while the second (63-8272) made its way to Korat for duty with the 13th TFS, 388th TFW. (Richard Kierbow via JEM Aviation Slides)

An F-105D (62-4261) of the 357th TFS rendezvous with a tanker before heading into the target area during Rolling Thunder operations in mid-1967. (USAF via Paul Minert)

was refined for use after early tests indicated some guidance and control problems, the 357th conducted the first USAF combat launch of a Standard ARM on 10 March 1968. A flight of four EF-105Fs fired eight missiles on the mission in support of a strike near Hanoi. Five missiles guided to the target, but only one radar van was confirmed destroyed. The use of the new missile in combat was cutback after the partial bombing halts were implemented during the spring of 1968, but the Wild Weasel program continued to progress. The RHAW system was vastly improved, and a new modification, first undertaken during November 1968, allowed the aircraft to fire the advanced AGM-78B. With these modifications, the EF-105Fs were redesignated F-105Gs, and the first arrived for service with the 357th during early 1969.

Strike operations continued in North Vietnam during the first three months of the 1968, although bad weather greatly reduced the number of missions flown. Commando Club and Combat Skyspot radar bombing missions were the primary means of delivering ordnance during this time. Targets struck included railyards, bridges, airfields, and military barracks and storage areas. Following the bombing halt of targets above the 20th parallel on 31 March and then above the 19th parallel on 4 April, the squadron shifted operations to striking supply and transport targets in the southern region of North Vietnam. Supply interdiction missions were also carried out in Laos, but this region did not become a major focus until after the Rolling Thunder campaign ended on 31 October 1968. The squadron lost at least seven F-105Ds and two EF-105Fs in combat during 1968. Two additional aircraft, one F-105D and one EF-105F, were lost to operational causes.

In May 1968, the 357th TFS received its second Presidential Unit Citation for its extraordinary heroism and military operations against North Vietnam during the period 29 January to 10 October 1966. During this time, the unit was credited with interrupting numerous links in the North Vietnamese supply lines and greatly impacting the enemy's war potential by destroying many important military storage and staging areas. Also received during 1968 was the Air Force Outstanding Unit Award with Combat "V" Device for the squadron's combat performance from 12 October 1966 to 11 April 1967.

Over the next two years, the 357th's operations generally followed those of its sister squadrons within the 355th TFW. Supply interdiction and armed recce duty in the Barrel Roll and Steel Tiger operating areas of Laos made-up the bulk of the unit's strike missions, while escort duty for both reconnaissance flights over North Vietnam and Gunship missions near the border region was performed by the Weasels. Four aircraft were lost while striking targets in Laos during 1969, and none were lost during 1970.

The squadron received its third and fourth Presidential Unit Citations in 1970. One was given for its participation in the Paul Doumer Bridge and Phuc Yen airfield strikes during 11-12 August and 24-28 October 1967 and the second for its combat record over the period 12 April 1968 to 30 April 1969. The 357th TFS also received a second Air Force Outstanding Unit Award with Combat "V" Device for operations over the period 12 April 1967 to 11 April 1968.

Concurrent with the planned inactivation of the 355th TFW and phase-out of Thud operations at Takhli, the 357th TFS flew its last combat mission during the first week of October 1970. Later that month, the unit redeployed its F-105Ds and Combat Martin F-105Fs to the U.S. under Operation Big Horn I. The squadron's Weasel Thuds and crews were retained in Thailand at Korat, where they augmented the formation of a new Wild Weasel detachment that grew in size to become the 6010th WWS on 1 November 1970.

The 357th TFS was inactivated on 10 December 1970. Subsequently, two additional decorations were received for the squadron's action over Southeast Asia. A third Air Force Outstanding Unit Award with Combat "V" Device was given for operations over the period 1 July 1969 to 24 November 1970, and the Republic of Vietnam Gallantry Cross with Palm was received for actions from 1 April 1966 to 10 December 1970.

Sporting the RU tail code used by the 357th TFS from late 1967, this EF-105F (63-8301) heads northward on an Iron Hand mission with a standard Weasel load of CBUs and Shrike missiles. Maj. Leo K. Thorsness flew this aircraft on his Medal of Honor mission of 19 April 1967. (Norm Taylor Collection)

The squadron was reactivated on paper within the 23rd TFW at McConnell on 15 March 1971. One week later, on 22 March, the unit moved to Davis-Monthan AFB, Arizona and remained non-operational within the 4453rd CCTW. Upon return to the 355th TFW on 1 July 1971, the squadron assumed operations with the A-7D Corsair II.

Major Leo K. Thorsness

On 19 April 1967, Maj. Leo K. Thorsness, a veteran 357th TFS Weasel pilot, led a flight of four Thunderchiefs on an Iron Hand mission in support of a raid against the Xuan Mai army barracks and storage supply area, roughly 37 miles southwest of Hanoi. Prior to reaching the target, Thorsness' radar warning system detected heavy SAM activity in the area. Ordering two of his Thuds to cover a different quadrant in the target area, Thorsness and his wingman stayed south, forcing the enemy missile crews to divide their attention. Upon identification of the SAM sites by his backseater, Capt. Harold E. Johnson, Thorsness fired a Shrike missile at one of the sites, destroying it. He then flew through heavy flak to silence another with cluster bombs.

In the second strike, Thorsness' wingman was badly hit by the AAA fire, forcing both crewmembers of the Weasel Thud to eject.

A second view of this 357th TFS EF-105F (63-8301) shows it being serviced and armed for its next mission at Takhli circa late 1968. (USAF via Stewart Hurd)

On locating the descending parachutes and positioning himself to gain a fix on their position, a third SAM site was located and attacked with a Shrike missile. At the same time, mechanical problems and MiGs forced the two other F-105s of the flight of four to call off the attack and return to Takhli, leaving Thorsness alone in the area.

As Thorsness circled the descending parachutes, Johnson spotted a MiG off their left wing. Thorsness attacked the MiG and shot it down with his 20-mm cannon as additional MiGs attempted to gain position on his tail. Low on fuel, he broke off the engagement and rendezvoused with a KC-135 tanker over Laos.

In the meantime, two A-1E Skyraiders and two Jolly Green rescue helicopters had arrived to search for the downed crew's location. After topping-off, Thorsness turned back to fly cover for the rescue force despite having only 500 rounds of ammunition left. He spotted several MiGs and initiated an attack, damaging one MiG and eluding the remaining enemy aircraft with a supersonic dash through a mountain pass.

Although he was now out of ammunition, Thorsness again set out for the rescue scene in an attempt to lure the MiGs away from the rescue operation. Before he returned, the MiGs found success by downing one Skyraider. Upon arrival, Thorsness found that a flight of four Thuds from Takhli had shown up to engage the MiG force, freeing himself to return to the tanker to get enough fuel to return to home base.

As he neared the tanker, Thorsness received a call for help from one of the Takhli Thuds who had become lost and was dangerously low on fuel. He directed the tanker to the lost pilot to avert the possibility of losing another pilot and aircraft. Without the tanker and critically low on fuel, Thorsness was forced to head for Udorn RTAFB, Thailand, approximately 200 miles closer than Takhli. On final approach, he placed the Thud in idle and glided the aircraft to a safe landing with the fuel gauge reading "empty".

After the Rolling Thunder campaign ended, the Weasels were intermittently tasked with electronic reconnaissance missions around North Vietnam to gather intelligence on the enemy's air defense system. This air-to-air photograph shows a brace of 357th TFS Thuds, consisting of an EF-105F (63-8339) and Combat Martin F-105F (62-4444), over the North during one such mission in December 1968. (Paul Minert Collection)

For his extraordinary deeds of heroism on this mission, Maj. Thorsness was awarded the Medal of Honor. Eleven days later and only eight missions short of the 100 required to complete a combat tour, he was shot down over North Vietnam while flying a Wild Weasel support mission against a strike on the Hanoi thermal power plant. Following his release after being held as a POW for nearly six years, Maj. Thorsness received this highest decoration for valor from President Nixon at the White House on 15 October 1973.

A Combat Martin F-105F (62-4444) of the 357th TFS formates with a KC-135 tanker during the return leg of a bombing sortie circa 1968. The large blade antenna atop the fuselage and displaced rear seat were the primary identification features of the Martin aircraft. (USAF via Jerry Geer)

This 357th TFS F-105D (62-4318) is seen outbound on a 24 February 1969 mission. Half of the eight M117 750-pounds bombs carried by this aircraft are fitted with "daisy cutter" fuse extenders to ensure detonation above the ground. (Stewart Hurd)

An early F-105G (63-8352) of the 357th TFS is prepared for an AGM-78 test sortie at Takhli on 15 April 1969. One year before, the 357th had the distinction of flying the first Standard ARM combat mission for the USAF with an EF-105F that had been equipped with the AGM-78A (Mod 0) equipment package. (USAF via James Geer)

Having delivered its ordnance, a 357th TFS F-105D (60-0504) returns from a mission over Laos on 30 October 1969. (Stewart Hurd)

A 357th Thud (62-4246) in the left slot position during a 4 December 1969 sortie from Takhli. The weapons load of six Mk-82 500-pound bombs indicates this aircraft was probably on a strike mission against enemy infiltration routes that supplied material to the South. (Stewart Hurd)

The Jolly Roger, an F-105D (61-0176) of the 357th TFS, stands ready for its next sortie at Takhli in February 1970. (John Coon via James Geer)

The Weasels were often used as standard tactical fighters subsequent to the end of the Rolling Thunder campaign. Here, a 357th TFS F-105G (62-4424) prepares to depart Takhli in early 1970 as part of a CBU flight carrying out an interdiction mission in Laos. (John Coon via James Geer)

Daisy Mae was the name of this 357th TFS F-105D (58-1172) pictured on a strike against the Ho Chi Minh Trail circa 1970. The aircraft carries SUU-30 cluster bombs on the centerline and Mk-82 500-pound bombs with "daisy cutter" fuse extenders on the outboard pylons. (Republic via Robert Robinson)

Seen on the boom refueling, *BUBBYE JEAN* is a 357th Thud (61-0060) hauling its bomb load to a target in 1970. (Paul Hoynacki via Jerry Geer)

421st Tactical Fighter Squadron

The 421st Tactical Fighter Squadron was the third unit within the 355th TFW to assume operations in the Thud. The squadron became operational at George on 5 March 1963, ten months after it was activated. After receiving its complement of F-105Ds and achieving IOC, the 421st trained as an operational squadron at George for about one year before moving with the 355th TFW to McConnell. Between 15 September and 23 November 1964, the unit successfully served a rotational tour at Incirlik AB, Turkey for nuclear alert duty while under Seventeenth Air Force control.

Under Operation Two Buck Three, the squadron deployed to Kadena AB, Okinawa on 7 April 1965 to support PACAF commitments while attached to the 313th AD. In addition to serving on back-up duty for resident squadrons that had deployed to Southeast Asia, the 421st TFS rotated aircraft and crews to Osan AB, Korea for nuclear alert duty. At Kadena, the squadron utilized the local ranges to complete all dart and AIM-9B standard training requirements. Eventually, the 421st rotated crews to Korat RTAFB, Thailand to augment combat operations being conducted by its sister unit, the 354th TFS, and later, the 357th TFS. The 421st ended its four-month duty in the Far East when it returned to McConnell and 355th TFW control on or about 20 August 1965.

As a result of the 355th TFW's relocation to Thailand, the 421st TFS was reassigned to the 835th AD on 8 November 1965, pending a PCS assignment to Southeast Asia. The unit moved to Korat during the third week of November with the bulk of personnel deploying by transport aircraft. The squadron was reassigned to the provisional 6234th TFW on 20 November, one day before the first group of personnel arrived in Thailand. At Korat, the unit assumed control of a group of TAC Thuds that had been serving with squadrons on temporary assignment in Thailand. To round out their complement of about 21 F-105Ds, a number of the unit's pilots ferried aircraft from the U.S. to Thailand.

This F-105D (59-1823) of the 421st TFS is seen high over the Pacific during the squadron's Two Buck Three deployment to Kadena AB, Okinawa during 1965. (D. Steigers via James Geer)

Although the 421st TFS operated out of Kadena for the entirety of its 1965 Far East tour, elements of the squadron visited other PACAF bases as it fulfilled theater commitments and training requirements. One of the unit's Thuds (59-1762) is seen here landing at Yokota AB after completing a range sortie in Japan on 4 May 1965. (Toyokazu Matsuzaki)

469th Tactical Fighter Squadron

The 469th Tactical Fighter Squadron was the last of four units activated within the 355th TFW at George on 13 April 1962 to become operational. The squadron gained operational status in October 1963, but remained a "paper unit" until being manned and equipped with F-105D/Fs at McConnell around July 1964. The 469th had been at full strength for only a few months when it was tasked to make its first overseas deployment.

Led by their commander, Lt. Col. A. J. Bowman, the 469th TFS departed McConnell without aircraft on 30 November 1964 for Yokota AB, Japan to relieve the 357th TFS from its temporary assignment in the Far East. Upon arrival, the squadron took over the 357th's aircraft and back-up role for PACAF. Almost immediately, three of the unit's four flights moved to Kadena AB, Okinawa, while another was sent to Osan AB, Korea for nuclear alert duty. A few days before 31 December 1964, the flight at Osan returned to Yokota, where it remained for about one week before moving to Kadena. The squadron's duty in Korea did not end at that point as it continued to support Fifth Air Force SIOP alert commitments by rotating flights to Osan.

On 5 January 1965, the squadron began rotating flights to Korat RTAFB, Thailand from Kadena to support early contingency operations against Communist forces in Southeast Asia. Here, the squadron performed 2nd AD directed missions. These missions were generally in the form of armed escort of reconnaissance aircraft, armed reconnaissance of major supply routes, strikes against known enemy positions, and top cover duty. This phase of the deployment was significant in that the 469th TFS recorded 69 combat support missions and 15 actual combat missions. Three aircraft were battle damaged and no aircraft were lost. The rotation of flights continued through the first week of March, at which time the 354th TFS arrived to replace the 469th and assume its role at both Kadena and Korat. After a one-week transition period, the squadron returned to McConnell without aircraft on or about 13 March 1965 after 104 days at the four locations.

After returning from overseas duty, 469th pilots flew training missions from McConnell and ferried F-105s between the Far East and Thailand to inspect and repair as necessary (IRAN) facilities at Crestview, Florida. During this time, many of the squadron's pilots

The 469th TFS deployed without aircraft from McConnell to Yokota AB, Japan on 30 November 1964 to replace the 357th TFS, which had been serving on back-up duty for PACAF during the previous four months. The process of passing operational command from one unit to the next was nearly complete when this flight of TAC-gained F-105s was caught on a low pass over Yokota shortly after the 469th's arrival. (Toyokazu Matsuzaki)

lost their combat-ready rating. By the fall 1965, the squadron had ended the ferrying duty and resumed full-scale operational training in preparation for a PCS move to Southeast Asia in November 1965.

Rather than continue its association with the 355th TFW at Takhli, the squadron was sent to Korat to operate under the control of the provisional 6234th TFW. Reassignment to the 6234th TFW took place on 8 November 1965, one week prior to its arrival. On 15 November 1965, 469th TFS personnel were on station and assumed control of about 21 F-105Ds that were forward deployed at the base. With the move complete, the 469th became the first Thud unit to be deployed PCS to Southeast Asia for combat operations.

Seen nearest the camera in this February 1965 photograph, a 469th F-105D (61-0054) prepares to launch out of Korat RTAFB, Thailand with a Thud (62-4281) from the 44th TFS, 18th TFW. Note the dark green and white checkered tail band that was applied to the 469th's aircraft during rotations to Korat. (Paul Minert Collection)

The 469th TFS was heavily tasked during its 1964-65 deployment as it supported PACAF commitments in Japan, Korea, Okinawa, and Thailand. In this view, a 469th Thud (61-0055) is seen refueling during a transit flight from Korat to Kadena in February 1965. (D. Steigers via Jerry Geer)

CHAPTER TWELVE

388th Tactical Fighter Wing

The history of the 388th Tactical Fighter Wing dates back to December 1942, when the 388th Bombardment Group (Heavy) was activated at Boise, Idaho with B-17s. The group moved to England in July 1943 and served in the war for two years as part of the Eighth Air Force. It returned to the U.S. during August 1945 and was inactivated.

The unit was re-established at Clovis AFB, New Mexico on 23 March 1953 as the 388th Fighter Day Wing. It was redesignated the 388th Fighter Bomber Wing three weeks prior to being activated on 23 November 1953. The wing trained with the F-86F for one year before being assigned to Etain-Rouvres AB, France during late 1954. Etain-Rouvres was a new base still under construction, so the wing's three squadrons were forced to operate out of three bases in Germany for most of 1955. The F-86s were flown until the fall of 1956, when the wing started converting to F-100D Super Sabres. The 388th was inactivated on 10 December 1957, when it was replaced by the 49th Fighter Bomber Wing.

The unit was reactivated on 1 May 1962 as the 388th Tactical Fighter Wing at McConnell AFB, Kansas and assigned to the Twelfth Air Force. Upon being organized on 1 October 1962, the wing was assigned four squadrons–the 560th, 561st, 562nd, and 563rd–and tasked to train as a combat-ready unit. Initially, only the 560th TFS gained operational status with F-100Ds. The other three squadrons remained non-operational until mid-1963, when the wing started its conversion to F-105Ds. All four squadrons had become fully equipped with the Thunderchief when the 388th TFW was inactivated and replaced by the 23rd TFW on 8 February 1964.

The 388th TFW was reactivated within PACAF on 14 March 1966 in preparation to establish the unit as the new parent organization at Korat RTAFB, Thailand. At that time, the provisional 6234th TFW resided at Korat with two PCS Thud squadrons. The tempo of the war, as well as plans to increase the number of squadrons at Korat, saw the need to bring a more stable control of operations at the base. On 8 April 1966, the 388th TFW replaced the 6234th TFW and assumed control of the 421st and 469th TFS. Although it was assigned to the Thirteenth Air Force, the 388th was attached to the Seventh Air Force for operational control.

The wing also gained control of a detachment of Wild Weasel F-100Fs formerly attached to the 6324th TFW. This detachment was established at Korat in late 1965 to combat the presence of the Russian-built SA-2 Guideline missiles in North Vietnam. The Weasel modification was extended to the Thud, and the first EF-105Fs arrived for duty at Korat in late May 1966. At about the same time, the 36th TFS at Yokota AB, Japan, and the 44th TFS at Kadena AB, Okinawa, were renumbered as the 34th and the 13th TFS respectively and assigned PCS to Korat to serve with the 388th TFW. Their arrival was delayed by about one month until the construction of additional ramp space was completed. Once on station, the 13th TFS absorbed the Weasel detachment and assumed the dual mission of strike and SAM suppression.

With the Rolling Thunder campaign continuing to escalate during the early summer of 1966, the 388th TFW was tasked to strike important targets throughout North Vietnam immediately upon its arrival in Thailand. On 29 May 1966, the wing teamed with the 355th TFW for a maximum effort strike on the massive Yen Bay military storage area. Exactly one month later, on 29 June, the wing's partnered again to destroy the Hanoi POL facility. One day after this highly successful strike, the wing carried out additional attacks on POL facilities near the Hanoi area. The wing received its first Air Force Outstanding Unit Award with Combat "V" Device for the POL raids on 29-30 June 1966.

Additional strikes on major POL facilities such as the Nguyen Khe and Viet Tri oil storage areas took place during July and August. Following the destruction of the Communist POL system, the

Standard TAC markings were the norm for the Thuds assigned to the 388th TFW while based at McConnell AFB, Kansas during the first half of the 1960s. This representative F-105D (61-0172) was shot at Sioux City MAP, Iowa in early 1964, possibly after the 388th had been replaced by the 23rd TFW. (Clyde Gerdes via Jerry Geer)

focus returned to transportation and military targets for the remainder of 1966. The intensity of Rolling Thunder during this time triggered a tremendous growth in the North Vietnamese air defense network. The total number of radar guided AAA guns and SAM sites increased significantly. MiG activity picked up considerably as well and the Thud strike forces became the primary targets of the NVAF. The frequent MiG encounters saw pilots of the 388th claim four aerial victories during the year, of which two were historically significant. On 29 June, Maj. Fred L. Tracy became the first F-105 pilot to shoot down a MiG. Three months later, on 21 September, 23-year old 1st Lt. Karl W. Richter became the youngest pilot to score a MiG kill in Vietnam. Nevertheless, the price of war was high for the 388th TFW in 1966 for as many as 48 F-105s were lost to hostile action and eight were claimed by operational accidents.

The bad weather due to the seasonal monsoon saw a reduction in the number of missions flown over North Vietnam during the early months of 1967. When the weather cleared, a series of attacks against the Thai Nguyen industrial complex were initiated. Located about 40 miles north of Hanoi, the complex produced nearly 300,000 tons of iron per year and manufactured pontoon and bridge sections used to repair destroyed bridges. Also located at Thai Nguyen was a thermal power station, army supply depot, and railway station. The first missions against Thai Nguyen took place on 10 March and continued into April. The 388th TFW dropped 169 tons of ordnance on the Thai Nguyen works and other important targets between 10 March and 1 May 1967. For their distinguished action

When the 388th TFW replaced the provisional 6234th TFW at Korat RTAFB, Thailand in April 1966, the wing gained control of the F-105D-equipped 421st and 469th TFS. Taken shortly after the wing's reactivation, this shot catches two 421st Thuds (58-1165 and 62-4326) on the tanker before they head into North Vietnam to strike a target with M118 3,000-pound bombs. (USAF via Stewart Hurd)

during this period, the wing was awarded the Presidential Unit Citation.

In April 1967, the 388th TFW went through a component change when the 44th TFS was transferred to Korat from the 18th TFW at Kadena AB, Okinawa to absorb the personnel, resources, and strike mission of the 421st TFS. That month also saw the arrival of modified EF-105Fs that had an improved radar bombing system to conduct night and all-weather strikes under what became known as the Commando Nail mission. These aircraft and their specially trained crews were initially organized as a separate provisional unit, but were absorbed by the 13th TFS in June 1967. Informally, they were known as "Ryan's Raiders" for PACAF chief John D. Ryan, who pushed to develop this capability within the USAF following the Navy's success with the all-weather A-6 Intruder.

The 388th TFW completed missions that pushed its total combat flying time in Southeast Asia over the 60,000 hour mark in the early summer of 1967. Major targets hit by the wing around this time included the MiG airfields at Hoa Lac and Kep, the Nguyen Khe storage area, the Vinh Yen army barracks, the Kep army barracks, the Ha Dong army barracks and supply depot, the Bac Le railroad yards, and the Bac Giang Railroad and Highway Bridge. Hitting these targets closed out the twelve-month period ending on 30 June 1967 for which the wing eventually received a second Air Force Outstanding Unit Award with Combat "V" Device.

The wing participated in operations against critical targets such as the Paul Doumer Bridge, the Yen Vien railroad yards, and the Lang Son railroad yards during August 1967. By October, the extensive use of the F-105 over North Vietnam and the corresponding steady loss of aircraft to enemy's air defenses forced the 388th TFW to scale back to three squadrons. Consequently, the 13th TFS was transferred to the 432nd TRW and re-equipped with F-4s, and its mission and makeup were absorbed by the 44th TFS. Little else changed that fall as the wing carried out missions against key supply and transportation targets such as the Yen Bai, Viet Tri, Phu Tho, and Kep railroad yards, as well as key points along the two main railroad lines into Hanoi.

Several follow-up strikes on the Paul Doumer Bridge and missions against the Phuc Yen and Kep airfields highlighted the wing's action in late 1967. The Phuc Yen raid was carried out on 24 October and was the largest single air strike of the war to date. The decision to bomb the previously banned base was prompted by the recent success of the NVAF MiGs in aerial combat. In another effort to counteract the MiG threat, the wing's 44th TFS added several specially equipped F-105Fs (known as Combat Martins) that were capable of blocking communications between the MiGs and their GCI centers. Aerial battles with the North Vietnamese enemy fighters saw the 388th down four additional MiGs during 1967.

For another year, the mission of flying combat in Southeast Asia was costly for the 388th TFW. The wing lost approximately 45 F-105s in 1967 to the enemy's air defense system, most of which fell to the heavy concentration of conventional anti-aircraft guns that defended the vital targets in the North Vietnam. October and November were especially difficult for as many as seventeen Thuds were lost in combat during that two-month period. Operational accidents claimed another six aircraft that year.

The seasonal northeast monsoon greatly scaled back Rolling Thunder operations during the first three months of 1968. On average, there were only three days per month during which visual strikes could be carried out in the far north. As a result, the wing carried out many Combat Skyspot and Commando Club radar bombing

The demands of the air war saw two additional Thud squadrons, the 13th and 34th TFS, added to the 388th TFW's roster in mid-1966. Here, a newly assigned 34th F-105D (60-0424) is seen hauling an incomplete load of Mk-82 500-pound Snakeye bombs over Southeast Asia during the late summer of 1966. (USAF via Stewart Hurd)

A pair of 388th TFW F-105Ds, belonging to the 13th (62-4287) and 421st TFS (60-0469), follows a specially equipped pathfinder F-100D Super Sabre into combat on 15 August 1966. The Thuds are carrying Mk-83 1,000-pound bombs. (USAF via Stewart Hurd)

missions. Important targets hit early in the year included the Dong Dau railroad bridge, the Dap Cau railroad bypass, the Phuc Yen airfield, and the Kim Lang army barracks. The bad weather saw the wing conduct an increasing number of Steel Tiger interdiction missions in the Laotian panhandle, where the unit flew strikes against troop and supply concentrations that were supporting the Communist offensive at the Marine Corps base at Khe Sanh.

President Johnson stopped the bombing north of the 20th parallel effective 1 April 1968. Four days later, the bombing restriction was moved down to the 19th parallel. These changes came as the wing neared the close of its second year in combat. In two years of war, the 388th TFW had flown about 38,500 sorties totaling 98,000 flying hours and had delivered approximately 86,650 tons of ordnance. Mission focus shifted to the southern panhandle of North Vietnam. Targets hit in this region during April included cargo-laden enemy barges and bridges around the Dong Hoi area, military storage areas, radar sites, and AAA positions. By the end of the month, the 388th TFW had surpassed 100,000 combat flying hours.

Over the summer of 1968, pilots of the 388th TFW continued to hit targets below the 19th parallel in North Vietnam. Highway bridges, railroad boxcars, tunnels, truck parks, POL storage areas, and air defense sites came under fire. Missions against major infiltration routes and military targets in Laos were also carried out during the second half of the year. Entering the fall, plans to gradually re-equip the wing with the new F-4E Phantom II variant were drawn up, but the F-105 served as the wing's sole strike aircraft through the announcement of the end of the Rolling Thunder campaign on 31 October 1968. The wing lost about 26 Thuds in Southeast Asia during 1968, nineteen in combat and seven to operational causes.

Providing support in the 388th TFW's conversion to the Phantom was the 33rd TFW at Eglin AFB, Florida. For some time, the 33rd had played a major role in re-equipping several combat wings in Southeast Asia with Phantoms. Typically, squadrons formed up under a 33rd designation and then transferred to Southeast Asia to assume the designation of a unit scheduled to re-equip with the F-4. The 33rd squadron then returned to Eglin in name and started working up again to convert another squadron. The wing's 40th TFS provided the 388th TFW its first formation asset in November 1968, and immediately upon arrival, the unit was designated the 469th TFS.

The gradual transition to the F-4E continued in 1969 with the 40th TFS arriving with a second formation squadron to re-equip the 34th TFS in May. Rather than converting the 44th TFS to the Phantom, PACAF transferred the unit and its Weasel Thuds to Takhli for assignment with the 355th TFW during October 1969. Throughout the transition, the wing's F-105s continued to support the Laotian supply interdiction campaign against the Ho Chi Minh Trail, and at least four Thuds were lost in that effort. The year 1969 also saw the 388th TFW receive its third Air Force Outstanding Unit Award with Combat 'V" Device for operations over the period 1 July 1967 to 30 June 1968.

During the fall of 1970, the inactivation of the 355th TFW and corresponding end of Thud operations at Takhli brought the F-105 back to Korat, as the important role of the Weasel Thuds in the ongoing war in Southeast Asia necessitated the need to retain them in Thailand. Specifically, the Weasels were active in performing "protective reaction" missions that primarily involved flying armed escort for tactical reconnaissance aircraft flying over North Vietnam. Another role involved escort duty for B-52 bombing missions in Cambodia. The Weasel Thuds were retained at Korat in the form of Detachment 1, 12th TFS. The first six F-105Gs from Takhli arrived in late September 1970, and additional aircraft were gained as the 355th TFW ended operations in October. The detachment advanced in status to become an element of the 388th TFW as the provisional 6010th WWS in November 1970.

The end of operations at Takhli also saw the 388th TFW add the EB-66C/E Destroyer in the form of the 42nd TEWS. After plans for the inactivation of the 355th TFW were announced, the 42nd moved to Korat for duty with the 388th TFW in September 1970. The primary use of the EB-66 at that time was as a tactical electronic reconnaissance platform in support of the interdiction campaigns in Laos. Another special purpose aircraft joined the wing in December 1970, when the EC-121R was assigned in the form of the 553rd RS. This Super Constellation variant was used as a radio relay aircraft for ground sensors that were "seeded" along the Ho Chi Minh Trail.

All of the 388th TFW's EF-105Fs were concentrated within the 13th TFS, which was tasked with a dual Wild Weasel and strike mission. On the hunt for SAMs over North Vietnam in this 1966 photograph is an early EF-105F (62-4446) named *Sneaky Pete*. (James Geer Collection)

As Rolling Thunder intensified, the North Vietnamese sent its MiGs up in greater numbers to protect its vital resources. As a result, the Thuds started carrying a Sidewinder missile on one pylon as illustrated here on the *THE MERCENARY*, an F-105D (60-0512) of the 34th TFS, 388th TFW preparing for an April 1967 strike against the North. (Don Larsen via Jerry Geer)

In late 1970, the wing's F-4Es and F-105Gs participated in the support force for the rescue attempt of American POWs at the Son Tay camp in North Vietnam. Otherwise, the 388th mainly supported the effort to stem the Communist flow of men and materials along the Ho Chi Minh Trail by flying Commando Hunt interdiction missions in the Steel Tiger operating area of the Laotian panhandle. Intermittent strays into North Vietnam under the "protective reaction" program also took place, but these missions did not increase in frequency until the following year. Three F-105Gs were lost in Southeast Asia in the short period of time the wing operated the aircraft in 1970, two in combat and one to operational causes.

The movement of North Vietnamese troops along Laotian infiltration routes saw the 388th TFW continue to support interdiction operations in 1971. Over the North, the enemy's challenge to the U.S. reconnaissance flights saw an increase in the number of retaliatory "protective reaction" strikes. The reprisals peaked late in 1971, when the wing participated in strikes on MiG airfields in the southern part of the country in November and another more extensive round of attacks mainly against air defense sites below the 20th parallel in December. Only one F-105G was lost in combat during 1971.

The 388th TFW underwent two squadron component changes in December 1971. The first action saw the 6010th WWS redesignated the 17th WWS. The second change involved the end of operations and subsequent inactivation of 553rd RS as a result of the EC-121R being phased-out of service. With these moves, the makeup of the 388th TFW at the end of 1971 included about 34 F-4Es assigned with the 34th and 469th TFS, fifteen F-105Gs with the 17th WWS, and twelve EB-66s with the 42nd TEWS.

By early 1972, the 388th TFW had received its fourth and fifth Air Force Outstanding Unit Awards with Combat "V" Device for exceptional performance in Southeast Asia. These awards were given for operations over the periods 1 July 1968 to 15 September 1969 and 10 October 1970 to 20 May 1971 respectively. The 388th's contributions to the war were evident, but a major North Vietnamese offensive into South Vietnam on the night of 30 March 1972 brought a new challenge, as well as a build-up of strength when reinforcements arrived to augment the wing's existing fighter force.

In response to the Communist invasion, President Nixon authorized a return to bombing targets in North Vietnam under an air campaign known as Freedom Train. This operation began on 6 April 1972 and allowed strikes as far north as the 20th parallel. A limited number of strikes were also carried out further north beginning on 16 April 1972 under the code name Freedom Porch Bravo. This series of attacks saw Strategic Air Command (SAC) B-52s teamed with tactical aircraft to destroy military storage facilities and POL dumps near Hanoi, Haiphong, Thanh Hoa, and Ham Rong. Units of the 388th TFW took part in the renewed bombing of the North

In late April 1967, the makeup of the 388th TFW changed when the 44th TFS arrived at Korat to absorb the personnel and equipment of the 421st TFS, which was transferred to the 15th TFW at MacDill AFB, Florida to become an F-4D operator. This 44th Thud (60-0444) was caught just before it departed on a 19 June 1967 mission from Korat. (Don Larsen via James Geer)

Throughout 1967, the 388th TFW maintained a high sortie rate as it continued to support the expanding air war over North Vietnam. This view of *THE TRAVELER*, an F-105D (61-0219) assigned to the 469th TFS, was taken in the Korat arming area during the midst of another launch cycle in May 1967. (Don Larsen via Jerry Geer)

As a result of the Thud's high attrition in Southeast Asia, the 388th TFW was reduced to a three-squadron wing in October 1967. At that time, the 44th TFS absorbed the mission and makeup of the 13th TFS, which moved to Udorn RTAFB, Thailand to join the 432nd TRW as an F-4D unit. Displaying the squadron's new JE tail code, this 44th Weasel (62-4446) was photographed on take-off from Korat in 1968. (USAF via James Geer)

The first squadron of the 388th TFW to give up its F-105s in favor of F-4Es was the 469th TFS. Their switch to Phantoms coincided with the close of the Rolling Thunder campaign, just a few weeks after this JV-coded 469th Thud (60-0464) was caught on an October 1968 bombing mission into the southern panhandle of North Vietnam. (USAF via James Geer)

A formation of JJ-coded F-105Ds (60-0518, 62-4361, and 61-0161) of the 34th TFS, 388th TFW heads for a Laotian target on 16 December 1968. Each aircraft is carrying six M117 750-pound bombs on the centerline and ECM pods on the outboard pylons. (USAF via Paul Minert)

from the outset, and the F-105Gs were particularly active in defending the strike packages from the prevalent SAM threat.

The escalation of the air war brought a corresponding build-up of air assets within the 388th TFW in April 1972. To bolster the Weasel force, twelve F-105Gs in the form of Detachment 1, 561st TFS deployed to Korat from McConnell AFB, Kansas under Operation Constant Guard I. The wing also added the 7th Airborne Command and Control Squadron (ACCS) and its specialized EC-130E Airborne Battlefield Command and Control Center (ABCCC) aircraft. Their mission was to provide a link between ground commanders and air offensive assets, including coordination of target requirements.

On 8 May 1972, a broader war against North Vietnam was initiated when Freedom Train was replaced by a new air campaign dubbed Linebacker. This operation was more strategic in nature and authorized the destruction of war support targets and communication lines throughout the North. Linebacker commenced with Operation Pocket Money, the aerial mining of North Vietnamese harbors and ports by the Navy on 9 May. Immediately following, the 388th TFW joined other USAF and Navy units in the effort to

This F-105D (59-1760) of the 34th TFS, 388th TFW is seen taxiing out for a mission during the winter of 1968-69. The following spring, the 34th became the second unit of the 388th TFW to re-equip with F-4Es, thus leaving the 44th TFS as the sole Thud operator at Korat. (USAF via James Geer)

In October 1969, the Thud era of the 388th TFW came to a temporary end when the 44th TFS was transferred to the 355th TFW at Takhli RTAFB, Thailand. This EF-105F (63-8329), *THE PROTESTOR'S PROTECTOR*, was photographed during the 44th's final days of operations at Korat. (Neil Schneider via Jerry Geer)

curtail the enemy's flow of weapons and supplies by bombing railroads, highways, bridges, and military stockpiles. Notable missions during the first phase of strikes saw the wing support attacks on a number of major bridges including the Paul Doumer, the Thanh Hoa, the Lang Giai, and the Bac Giang. By the end of May 1972, the vital supply lines were cut, and the focus turned to other targets such as airfields, industrial facilities, military storage sites, and power plants.

In June 1972, the 388th TFW grew in size again when the F-4D-equipped 35th TFS, 3rd TFW out of Kunsan AB, Korea was temporarily attached to augment the F-4Es of the 34th and 469th TFS. With its three squadrons of F-4s, two squadrons of F-105Gs, one squadron of EB-66s, and one squadron of specialized C-130s, the wing continued to carry out Linebacker operations throughout the summer and fall of 1972. In October, the success of the bombing pushed the North Vietnamese to adopt a more positive line at the negotiating table, and the attacks in the Hanoi region were gradually restricted and reduced as talks progressed. In a conciliatory move, the U.S. ended the Linebacker campaign when it terminated all operations north of the 20th parallel on 22 October 1972.

The fall of 1972 brought not only a change in bombing operations over the North, but also significant changes in the makeup of air assets at Korat. In September, a portion of Detachment 1, 561st TFS departed upon the arrival of six Wild Weasel F-4Cs from the 67th TFS, 18th TFW out of Kadena AB, Okinawa. Early October saw the wing lose two F-4 components under separate actions. First, the 35th TFS returned home after four months of combat duty, and second, the 469th TFS disbanded. To fill the void from these actions, 72 A-7Ds from the 354th TFW out of Myrtle Beach, South Carolina deployed to Korat, although they were not directly controlled by the 388th TFW.

Bombing continued in the southern region of North Vietnam in the early winter of 1972, but a stalemate in negotiations spurred President Nixon to launch a brief, all-out massive air assault against Hanoi and Haiphong known as Linebacker II. The operation was carried out between 18-29 December 1972 and involved around-the-clock attacks against electrical power plants and broadcast stations, railways and railyards, port and storage facilities, and airfields. Unlike any previous air campaign against North Vietnam, this offensive employed SAC B-52s over Hanoi. In general, USAF operations consisted of F-4 and A-7 tactical strikes during the day and B-52 and F-111 bombing runs at night.

With the bulk of its air assets being dedicated to specialized missions, the 388th TFW's primary role in Linebacker II was strike force protection. The heavy concentration of SAMs surrounding the North's urban centers made the 388th's Wild Weasel F-105Gs and F-4Cs, as well as its EB-66 electronic countermeasures aircraft, critically important to limiting the loss of aircraft and airmen. The B-52's size and lack of maneuverability made it particularly vulnerable to the SAM threat. Nearly 900 SA-2 missiles were fired at the big bombers during Linebacker II, but the Weasels highly effective anti-SAM measures forced the North Vietnamese to resort to less accurate methods of firing the SA-2 missiles. Nonetheless, the enemy shot down fifteen B-52s with SAMs during the campaign, of which many were downed by the crude tactic of launching a barrage of the missiles unguided at the bombers during their final approach to the target.

Despite the extreme demands placed on the Weasels during Linebacker II, no aircraft were lost. In previous action during 1972, the 388th TFW lost eight F-105Gs, six in combat and two to operational mishaps. At the beginning of 1973, military operations continued in the northern areas south of the 20th parallel, but the effec-

The 388th TFW resumed its association with the Thud when the Weasel aircraft from the inactivating 355th TFW at Takhli were transferred to Korat beginning in late September 1970 to form Detachment 1, 12th TFS. This unit quickly grew in size to become the 6010th WWS in November 1970. One of the new squadron's ZB-coded F-105Gs (63-8266) is seen here on the wing of a tanker in July 1971. (Richard Kierbow via JEM Aviation Slides)

In a move that amounted to little more than a numeric change, the 17th WWS replaced the 6010th WWS as the sole Thud-equipped Weasel unit of the 388th TFW in December 1971. This F-105G (63-8300) is seen parked on the Korat ramp in early 1972. (Don Logan via Jerry Geer)

An F-105G (63-8301) of the 17th WWS, 388th TFW gets ready to leave Korat on a mission in the spring of 1972. During that time, the renewed bombing of North Vietnam under Operation Freedom Train brought a tremendous increase in operational tempo for the squadron. (Don Logan via Paul Minert)

In April 1972, Operation Constant Guard I bolstered the Wild Weasel force in Southeast Asia by deploying twelve F-105Gs of Detachment 1, 561st TFS from McConnell AFB, Kansas to Korat. The unit, seen here shortly after their arrival in Thailand, augmented the 17th WWS while operating under the control of the 388th TFW. (Tom Waller via James Geer)

tiveness of the eleven day Linebacker II campaign forced the North Vietnamese leadership to return to the negotiating table to talk in earnest. Combat operations in North and South Vietnam ended with the signing of the Paris Peace Accords on 27 January 1973. About three weeks later, on 21 February 1973, combat missions in Laos ceased when a peace agreement between the various fighting factions was formalized.

The peace agreements brought immediate changes to the makeup and mission of air units at Korat. The Weasel presence was reduced with the departure of the F-4Cs of the 67th TFS in February 1973. The mission for the 388th's remaining F-105Gs within the 17th WWS and Detachment 1, 561st TFS was relegated to supporting B-52 operations in Cambodia or RF-4C recce missions that monitored the terms of the peace agreements. The importance of troop interdiction in Cambodia saw the 388th TFW gain an A-7D unit, the 3rd TFS, after a portion of the TDY element of the 354th TFW was withdrawn from Southeast Asia in March 1973.

Combat operations ended for the 388th TFW on 15 August 1973 when a Congressional-imposed ban on funding military activities in or over Southeast Asia became law. The wing received two additional awards for operational periods that ended in 1973. First, the Republic of Vietnam Gallantry Cross with Palm was given for its long-term contribution to the war over the period 8 April 1966 to 28 January 1973. Second, a sixth Air Force Outstanding Unit Award with Combat "V" Device was earned for combat operations from 18 December 1972 to 15 August 1973.

After the final ceasefire, the 388th TFW trained to maintain combat readiness while processing through a series of air asset redeployments and realignments related to the downsizing of forces in Southeast Asia. The return of aircraft to the U.S. occurred at a steady pace with the F-105Gs of the 561st TFS being the first to depart in September 1973, followed by the EB-66s of the 42nd TEWS in January 1974, and the C-130s in 7th ACCS in May 1974. The departure of the 8th TFW at Ubon RTAFB, Thailand saw the wing gain the AC-130H Spectre when the 16th Special Operations Squadron (SOS) moved from the former base to Korat in July 1974. In a historic move that not only concluded the wing's long affiliation with the Thud, but also ended the aircraft's ten-year presence

The Weasels remained heavily tasked throughout the Linebacker campaign as most strikes into North Vietnam required SAM suppression support. This F-105G (62-4427) from Detachment 1, 561st TFS was photographed on a July 1972 mission from Korat. (Paul Hoynacki via James Geer)

in Thailand, the F-105Gs of the 17th WWS returned to the U.S. in October 1974.

Subsequent to the Thud's departure, the 388th TFW remained in Thailand for just over one year. It ceased all aircraft operations on 28 November 1975 in preparation for a return to the U.S. One month later, on 23 December, the 388th moved in name only to Hill AFB, Utah, where it was soon equipped with F-4Ds.

Wing commanders during the 388th TFW's brief period of flying the F-105 out of McConnell were Col. Richard C. Banbury (1 October 1962) and Col. Olin E. Gilbert (1 October 1963). At Korat, no less than nineteen individuals commanded the wing from 1966 through 1974 including Col. Monroe S. Sams (8 April 1966), Brig. Gen. William S. Chairsell (17 August 1966), Col. Edward B. Burdett (1 August 1967), Col. Jack C. Berger (18 November 1967), Col. Neil J. Graham (22 November 1967), Col. Norman P. Phillips (19 January 1968), Col. Paul P. Douglas, Jr. (24 January 1968), Col. Allen K. McDonald (23 July 1968), Col. Paul P. Douglas, Jr. (19 August 1968), Col. Allen K. McDonald (15 December 1968), Col. John A. Nelson (11 June 1969), Col. James M. Breedlove (5 December 1969), Col. Ivan H. Dethman (20 June 1970), Col. Irby B. Jarvis, Jr. (1 August 1970), Col. Webb Thompson (26 July 1971), Col. Stanley M. Umstead, Jr. (15 December 1971), Col. Richard E. Markling (5 August 1972), Col. Mele Vojvodich, Jr. (25 January 1973), Col. Robert K. Crouch (1 July 1973), Col. Thomas H. Normile (3 January 1974), and Col. John P. Russell (3 July 1974). The 388th TFW did not operate the F-105 between 10 October 1969 and 1 November 1970, but the commanders during that time are listed for continuity purposes.

Both Thud squadrons operating out of Korat are represented in this October 1972 shot of two F-105Gs holding on the wing of a KC-135 tanker enroute to North Vietnam. The JB-coded aircraft (62-4416) belonged to the 17th WWS, while the WW-coded machine (63-8265) was assigned to Detachment 1, 561st TFS. (Barry Miller via Jerry Geer)

This F-105G (63-8291) of the 17th WWS, 388th TFW is seen at Korat on 29 January 1973, just two days after the Paris Peace Accords took effect to end the fighting in North and South Vietnam. The aircraft carries the name *MUTTLEY THE FLYING DOG* on the air intake. (Don Larsen via Norm Taylor)

A brace of escort F-105Gs (63-8320 and 62-4434) of Detachment 1, 561st TFS awaits refueling while an RF-4C of the 14th TRS, 432nd TRW replenishes its tanks for a recce mission over North Vietnam in February 1973. These photo flights were flown regularly after the truce was signed to monitor the North's compliance with the terms of the agreement. (Don Kilgus via Robert F. Dorr)

After the final ceasefire, the 17th WWS maintained combat readiness as an element of the 388th TFW until redeploying to the U.S. under Operation Coronet Exxon in October 1974. This F-105G (62-4446) was shot at Korat circa March 1973. (Don Larsen via Paul Minert)

Wild Weasel Detachment

Control of the Wild Weasel Detachment at Korat shifted from the provisional 6234th TFW to the 388th TFW on 8 April 1966. The unit was formed on 25 November 1965, when a small number of F-100F Wild Weasel aircraft arrived to evaluate newly installed RHAW equipment against the North Vietnamese SAM threat. The deployment was to last 90 days but was extended considerably. The F-100F Weasel program proved successful, although lessons learned from combat dictated the need for a higher performance aircraft.

As the follow-on Wild Weasel aircraft, the first EF-105Fs arrived at Korat on 28 May 1966. The early EF-105F combat missions were led by Weasel F-100Fs and involved flights in the lower threat areas of southern North Vietnam. The first orientation flight took place on 3 June 1966, and four days later, the first radar kill for an EF-105F took place when a GCI radar site was destroyed with rocket fire. Mission progressed into the Hanoi area by mid-June, and the EF-105F Weasels successfully attacked several radar control vans during the second half of the month.

On 29 June 1966, the Weasels destroyed at least one SAM site while escorting the main strike force that hit the Hanoi POL complex. Less than a week later, on 5 July, Maj. Bill Robinson and his EWO, Maj. Peter Tsouprake, led a Weasel flight into the immediate Hanoi area that destroyed four SAM sites. For their action that day, Robinson and Tsouprake became the first Weasel crew to be awarded the Air Force Cross. The celebration was short lived as the following day the Thud team lost its first aircraft and crew when an EF-105F flown by Maj. Roosevelt L. Hestle, Jr. and Capt. Charles E. Morgan was shot down by anti-aircraft fire on a mission near Hanoi.

The F-100F Weasel team flew their last combat mission on 11 July 1966. They subsequently returned to the U.S. at Nellis AFB, Nevada to train the next generation of Weasels. Shortly after their departure, the Wild Weasel Detachment was discontinued, and the cadre of Weasel Thuds left behind was formed into a flight within the recently arrived 13th TFS, 388th TFW.

Detachment 1, 12th Tactical Fighter Squadron

Detachment 1, 12th Tactical Fighter Squadron was formed at Korat in the fall of 1970 as a result of the planned end of F-105 operations at Takhli and the corresponding need to retain the Wild Weasel Thuds assigned to the inactivating 355th TFW in Southeast Asia. Outside of supporting strike operations in Laos, the Weasels were being utilized on intermittent "protective reaction" duty in support of tactical reconnaissance missions over North Vietnam or Gunship operations near the North Vietnamese border. Another important role driving the need to retain the Weasel assets in Thailand was their use in support of B-52 bombing runs in Cambodia.

Placed under the operational control of the 388th TFW, Detachment 1, 12th TFS came into existence when it received a mix of six EF-105Fs and F-105Gs from Takhli on 24 September 1970. Over the next two weeks, the unit gained additional aircraft as the 355th TFW ended operations. Other personnel and assets came from the 12th TFS at Kadena, which had maintained a flight of Weasel crews and aircraft since mid-1968. The growth of the detachment brought a change in designation to the provisional 6010th WWS, 388th TFW on 1 November 1970.

13th Tactical Fighter Squadron

The 13th Tactical Fighter Squadron was organized and activated on 15 May 1966 within the 18th TFW at Kadena AB, Okinawa as a new Thud squadron to be assigned PCS at Korat to serve with the 388th TFW. The unit was formed from the assets of the 44th TFS; however, pilots were drawn from all of 18th TFW's squadrons. Upon being activated, the 13th TFS was detached to the 388th TFW, although it was not until mid-June 1966 that the squadron moved to Korat.

About two weeks after arriving in Thailand, the 13th TFS assumed the dual mission of strike and suppression of enemy air defenses when Korat's Wild Weasel Detachment of EF-105Fs was formed as a separate flight within the squadron. The Weasels flew two basic types of missions: as an element of a strike force package tasked to suppress SAMs that threatened the bombers, and as a member of a hunter-killer team where they were paired with standard fighter-bombers to find and destroy SAM sites.

As the only Weasel-equipped unit at Korat, the 13th TFS supported every major strike in the North carried out by the 388th TFW. The emphasis during the second half of 1966 remained with POL facilities and transportation oriented targets. The squadron had about twelve Weasel Thuds by September 1966, and despite the fact that they were used extensively in the heavily defended Hanoi area, only one EF-105F was lost. While supporting the Weasels or bombing targets in the North, six of the squadron's F-105Ds were shot down.

The Weasel role had become the primary mission of the squadron by the close of 1966, and the vital role of the EF-105F SAM suppressors saw the unit support a variety of operations over the North. To open 1967, the squadron led Iron Hand flights participating in the highly successful anti-MiG sweep code named Operation Bolo. The mission was carried out on 2 January and involved F-4 Phantoms luring MiGs into air-to-air combat. In more traditional fashion, the 13th was involved in both the strike and Weasel roles in raids against the Thai Nguyen iron and steel works beginning on 10 March 1967.

The 13th TFS gained another specialized mission known as Commando Nail on 1 June 1967. On that day, the squadron absorbed a recently established provisional unit that was equipped with a small number of EF-105Fs that had been modified with an upgraded radar bombing system for night and all-weather strikes. General John D. Ryan, PACAF commander, pushed to develop this capability in the USAF after the Navy had achieved success in the all-weather mission with the A-6 Intruder. Accordingly, the aircraft

An EF-105F of the 13th TFS is about to refuel from a KC-135 tanker during Rolling Thunder operations in 1966. The aircraft is carrying CBUs on the inboards and Shrikes on the outboard pylons. (USAF via Stewart Hurd)

BELOW: With a Kaman HH-43 rescue and crash fire fighting helicopter hovering overhead, an Iron Hand flight, comprised of two 13th TFS EF-105Fs teamed with two F-105Ds under the hunter-killer concept, is seen lined up for take-off on the Korat runway circa late 1966. (USAF via Stewart Hurd)

Miss Molly was the name of this 13th TFS EF-105F (63-8356) seen on a visit to Da Nang AB, South Vietnam in March 1967. Note the four SAM site kill marks between the canopies. (Neil Schneider via Jerry Geer)

This EF-105F (63-8329) of the 13th TFS was also photographed while transient at Da Nang in early 1967. The squadron's subtle markings included a yellow nose gear radar reflector and canopy name block. (Neil Schneider via Jerry Geer)

In addition to its primary role as a Wild Weasel unit, the 13th TFS maintained a secondary general-purpose strike responsibility. Armed with six M117 750-pound bombs, this F-105D (58-1157) dubbed *BUBBLES I* is seen taxiing out at Korat for a 1967 bombing mission. (Don Larsen via Jerry Geer)

HALF FAST, an EF-105F (63-8317) assigned to the 13th TFS in the spring of 1967, gets ready to take the runway after stopping at the "last chance" checkpoint. (Don Larsen via Jerry Geer)

A 13th TFS EF-105F (63-8298), *SAM DODGER*, takes off from Korat for yet another Wild Weasel mission over North Vietnam on 29 May 1967. (Don Larsen via James Geer)

and their crews were known as "Ryan's Raiders", and they carried out some of the most hazardous bombing missions in the Rolling Thunder campaign.

Missions against vital targets continued into the late spring and summer of 1967. The Weasels were involved in nearly every raid in the far reaches of North Vietnam, and the "strike" pilots flew missions against critical military, industrial, and transportation targets. Action during May and June was particularly heavy as targets such as the Kep airfield, the Hoa Lac airfield, the Vinh Yen army barracks, the Yen Bai railroad yards, and the Bac Giang Bridge and adjacent railyards were hit. The unit found itself engaging MiGs in greater numbers during this time. On 3 June, the 13th TFS was credited with its first aerial victory when Maj. Ralph L. Kuster, Jr. shot down a MiG-17 with his Vulcan cannon while on a mission against the Bac Giang Bridge.

The month of August 1967 was marked by the squadron's involvement in a large-scale raid on the previously untouched Paul Doumer Bridge. The mission took place on 11 August, and a Weasel flight led by Squadron Commander Lt. Col. James McInerney and his EWO, Capt. Fred Shannon, escorted the strike force that successfully dropped several spans on the bridge. For their efforts against the enemy's air defenses that day, McInerney and Shannon earned the Air Force Cross. Other highlights that month saw the squadron provide Weasel escort for missions against the Lang Son and Yen Vien railyards, which were attacked on 13 and 23 August respectively.

Several years of extensive aircraft losses due to the Thud's operational responsibility over the North required the 388th TFW to downsize to three squadrons in the fall of 1967. Consequently, the 13th TFS assumed a non-operational status on 18 October 1967, and its resources and mission were absorbed by the 44th TFS. Three days later, the 13th TFS designation moved to Udorn RTAFB, Thailand, where it was attached to the 432nd TRW and equipped with F-4Ds. The 13th lost six aircraft (three F-105Ds, one Commando Nail F-105F, and two EF-105Fs) over North Vietnam during 1967 prior to ending operations at Korat.

The squadron earned two Air Force Outstanding Unit Awards with Combat "V" Device for operations in the F-105. The first was given for the POL raids in the immediate Hanoi area on 29-30 June 1966, and the second was received for combat operations during the period 1 July 1966 to 30 June 1967. The 13th TFS was also awarded with the Presidential Unit Citation for their role in the destruction of Thai Nguyen complex and other critical targets over the period 10 March to 1 May 1967.

Ryan's Raiders

The bad weather over North Vietnam was a constant hindrance to bombing operations during the first two years of the Rolling Thunder campaign. In particular, the seasonal northeast monsoon at the beginning of each year allowed the enemy time to rebuild previously destroyed targets and step-up the infiltration of supplies and troops to the South. The cover of night was no different, and the North Vietnamese took advantage of the opportunities. The Navy found success in countering these obstacles with the all-weather A-6 Intruder. Not to be outdone by the Navy, the USAF started a program to develop its own night, all-weather radar bombing capability during early 1967. General John D. Ryan, PACAF commander, was at the forefront of the effort, and the aircraft and crews that would carry out the mission aptly became known as "Ryan's Raiders".

The program was started on 4 March 1967 under Operation Northscope at Yokota AB, Japan. Here, a small number of EF-105F Wild Weasels (and later several standard F-105Fs) were modified with an improved R-14A radar that expanded presentation for sharper target definition and an optimized toss-bomb computer that improved delivery accuracy. Although the aircraft were modified EF-105Fs, the crews initially chosen to pioneer the mission were not Weasel qualified. Instead, the two-man crew was made of two rated pilots. An instructor pilot filled the front seat, and a pilot fresh from RTU training or one with previous navigator experience served as a bombardier in the backseat. After developing tactics and perfecting radar bombing techniques at Yokota, the first set of four crews arrived at Korat for duty with the 388th TFW on 24 April 1967. Four additional crews followed on 8 May, and another group of equal size arrived on 22 May. After initially being organized as a separate provisional unit, the Raider team was absorbed by the 13th TFS on 1 June 1967.

The new highly specialized mission of striking targets at night and bad weather with self-contained radar was code named Commando Nail. Under the leadership of Col. Fred A. Treyz, the Raiders flew their first mission on 26 April 1967, when they hit the Yen Bai railyards and the ferry crossing at Ron's Ferry. During the next 80 days, the team flew 98 sorties over North Vietnam. The typical mission profile was to strike a single target in the North at altitudes of 500 to 2,000 feet. Inherently, the chosen targets were heavily defended, and the perils of flying the nocturnal missions were epitomized by the loss of two aircraft and crews during the first month of operations.

An early Commando Nail F-105F (63-8312) of the 13th TFS prepares for a brief test hop at Korat on 23 June 1967. Note the tan and SAC green underside camouflage scheme used by the Raiders to help conceal the aircraft during night bombing missions. (Don Larsen via Jerry Geer)

The losses and experience of combat brought operational changes to the Raider program. Most important was the need to further integrate the program with Weasel operations. Since they were flying Weasel equipped Thuds, Raider crewmember requirements were revised to call for the front and backseater to be Weasel qualified. This change saw the second generation of Raider crews responsible for flying Weasel missions during the day and Commando Nail missions at night. Another significant change incorporated the standard EF-105F Weasels into the Raider nighttime strike package for added defensive measures.

By the fall of 1967, the Raiders had recorded over 400 combat sorties over North Vietnam, many of which were in the immediate Hanoi area. However, the loss of a third aircraft and crew on a night mission near the Chinese border on 4 October 1967 brought an end to the low-level strikes in the far reaches of the North. Two weeks later, on 18 October, the Raider team joined the 44th TFS following the transfer of the 13th TFS to the 432nd TRW at Udorn RTAFB, Thailand. From that point, Raider operations primarily consisted of night interdiction missions in the southern panhandle of North Vietnam. In limited duty, the Raiders were also employed in a role known as Commando Nail Papa. On these missions, they served on pathfinders for large F-105D strike forces bombing targets in bad weather.

The Raider program was officially discontinued shortly after the Rolling Thunder campaign ended on 31 October 1968. Overall, the program's objective of pioneering the night, all-weather radar bombing mission for the USAF was considered moderately successful; nevertheless, the experience and tactics gained by the elite crews and aircraft proved valuable and were incorporated in future night fighter operations carried out by F-4s and F-111s.

17th Wild Weasel Squadron

The 17th Wild Weasel Squadron was activated within the 388th TFW on 1 December 1971 to replace the provisional 6010th WWS. With about fifteen F-105Gs, the squadron continued its forerunner's mission of supporting the war in Southeast Asia by participating in the "protective reaction" program that correlated to the reconnaissance of Communist troop and air defense positions in North Vietnam. Other duty involved escorting U.S. aircraft operating against the Ho Chi Minh Trail in Laos when SAMs or radar controlled anti-aircraft fire were known to be a threat.

Ten days after being activated, the 17th suffered its first loss when an F-105G was downed by a SAM while operating against enemy defensive positions protecting key Communist infiltration routes near the North Vietnamese-Laotian border. The pilot, Lt. Col. Scott W. McEntire, was killed, while the EWO, Maj. Robert E. Belli, ejected and was recovered. The increasing number of SAM sites in the southern panhandle of North Vietnam, as well as the continued build-up of troops in this area, prompted a series of "protective reaction" strikes in the final days of 1971. This limited campaign, known as Proud Deep Alpha, saw the 17th WWS participate in an extensive operation against military, supply, and air defense targets south of the 20th parallel over the period 26-30 December.

In early 1972, the 17th WWS was tasked to support additional strikes against North Vietnam when the enemy continued its logistical preparations for a major offensive against South Vietnam. A maximum effort strike was carried out against suspected North Vietnamese supply and staging positions in the DMZ on 16-17 February. On the second day of the attacks, the squadron lost an F-105G

The 17th WWS was activated at Korat in December 1971 through the redesignation of the provisional 6010th WWS. Initially, the 17th's aircraft retained the ZB tail code of its forerunner as illustrated by this F-105G (63-8345) depicted at Korat in early 1972. (Don Logan)

The Communist offensive into South Vietnam in the early spring of 1972 brought a return to sustained air operations over North Vietnam. This 17th WWS F-105G (63-8292) is seen on a SAM suppression mission in support of Freedom Train bombing strikes against the North in April 1972. (Don Logan via Jerry Geer)

crewed by Captains James Cutter and Ken Fraser most likely to a SAM. Both crewmembers ejected, were captured, and spent the remainder of the war as POWs.

The long awaited Communist offensive into South Vietnam in the early spring of 1972 brought a return to sustained operations over North Vietnam for the 17th WWS. The renewed bombing began on 6 April and attacks as far north as the 20th parallel were conducted under a campaign dubbed Freedom Train. Beginning on 16 April, the squadron flew further north while participating in a series of strikes against military storage facilities and POL dumps near Hanoi, Haiphong, Thanh Hoa, and Ham Rong. These attacks were called Freedom Porch Bravo and saw the unit provide SAM suppression support for not only tactical aircraft, but also SAC B-52s. As the only Weasel squadron in Southeast Asia when the bombing resumed over the North, the mission load of the 17th WWS was extreme through mid-April, at which time reinforcements arrived at Korat in the form of twelve F-105Gs of Detachment 1, 561st TFS.

On 10 May 1972, the 17th WWS began participating in more intensive operations in North Vietnam when a new campaign known as Linebacker superseded Freedom Train. The squadron's Wild Weasel mission saw it play a vital role in protecting strike elements

A heavily weathered F-105G (63-8300) of the 17th WWS taxis out for a mission at Korat in the spring of 1972. Standard for the time, the aircraft carries an asymmetrical load consisting of a Standard ARM on the right inboard, a Shrike on the left outboard, an ECM pod of the right outboard, and fuel tanks on the centerline and left inboard stations. (Don Logan via Paul Minert)

that attacked major bridges, airfields, industrial facilities, military storage sites, and power plants in the North. The typical Iron Hand mission profile required the Weasels to be the "first in and last out" of the target area, clearing the strike package ingress and egress routes of SAM threats. A common variation of the Iron Hand mission saw the F-105Gs work in tandem with F-4Es to find and destroy SAM sites as hunter-killer teams.

The squadron lost four aircraft while supporting Linebacker operations throughout the summer and early fall of 1972. The first loss took place on 11 May, when an Atoll missile from a MiG-21 downed an F-105G flown by Majors William Talley and James Padgett. Both crewmembers ejected and were taken POW. The second loss occurred on 29 July, when a bad AGM-45 Shrike missile damaged a Thud while it was attempting to evade a threatening MiG. The crewmembers bailed out over the Gulf of Tonkin and were rescued. SAMs downed the third and fourth F-105Gs on 17 and 29 September respectively. Capt. Thomas Zorn and 1st Lt. Michael Turose were killed on the earlier date, while Squadron Commander Lt. Col. James O'Neil was taken POW and Capt. Michael Bosiljevac was listed as MIA on the latter.

The Linebacker campaign ended on 22 October 1972 as a result of progressing diplomatic talks between the U.S. and North Vietnam. Although this was the case, the 17th WWS remained active over the North for the next two months as President Nixon allowed air attacks in the southern panhandle region below the 20th parallel. A breakdown in the peace negotiations brought a return to operations further north when an eleven-day air assault known as Linebacker II began on 18 December 1972. This offensive involved intensive air strikes by tactical aircraft and B-52s against industrial and military targets in the Hanoi and Haiphong region.

The 17th WWS was instrumental in protecting strike elements during Linebacker II as the 23 October bombing cessation gave the enemy time to reinforce and expand its SAM defenses in the Hanoi region. The around-the-clock bombing during the brief campaign often required the crews to fly as many as three missions each day. Particularly important was the squadron's role in providing SAM suppression for the cells of conventionally armed B-52s hitting Hanoi's periphery at night. In support of these raids, the Weasels flew the traditional Iron Hand mission versus operating alongside F-4s in hunter-killer teams due to constant bad weather over North

A pair of F-105Gs (62-4423 and 62-4416) of the 17th WWS refuels enroute to North Vietnam during early Linebacker operations in the late spring of 1972. (Don Logan via Paul Minert)

This 17th WWS F-105G (63-8306) was marked with the squadron's newly adopted JB tail code when photographed at Korat circa mid-1972. By this time, most of the unit's aircraft had been upgraded to full G-model standard with the addition of the ALQ-105 (QRC-380) ECM fairings on the lower fuselage sides. (Republic via Jerry Geer)

A F-105G (63-8266) of the 17th WWS on the prowl over North Vietnam in August 1972. (Paul Hoynacki via Jerry Geer)

During the late 1972 time frame, the 17th WWS began applying sharkmouths and black tail bands to its aircraft. This F-105G (63-8316) shows the revised markings in this view taken at Korat on 29 January 1973. (Don Larsen via Norm Taylor)

Vietnam. The Weasels' effectiveness forced the North Vietnamese to launch the SAMs without radar guidance, but an estimated 884 missiles were fired at the B-52s and fifteen were downed. Despite the intensity of the Linebacker II operations, the 17th WWS carried out their mission without incurring any losses.

The success of Linebacker II brought a return to meaningful negotiations and a corresponding reduction in the air war. During the first two weeks of 1973, the 17th WWS supported strike operations against targets in southern part of North Vietnam, but these attacks ceased after a major breakthrough in the peace talks indicated an agreement was forthcoming. The war in North and South Vietnam ended with the signing of the Paris Peace Accords on 27 January 1973. The end of fighting in Laos followed on 21 February 1973, leaving Cambodia as the lone war zone. From that point, the 17th carried out combat missions on a significantly reduced scale. The few missions flown were in support of B-52 operations against Communist positions in Cambodia or RF-4C reconnaissance missions that monitored the North's compliance with the peace agreements.

Although the war ended in North and South Vietnam on 27 January 1973, the 17th WWS continued to fly combat missions in support of the ongoing fighting in Laos and Cambodia. Named *PATIENCE*, this 17th WWS F-105G (63-8336) awaits the arrival of its crew at Korat on 2 February 1973. (Don Larsen via James Geer)

A 17th WWS F-105G (62-4446) powers through Southeast Asian skies on a flight in March 1973. (Tom Lynn via Jerry Geer)

The 17th WWS was about to enter a training routine when this F-105G (63-8291) was photographed at Korat in August 1973. That month, a Congressional-imposed ban on the funding of military activities in Southeast Asia took effect to end the American role in the war. (Jerry Geer Collection)

The squadrons remaining in Thailand after the truce settlement participated in Commando Scrimmage war exercises to maintain combat readiness and deter North Vietnamese aggression. This 17th WWS F-105G (63-8316) carries an inert Shrike missile during one such training operation in 1974. (Jerry Geer Collection)

Operations in Cambodia ended on 15 August 1973 after Congress terminated the funding of all combat activities in Southeast Asia. Within one month, the 17th WWS was the last F-105 organization in Southeast Asia after Detachment 1, 561st TFS returned to the U.S. For the next year, the squadron entered into a training program to maintain combat readiness and participated in Commando Scrimmage war exercises that were intended to deter the North Vietnamese from attacking South Vietnam.

The F-105Gs of the 17th WWS returned to the U.S. under Operation Coronet Exxon beginning in late October 1974. Maj. Wayne Hauth led the last flight of Thuds out of Korat on 29 October, ending the aircraft's ten-year presence in Thailand. On that same day, the 17th WWS assumed a non-operational status in preparation for its deactivation on 15 November 1974. Upon redeployment from Thailand, the personnel and equipment of the 17th WWS were used to form the 562nd TFS, 35th TFW at George AFB, California.

During its service in Southeast Asia, the 17th WWS lost six aircraft in combat. Honors included the Air Force Outstanding Unit Award with Combat "V" Device for operations from 18 December 1972 to 15 August 1973 and the Republic of Vietnam Gallantry Cross with Palm for efforts during the period 1 December 1971 to 29 October 1974.

34th Tactical Fighter Squadron

The 34th Tactical Fighter Squadron was organized and activated within PACAF on 15 May 1966 as part of a plan to add two additional PCS squadrons at Korat. The 41st AD at Yokota AB, Japan formed the 34th from assets of the 36th TFS. The original plan was for the 36th TFS to go to Korat, but the Japanese government complained that they did not want a combat unit going to war from Japanese soil, so the squadron was renamed the 34th TFS and the 36th stayed in Japan in name only. Upon activation, the 34th TFS was assigned to the 41st AD, but was detached to the 388th TFW.

Although it got its aircraft from the 36th TFS, the unit's pilots were made-up from volunteers from all of Yokota's F-105 squadrons. To volunteer, pilots had to have less than 50 combat missions. The fighting spirit of the eligible pilots, coupled with the career importance of completing 100 combat missions, brought twice as many volunteers than were needed. In charge of selecting who went with the 34th TFS to Korat was Squadron Commander Lt. Col. Howard F. Hendricks and Operations Officer Maj. Richard P. Fitzgerald.

The squadron's move to Thailand was delayed by about one month while additional ramp space and facilities were constructed at Korat. After receiving orders to move, the 34th TFS sent 21 F-105Ds on a flight plan that called for an intermediate servicing stop at Kadena AB, Okinawa before proceeding to Thailand. While at Kadena, the 34th was informed that there still was not enough concrete ramp space for the squadron. As a result, they returned to Yokota for two weeks while additional concrete was poured.

By about mid-June, the squadron was on duty at Korat and integrated into the 388th TFW's operational mission of supporting the air war against North Vietnam. On 29 June 1966, a portion of the unit participated in the highly successful Hanoi POL strike. Missions on POL targets, plus attacks on bridges, rail routes, and military storage and staging areas were carried out during the second half of 1966. Other action saw pilots teamed with the 13th TFS Weasels on Iron Hand SAM suppression sorties. While flying in an Iron Hand element on 18 August 1966, Maj. Kenneth T. Blank shot down a MiG-17 with his 20-mm cannon to gain the 34th TFS its first aerial victory of the war. The enemy also found success as the 34th had at least five aircraft shot down during its first six months of combat.

Seen in the landing pattern at Yokota in May 1966, this F-105D (62-4308) was one of about 21 Thuds that deployed to Thailand when the former 36th TFS was sent to Korat on a PCS basis as the new 34th TFS. A close look at the form of the removed markings at the top of the tail reveals this aircraft was previously used by the 335th TFS, 4th TFW. (Toyokazu Matsuzaki)

The fresh appearance of this F-105D (60-0449) of the 34th TFS hints that it had only recently joined the squadron as a replacement aircraft when photographed during a visit to Da Nang in September 1966. (Terry Love via Jerry Geer)

After a lull in the number of sorties in the North during the seasonal monsoon of early 1967, the 34th TFS participated in the all-out effort to destroy the iron and steel plant, power station, military storage area, and railroad station at Thai Nguyen beginning on 10 March. Intense action continued into the spring and early summer as the unit was involved in the destruction of key military airfields and power facilities, as well as systematic strikes against rail transportation targets. An indication of the unit's heavy flying schedule took place in May 1967, when it surpassed 10,000 combat flying hours in less than one year of combat.

The second half of 1967 was marked by a significant escalation in the air war over the North, and the 34th TFS was engaged in nearly every major strike carried out by the 388th TFW during that time. Notable missions included the Paul Doumer Bridge raid on 11 August and the attack on the Yen Vien railroad yards on 23 August. In the latter mission, 34th pilots faced heavy MiG opposition after bombing the target. During the ensuing air battles, 1st Lt. David B. Waldrop most likely gunned down two MiG-17s, but received credit for only one kill due to insufficient evidence for one of the claims. Waldrop's flight leader, Maj. Billy R. Givens, fired more

This 34th TFS F-105D (58-1167) named *MISS UNIVERSE* was forced to recover at Da Nang after its right stabilator was shot off during a 1966 mission over North Vietnam. (Neil Schneider via Jerry Geer)

than 900 rounds of 20-mm at another MiG for a probable kill, but again the claim was denied due to a lack of definitive data to substantiate the victory.

Enemy support and supply line targets in the North continued to be the focus of many missions for the 34th TFS in late 1967. Outside of missions against major railroad yards and bridges, squadron pilots flew on strikes against the Phuc Yen and Kep airfields. Participating in the destruction of enemy targets was particularly costly during the last three months of the year as the squadron lost seven Thuds in combat. For all of 1967, the 34th TFS lost about thirteen F-105s to the enemy's air defense system, while an operational mishap claimed one additional aircraft.

In early 1968, the squadron's operations in the Hanoi area were limited due to adverse weather conditions, but some strikes were carried out in this region using Combat Skyspot and Commando Club radar bombing techniques. When diverted because of weather, the 34th TFS spent time striking targets in Laos or supporting the Marines at Khe Sanh, where the North Vietnamese had launched a major offensive on an American base. By mid-March, the squadron had resumed flying most of its missions in the North, which continued until President Johnson restricted bombing to the southern panhandle of North Vietnam in early April 1968.

Although the bombing of the North was limited to the lower regions, the 34th TFS remained active and struck key links in the supply and transportation network along major infiltration routes. Many targets were struck in the Dong Hoi area, where the unit destroyed highway and railroad ridges, truck parks, military storage areas, and air defense sites. The action in the southern panhandle continued until the halt of all air attacks against North Vietnam, effective on 1 November 1968. From that point, the squadron operated extensively in Laos in support of the interdiction effort against the Ho Chi Minh Trail. During 1968, the squadron lost eleven F-105s, eight in combat and three to operational causes.

The 34th continued to fly strike missions in Laos in the Thud through the spring of 1969. Three aircraft were shot down prior to May 1969, at which time the squadron became the second unit of the 388th TFW to re-equip with F-4Es. The conversion to the Phantom was undertaken by the "formation asset" program that saw a squadron form-up in the U.S. and transfer to Southeast Asia to assume the designation of a unit due for conversion. The 40th TFS, 33rd TFW at Eglin AFB, Florida provided the 388th TFW with two F-4E formation assets, and the second of these arrived in May as the new 34th TFS. The remaining F-105 units in Thailand absorbed the assets and personnel of the former 34th TFS.

The 34th TFS received one Presidential Unit Citation and several Air Force Outstanding Unit Awards with Combat "V" Device for operations in the F-105. The Presidential Unit Citation was given for the unit's contribution in the destruction of the Thai Nguyen iron and steel works and other primary targets in North Vietnam during the period 10 March to 1 May 1967. One Outstanding Unit Award was given for the 34th's role on POL strikes against Hanoi during 29-30 June 1966, while a second and third were given for distinguished service over the periods 1 July 1966 to 30 June 1967 and 1 July 1967 to 30 June 1968 respectively. A fourth Outstanding Unit Award noting operations over the period 1 July 1968 to 15 September 1969 was partially attributed to operations in the F-105. Likewise, the 34th received the Republic of Vietnam Gallantry Cross with Palm for combat operations from 15 May 1966 to 29 January 1973.

BLITZKREIG, an F-105D (61-0208) of the 34th TFS, is seen in the Korat arming area prior to a mission circa April 1967. Note the squadron painted the nose gear radar reflector and canopy name block in black to identify their aircraft during this time. (Don Larsen via Jerry Geer)

Pictured on the Korat ramp in April 1967 is *THE AVENGER*, a 34th TFS Thud (61-0194) bombed-up and ready for its next sortie. (USAF via James Geer)

Known as *DRAGON JANE*, this F-105D (58-1169) of the 34th TFS is seen taxiing out at Korat for a June 1967 mission. (Don Larsen via Jerry Geer)

A 34th TFS F-105D (59-1760), *War Lord II*, glides in for landing at Korat during the summer of 1967. (Don Larsen via Jerry Geer)

The 34th TFS was assigned the JJ tail code when this unit identification system was introduced in late 1967. This F-105D (60-0518) was caught while enroute to a target in northern Laos on 16 December 1968. (USAF via Paul Minert)

This photograph, taken at Korat on 22 January 1969, shows a 34th TFS Thud (60-0505) parked in its revetment awaiting to be armed for its next mission. (USAF via Jerry Geer)

In the twilight of its service with the 34th TFS, an F-105D (61-0093) taxis out for a sortie on 8 April 1969. One month later, the 34th became the second squadron of the 388th TFW to relinquish its Thuds for F-4E Phantoms. (Neil Schneider via Jerry Geer)

44th Tactical Fighter Squadron

The 44th Tactical Fighter Squadron was reassigned from the 18th TFW to the 388th TFW on 25 April 1967. The unit originally began operating the F-105D within the 18th TFW at Kadena AB, Okinawa in late 1962. Two years later, the 44th began participating in rotational combat deployments to Southeast Asia. In mid-1966, the squadron's resources were used to form the 13th TFS at Korat. From that point, the squadron was maintained with minimal assets until being relegated to "paper unit" status at the end 1966. Upon reassignment to the 388th TFW, the 44th TFS returned to operational status by absorbing the personnel, equipment, and resources of the 421st TFS.

At the time of 44th's reactivation in the spring of 1967, the Rolling Thunder campaign was at its peak of intensity as U.S. strike forces were focused on the destruction of Hanoi's industrial base. As a strike squadron equipped with about 21 F-105Ds, the 44th joined the effort to destroy critical targets in the North such as major power plants, steel and cement plants, railyards, bridges, airfields, and military storage and staging areas. The intensity of the bombing brought heavy action from the NVAF MiG force, and the 44th TFS achieved its first aerial victory less than one month after its arrival in Thailand. The kill took place on 13 May 1967, when Maj. Maurice E. Seaver, Jr. downed a MiG-17 with his 20-mm cannon after pulling out from a bomb run on the Vinh Yen army barracks.

In the summer-fall period of 1967, the squadron flew many missions against transportation targets along the main road from China into Hanoi, and it also played an important role in the first strike on the Paul Doumer Bridge in August. Despite flying daily missions against heavily defended targets in North Vietnam, the unit lost only two F-105Ds in combat through September; however, the Thud's high loss rate over several years of combat and the corresponding lack of replacement aircraft forced the 388th to reduce to a three-squadron wing. Changes instituted as a result of the cutback saw the 44th TFS absorb the makeup and mission of the 13th TFS on 18 October 1967. The 13th TFS was transferred without personnel and equipment to Udorn RTAFB, Thailand to become an F-4D unit with the 432nd TRW.

When the 44th TFS absorbed the 13th TFS, its primary mission became that of suppressing SAMs and radar controlled AAA sites in the Wild Weasel role. Accordingly, the squadron gained the EF-105Fs that formerly belonged to the 13th TFS. Another mission inherited from the 13th TFS was the Ryan's Raiders night, all-weather radar bombing role in Commando Nail F-105Fs. By the

The 44th TFS came out of an operational hiatus when it was transferred from the 18th TFW to the 388th TFW on 25 April 1967 to absorb the 421st TFS. Seen at Korat shortly after the 44th's arrival, this F-105D (62-4326) is poised to launch for a mission over North Vietnam. (Don Larsen via Jerry Geer)

A 44th TFS F-105D (60-0497), *MISS T*, holds at the "last chance" area awaiting take-off in May 1967. Note the seldom used dual AIM-9 Sidewinder missile launcher on the outboard pylon. (Don Larsen via Jerry Geer)

end of the year, the squadron added another specialized mission that involved jamming communications between enemy MiGs and their GCI centers in modified F-105Fs known as Combat Martins.

The 44th's new diversified mission made it a key element of the 388th TFW. The Weasels flew support for all major raids in the North during the last three months of 1967, including missions against the Phuc Yen airfield, the Kep airfield, and the Paul Doumer Bridge. Other action saw the Raiders fly night interdiction strikes in the southern panhandle of North Vietnam. Although the Thud loss rate reached its highest point in the war during late 1967, the 44th TFS lost only one EF-105F in combat during the final months of that year.

In early 1968, the 44th TFS continued to fly Weasel missions in the far reaches of North Vietnam, but bad weather in this area saw the unit often diverted to support strike operations in the panhandle region. After the partial bombing halt of the North was announced on 31 March 1968, the 44th focused on seeking out SAM, AAA, and radar sites in southern North Vietnam below the 19th parallel. Around this time, the Commando Nail mission carried out by Raiders was discontinued as the 497th TFS, 8th TFW assumed the night fighter role with its F-4Ds.

Operations in the lower regions of North Vietnam continued until Rolling Thunder ended on 31 October 1968. The 44th TFS lost two EF-105Fs in action over the North in 1968, while another was downed in Laos. With the termination of the bombing of the North, missions were almost exclusively carried out over Laotian airspace. In its limited secondary role of strike operations, the 44th lost one F-105D over Laos in 1969. Although the threat of SAMs

This view of *Miss Mi Nookie*, an F-105D (62-4283) assigned to the 44th TFS in mid-1967, shows the blue nose gear radar reflector and canopy name block markings used by the squadron to distinguish their aircraft during this period. (Don Larsen via Jerry Geer)

The sound of thunder: a 44th TFS Thud (60-0434) cuts in the afterburner on take-off from Korat in the summer of 1967. (Don Larson via Jerry Geer)

In October 1967, the 44th TFS absorbed the mission and makeup of 13th TFS, thus changing its primary mission to the suppression of enemy air defenses in the Wild Weasel role. This EF-105F (63-8284) carries the squadron's new JE tail code when photographed during a visit to Yokota AB, Japan on 20 April 1968. (Yasuhiko Takahashi)

An EF-105F (62-4428) of the 44th TFS taxis back to the Korat flightline after completing a December 1968 mission. (USAF via James Geer)

was minimal in this region, the Weasel role remained important as the enemy had protected infiltration routes with an extensive AAA network.

By mid-1969, the 44th TFS was the only squadron within the 388th TFW flying the F-105 as its sister units had re-equipped with the F-4E. This time also saw the Weasels return to North Vietnam when they were tasked to participate in attacks against air defense sites under a concept known as "limited duration, protective reaction strikes". The first of these intermittent attacks took place in June after an RF-4C was downed by AAA fire while on a reconnaissance mission over the North. From that point, the perils of the recce flights over this region brought directives that required the squadron to occasionally fly armed escort on these missions. The "protective reaction" program also saw the 44th Weasels periodically carry out strikes on enemy forces just inside the North Vietnamese border when they threatened American aircraft performing operations in Laos or South Vietnam.

In an effort to ease logistics of the remaining F-105 assets in Southeast Asia, the 44th TFS was detached from the 388th TFW and relocated from Korat to Takhli on 10 October 1969. Five days later, the squadron was reassigned to the 355th TFW to operate alongside the 333rd, 354th, and 357th TFS in a revised mission that placed a higher emphasis on strike operations. As a component of the 388th TFW, the 44th earned the Presidential Unit Citation for missions against the Thai Nguyen iron and steel works and other important industrial targets in North Vietnam during the period 25 April to 1 May 1967. In addition, three Air Force Outstanding Unit Awards with Combat "V" Device for the 44th's performance over the individual periods 25 April to 30 June 1967, 1 July 1967 to 30 June 1968, and 1 July 1968 to 15 September 1969.

In addition to the Weasel role, the 44th TFS also inherited the Commando Nail night, all-weather radar bombing mission from the 13th TFS, albeit these flights ended with the close of the Rolling Thunder campaign. Previously modified to fly these strikes, this EF-105F (62-4446) is seen returning from a standard bombing sortie in 1969. (USAF via Jerry Geer)

Another unique mission carried out by the 44th TFS was the MiG ground-control intercept jamming role in specially equipped F-105Fs dubbed Combat Martins. This post-strike view shows two Martin aircraft (63-8281 and 63-8268) and two 34th TFS F-105Ds (61-0127 and 59-1760) refueling on the way back to Korat. (USAF via James Geer)

All systems indicate readiness so a ground crewman gives the "go" sign to the pilot and his EWO as he guides their 44th TFS EF-105F (63-8327) out of its revetment for a mission from Korat in July 1969. (USAF via James Geer)

ABOVE: The 44th TFS continued to support strike operations while tasked with the Weasel mission, thus it retained a good number of F-105Ds in connection with this secondary role. This fully loaded D-model (62-4360) is seen heading for a Laotian target in 1969. (Michael Hudson via Paul Minert)

OPPOSITE
TOP: With no air strikes being carried out in North Vietnam during 1969, the Weasels were available to support the interdiction campaign against hostile communication lines in Laos. Here, a 44th TFS EF-105F (63-8284) is seen refueling before striking enemy positions along the Ho Chi Minh Trail. (Michael Hudson via Paul Minert)

CENTER: *THE JEFFERSON AIRPLANE*, an EF-105F (63-8302) of the 44th TFS, took its namesake from a popular rock music group of the day. It was photographed between missions at Korat on 20 July 1969. (Neil Schneider via Jerry Geer)

BOTTOM: This "buttoned-up" 44th TFS F-105D (61-0153) at Korat on 20 July 1969 is loaded with four M117 750-pound bombs on the centerline and a pair of SUU-30 cluster bombs on the outboard pylons. (Neil Schneider via Jerry Geer)

JE
153
63
153

A 44th TFS crew chief services the strike camera of his EF-105F (63-8347) at Korat circa mid-1969. (USAF via James Geer)

421st Tactical Fighter Squadron

The 421st Tactical Fighter Squadron was reassigned from the 6234th TFW to the 388th TFW on 8 April 1966. The unit's history with the Thud dates back to 1963, when it gained operational status as a component of the 355th TFW at George AFB, California. It was equipped with F-105Ds and moved to McConnell with the 355th TFW in mid-1964. The squadron made several overseas deployments before being assigned PCS to Korat with the provisional 6234th TFW in November 1965. Upon reassignment to the 388th TFW, the 421st TFS continued its combat mission in support of the war in Southeast Asia.

The spring of 1966 saw the 421st TFS engaged in systematic strikes on key links along North Vietnam's transportation system. The road and highway network to the north of Hanoi was a major focus. Important targets along this line were heavily defended, exemplified by the loss of two 421st Thuds on a strike against the Bac Giang Bridge on 23 April. Other primary targets hit during this time included air defense sites and military storage and staging areas. The highlight of this action took place on 29 May, when the squadron participated in the maximum effort strike on the Yen Bay military storage facility.

The squadron joined the effort to destroy the North Vietnamese POL supply network beginning in the mid-summer of 1966. This campaign began on 29 June, when a massive raid took place on the Hanoi POL complex. On that mission, Maj. Fred L. Tracy became the first Thud pilot to shoot down a North Vietnamese MiG. Tracy got the kill when he encountered four MiG-17s northwest of Hanoi while flying in a flight of four F-105s on Iron Hand duty in support of the strike. He took nine rounds of 23-mm fire from one of the MiGs, which pierced the cockpit and knocked out his instrument panel. Despite the damage, he executed a high G barrel role to place the MiG in his twelve o'clock position and fired 200 rounds of 20-mm, hitting the MiG about ten times.

Encounters with MiGs continued in the second half of 1966 as the squadron continued to fly missions against transportation, military, and POL targets in the North. The 421st TFS got its second aerial victory when 1st Lt. Karl W. Richter downed a MiG-17 with his 20-mm gun on 21 September 1966. He was flying in the number three position in a flight of one EF-105F and three F-105Ds on an Iron Hand mission against SAM sites in support of a large strike force directed against the Dap Cau highway and railroad bridge. At age 23, Richter was the youngest American pilot to score a MiG kill in Vietnam. He flew his 100th mission over North Vietnam on 13 October 1966 and became one of the first pilots to volunteer for a concurrent tour in Southeast Asia. On 28 June 1967, flying his 198th mission, he was shot down while striking a bridge in the southern panhandle of North Vietnam. He ejected safely, but sustained fatal injuries on landing when his parachute collapsed.

Industrial facilities were added to the list of authorized targets in November 1966, although the effort to destroy these sites in earnest did not begin until early 1967. The first major facility to fall under attack was the iron and steel works at Thai Nguyen. The first strike on the facility took place on 10 March and several more followed during the next two weeks. The 421st TFS played a significant role on the attacks against the Thai Nguyen works and other power and industrial plants during the spring of 1967. For their performance during this time, the squadron was awarded the Presidential Unit Citation.

On 25 April 1967, the 421st TFS closed out its association with the F-105 when its personnel, equipment, and resources were absorbed by the 44th TFS. In addition to winning the Presidential Unit Citation, the 421st TFS earned two Air Force Outstanding Unit Awards with Combat "V" Device as an element of the 388th TFW. The first was given for POL raids in the Hanoi area during 29-30 June 1966, and the second was received for combat operations over the period 1 July 1966 to 24 April 1967. On the other hand, the mission of bombing targets in Southeast Asia was costly for the 421st TFS during its one-year tenure with the 388th TFW. The squadron lost at least eighteen F-105s in combat and four to operational accidents.

Immediately after being replaced by the 44th TFS, the 421st designation was reassigned to TAC in a non-operational state with the 15th TFW at MacDill AFB, Florida. On 1 July 1967, the 421st moved to Homestead AFB, Florida, where it remained inactive while assigned to the 4531st TFW. The squadron was then maintained "on-paper" within the 23rd TFW at McConnell AFB, Kansas from 14 December 1967 to 16 April 1969 before returning to PACAF and gaining operational status as an F-4E operator. It temporarily served at Kunsan AB, Korea within the 475th TFW before joining the 366th TFW at Da Nang AB, South Vietnam on 25 June 1969.

1st Lts. Karl W. Richter (right) of the 421st TFS, 388th TFW and Fred A. Wilson of the 333rd TFS, 355th TFW pose at Korat shortly after each scored MiG-17 kills on 21 September 1966. At that time, Richter was the youngest pilot to record a MiG kill in Vietnam. (USAF via James Geer)

BELOW: An F-105D (62-4326) of the 421st TFS returns from a strike over North Vietnam in the late spring of 1966. (USAF via Stewart Hurd)

Armed with CBUs and Shrike missiles, a 421st TFS F-105D (59-1759) works it way northward as part of an Iron Hand flight in November 1966. While supporting Wild Weasel operations, the D-models were teamed with EF-105Fs in the hunter-killer role. (Jerry Arruda via Norm Taylor)

The tempo of the air war required ground crews to work around-the-clock to keep the Thuds ready for combat. This 421st TFS F-105D (58-1152), *Das Jaeger*, is seen undergoing night maintenance at Korat in March 1967. (USAF via Paul Minert)

A 421st Thud (62-4359) named *12 O'CLOCK HIGH* taxis for a mission in April 1967, shortly before the squadron was replaced by the 44th TFS. Unit markings on this aircraft included a red nose gear radar reflector and canopy name block, as well as red trim with superimposed white stars on the main landing gears. (Don Larsen via Jerry Geer)

469th Tactical Fighter Squadron

The 469th Tactical Fighter Squadron was reassigned from the 6234th TFW to the 388th TFW on 8 April 1966. The unit was activated within the 355th TFW during 1962 as one of four squadrons to be equipped with the Thud; however, it was not until mid-1964 that it received F-105Ds at McConnell. The squadron deployed to the Far East for three months beginning in late 1964, during which time a portion of the unit rotated to Thailand for early contingency operations in Southeast Asia. In November 1965, the 469th became the first squadron to be assigned PCS to Thailand when it moved to Korat for combat duty as an element of the provisional 6234th TFW.

The mission of flying daily against Communist targets in Southeast Asia continued upon the 469th's reassignment to the 388th TFW. Strike and armed recce missions were flown in Laos, but most action concentrated on the destruction of transportation lines, military storage and staging areas, and air defense sites in North Vietnam through the spring of 1966. The 469th TFS lost several pilots to hostile forces during this time including Squadron Commander Lt. Col. William E. Cooper, who was declared MIA after being shot down on a 24 April mission against the Bac Giang Bridge. The losses continued into the second half of 1966 as the squadron faced heavy enemy opposition over the North. During its first nine months of service with the 388th TFW, the 469th TFS lost fifteen F-105s in combat and four to operational causes. The unit's loss total for all of 1966 was second only to the 354th TFS, 355th TFW at Takhli. On a positive note, the 469th destroyed its first enemy aircraft during 1966, when Maj. Roy S. Dickey gunned down a MiG-17 during a strike against a railroad yard near Hanoi on 4 December.

Action during early 1967 was marked by the 469th's participation in a series of strikes against the iron and steel works at Thai Nguyen beginning on 10 March. Important targets hit in the spring period were the MiG airfields at Hoa Lac and Kep, the Viet Tri thermal power plant, and numerous army barracks and storage facilities. All the while, the effort to destroy critical transportation targets in the North continued, and the 469th TFS was involved in many attacks on railroad yards and bridges during the first half of the year. On a 3 June 1967 mission against the Bac Giang Bridge and adjacent railroad yards, Capt. Larry D. Wiggins downed a MiG-17 to get the 469th its second aerial victory of the war. He was in a lead flight providing flak suppression for the strike force when he encountered the MiG and destroyed it with an AIM-9B missile and 20-mm fire combination.

In July 1967, the 469th became the first F-105 unit to accumulate 20,000 combat flying hours. The heavy mission load continued into the second half of the 1967 as the war gradually expanded. Over this period, the squadron flew missions against vital targets such as the Paul Doumer Bridge, the Lang Son railway yards, the Yen Vien railroad yards, the Phuc Yen airfield, the Kep airfield, the Bac Mai airfield, and the Canal des Rapides Bridge. For a second year, the 469th TFS paid a high price to accomplish its mission in Southeast Asia as no less than eighteen F-105Ds were lost in combat and two were claimed by operational accidents. These losses combined with those previously recorded gave the 469th the unfortunate distinction of losing more aircraft than any other Thud squadron up to that point in the war.

Poor weather limited the number of missions in the far reaches of North Vietnam during the early part of 1968, but some strikes were carried out using the Commando Club radar bombing tactic. With clearer cloud conditions over Laos, the squadron flew a good number of Steel Tiger strikes against troop and supply concentrations, truck parks, and truck convoys. The squadron's diligence in carrying out its mission against the enemy was emphasized when it surpassed 30,000 combat flying hours on 13 March 1968. Since its

The 469th TFS helped pioneer many tactics of the highly successful hunter-killer mission concept while flying alongside F-100Fs and EF-105Fs during early Wild Weasel operations from Korat. This view shows a 469th Thud firing an AGM-45 Shrike at a North Vietnamese SAM site in May 1966. (USAF via Stewart Hurd)

This 469th TFS F-105D (62-4347), *Little Lois Ann*, diverted to Da Nang after a 1966 mission over North Vietnam. In June 1970, this aircraft became the third Thud to attain the 4,000 flying hours mark while serving with the 333rd TFS, 355th TFW. (Neil Schneider via Jerry Geer)

FLYING ANVIL IV, an F-105D (59-1750) of the 469th TFS, was photographed during a visit to Da Nang circa early 1967. (Neil Schneider via Jerry Geer)

Ground crews have completed their "last chance" checks on *THE RED BARON*, an F-105D (60-0422) assigned to the 469th TFS during 1967. Note the experimental triangle identification marking on the tail. (Don Larsen via Jerry Geer)

THE GREAT PUMPKIN, with Peanut's famous Snoopy character, was applied to this 469th TFS F-105D (60-0421) seen taxiing out to the runway for an April 1967 Rolling Thunder strike from Korat. (Don Larsen via Jerry Geer)

arrival in Thailand, the unit had participated in every major air raid of the war, totaling 135,000 tons of ordnance dropped on key military targets in North Vietnam.

Beginning in April 1968, the destruction of Communist targets in the lower part of North Vietnam became the primary focus for the 469th TFS after President Johnson ended bombing operations above the 19th parallel. In particular, mid-1968 found the squadron carrying out strikes against bridges, rail lines, barges, truck parks, and military storage areas in the Dong Hoi region. This time also saw the 469th spend a considerable amount of their time attacking key points along major infiltration routes in Laos. The squadron's split flying time over North Vietnam and Laos continued until Rolling Thunder ended on 1 November 1968.

In the fall of 1968, the 469th received word that it would be the first unit within the 388th TFW to re-equip with the F-4E. Fittingly, the aircraft that was responsible for flying 75 percent of the bombing missions over the North since the beginning of the war was not replaced until just after the end of the Rolling Thunder campaign.

This 469th Thud (59-1737) is loaded with six M117 750-pound bombs on the centerline and rocket pods on the outboard pylons, possibly for a Wild Weasel support mission. This photograph was taken at Korat in May 1967. (Don Larsen via Jerry Geer)

About two weeks prior to the Phantom's arrival, on 30 October 1968, the 469th TFS set another milestone by becoming the first Thud squadron to amass 40,000 combat flying hours in Southeast Asia.

The transition to Phantoms took place on 17 November 1968 under the "formation asset" program that saw the 40th TFS, 33rd TFW work-up in the F-4E at Eglin AFB, Florida and transfer to Southeast Asia as the new 469th TFS. During the week preceding the 40th's arrival at Korat, the 469th's aircraft and aircrews were dispersed to the remaining Thud units in Thailand. During 1968, the squadron lost seven F-105Ds to hostile fire and three to operational causes.

While operating the F-105 with the 388th TFW, the 469th TFS earned one Presidential Unit Citation and numerous Air Force Outstanding Unit Awards with Combat "V" Device. The Presidential Unit Citation was given for the squadron's role in the destruction of the Thai Nguyen industrial facility and other targets in North Vietnam over the period 10 March to 1 May 1967. One Outstanding Unit Award was given for the 469th's participation on POL strikes in the immediate Hanoi area during 29-30 June 1966, while three others were received for performance over individual periods 1 July 1966 to 30 June 1967, 1 July 1967 to 30 June 1968, and 1 July 1968 to 15 September 1969. The latter award noted a period during which time the squadron flew both the F-105 and F-4.

An F-105D (60-5376) of the 469th TFS leaves the tanker after refueling on the way back to Korat following a strike in North Vietnam during the final weeks of the Rolling Thunder campaign. The JV tail code was added in late 1967. (USAF via James Geer)

Like its sister units within the 388th TFW, the 469th TFS followed the practice of applying its squadron color of green to the nose gear radar reflector and canopy name block to differentiate its aircraft before tail codes came into use. *MR. TOAD*, an F-105D (59-1749) preparing to depart Korat for a mission in the early summer of 1967, displays these discreet unit markings. (Don Larsen via James Geer)

560th Tactical Fighter Squadron

The 560th Tactical Fighter Squadron was activated within the 388th TFW at McConnell on 1 October 1962 and was the sole unit of the four squadrons activated on that date to immediately assume operations. The squadron initially trained as an operational unit in F-100Ds before converting to F-105Ds during late 1963. The unit was working on obtaining a combat-ready rating in the Thunderchief when the 388th TFW was inactivated and replaced by the 23rd TFW at McConnell on 8 February 1964. The 560th TFS was reassigned to the new wing without a change in mission status.

561st/562nd/563rd Tactical Fighter Squadrons

The 561st, 562nd, and 563rd Tactical Fighter Squadrons were activated within the 388th TFW at McConnell on 1 October 1962. Unlike their sister unit, the 560th TFS, the squadrons did not gain operational status until 30 June 1963. They were equipped with F-105Ds and primarily spent the second half of 1963 training with the 4520th CCTW at Nellis AFB, Nevada. On 8 February 1964, the squadrons received a new assignment when the 23rd TFW replaced and 388th TFW as the parent organization at McConnell.

Detachment 1, 561st Tactical Fighter Squadron

Detachment 1, 561st Tactical Fighter Squadron was formed at McConnell on 6 April 1972, when the 561st TFS, 23rd TFW split into Advance and Rear echelons after being ordered to Southeast Asia in the build-up of air power following the North Vietnamese Easter invasion. As the Advance echelon, Detachment 1, 561st TFS deployed twelve F-105Gs to Korat over the five-day period 7-12 April under Operation Constant Guard I. Upon arrival, the unit was placed under the operational control of the 388th TFW and commenced combat operations in support of the renewed bombing of North Vietnam.

The addition of Detachment 1, 561st TFS at Korat brought much needed relief to the mission load of the 17th WWS, which was the sole Weasel unit in Southeast Asia when the bombing of the North resumed under Operation Freedom Train on 6 April 1972. During the detachment's first month on station, it suppressed SAM and radar controlled AAA sites for strike forces carrying out attacks in the southern panhandle of North Vietnam. In addition, the unit flew a number of missions in support of Freedom Porch Bravo strikes against military storage facilities and POL dumps in the Hanoi and Thanh Hoa region. Early operations over the North cost the detachment one aircraft and its crew when an F-105G flown by Captains Alan P. Mateja and Orvin C. Jones, Jr. was shot down by a SAM on 15 April.

These Detachment 1, 561st TFS aircraft are seen parked at Korat shortly after arriving on their Constant Guard I deployment on 12 April 1972; combat missions began on the same date. (Don Logan via Jerry Geer)

On 10 May 1972, Detachment 1, 561st TFS began supporting a wider war against North Vietnam under Operation Linebacker. It carried out its Weasel role by flying both standard and hunter-killer Iron Hand missions in support of strikes against war related resources and lines of communication throughout North Vietnam. With nearly 300 SAM sites scattered throughout the North and 1,500 AAA sites defending the high valued targets, the detachment's mission and operational tempo was demanding throughout the summer of 1972. By early September, a number of the unit's pilots and EWOs had completed their combat tour requirements and returned home. Additional crews were rotated to Korat from McConnell to reinforce the detachment's strength, but the transition resulted in a reduction of the unit's size by about one-third.

Linebacker operations concluded on 22 October 1972 after North Vietnamese peace overtures gave promise to an end of the war. Detachment 1, 561st TFS conducted its mission during the Linebacker campaign without losing any aircraft to hostile action, but one Thud was claimed by an operational accident on 17 May, when it crashed off the end of the runway at Korat after returning from an aborted mission. After the Linebacker offensive ended, the unit spent the next two months primarily supporting attacks on military positions and transportation lines in the southern half of North Vietnam. On 16 November 1972, the detachment lost an F-105G when Maj. Norbert Maier and his EWO, Capt. Kenneth Thaete, were shot down while escorting B-52s on a night strike near Thanh Hoa. Both crewmembers ejected and spent 38 hours on the ground before being rescued.

Detachment 1, 561st TFS returned to the far reaches of North Vietnam between 18-29 December 1972, when a deadlock in the peace negotiations pushed President Nixon to launch a maximum assault on Hanoi dubbed Operation Linebacker II. During the brief campaign, the unit flew Iron Hand missions in support of day and night attacks against power and industrial plants, port and storage facilities, railways and railyards, bridges, and airfields. The Wea-

A newly arrived 561st TFS F-105G (63-8342) sits on the flightline at Korat waiting to be turned around for its first combat mission. This aircraft was shot down over North Vietnam on 15 April 1972, just three days after deploying to Thailand. (Don Logan via Jerry Geer)

Two F-105Gs (63-8313 and 63-8332) of Detachment 1, 561st TFS formate on a tanker enroute to North Vietnam in June 1972. Visible are inboard AGM-78B Standard ARMs and outboard ECM pods, the latter required because these aircraft have yet to be fitted with the QRC-380 jamming blisters on the lower fuselage sides. (Richard Kierbow via JEM Aviation Slides)

sels' most challenging role during this offensive involved SAM suppression duty for B-52s on night bombing raids on the outskirts of Hanoi. The North Vietnamese fired nearly 900 SA-2s at the B-52s during the operation, but the Weasels' measures to counter the extensive SAM and AAA defenses helped limit the number of bombers lost to fifteen.

Subsequent to the destruction imposed during Linebacker II, the scale of the war in Southeast Asia greatly diminished in early 1973 with peace agreements to end the fighting in North and South Vietnam on 27 January and in Laos on 21 February. Although the ceasefires lessened the need for Weasel assets in Southeast Asia, Detachment 1, 561st TFS remained at Korat as a precaution against renewed tensions between the warring parties. The fragility of the peace agreements was emphasized by the ongoing war in Cambodia. The bombing in that region saw the unit intermittently tasked to support B-52 operations against Communist troop and supply positions. Other action saw the Weasels periodically charged to escort RF-4C reconnaissance flights over North Vietnam that monitored Hanoi's adherence with the terms of the truce.

The arrival of additional personnel and aircraft saw Detachment 1 return to a strength of twelve F-105Gs by 15 June 1973. For another two months, the unit carried out its limited combat support role until Congress cutoff the funding of military activities in and over Southeast Asia on 15 August 1973. Shortly thereafter, preparations began for the return of the detachment's personnel and equipment to the U.S. at George AFB, California, where the 561st TFS was now assigned to the 35th TFW. The redeployment was carried out under Operation Coronet Bolo IV and entailed the movement of the F-105Gs from Korat to George over the five-day period 5-10 September 1973.

During its time in Southeast Asia, Detachment 1, 561st TFS lost two aircraft in combat and one to operational causes. Decorations for its achievements included the Air Force Outstanding Unit Award with Combat "V" Device for operations from 6 April 1972 to 27 January 1973. During this period, the unit recorded 6,000 combat hours while flying over 1,900 sorties.

The mission load for the 561st Weasels remained high throughout the summer of 1972 as Linebacker operations continued at a fast and furious pace. This F-105G (63-8332), *DRAGGIN ASS*, is seen over the North on an Iron Hand sortie in July 1972. (Paul Hoynacki via James Geer)

The 561st tail code changed from MD to WW shortly after the squadron gained a new parent unit, the 832nd AD, at its stateside home at McConnell AFB, Kansas in July 1972. The new letters are displayed here by *TRUCKIN' MAMA*, a well-armed F-105G (62-4439) of Detachment 1 getting ready to taxi out at Korat for a September 1972 mission. (Barry Miller via Jerry Geer)

An airborne view of *TUFFY*, an F-105G (63-8319) assigned to Detachment 1, 561st TFS at Korat in the fall of 1972. (Paul Hoynacki via Jerry Geer)

High over Laos alongside a tanker, a Detachment 1, 561st TFS Thud (63-8265) is seen with a 17th WWS counterpart (62-4416) during an October 1972 Linebacker mission. Mixed flights such as this were rare as the two Weasel units generally flew with aircraft from their own squadrons. (Barry Miller via James Geer)

27 January 1973: the war in North and South Vietnam is over and the combat-weary aircraft of Detachment 1, 561st TFS take a well-earned break from operations at Korat. (Don Larsen via James Geer)

The bulk of the 561st TFS remained in Southeast Asia for a good portion of 1973 even though the level of fighting was a fraction of that occurring during the prior year. This F-105G (63-8292) is being serviced on the Korat ramp circa February 1973. (Don Larsen via Paul Minert)

A Detachment 1, 561st TFS F-105G (63-8351) awaits its next sortie at Korat in March 1973. By this time, the Weasels' combat role was limited to intermittent escort duty for B-52 bombing operations in Cambodia or RF-4C reconnaissance flights over North Vietnam. (Don Kilgus via Robert F. Dorr)

This 561st Thud (63-8320) was photographed over the Pacific during the squadron's Coronet Bolo IV redeployment from Thailand to the U.S. in September 1973. Three claimed MiG kills are prominently displayed on the nose of the aircraft. (Jerry Geer Collection)

6010th Wild Weasel Squadron

The 6010th Wild Weasel Squadron was a provisional unit that was activated within the 388th TFW on 1 November 1970 from the assets of Detachment 1, 12th TFS. The former unit was established in September 1970 at Korat as a result of the need to retain the Weasel Thuds assigned to the inactivating 355th TFW in Southeast Asia. Initially equipped with a mix of EF-105Fs and F-105Gs, Detachment 1, 12th TFS grew in size during October and had a complement of about twelve aircraft when it was replaced by the 6010th WWS.

Although the Rolling Thunder campaign had ended two years earlier, the Weasel Thuds were still playing an important role in the war in Southeast Asia in late 1970. In particular, they were regularly being utilized as armed escorts under the "protective reaction" program for tactical reconnaissance missions over North Vietnam or in support of U.S. aircraft performing missions in Laos and South Vietnam in the border regions. Other "protective reaction" duty saw the Weasels support periodic one-time attacks on specific targets in retaliation to North Vietnamese threats against recce aircraft.

The first major operation for the 6010th WWS was its participation in the support force for the Son Tay raid to free American POWs. The mission took place in the cover of darkness on 20 November 1970, and the Weasels' role was to draw SAM fire off the helicopter-borne assault team. The Weasels had a personal interest in the rescue attempt as 47 electronic warfare crewmembers were confirmed prisoners at North Vietnamese camps. Unfortunately, the rescue team found no POWs as Son Tay had been closed down some four months earlier due to a problem with the camp's water supply. During the mission, SAMs were launched, and two F-105Gs sustained damage from near miss explosions. One was able to make it back to Thailand and landed safely at Udorn. The other made it to Laos before Maj. Don Kilgus and his EWO, Capt. Ted Lowry, were forced to eject. After spending several hours on the ground, they were recovered by one of the helicopters from the original Son Tay assault force.

The heavy air defenses faced in the ill-fated Son Tay raid, as well as the loss of another F-105G on a "protective reaction" mission in December 1970, illustrated the enemy's vigorous resistance to any U.S. flights over North Vietnam. Over the next year, the constant challenge to American reconnaissance flights saw the 6010th involved in a series of brief campaigns against Communist air defense positions in the North. The first of these limited strikes took place in February 1971 against SAM sites in the Ben Karai Pass area. The operation was carried out under the code name Louisville Slugger and was successful in destroying several SAM transporters.

On 21-22 March 1971, the 6010th WWS participated in a more extensive round of "protective reaction" strikes code named Operation Fraction Cross Alpha. The campaign followed another North Vietnamese threat to a U.S. recce aircraft and involved armed reconnaissance and attack missions against air defense sites and war support targets in the North. The intermittent "protective reaction" strikes continued throughout 1971, and the squadron was credited

The 6010th WWS was created on 1 November 1970 from the assets of Detachment 1, 12th TFS, a unit that had been formed at Korat just over one month earlier as a result of the transfer of the Weasel Thuds from the inactivating 355th TFW at Takhli. As seen on this F-105G (62-4425) at Korat in early 1971, the squadron retained the ZB tail code of its predecessor. (Paul Minert Collection)

with supporting notable campaigns against POL facilities at Dong Hoi in September and MiG airfields at Quang Lang, Vinh, and Dong Hoi in November.

The 6010th WWS was inactivated on 1 December 1971, when it was replaced by the 17th WWS. The squadron lost three F-105Gs in Southeast Asia, two to hostile action and one to operational causes.

A lineman directs a 6010th WWS F-105G (63-8300) to a parking spot on the transient ramp at Phu Cat AB, South Vietnam on 5 May 1971. The first letter of the holdover ZB tail code served as a reminder of the unit's origin and ongoing affiliation with the 12th TFS, a constituent of the 18th TFW at Kadena AB, Okinawa. (Norm Taylor)

This uncoded F-105G (63-8339) of the 6010th WWS was photographed at Phu Cat during a visit in June 1971. (Norm Taylor via Jerry Geer)

A 6010th WWS F-105G (62-4423) takes off for a "protective reaction" mission over North Vietnam during the late summer of 1971. The aircraft is carrying an AGM-78B Standard ARM on the right inboard and two AGM-45 Shrikes on the outboard pylons. (T. Sokol via James Geer)

CHAPTER THIRTEEN

832nd Air Division

The 832nd Air Division served under the Twelfth Air Force between 8 October 1957 and 1 July 1975 as a unit responsible for maintaining a combat-ready force of tactical aircraft. Headquartered at Cannon AFB, New Mexico, the division controlled a succession of fighter wings based in the western part of the U.S. during its existence. It became associated with the Thud on 1 July 1972, when it gained control of the 561st, 562nd, and 563rd TFS at McConnell AFB, Kansas upon transfer of the 23rd TFW to England AFB, Louisiana. The 562nd and 563rd TFS were phasing down operations at the time of their reassignment and were inactivated on 31 July 1972; however, the F-105G-equipped 561st TFS retained operational status due to the vital nature of the Wild Weasel mission.

The 561st TFS first began operating the Thud when it was equipped with F-105Ds in 1963 within the 388th TFW. The unit was reassigned to the 23rd TFW in early 1964 and maintained combat-ready operations until transitioning to the F-105 RTU role in 1966. The 561st ended its training role in late 1970 and became the only operational Wild Weasel squadron in TAC when it transitioned to F-105Gs. In early April 1972, the squadron split into Advance and Rear echelons. The Advance echelon deployed to Korat RTAFB, Thailand for combat duty as Detachment 1, 561st TFS with twelve F-105Gs and nearly 200 personnel.

Commanded by Lt. Col. Richard E. Moser, the 561st TFS was still operating as a split unit when it was reassigned to the 832nd AD. The Rear echelon carried out routine training operations at McConnell with no more than six aircraft through the summer of 1972. Some of the unit's crews, aircraft, and support personnel returned to the U.S. in the early fall of 1972, but a significant portion of the squadron remained in Thailand to support the ongoing war in Southeast Asia. The 561st maintained its split unit status into 1973, and although the war had greatly diminished by the early summer of that year, additional resources were sent to Thailand to return Detachment 1 to a strength of twelve F-105Gs.

A 561st TFS F-105G (62-4427), *DAMN OKIE*, sits idle on the McConnell flightline on 9 September 1972. Lacking the ECM fuselage blisters, this aircraft had just returned from Southeast Asia for overhaul and further modification at the Sacramento Air Material Area. (Bob Pickett via Kansas Air Museum)

The anticipated end of the war in Southeast Asia and corresponding return of the F-105Gs to the U.S. prompted TAC to formulate plans to establish a new foundation for Wild Weasel operations. The 35th TFW at George AFB, California was chosen for the role in the early spring of 1973, and the 561st was the first Weasel outfit to join the wing. The squadron started its move in April 1973, when C-130Es from the 313th Troop Carrier Wing out of Forbes AFB, Kansas began transporting the unit's equipment to George. On 1 July 1973, the 561st TFS was ready to transfer its Thuds from McConnell to George, prompting it to be attached to the 35th TFW. Led by their new commander, Lt. Col. Donald R. Yates, the six F-105Gs of the Rear echelon departed McConnell on 3 July, ending an eleven-year run of active duty Thud operations at the base. Just under two weeks after arriving at George, on 15 July 1973, the 561st was reassigned to the 35th TFW.

The WW tail code was adopted by the 561st TFS in late July 1972, about one month after it was reassigned from the 23rd TFW to the 832nd AD. This F-105G (63-8296) was photographed during a refueling stop at Malmstrom AFB, Montana on 27 April 1973. (Paul Minert Collection)

An F-105G (63-8303) of the 561st TFS is displayed at a June 1973 open house at McConnell. Visible in the background is a KC-135A of the resident 91st AREFS, 384th AREFW. (Jerry Geer)

On 3 July 1973, the 561st TFS left McConnell for George AFB, California to become part of the 35th TFW. This F-105G (62-4423) was configured for the cross-country trip when photographed one day before the squadron's departure. (Bob Pickett via Kansas Air Museum)

This view shows six 561st F-105Gs in a neat line-up at McConnell on 2 July 1973 awaiting transfer to George. These were the only aircraft involved in the move as the bulk of the unit was still on TDY in Thailand. (Bob Pickett via Kansas Air Museum)

CHAPTER FOURTEEN

835th Air Division

The 835th Air Division served under the Twelfth Air Force between 24 June 1964 and 30 June 1971 as a unit responsible for maintaining a combat-ready force of tactical aircraft. Headquartered at McConnell AFB, Kansas, the division controlled the F-105-equipped 23rd TFW from 24 June 1964 to 30 June 1971 and 355th TFW from 21 July 1964 to 8 November 1965, as well as the F-4-equipped 49th TFW from 1 February 1970 to 30 June 1971. Subsequent to the 355th TFW's move from McConnell to Takhli RTAFB, Thailand, the 835th AD directly controlled several F-105 squadrons awaiting their PCS assignment to Southeast Asia. Units assigned included the 354th TFS from 8-27 November 1965 and the 421st TFS from 8-20 November 1965. The 357th TFS was also assigned between 8 November 1965 to 29 January 1966, but it was detached to the 23rd TFW during that entire period.

A close-up of the 835th AD insignia on an F-105D (60-0535) of the 562nd TFS, 23rd TFW at McConnell AFB, Kansas in June 1970. (Jerry Geer)

CHAPTER FIFTEEN

4520th Combat Crew Training Wing

The 4520th Combat Crew Training Wing was established on 1 July 1958 as a result of a major reorganization and reassignment of the training operations at Nellis AFB, Nevada. On that day, Nellis was transferred from Air Training Command (ATC) to TAC, and the 4520th CCTW replaced and absorbed the resources of the 3595th CCTW. Tasked with training pilots in the F-100 Super Sabre, the flying organizations of the 3595th CCTW were the 3594th, 3595th, 3597th, 3598th CCTS, and the 3595th ADF (Thunderbirds). Respectively, these units were redesignated the 4521st, 4524th, 4522nd, 4523rd CCTS, and the 4520th ADF (Thunderbirds). Like its predecessor, the new wing included an intermediate organization, the 4520th Combat Crew Training Group (CCTG), which controlled all flying units except for the Thunderbirds. The 4520th CCTW was assigned to the Twelfth Air Force and maintained the primary mission of post-graduate level flight training.

Another aspect of the July 1958 reorganization saw the 4520th CCTW gain control of the 4525th School Squadron (USAF Fighter Weapons School). The school, tasked with the mission of training weapons program instructor pilots, had been inactive over the last year. The reorganization revitalized the program under TAC, and the school was equipped with F-100s. Under ATC, Nellis had maintained a separate branch for test, research, and development. TAC established a similar program at Nellis during February 1959 and placed it within the Fighter Weapons School.

The F-105 entered service with the 4520th CCTW during 1960. In April of that year, the 4526th CCTS was activated within the wing to serve as TAC's training squadron for the new aircraft. The unit's first F-105D arrived at Nellis on 1 August. This was the first delivery of a D-model production variant to TAC, and in a ceremony held on 28 September, the wing formally accepted this aircraft for the command. Over 40 F-105s were in service with the wing before the end of the year. Despite the addition of the new aircraft, the wing continued its large F-100 training program. About 110 Super Sabres were divided between the 4521st, 4523rd, and the 4524th CCTS at the end of 1960.

The wing went through a series of organizational changes over the next two years. On 1 April 1961, the 4520th CCTG was discontinued, which resulted in the training squadrons being assigned at wing level. Eight months later, on 1 November, the 4520th CCTG was re-established and again assumed control of all training operations, including the Fighter Weapons School function. More significant were the aircraft realignment and training function changes during the fall of 1962. The entire F-100 combat crew training program was transferred to Luke AFB, Arizona, which in turn shifted its F-86 Allied pilot training mission under the Military Assistance Program (MAP) to Nellis. This exchange saw the 4523rd CCTS join the 4526th CCTS in training pilots with the wing's fleet of about 70 F-105s, while the 4521st CCTS transitioned to the MAP training mission with about twenty F-86s. As of this writing, it is unclear to the author as to the fate of the 4524th CCTS.

The wing's F-105 training program was slowed briefly beginning in mid-October 1962, when the 4520th CCTW was charged to support the 4th TFW in their alert duty during the Cuban Missile Crisis. At that time, many of the 4th's aircraft were rotating through the Look-Alike modification program; thus, when ordered to deploy three squadrons to McCoy AFB, Florida, the wing needed replacement aircraft. The 4520th CCTW supplied a mix of about twenty F-105B/Ds and aircrew until the crisis subsided and the alert duty ended on 29 November 1964.

The 4520th CCTG was discontinued for a second time on 1 November 1963, which again resulted in a reassignment of all flying units to the 4520th CCTW. Other significant events during 1963 included the acceptance of the first production F-105F for the USAF on 7 December and the decision to modernize the F-100C-equipped

Thunderbirds with the F-105B for the 1964 performance season. Redesignated the 4520th Air Demonstration Squadron (ADS) back in October 1960, the demonstration team's experience with the Thunderchief was short-lived. A serious accident during May 1964, as well as modifications directed as a result of the accident, prevented the unit from using the aircraft, and the team reverted back to the Super Sabre.

The 4520th CCTW lost control of the Fighter Weapons School on 1 March 1964. Now designated the 4525th Student Squadron, the school was attached to the recently formed Tactical Air Warfare Center (TAWC) at Eglin AFB, Florida for operational control without a change in assignment or location. The following year saw the school introduce weapons instruction courses in the F-105 and F-4. The growth of the program and a pending reorganization at Nellis prompted TAC to discontinue the 4525th Student Squadron on 1 January 1966. On that day, the Fighter Weapons School was established as a named unit and attached to the 4520th CCTW.

On 5 May 1965, Headquarters USAF asked TAC to review the Command's Center organization and establish the USAF TFWC at Nellis. In response to this directive, the 4520th CCTW commander, Brig. Gen. Frank K. Everest, Jr., appointed a steering committee consisting of senior officers at Nellis who organized a working panel. A local refined plan dubbed Project Sand Dune evolved and was published on 21 May 1966. The plan emphasized the need to develop forces and weapons systems for the conduct on non-nuclear limited warfare in all functional areas of tactical air operations. The TFWC was officially activated on 26 August 1966. Modeled after Sand Dune, the TFWC was organized and established as the parent organization at Nellis on 1 September 1966. As a result, the 4520th relinquished its position as the highest echelon of command at Nellis and became assigned to the TFWC.

Another major change coinciding with the formation of the TFWC was the establishment and activation of the 4525th FWW. In essence, the 4525th FWW was a new designation for the USAF Fighter Weapons School. Like the 4520th CCTW, the 4525th FWW was assigned to the TFWC. A further change on 1 September 1966 saw the 4520th ADS relieved from assignment to the 4520th CCTW and placed under the control of the TFWC.

Concurrent with the development of plans to form the TFWC at Nellis, TAC took steps to gear its F-105 training program to the support the Southeast Asian war. To meet the increase in demand for combat pilots, the 23rd TFW at McConnell AFB, Kansas and the 4th TFW at Seymour Johnson AFB, North Carolina converted to a pilot training mission during 1966. This move was part of a long-term plan to eventually reduce the size of the F-105 training program at Nellis to accommodate the establishment of the TFWC and the corresponding growth of weapons development programs through the 4525th FWW. Other changes driven by the effort to support the war involved the modification of the pilot training syllabus to place a higher emphasis on the use of conventional weapons versus nuclear.

By early 1967, the 4526th CCTS was the only flying squadron under the 4520th CCTW with operational status. The 4523rd CCTS ceased operations during the second half of 1966 as a result of the reduction in the F-105 training program. The 4521st CCTS was inactivated on 3 January 1967, six months after it had completed its last F-86 MAP course.

During the spring of 1967, Nellis was named to receive the F-111 Aardvark, and plans to transfer the remaining F-105s serving with the 4520th CCTW to McConnell were announced. In preparation to receive the new aircraft, the 4480th TFW was activated and organized at Nellis on 15 July 1967 and assigned to the TFWC. The first F-111 arrived on 23 September 1967, and five week's later, personnel of the 4520th CCTW began transferring to the 4480th TFW. Training operations in the F-105 wound down over the next several months, and personnel that were slated to remain with the training program gradually moved to McConnell. On 20 January 1968, the 4520th CCTW and all subordinate components were inactivated. On that same day, the 4480th TFW was replaced by the 474th TFW.

4520th Air Demonstration Squadron (Thunderbirds)

The decision to modernize the F-100C-equipped 4520th Air Demonstration Squadron (Thunderbirds) with the F-105B took place during May 1963. Flight testing of F-105Bs modified to evaluate the aircraft for use with the demonstration team ensued a few months later at Eglin AFB, Florida. The tests, conducted by Republic pilots and technicians, involved fitting several F-105Bs with special instruments to monitor the aircraft's vibration and fin temperature characteristics while flying in tight formations.

Nine modified F-105Bs were delivered to the Thunderbirds beginning in December 1963. The final aircraft arrived on 16 April 1964, ten days before the first scheduled performance with the new aircraft. In their final configuration, the Thunderbird F-105Bs had their 20-mm cannon and ammunition can replaced with a baggage compartment, a smoke system installed in the internal bomb bay, and landing gear and flaps replaced with those found on the F-105D. Four of the aircraft had their conventional vertical tail replaced with a special steel tail. This change was required to allow the aircraft to withstand the increased stress associated with flying in the slot position or when performing the "knife edge" maneuver.

The Thunderbirds flew their F-105s for only six shows. On 9 May 1964, Capt. Gene Devlin was killed when his F-105B broke in half on a pitch-up out of the diamond formation to land on arrival at Hamilton AFB, California for an airshow. The accident was one in a series of unrelated crashes that saw the F-105 fleet grounded for inspection and modification. Due to the modifications directed as a result of the accidents, the Thunderbird's tenure with the F-105 ended, and the team hastily re-equipped with eight F-100Ds to complete the 1964 performance schedule. The F-105Bs were returned to combat configuration and transferred to the New Jersey Air Guard's 141st TFS, 108th TFG at McGuire AFB.

This F-105B (57-5788) was equipped with special instruments while undergoing vibration and fin temperature tests at Eglin AFB, Florida prior to delivery to the Thunderbirds. Here, Republic test pilot Carl Ardrey is at the controls preparing to conduct another flight of the evaluation program in March 1964. (USAF via James Geer)

The USAF Thunderbirds execute a nice four-ship formation take-off in their new F-105Bs at Nellis AFB, Nevada in mid-April 1964, shortly before the air demonstration team carried out their first show. (USAF via James Geer)

The colorful markings used by the Thunderbirds on its F-105Bs are illustrated in this view at one of its jets (57-5814) flying in formation with a civil F8F Bearcat in April 1964. (Jerry Geer Collection)

4523rd Combat Crew Training Squadron

Having previously trained pilots to fly the F-100 Super Sabre, the 4523rd Combat Crew Training Squadron began functioning in the F-105 pilot training role during October 1962. The change in the unit's mission was due to the growth of the Thud training operation at Nellis and the corresponding transfer of the 4520th CCTW's F-100 training program to Luke AFB, Arizona. The 4523rd CCTS was the second Thud training squadron within the 4520th CCTW and joined the 4526th CCTS in operating about 70 Thuds. The unit trained F-105 pilots until early 1967, at which time it assumed a non-operational status when the 4520th CCTW scaled back to one active squadron. The 4523rd CCTS was inactivated on 20 January 1968.

4526th Combat Crew Training Squadron

The 4526th Combat Crew Training Squadron was organized and activated within the 4520th CCTW on 1 April 1960 to train pilots in the F-105. The squadron received its first Thud on 1 August 1960 and by the end of the year was equipped with a mix of 43 F-105B/Ds. Training courses began in March 1961, and the unit's program grew considerably over the next few years as the Thud rapidly entered operational service. The demand to train pilots saw the 4526th gain over 70 F-105s by mid-1961. Later, the squadron was joined by the 4523rd CCTS in training pilots with the large fleet of aircraft. The two-seat F-105F began arriving during December 1963 and displaced many of the unit's F-105Ds over the course of 1964. The 4526th CCTS trained Thud pilots until it was inactivated on 20 January 1968.

Combat Crew Training at Nellis

The 4526th CCTS started its first F-105 transition course during March 1961. Due to the aircraft's high performance and sophisticated weapons system, early pilot eligibility requirements generally called for a minimum of 1,000 hours of total flying time, of which at least 200 were required in Century series aircraft. To expedite the process of getting the new F-105D into squadron use, a two-month course was designed to familiarize pilots with basic flight, navigation, and weapons systems characteristics.

The majority of the 21 students in the first class came from the 22nd TFS, which was the first unit of the 36th TFW at Bitburg AB, Germany to transition to the F-105D from the F-100C. The course involved about 45 hours of flight time and extensive ground training. Only 5 1/2 hours of the flying time was devoted to aircraft transition. More than half of the total flying time, 24 1/2 hours, was devoted to radar navigation and simulated combat missions. The combat program included a heavy dose of nuclear weapons training and limited conventional air-to-ground weapons training. Only minimal air-to-air combat training was conducted. After completing the course, pilots took their basic understanding of the F-105 to their operational squadrons and reached proficiency in the aircraft after extensive field training.

Beginning in early 1964, pilots fresh from advanced flight school became eligible to enter the F-105 training program. Consequently, a new six-month course was developed to provide the students with a thorough indoctrination of the aircraft's flight characteristics and complex weapons and navigation systems. The program totaled 739 hours, of which 120 were actual time in the air. By the time this program was introduced, the two-seat F-105F was available and proved valuable in training the less experienced pilots.

The F-105B served in small numbers with the 4520th CCTW from the outset of the training program. This example (57-5834) was photographed at Nellis on 7 October 1960. (Doug Olson)

An early production F-105D (58-1170) of the 4520th CCTW at Nellis on 7 October 1960 displays the bare metal finish and standard TAC markings that were typical of the era. (Doug Olson)

Holding tight formations in the Thud was never easy since the aircraft was not real sensitive to adjustments in speed. Here, student pilots training with the 4520th CCTW practice this maneuver over the Nevada desert in mid-1961. (Republic via Paul Minert)

A superb in-flight photograph of an F-105D (59-1750) of the 4520th CCTW on a training mission circa July 1961. (Republic via Paul Minert)

The practice bomb dispenser fitted to the outboard pylon of this 4520th CCTW F-105D (59-1721) confirms that it has been prepared for a conventional weapons training sortie. This shot was taken at Nellis on 23 March 1963. (Doug Olson)

The 4520th CCTW received its first F-105F in December 1963 and gained a sizeable number of this two-seat Thud variant during the following year. This F-model (63-8304) in aluminized lacquer finish is seen on 30 October 1965 at the Sacramento Air Material Area at McClellan AFB, California. (Doug Olson)

Camouflage replaced the silver finish on all F-105s during the mid-1960s. As before, the aircraft of the 4520th CCTW lacked distinctive unit markings in the new paint as illustrated by this F-105B (57-5808) at Nellis on 15 March 1967. (Doug Olson)

An F-105F (62-4433) of the 4520th CCTW sits on the Nellis ramp awaiting its next training sortie on 15 March 1967. (Doug Olson)

By the time this F-105F (63-8263) was photographed at Nellis in November 1967, the 4520th CCTW was conducting its final instruction course as it was only two months away from being inactivated. (USAF via Kirk Minert)

4525th Student Squadron/ USAF Fighter Weapons School

Associated with the USAF Fighter Weapons School, the 4525th Student Squadron's history with the 4520th CCTW dates back to its assignment with the wing on 25 July 1958. Before this time, the unit (designated a School Squadron prior to 1 April 1963) was basically in a dormant state due to aircraft unavailability within ATC. Upon reassignment to the 4520th CCTW, TAC revived the program, and the 4525th School Squadron resumed the mission of training instructor pilots and managers to supervise fighter weapons programs.

The 4525th was equipped with about 30 F-100D/Fs by the early 1960s. Operational squadrons flying the Super Sabre rotated to Nellis for training by the 4525th's instructors. Other important functions performed by the school included the improvement of weapons systems in the areas of academics, operations, and training. Working closely with this aspect of the school's mission was the Test, Research, and Development (TR&D) Division at Nellis. The F-105D was brought into the school's inventory within the TR&D Division during the spring of 1962. A few years later, a training syllabus tailored for the Thunderchief was developed, and the first F-105 Fighter Weapons Instructor Course (FWIC) began on 1 March 1965. Instruction courses in the F-4 were added during mid-1965, and the school's tremendous growth helped prompt the reorganization of TAC's advanced weapons programs.

The organizational structure of TAC's weapons development programs began to evolve during late 1963. The TAWC was established at Eglin AFB, Florida on 1 November 1963 with the role of providing a link between the development of new weapons and their implementation into operational service. Accordingly, on 1 March 1964, the 4525th was attached to this organization due to the nature of its weapons development function. One year later plans to establish the TFWC at Nellis began to unfold. The pending reorganization at Nellis saw the inactivation of the 4525th Student Squadron on 1 January 1966, and the USAF Fighter Weapons School was established as a named unit under the 4520th CCTW.

On 1 September 1966, the school was converted into the 4525th FWW. The F-100, F-105, and F-4 training programs were converted into the 4536th, 4537th, and 4538th FWS respectively.

The Advent of the Wild Weasel College

The air war in Southeast Asia hastened the development of new weapons and tactics, of which many were incorporated in the advanced training program of the USAF Fighter Weapons School. The requirement to train crews in the Wild Weasel mission was no exception. The Weasel mission involved the use of RHAW equipment and anti-radiation missiles to counter the North Vietnamese SAM threat. The first appearance of a SAM in North Vietnam took place during the summer of 1965, and shortly thereafter, American aircraft began falling to the Soviet-built missiles.

The first aircraft chosen for the Wild Weasel role was the F-100F. After training under a veil of secrecy at Eglin AFB, Florida, a small group of RHAW modified F-100Fs and their crews deployed to Southeast Asia during November 1965. Although several aircraft were lost, the program was deemed a success; however, it was clear that a higher performance aircraft was needed to increase the effectiveness of the mission. The two-seat F-105F was chosen as the follow-on aircraft. Modifications of the first group of RHAW modified F-105Fs (unofficially dubbed EF-105Fs) took place beginning in January 1966. At the same time, a portion of the crews from the F-100F program returned from Southeast Asia to establish a new Wild Weasel instruction course at Nellis.

In charge of organizing the new training program was Col. Garry A. Willard, Jr. As the individual who guided the F-100F Weasel operation, Willard brought tremendous experience and leadership to the new program. The first F-105 Wild Weasel course was held during spring of 1966 and was staffed entirely by veterans of the first F-100F Weasel deployment. The first class was made-up of pilots with a minimum of 1,000 hours in the Thud and experienced EWOs from B-52s or EB-66s. For about four weeks, the crews were trained in the fundamentals of Weasel tactics and techniques in the new EF-105F before deploying to Southeast Asia in May 1966. The training course was later refined and extended as knowledge was brought back from returning crews. It developed into the core mission of the 4537th FWS and became known as the "Wild Weasel College".

Test, Research, and Development Division

Operating within the USAF Fighter Weapons School, the Test, Research, & Development Division at Nellis was part of the Operational Training and Evaluation (OT&E) Division at Headquarters TAC. The TR&D Division's primary mission was to assist in the development of tactics and techniques for all fighter weapons systems used by TAC. Additionally, the section maintained a worldwide liaison team available to requesting commands. This team presented lectures and briefings on the latest weapons employment techniques, conducted training missions upon request, checked harmonization and fire control system problems, and in general, aided commanders in attaining combat proficiency.

In line with TAC's rapid deployment of the Thunderchief to operational service during the early 1960s, the TR&D Division received a small group of F-105Ds during the spring of 1962 to assist in the development of weapons tactics and instruction courses for the aircraft. During mid-1966, the division played an important support role in the development of Wild Weasel tactics and training in the EF-105F. Upon the reorganization of Nellis on 1 September 1966, the TR&D function was transferred to the newly established 4525th FWW.

RIGHT: The TR&D Division, a unit operating within the USAF Fighter Weapons School, was equipped with several F-105Ds in 1962 to assist in the development of new weapons and tactics for the aircraft. One of the unit's Thuds (60-0531) is seen here on static display at an open house at George AFB, California in June 1962. (James Geer Collection)

With 750-pound bombs carried on the outboard pylons, a TR&D Division F-105D (59-1766) takes off from Nellis to commence its participation in TAC's Fighter Weapons Meet in September 1962. (USAF via James Geer)

The tail markings of the TR&D Division show up well on this F-105D (59-1766) at Nellis on 22 September 1962. The design consisted of a standard TAC shield and lightning bolt superimposed on a broad black and yellow checkered band with red borders that included the words *RESEARCH* and *DEVELOPMENT*. (Doug Olson)

CHAPTER SIXTEEN

4525th Fighter Weapons Wing

The 4525th Fighter Weapons Wing was organized and assigned to the Tactical Fighter Weapons Center with four squadrons on 1 September 1966. In reality, the 4525th FWW was a new designation for the USAF Fighter Weapons School, which had been a named unit attached to the 4520th CCTW. On that day, the USAF Fighter Weapons School was discontinued as a named unit and established as a named activity assigned to the 4525th FWW. Other named activities assigned to the wing were Operational Test and Evaluation and Combat Analysis. A subsequent reorganization on 1 October 1967 transferred the Combat Analysis function to the TFWC.

Instruction courses and weapons development programs previously carried out by the USAF Fighter Weapons school were organized into the 4536th FWS (F-100s), 4537th FWS (F-105s), and the 4538th FWS (F-4s). The 4539th FWS (F-111s) was assigned on 1 September 1966, but did not gain operational status until about mid-1968. Traditional weapons instruction courses were carried out in all units, but the 4537th FWS placed a heavy emphasis in Wild Weasel training.

The Wild Weasel training mission came to Nellis during early 1966, when crews from the F-100F Weasel program returned from Southeast Asia to establish instruction courses in the new EF-105F. Initially, brief four to six-week courses were developed to get crews ready for combat as quickly as possible. As experience was brought back from the war, the courses expanded and eventually covered all aspects of the Weasel mission. Graduates from the 4537th's "Wild Weasel College" completed about twenty simulated SAM suppression missions and received extensive ground training in the Weasel's electronics and weapons systems.

During the summer of 1967, the 4537th FWS added the Wild Weasel/Commando Nail training course. The Commando Nail mission was developed under Operation Northscope at Yokota AB, Japan during the spring of 1967. Northscope involved the modification of a small number of EF-105Fs (and later several standard F-105Fs) to enable them to carry out night, all-weather radar bombing missions over North Vietnam. Initially, crews selected for the mission were not Weasel qualified even though they would be flying modified EF-105Fs. After training at Yokota, they deployed to Thailand for combat duty. The program struggled from the outset, and a subsequent review of the tactics called for all Commando Nail crews to be Weasel qualified. The 4537th's graduated its first Wild Weasel/Commando Nail class with four aircrews on 19 August 1967.

On 28 January 1968, six EF-105Fs from the 4537th FWS departed Nellis for Osan AB, Korea following the North Korean seizure of the USS *Pueblo*. The deployment was code named Combat Fox and was part of the build-up of tactical air power in Korea under Operation Coronet Wasp. The order was unusual for a noncombat squadron, but the 4537th had the only Weasel Thuds in the USAF inventory that were not tied up in the war in Southeast Asia. The crews (a mix of instructors and new graduates of the Weasel College) sat on high alert at Osan until May 1968, but engaged no enemy. After tensions subsided, a portion of the crews and aircraft were reassigned to the 12th TFS, 18th TFW at Kadena AB, Okinawa, while others were either sent to Southeast Asia or returned to the U.S.

The 4537th FWS added three T-39F Wild Weasel trainers to its fleet during 1968. These specially modified aircraft carried all the electronics found on the Weasel Thuds and were used to train EWOs during the early phase of the instruction program. That year also saw the beginning of development and training with the new AGM-78A Standard ARM. By 1969, additional upgrades to the aircraft's RHAW system and modifications that allowed the Weasel Thuds to fire the AGM-78B brought the arrival of the F-105G.

The 4525th FWW was inactivated on 15 October 1969. On that day, the 57th FWW was activated at Nellis, and all functions, personnel, and equipment of the 4525th were assigned to the new wing. In accordance with the change, the 4536th, 4537th, 4538th, and 4539th FWS were redesignated the 65th, 66th, 414th, and 422nd FWS respectively.

A 4537th FWS EF-105F (63-8340) taxis out for take-off at Nellis in late 1967. Note the thin stripe below the checkered tail band and nose gear radar reflector were painted either light blue or red to reflect assignment to the Wild Weasel training program or Test and Evaluation function respectively. (USAF via Kirk Minert)

Lacking unit markings, this 4537th FWS EF-105F (63-8296) is seen at Hickam AB, Hawaii on 29 January 1968 during an intermediate servicing stop enroute to Osan AB, Korea under Operation Coronet Wasp/Combat Fox, a mobilization in response to the Pueblo Incident. (USAF via James Geer)

Several F-105Ds were allocated to the 4537th for use in the squadron's weapons development program. This example (60-0432) was shot at Nellis on 13 March 1968. (Doug Olson)

ABOVE: Graduates of the "Wild Weasel College" were immediately sent to Southeast Asia to join combat units in Thailand. The EF-105F (63-8333) seen here at Nellis on 13 March 1968 was one of about twelve aircraft used by the 4537th FWS to train new Weasel crews. (Doug Olson)

OPPOSITE

TOP: Parked on the Nellis ramp in April 1968, this 4537th FWS EF-105F (63-8304) in reverse camouflage is carrying an inert Shrike missile for its next training sortie. (Duane Kasulka via Jerry Geer)

CENTER: The 4537th provided Wild Weasel/Commando Nail qualified crews with dedicated instruction courses starting in the early summer of 1967. Equipped to perform both of these specialized missions, this aircraft (62-4419) was on strength with the squadron for test work when photographed at Nellis in April 1968. (Duane Kasulka via Jerry Geer)

BOTTOM: An F-105D (60-0432) of the 4537th FWS displays a recently applied WC tail code while appearing at an October 1968 airshow. In connection with their role in the test mission area, all of the squadron's D-models carried a red stripe below the checkered tail band. (Jerry Geer)

8304

4419

WC
432

Seen at Nellis on 30 November 1968, this EF-105F (62-4438) was another aircraft assigned to the Test and Evaluation function of the 4537th FWS. (T. Coxall via James Geer)

The aircraft of the 4537th FWS were known for their immaculate appearance, as exemplified by this EF-105F (63-8304) depicted at an airshow in May 1969. (Jerry Geer)

CHAPTER SEVENTEEN

6234th Tactical Fighter Wing

The 6234th Tactical Fighter Wing was established under the Thirteenth Air Force on 5 April 1965 as a provisional unit responsible for the management of combat operations at Korat RTAFB, Thailand. Its primary function was to provide a central command for F-105 units operating on a TDY basis out of Korat in support of the air war in Southeast Asia. From its activation through the late fall of 1965, the wing administered an increasing number of combat missions against lines of communication and military targets in North Vietnam. Squadrons that were attached to the 6234th TFW during that time included the 12th TFS from 15 June to 25 August 1965; 44th TFS from 21 April to 23 June 1965 and 19-29 October 1965; 67th TFS from 5-26 April 1965 and 16 August to 23 October 1965; 354th TFS from 5 April to 12 June 1965; and the 357th TFS from 12 June to 8 November 1965.

November 1965 was a transition month for the 6234th TFW as the air war had escalated to the point that the USAF decided to phase-out the rotation of F-105 squadrons into the combat theater in favor of moving stateside units PCS to bases in Thailand. Moving to Korat for assignment with the 6234th TFW were the 421st and 469th TFS, both having previously been a part of the 355th TFW at McConnell AFB, Kansas. Also arriving at Korat in November and placed under the control of the 6234th TFW was a detachment of F-100F Wild Weasels that deployed from Eglin AFB, Florida to test newly installed RHAW equipment against the North Vietnamese SAM threat.

With its two permanently assigned F-105 squadrons, the 6234th TFW continued to support the Rolling Thunder campaign by hitting army barracks, ammo storage depots, air defense sites, and transportation related targets. A good number of missions were flown in the far reaches of North Vietnam, where the two rail lines between Hanoi and the Chinese border came under attack. Between 25 December 1965 and 30 January 1966, President Johnson suspended the bombing of North Vietnam in the hope that Hanoi would step to the negotiating table. During this bombing halt, combat operations for the wing primarily consisted of flying strike and armed recce missions along the Ho Chi Minh Trail in Laos.

With the peace gesture all but ignored by Hanoi, Johnson launched another phase of Rolling Thunder beginning on 31 January 1966. Destroyed supply lines that had been rebuilt by the North Vietnamese during the bombing pause were some of the first targets to come under attack. Over the next two months, the tempo of operations gradually increased and the expansion of the air war brought plans to establish a new parent organization at Korat in anticipation of moving additional F-105 squadrons to the base. As a result, the 6234th TFW was discontinued on 8 April 1966 and replaced by the 388th TFW. Commanders of the 6234th TFW during its one-year existence were Col. William D. Ritchie, Jr. (5 April 1965) and Col. Monroe S. Sams (14 December 1965).

421st Tactical Fighter Squadron

The 421st Tactical Fighter Squadron was reassigned from the 835th AD to the provisional 6234th TFW on 20 November 1965. The unit began flying F-105Ds in early 1963, when it gained operational status within the 355th TFW at George AFB, California. The 421st moved to McConnell AFB, Kansas with the 355th TFW in mid-1964 and made several overseas deployments over the next year, including a four-month rotational assignment to Kadena AB, Okinawa. Here, the squadron backed-up 18th TFW units on TDY in Southeast Asia and eventually rotated crews to Korat for combat duty. When the 355th TFW moved to Thailand on 8 November 1965, the 421st TFS was temporarily reassigned to the 835th AD pending its PCS move from McConnell to Korat.

These 421st TFS F-105Ds (62-4409 and 61-0095) are seen passing through Yokota AB, Japan on their way to Korat RTAFB, Thailand in November 1965. The haste to get the squadron to Southeast Asia resulted in many aircraft deploying with all or part of their old 355th TFW tail markings still in place. (Yukio Enomoto)

Upon arrival of the first group of personnel on or about 21 November 1965, the 421st TFS gained control of a number of Thuds that were already present at the base. A portion of the unit's pilots had to ferry F-105s from the U.S. to Thailand to give the squadron a full complement of about 21 aircraft. After receiving orientation lectures on current intelligence, rules of engagements, and local flying conditions, the 421st TFS commenced combat operations in support of the Rolling Thunder campaign against North Vietnam. In addition to flying strike missions against military and transportation targets, the unit was tasked to support early F-100F Wild Weasel operations against SAM sites. Notable missions during the squadron's first month of action involved attacks on several major bridges northeast of Hanoi including the Cao Nung, the Lang Luong, and the Bac Can.

The squadron lost is first aircraft on 21 December, when one of its F-105Ds crashed in Laos after being hit by enemy fire while flying an armed recce mission in North Vietnam. The pilot ejected safely and was rescued. Four days later, on 25 December, the U.S. suspended air operations over the North in an attempt to lure Hanoi's leadership to negotiations. For the next 37 days, the 421st TFS primarily flew supply interdiction missions in Laos while the U.S. waited for a positive response from the North Vietnamese. The 421st returned to North Vietnam on 31 January 1966, when Rolling Thunder resumed after Hanoi formally rejected the peace overture.

Over the next two months, the 421st TFS destroyed bridges, rail lines, highways, airfields, and ammo storage areas in support of the war in the North. Bad weather during much of this period saw the unit conduct many radar strikes with B-66 pathfinder aircraft. Missions also continued in Laos, and operations in that region accounted for the first loss of 1966, when an F-105D was downed by enemy fire while operating against Communist positions along the Ho Chi Minh Trail on 26 February. For a second time, the pilot exited the aircraft and was recovered. Just under one month later, on 24 March, the squadron lost its first pilot when Capt. Robert E. Bush was killed while on a Rolling Thunder strike mission in North Vietnam.

An F-105D (59-1823) of the 421st TFS enroute to a target in North Vietnam, as it approaches a KC-135 tanker for aerial refueling. This photograph was taken in early December 1965, shortly after the squadron commenced combat operations as an element of the provisional 6234th TFW. (USAF via James Geer)

On 8 April 1966, the 421st TFS received a new assignment when the 388th TFW replaced the provisional 6234th TFW as the parent organization at Korat. Decorations earned by the 421st while serving with the 6234th TFW included the Presidential Unit Citation for combat operations over the period 20 November 1965 to 8 April 1966.

469th Tactical Fighter Squadron

The 469th Tactical Fighter Squadron was reassigned from the 355th TFW to the provisional 6234th TFW on 8 November 1965, making it the first F-105 unit to be deployed on a PCS basis in Thailand. The squadron started operating F-105Ds within the 355th TFW at McConnell AFB, Kansas in mid-1964. It deployed to the Far East later that year and eventually rotated aircraft and crews to Thailand for early contingency operations in Southeast Asia. After returning home, the 469th spent a good portion of 1965 ferrying F-105s between the U.S. and Thailand before returning to combat-ready operations in preparation for its move to Korat.

The unit arrived at Korat by military transport on 15 November 1965 and gained control of about 21 F-105Ds that had been operating with previous TAC and PACAF squadrons on temporary assignment in Thailand. Led by their commander, Lt. Col. William E. Cooper, the 24 pilots of the 469th TFS were a veteran group with an average of 1,500 flying hours per pilot, with over 1,000 of those hours being in jet fighters. Since the 469th was manned with pilots from other Thud squadrons in mid-1964, most had flown the aircraft for more than two years before arriving PCS at Korat.

The 469th lost its first aircraft and pilot when it began combat operations in support of the Rolling Thunder campaign on 16 November 1965. Capt. Donald G. Green was killed when he crashed at sea after a SAM hit his F-105 while on a mission in the Haiphong Harbor area. A second aircraft was lost over North Vietnam on 18

Seen at Korat on 14 November 1965, this F-105D (62-4334) was one of the aircraft inherited by the 469th TFS when it deployed on a PCS basis to Southeast Asia. Derived from the 36th TFS at Yokota, this Thud had been carrying out augmentation duty with the provisional 6234th TFW prior to the 469th's arrival. (USAF via James Geer)

Two F-105s from the 469th TFS return from a strike over North Vietnam in the early spring of 1966, each having jettisoned their external fuel tanks during the mission. Note the near aircraft (59-1769) still retains the markings from its previous assignment with the 355th TFW at McConnell AFB, Kansas. (Jim Heston via Robert F. Dorr)

November, but the pilot ejected and was recovered by helicopter. No additional losses were incurred while the squadron carried out missions against military targets and lines of communication in the North until operations in that region were suspended on Christmas Eve 1965.

After spending just over one month striking targets in Laos and South Vietnam, the 469th TFS returned to North Vietnam when Rolling Thunder resumed on 31 January 1966. On the opening day of the renewed campaign, the unit lost another pilot when Capt. Eugene "David" Hamilton was listed MIA after his F-105 was downed by 37-mm AAA fire near Vinh. The renewed bombing was plague by bad weather from the outset, and radar bombing techniques were used when visual attacks were not possible. In March, the squadron played a significant role in restricting the movement of enemy supplies and ammunition by flying a large number of interdiction strikes on the Barthelmy and Mu Gia passes near the North Vietnamese-Laotian border. The 469th lost two more Thuds in combat over the North on 7 and 23 March, but in each downing the pilot ejected and was rescued.

The 469th's tenure as an element of the provisional 6234th TFW ended when the 388th TFW replaced the former wing as the parent organization at Korat on 8 April 1966. During its time with the 6234th TFW, the squadron lost two pilots and five aircraft in combat. Awards received included the Presidential Unit Citation for outstanding combat performance over the period 8 November 1965 to 8 April 1966.

CHAPTER EIGHTEEN

6235th Tactical Fighter Wing

The 6235th Tactical Fighter Wing was established under the 2nd AD on 8 April 1965 as a provisional unit responsible for the management of combat operations at Takhli RTAFB, Thailand. In this role, the wing controlled all F-105 and RB-66 units operating on a TDY basis out of Takhli in support of the air war in Southeast Asia. Squadrons serving with the wing carried out strike, armed reconnaissance, close air support, and electronic warfare missions in Laos and North Vietnam. The 6235th TFW was discontinued on 8 November 1965 when the 355th TFW was transferred PCS to Takhli from McConnell AFB, Kansas.

F-105 squadrons attached to the 6235th TFW included the 35th TFS from 4 May to 26 June 1965 and 19 October to 8 November 1965; 36th TFS from 10 April to 4 May 1965 and 26 August to 28 October 1965; 80th TFS from 27 June to 26 August 1965; 334th TFS from 2 September to 8 November 1965; 562nd TFS from 13 August to 8 November 1965; and the 563rd TFS from 10 April to 15 August 1965. RB-66 units attached to the wing included a detachment from the 9th TRS from circa 15 July to 20 October 1965 and the 41st TRS from 20 October to 8 November 1965.

CHAPTER NINETEEN

Air Force Reserve

457th Tactical Fighter Squadron

506th Tactical Fighter Group/ 301st Tactical Fighter Wing

The 457th Tactical Fighter Squadron was activated on 8 July 1972 at Carswell AFB, Texas. Equipped with F-105D Thunderstick II aircraft and several F-105Fs, the squadron was initially assigned to the 506th TFG, a subordinate unit of the 301st TFW. On 25 March 1973, the 506th TFG was discontinued, and the 457th TFS began reporting directly to the 301st TFW. Throughout the 1970s, the 457th carried out routine training operations and maintained the capability to deploy aircraft and personnel as required for combat operations. The squadron's mobility was put to the test when it deployed overseas to Norvenich AB, West Germany between 12-27 August 1977 for training with Luftwaffe units. In 1981, the unit added several standard F-105Ds to augment its fleet of Thunderstick II aircraft. The 457th TFS started to phase-out its Thuds in favor of the F-4D Phantom II in late 1981 and completed the transition process early in the following year.

BELOW: An F-105D Thunderstick II (61-0075) on the transient ramp at Kelly AFB, Texas on 29 October 1972 shows the early markings of the 457th TFS. The TH tail code stood for "Texas Humpbacks", in reference to the enlarged dorsal fairing of its aircraft. (Norm Taylor via James Geer)

Thuds line the 457th TFS flightline in this view taken at Carswell AFB, Texas in June 1973. (Jerry Geer)

This 457th TFS F-105D Thunderstick II (60-0528) at Carswell in June 1973 is fitted with a practice bomb dispenser for its next training sortie. (Jerry Geer)

The 457th TFS gained experience in the NATO operational environment when it deployed to Germany to train with Luftwaffe units in August 1977. Here, two F-105D Thunderstick IIs (61-0044 and 60-0533) and an F-104G of JBG 31 return to Norvenich AB after a practice bombing mission. (Paul Minert Collection)

The tri-colored tail band on this 457th Thud (60-0471) indicated its assignment to the commander of the squadron's upper echelon, the 301st TFW. This photograph was taken at Carswell on 27 September 1978. (Jerry Geer Collection)

In early 1981, a small number of standard F-105Ds were added to the 457th's roster. This example (62-4299) is seen at Carswell on 19 March 1981. (Charles Stewart via Paul Minert)

This F-105F (63-8261) at Carswell in 1981 was one of several that served with the 457th TFS for training purposes. (Jim Goodall via James Geer)

Seen at Buckley ANGB, Colorado in August 1981, this F-105D Thunderstick II (61-0096) displays the wraparound camouflage that began appearing on some of the 457th TFS aircraft during that year. (Paul Minert Collection)

465th Tactical Fighter Squadron

507th Tactical Fighter Group/ 301st Tactical Fighter Wing

The 465th Tactical Fighter Squadron was activated on 20 May 1972 at Tinker AFB, Oklahoma. Equipped with F-105D/Fs, the squadron initially reported to 507th TFG, which was a subordinate unit of the 442nd Tactical Airlift Wing until being reassigned to the 301st TFW at Carswell AFB, Texas on 25 July 1972. The 465th began reporting directly to the 301st TFW when its parent group was inactivated on 25 March 1973. About 2 1/2 years later, on 17 October 1975, the 507th TFG was reactivated under the 301st TFW and regained control of the 465th TFS. For more than seven years, the 465th maintained a peacetime readiness posture in its F-105s. Notable accomplishments during its time of flying the Thud include a major contribution to the first AFRES involvement in Red Flag during the fall of 1976 and an overseas deployment to Norvenich AB, West Germany with the 457th TFS, 301st TFW between 12-27 August 1977. The squadron exchanged its Thuds for F-4Ds in fall of 1980.

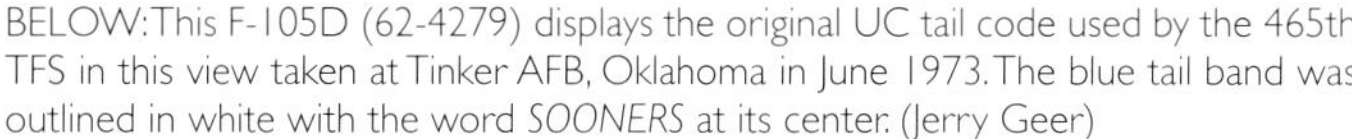

BELOW: This F-105D (62-4279) displays the original UC tail code used by the 465th TFS in this view taken at Tinker AFB, Oklahoma in June 1973. The blue tail band was outlined in white with the word *SOONERS* at its center. (Jerry Geer)

Also carrying the early markings of the 465th TFS, this F-105F (63-8331) was photographed during a cross-country refueling stop on 12 June 1973. (Paul Minert Collection)

Around the fall of 1973, the 465th TFS tail code changed to SH and the *SOONERS* script was removed from the tail band. The revised markings are illustrated by this F-105D (61-0152) pictured at NAS Miramar, California in September 1975. (James Geer Collection)

An F-105D (61-0069) of the 465th TFS sits ready for its next training sortie at Tinker in April 1976. This aircraft downed a North Vietnamese MiG-17 on 3 June 1967 while being flown by Capt. Larry D. Wiggins of the 469th TFS, 388th TFW. (Jerry Geer)

A 465th TFS F-105F (63-8365) prepares for a mission at Norvenich AB during a joint AFRES operation that saw a portion of the unit deploy overseas to Germany with the F-105D Thunderstick II-equipped 457th TFS from Carswell AFB, Texas. (Jerry Geer Collection)

Technicians service an F-105F (63-8287) of the 465th TFS at Tinker on 25 May 1978. Later transferred to the 466th TFS, this aircraft was one of the last Thuds to be retired from service in a ceremony at Hill AFB, Utah on 25 February 1984. (Bob Niedermeier via James Geer)

This pair of 465th TFS F-105Ds (62-4375 and 61-0146) was photographed while transient at Forbes Field, Topeka, Kansas on 23 October 1979. (Jerry Geer)

In the twilight of its service with the 465th TFS, this F-105D (61-0088) is seen taxiing past a row of 466th TFS F-105Bs during a tactical bombing and gunnery competition between AFRES Thud squadrons at Tinker in April 1980. (Jack Keefer via James Geer)

466th Tactical Fighter Squadron

508th Tactical Fighter Group/ 301st Tactical Fighter Wing/ 419th Tactical Fighter Wing

The 466th Tactical Fighter Squadron was activated on 1 January 1973 at Hill AFB, Utah. It was equipped with F-105Bs upon activation and retained this Thud variant as its primary mission aircraft until converting to F-105D/Fs in 1980. The squadron was initially assigned to the 508th TFG, which reported to the 301st TFW at Carswell AFB, Texas. On 25 March 1973, the 508th TFG was inactivated, and the 466th TFS began reporting directly to the 301st TFW. The 508th TFG was reactivated at Hill on 17 October 1975 and regained control of the 466th TFS as an intermediary in the chain of command to the 301st TFW. The 466th's association with the 301st TFW ended when the 508th TFG was discontinued on 1 October 1982, and the command structure at Hill was upgraded to wing status as the 419th TFW.

Notable events during the squadron's eight-year run of operating the F-105B included two deployments to NAS Barbers Point, Hawaii. The first took place in January 1978 under the name Coronet Crane and saw ten aircraft deployed for various forms of training, including the delivery of live ordnance. The second visit to Barbers Point occurred exactly one year later under Coronet Intake and involved the deployment of twelve aircraft for intensive training tied to the unit's Operational Readiness Inspection (ORI).

The squadron began its transition to F-105D/Fs in April 1980 and formally completed the conversion process with the departure of the last F-105B on 5 January 1981. Highlighting the unit's operations with the D-model was a deployment of eighteen aircraft to Skrydstrup, Denmark in August 1981 under Coronet Rudder. Here, the squadron took part in Operation Oksboel 81, a NATO war exercise hosted by the Royal Danish Air Force. The 466th was the sole remaining F-105 unit in the USAF by the mid-1983, although a gradual phase-down in Thud operations had started in preparation for the unit's conversion to F-16A/Bs in early 1984. The last F-105s were retired from service in a ceremony at Hill on 25 February 1984.

Initially, the 466th TFS limited their markings to a simple HI tail code as seen on this F-105B (57-5816) at Hill AFB, Utah on 11 June 1973. The squadron later enhanced the appearance of its aircraft by adding a yellow tail band outlined in black. (Paul Minert Collection)

An F-105B (57-5803) of the 466th TFS prepares to depart Buckley ANGB, Colorado after a transient stop in June 1974. That year, the squadron made several visits to Buckley to participate in a series of joint training exercises named Hot Wheels. (Brian Rogers via Jerry Geer)

This 466th TFS F-105B (57-5831) is seen during a break in operations at Hill in June 1977. Dissimilar Air Combat Training (DACT) became an important part of the 466th's routine during the late 1970s as Operation Rattler was undertaken to bring units with different aircraft to Hill to train with the squadron. (Jerry Geer)

A wraparound camouflaged F-105B (57-5838) of the 466th TFS at Davis-Monthan AFB, Arizona on 2 August 1980. Named *Xanadu*, this aircraft recorded the last B-model sortie when it was flown to Volk Field, Wisconsin for preservation on 5 January 1981. (Brian Rogers via Jerry Geer)

ABOVE: The 466th's markings generally remained unchanged when the unit transitioned to the later D-model Thud variant. One minor exception was the addition of the squadron insignia on the tail as seen on this aircraft (61-0065) at McConnell AFB, Kansas on 19 February 1981. (Chuck Stewart via Terry Love)

OPPOSITE
TOP: The transatlantic ferry flight to Skrydstrup, Denmark under the 466th's Coronet Rudder deployment for exercise Oxbol started from Westover AFB, Massachusetts, where these four Thuds are seen awaiting the long overseas trip on 14 August 1981. (Frank Carberry via Jerry Geer)

CENTER: Photographed at Andrews AFB, Maryland on 3 October 1981, *My Karma* was an F-105D (62-4301) of the 466th TFS that carried an early variation of the European One paint scheme. This camouflage finish became standard dress for USAF combat aircraft during the mid-1980s. (Frank MacSorley)

BOTTOM: This F-105D (62-4259) was shot at Travis Field, Savannah, Georgia on 4 August 1982 while the 466th TFS was participating in a fighter competition to select an AFRES representative for the following Gunsmoke bombing and gunnery meet at Nellis AFB, Nevada in 1983. (Norm Taylor via Jerry Geer)

HI
AF
62 361
AFRES
HI
259
HI

HI
301

HI
259

As the last Thud operator, the 466th received numerous requests to send aircraft to airshows during the type's final year of service with the squadron. Depicted at one such event on 8 May 1983, this F-105D (62-4299) was named *Desert Fox* in reference to its experimental tan camouflage scheme. (Ray Leader via James Geer)

A number of 466th TFS F-105Ds carried the standard wraparound camouflage scheme as evidenced by this aircraft (62-4375), captured here on 23 June 1983 while deployed to Nellis for Red Flag. (Paul Minert Collection)

Four F-105Fs were assigned to the 466th TFS including this aircraft (63-8261) seen at CFB Toronto, Ontario circa August 1983. (Yves Richard via Jerry Geer)

ABOVE: Dubbed *Star Dust 6*, this high-time Thud (62-4347) of the 466th TFS is seen at an open house at Richards Gebaur AFB, Missouri in August 1983. Upon making its last flight on 3 October 1983, this aircraft had recorded 6,730.5 flying hours. (Jerry Geer)

RIGHT: This in-flight view of a 466th TFS F-105D (62-4253) was taken in October 1983, possibly as the aircraft was enroute to Davis-Monthan AFB for retirement at the MASDC. (Chuck Hanna via Jerry Geer)

BELOW: One of the last of its type in operational service, this 466th TFS F-105F (63-8309) is being prepared for another sortie at Hill on 25 October 1983. (Keith Svendsen via Paul Minert)

CHAPTER TWENTY

Air National Guard

New Jersey ANG

119th Tactical Fighter Squadron
177th Tactical Fighter Group

The 119th Tactical Fighter Squadron traces its roots back to September 1917, when it came into existence as the 119th Aero Squadron at Hampton, Virginia. It served as an active duty training squadron during World War I before being demobilized in May 1919. The unit was reactivated in January 1930 and assigned to the New Jersey Guard as an Observation Squadron at Newark AP with O-2s, O-17s, BT-1s, and PT-1s. Over the next ten years, the unit trained with a variety of aircraft including O-38s, O-46s, O-47s, and BC-1s. The squadron processed through a series of moves starting in March 1942 while on active duty during World War II. The 119th was inactivated in May 1944 and remained dormant for two years before resurfacing as a Fighter Squadron in the New Jersey Guard in May 1946. The unit received P-47Ds in early 1947 and operated the Thunderbolt until being re equipped with F-51Hs in 1952.

In 1955, the 119th entered the jet age when it became a Fighter Interceptor Squadron with F-86Es. A move to McGuire AFB took place the following year, and in 1958, the unit converted to F-84Fs before moving again to Atlantic City and becoming a Tactical Fighter Squadron. A switch to F-86Hs occurred in 1962, followed by a transition to F-100C/Fs in 1965. The squadron was called to active duty in January 1968 as a result of the *Pueblo* Incident and spent the next year and a half at Myrtle Beach AFB, South Carolina training Super Sabre pilots. In June 1970, the 119th TFS became the second

Heading a line-up of twelve Thuds at Atlantic City IAP in early 1972, this F-105B (57-5812) shows the minimal markings used by the 119th TFS. The practice of applying the state's name in white above the serial number was also followed by the 141st TFS at McGuire AFB. (Paul Minert Collection)

Guard unit in the state to fly the Thunderchief when it started to transition to F-105Bs. The squadron flew the Thud for only 2 1/2 years, but did manage to gain proficiency in the aircraft through intensive training and participation in readiness exercises. It began exchanging its F-105Bs for F-106A/Bs in October 1972 and completed the conversion process in January 1973.

A 119th TFS F-105B (57-5813) arrives back at Kelly AFB, Texas on 25 March 1972 after completing a mission for Gallant Hand '72, this being one of several training exercises attended by the unit during its brief run of flying the Thud. (Norm Taylor)

District of Columbia ANG

121st Tactical Fighter Squadron
113th Tactical Fighter Wing

The 121st Tactical Fighter Squadron dates its origin to July 1940, when it was designated the 121st Observation Squadron and allotted to the District of Columbia Guard. The squadron gained federal recognition in the spring of 1941 at Bolling Field, Washington and was equipped with O-38s, O-46s, and O-58s. The unit evolved into the 121st Liaison Squadron by mid-1943 and was called to active duty during World War II, flying L-4s and L-5s out of Algeria, Italy, and France. After the war, the squadron returned to the U.S. at Muskogee Airfield, Oklahoma, where it was inactivated in November 1945. Six months later, the unit was allotted back to the District of Columbia Guard as the 121st Fighter Squadron. It regained federal recognition later that year at Andrews Airfield and received P-47s in early 1947.

The unit converted to F-84Cs in late 1949 and became a Fighter Interceptor Squadron in February 1951, when it was called to active duty during the Korean War and sent to New Castle County AFB, Delaware. In line with its new mission, the squadron was re-equipped with F-94Bs in mid-1951 and operated this aircraft until it returned to Andrews in late 1952. Over the next six years, the 121st successfully operated F-51Hs, F-86As, F-86Es, and F-86Hs in the interceptor role before becoming a Tactical Fighter Squadron in November 1958. In mid-1960, the squadron began a long-term association with the Super Sabre when it received F-100C/Fs. Between January 1968 and June 1969, the 121st operated as an F-100 RTU unit at Myrtle Beach AFB, South Carolina, when it was called to active duty as a result of the *Pueblo* Incident.

By July 1971, the 121st TFS had given up its trusted F-100C/Fs for F-105D/Fs. Allocated many war veteran Thuds formerly assigned to the 355th TFW in Thailand, the squadron's early experience with the aircraft involved making repairs to the damage and associated temporary fixes received during the Vietnam War. Nonetheless, the unit attained a combat-ready rating in its allotted time and subsequently maintained readiness by following routine training directives in line with its mission as a TAC-gained unit. The 121st deployed to Europe for the two week period 23 October to 6 November 1976 under Coronet Fife, an operation that teamed the squadron with the Virginia ANG's 149th TFS, 192nd TFG to send sixteen Thuds to RAF Lakenheath, England for experience in flying in overseas environments. Five F-105Ds and a single F-105F from the 121st TFS participated in the deployment that saw crews train with various NATO forces in England and Western Europe. After flying the Thud for ten years, the 121st TFS started to re-equip with F-4Ds in July 1981 and relinquished its final F-105s in January 1982.

The Thuds of the 121st TFS carried the district's name on the tail and squadron insignia on the fuselage as illustrated by this F-105D (60-0535) at Andrews AFB, Maryland on 24 April 1973. Although not seen on this aircraft, the ANG badge was typically applied to the tail. (Jim Sullivan via Jerry Geer)

Ground support personnel service a 121st TFS F-105F (62-4413) at Andrews on 21 April 1974. Note the wing insignia was on the right side of the forward fuselage. (Don Spering via James Geer)

This 121st TFS Thud (61-0166) at Andrews in June 1974 carries a practice bomb dispenser and rocket pods for an air-to-ground training mission. (Frank MacSorley via Paul Minert)

An F-105D (60-0504) of the 121st TFS between Red Flag missions at Nellis AFB, Nevada on 29 March 1980. This veteran of the war in Southeast Asia sports two claimed MiG kills just below the cockpit. (Paul Minert Collection)

The 121st TFS deployed this F-105F (63-8357) to Red Flag in March 1980 to take advantage of the additional training opportunities provided by the type's second seat. (Brian Rogers via Jerry Geer)

Enroute to the bombing range, a 121st TFS F-105D (58-1173) formates with a KC-135 tanker during a July 1980 training sortie. (Frank MacSorley via Paul Minert)

This F-105D (60-0496) of the 121st TFS was photographed at Andrews in May 1981, just a few months before the unit started its transition to the F-4D Phantom II. (Frank MacSorley via Paul Minert)

One of the last Thud sorties to be recorded by the 121st TFS is about to be flown by this F-105D (61-0056) on a bitterly cold day at Andrews in January 1982. (Katsuhiko Tokunaga via Jerry Geer)

Kansas ANG

127th Tactical Fighter Training Squadron 184th Tactical Fighter Training Group

The 127th Tactical Fighter Training Squadron traces its heritage to July 1940, when it was designated the 127th Observation Squadron and allotted to the Kansas Guard. After gaining federal recognition at Wichita MAP in August 1941, the squadron was equipped with one BC-1A, one O-38E, one C-47, and four L-1s. Two months later, the unit was ordered to active duty as part of the World War II call-up. After several years of training at a variety of locations in the U.S., the 127th became a Liaison Squadron with L-4s, L-5s, and UC-24s. It subsequently carried out duty assignments in India and Okinawa before being inactivated after the war in October 1945. The unit returned to the Kansas Guard at Wichita in September 1946, when it was reorganized and redesignated the 127th Fighter

Squadron and equipped with F-51Ds. Just over three years later, in December 1949, the squadron transitioned to F-84Cs.

The outbreak of the Korean War resulted in mobilization of the 127th into Federal service in October 1950. One month later, it became a Fighter Bomber Squadron and transferred to Alexandria AFB, Louisiana to join other units in the formation of the 137th Fighter Bomber Wing. A switch to F-84Es in the spring of 1952 preceded a deployment to Chaumont AB, France. In July 1952, after 21 months on active duty, the 127th returned to state control in Wichita and was again assigned F-51Ds. In June 1954, F-80Cs were assigned, and the squadron's mission changed to Fighter Interceptor when F-86Ls were received in January 1958. The unit converted to F-100C/Fs in the spring of 1961 and became the 127th Tactical Fighter Squadron with their new aircraft. In January 1968, following the North Korea seizure of the USS *Pueblo*, the unit was ordered to active duty and deployed to Kunsan AB, South Korea. Here, the squadron was assigned to the 354th TFW until release from active duty and return to state control in June 1969.

On 20 January 1971, the squadron received two F-105s to start its conversion from a combat-ready unit with F-100s to the mission of training pilots to fly the Thud. The unit was redesignated the 127th Tactical Fighter Training Squadron on 25 March 1971, when it was fully equipped with eighteen F-105D/Fs. The squadron officially took over the F-105 RTU function from the 23rd TFW in August 1971, and for the next eight years, it carried on McConnell's role as the center of Thud training by cranking out crews for the Guard and Reserve. On 7 August 1979, the unit received its first F-4Ds, and on 8 October 1979, it was redesignated the 127th Tactical Fighter Squadron as it assumed both an operational and training mission with its new Phantoms. The last of the unit's Thuds had departed by the end of 1979.

Many of the Thuds transferred to the 127th TFTS were combat veterans that had previously served with the 355th TFW in Thailand. Seen at McConnell in October 1971, this newly assigned F-105D (62-4253) displays obvious signs of having carried the RK tail code of the 333rd TFS. (Jerry Geer)

This view of an F-105D (62-4361) at McConnell in October 1971 illustrates the full original markings used by the 127th TFTS. A red band bordered in white was carried on the tail with a circular style ANG badge. (Jerry Geer)

An F-105D (61-0154) of the 127th TFTS at rest on the McConnell ramp in April 1974. Note the group badge was carried on the left side of the forward fuselage just below the cockpit. (Jerry Geer)

With a practice bomb dispenser fitted to the centerline, this 127th TFTS Thud (62-4387) was prepared for a range sortie when photographed at McConnell in April 1976. By this time, the new shield style ANG badge was carried on the tail. (Jerry Geer)

The 127th TFTS operated a good number of two seat F-105Fs to facilitate the training of new pilots. This F-model (62-4418) is seen taxiing out for a mission in April 1976. (Jerry Geer)

Towards the end of the time period the 127th flew Thuds, the squadron added the state's name to the center of the red tail band as seen on this F-105D (61-0107) at McConnell in April 1979. (Jerry Geer)

A 127th TFTS F-105F (63-8288) sits silently at McConnell during a lull in training operations in April 1979. (Jerry Geer)

With the 127th's transition to the F-4D drawing near, a combined sixteen-year run of Guard and active duty Thud operations at McConnell was nearing an end when this F-105D (62-4253) was captured on 21 July 1979. (Bob Pickett via Kansas Air Museum)

Georgia ANG

128th Tactical Fighter Squadron
116th Tactical Fighter Wing

The history of the 128th Tactical Fighter Squadron dates back to July 1940, when it was designated the 128th Observation Squadron and allotted to the Georgia Guard. The unit was extended federal recognition in May 1941 at Candler Field, Atlanta MAP and was equipped with O-38Es, O-46As, and a single BC-1A. Five months later, the squadron was called to active duty and subsequently spent the next several years progressing through a succession of moves and designations. A change in identity to the 840th Bomb Squadron preceded a move to Europe in spring of 1944 for combat duty in B-17Gs with the 483rd Bomb Group. The unit was inactivated at Pisa, Italy shortly after the war, but was allotted back to the Georgia Guard in May 1946 as the 128th Fighter Squadron. It regained federal recognition in August 1946 at Marietta AB (later named Dobbins AFB) and was equipped with P-47Ns.

The unit re-equipped with F-84Ds in October 1950 after being called to active due to the Korean War. It subsequently operated out of Alexandria AFB, Louisiana with the 137th Fighter Bomber Wing for nearly two years before returning back to state control at Dobbins with newly assigned F-51Hs in July 1952. The 128th was redesignated a Fighter Bomber Squadron in December 1952, when it switched back to flying F-84Ds. In July 1955, the unit started operating in the air defense role when it became the 128th Fighter Interceptor Squadron and flew F-84Fs and F-86Ls in succession. Another change in mission took place in April 1961, when the unit was redesignated the 128th Air Transport Squadron and equipped with C-97Fs. The unit continued to operate in the transport mission as the 128th Military Airlift Squadron from January 1966 with C-124Cs. The spring of 1973 brought a return to fighter operations when the unit was equipped with F-100D/Fs and redesignated 128th Tactical Fighter Squadron.

The 128th started its conversion from its tactical air-to-ground mission in F-100s to the Wild Weasel mission in F-105G/Fs in the fall of 1978. The first Thud arrived in September, and a steady delivery of aircraft from the 35th TFW at George AFB, California brought the unit up to full strength by mid-1979. The veteran F-105s arrived for service with the 128th TFS in need of considerable maintenance, and it took the unit nearly two years to bring the aircraft up to Guard standard. Despite the maintenance challenges, the 128th was able to achieve combat readiness in eleven months after converting to the Thud. The squadron performed exceptionally well during its time with the F-105, demonstrated by the receipt of two Air Force Outstanding Unit Awards and the Winston P. Wilson Trophy for being the most operationally ready fighter unit in the ANG. By late 1982, the 128th TFS was the last Guard unit flying the F-105, although it had received several F-4Ds to start its conversion to the Phantom. The unit retired its last Thud on 25 May 1983, bringing the aircraft's career with the Guard to an end after nearly 20 years of service.

The 128th TFS Thuds carried the same sabre-toothed sharkmouths made famous by the 17th WWS in Thailand. Showing the revived design in this view is an F-105G (63-8265) arriving at Lambert Field, St Louis, Missouri for an airshow in May 1980. (Jerry Geer)

An F-105G (63-8363) of the 128th TFS while transient at Davis-Monthan AFB, Arizona on 27 July 1980. The tail markings included an ANG badge and a yellow band bordered in black with the state's name at its center. (Brian Rogers via Jerry Geer)

This 128th TFS F-105G (62-4444) had served as a Combat Martin jammer before being modified to perform the Wild Weasel mission. This photograph was taken at Nellis AFB, Nevada on 1 February 1981. (Ray Leader via Paul Minert)

A newly applied wraparound camouflage finish is displayed by this F-105G (63-8265) of the 128th TFS visiting Andrews AFB, Maryland in May 1981. (Frank MacSorley via Terry Love)

This F-105G (63-8292) was one of several 128th TFS aircraft deployed to Nellis in early 1982 to participate in Red Flag. (Ray Leader via Paul Minert)

Old warrior in a classic pose: a 128th TFS F-105G (63-8275) pictured in the late afternoon sun at Forbes Field, Topeka, Kansas on 1 October 1982. (Jerry Geer)

Seen high over southern Georgia on 14 October 1982, an F-105G (63-8316) of the 128th TFS maintains a steady course to the practice range for air-to-ground training. (Ray Leader via Jerry Geer)

Final checks are complete so ground crews "pull chocks" for this 128th TFS F-105G (62-4423) preparing to depart Dobbins AFB, Georgia for a training mission on 26 October 1982. (Ray Leader via Paul Minert)

Parked next to one of its F-4 successors at Dobbins, this F-105F (63-8325) was one of a handful of Thuds still serving with the 128th TFS when this shot was taken on 20 April 1983. (Ray Leader via Paul Minert)

The last 128th TFS Thud (63-8299) is seen at Dobbins on 24 May 1983, one day before it flew to NAS Patuxent River, Maryland for disposal. The special markings were applied to commemorate the retirement of the F-105 from ANG service. (Ray Leader via James Geer)

New Jersey ANG

141st Tactical Fighter Squadron
108th Tactical Fighter Wing

The 141st Tactical Fighter Squadron first came into existence in September 1942, when it was activated as the 341st Fighter Squadron at Mitchell Field, New York and equipped with P-47Ds. The unit took its Thunderbolts to the Pacific theater in mid-1943 and participated in a number of campaigns during World War II. After the war, the squadron flew P-51Ds and served as part of the occupational forces in Japan before being inactivated in May 1946. That same month, the unit was reconstituted and redesignated the 141st TFS and allotted to the New Jersey Guard. Almost immediately, the squadron gained federal recognition at Mercer County AP and was equipped with P-47Ds. In March 1951, the unit was ordered to active duty as part of the Korean War call-up and relocated to Turner AFB, Georgia, where it became a Fighter Bomber Squadron. It moved to Godman AFB, Kentucky in late 1951 and remained under federal control for another year before returning to the New Jersey Guard and receiving F-51Hs.

The squadron started flying jet fighters in February 1954, when it moved to McGuire AFB and converted to F-86As. In July 1955, the 141st started operating in the air defense role as a Fighter Interceptor Squadron. The squadron received F-86Es in early 1956, and after being equipped with F-84Fs in the fall of 1958, the unit was redesignated the 141st Tactical Fighter Squadron. From October 1961 to August 1962, the squadron was deployed to Chaumont AB, France while on active duty in support of the Berlin Crisis. After returning to McGuire, the unit operated F-86Hs for about a year and a half before it became the first ANG unit to fly twice the speed

An F-105B (57-5795) at McGuire AFB, New Jersey in July 1965 illustrates the original markings used by the 141st TFS. The aircraft is painted in silver lacquer, and it has the state's name with a circular style ANG badge applied to the tail. (Roger Besecker via Jerry Geer)

Also seen at McGuire in July 1965, this 141st TFS F-105B (57-5836) is fitted with a target tow system for air-to-air gunnery training. (Roger Besecker via Jerry Geer)

of sound when it converted to F-105Bs in April 1964. The 141st TFS maintained a combat-ready posture in the Thud for the next seventeen years and earned several Air Force Outstanding Unit Awards for exceptional operations during that time. The unit traded its F-105Bs for F-4Ds in the spring of 1981.

The 141st's Thuds retained the state's name on the tail after camouflage became standard. This F-105B (57-5839) was photographed at McGuire on 5 July 1972. (James Geer Collection)

Heading a line-up at McGuire in August 1976, this F-105B (57-5802) was one of at least six 141st TFS Thuds that had formerly served with the USAF Thunderbirds. Note the shield style ANG badge was now carried on the tail. (Paul Minert Collection)

Later markings used by the 141st TFS are displayed by this F-105B (57-5804) depicted at McGuire on 23 October 1977. An orange band bordered in black was painted on the tail, and the squadron and wing insignias were added to the left and right side of the forward fuselage respectively. (Paul Minert Collection)

This F-105B (57-5791) of the 141st TFS is parked amongst a variety of fighter and attack types while attending an open house at Griffiss AFB, New York in July 1978. (Ronald Harrison via Jerry Geer)

A becalmed 141st TFS Thud (57-5789) sits on the transient ramp at Davis-Monthan AFB, Arizona on 30 March 1980. (Brian Rogers via Jerry Geer)

High somewhere over the Northeast, an F-105B (57-5783) of the 141st TFS poses for the camera during a routine training flight circa 1980. (Chuck Stewart via Paul Minert)

Virginia ANG

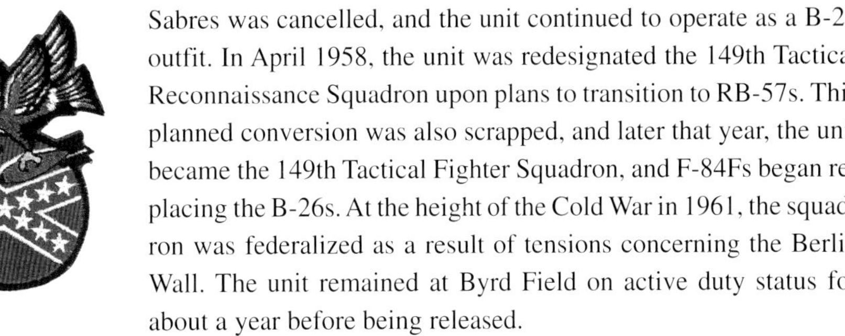

149th Tactical Fighter Squadron
192nd Tactical Fighter Group

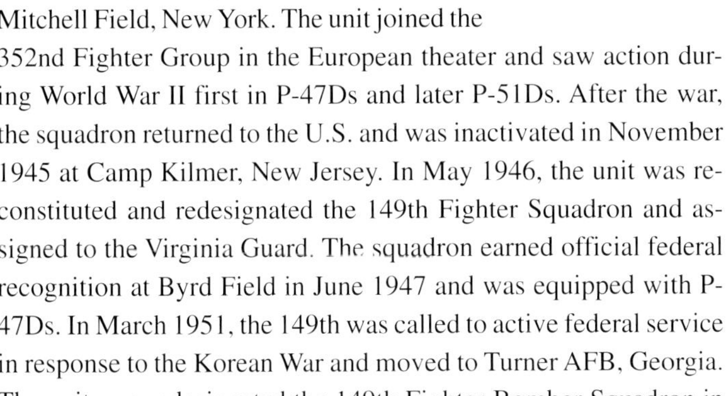

The history of the 149th Tactical Fighter Squadron goes back to September 1942, when the 328th Fighter Squadron was organized at Mitchell Field, New York. The unit joined the 352nd Fighter Group in the European theater and saw action during World War II first in P-47Ds and later P-51Ds. After the war, the squadron returned to the U.S. and was inactivated in November 1945 at Camp Kilmer, New Jersey. In May 1946, the unit was reconstituted and redesignated the 149th Fighter Squadron and assigned to the Virginia Guard. The squadron earned official federal recognition at Byrd Field in June 1947 and was equipped with P-47Ds. In March 1951, the 149th was called to active federal service in response to the Korean War and moved to Turner AFB, Georgia. The unit was redesignated the 149th Fighter Bomber Squadron in late 1951 and subsequently relocated to Godman AFB, Kentucky.

The unit returned to state control at Byrd Field in December 1952 and was reorganized as the 149th Bomb Squadron with B-26B/Cs assigned as the mission aircraft. In June 1957, the unit was redesignated the 149th Fighter Interceptor Squadron on being scheduled to get F-86Es; however, the plan to equip the squadron with Sabres was cancelled, and the unit continued to operate as a B-26 outfit. In April 1958, the unit was redesignated the 149th Tactical Reconnaissance Squadron upon plans to transition to RB-57s. This planned conversion was also scrapped, and later that year, the unit became the 149th Tactical Fighter Squadron, and F-84Fs began replacing the B-26s. At the height of the Cold War in 1961, the squadron was federalized as a result of tensions concerning the Berlin Wall. The unit remained at Byrd Field on active duty status for about a year before being released.

On 19 February 1971, the squadron received its first F-105 for maintenance training to initiate the unit's conversion to Thunderchiefs. The training was critical as the squadron inherited a fleet of combat veteran Thuds that required extensive maintenance to get them operationally ready. The unit's special tasking during the next ten years included several deployments to Red Flag live-fire exercises at Nellis AFB, Nevada and an overseas deployment to RAF Lakenheath, England. Named Coronet Fife, the visit to England took place from 23 October to 6 November 1976 and saw the squadron deploy seven F-105Ds and three F-105Fs in an operation that teamed the unit with 121st TFS, 113th TFW to send sixteen Thuds to Europe for training with NATO units. The 149th TFS started retiring its Thuds in the summer of 1981 and flew the aircraft in decreasing numbers until completing its conversion to A-7Ds in early 1982.

For a short time after receiving the Thud, the 149th TFS flirted with the simple markings displayed by this F-105F (63-8261) at Byrd Field, Richmond, Virginia in July 1972. The sole indicator of the aircraft's assignment was the state's name above the circular style ANG badge. (Jim Sullivan via Jerry Geer)

This F-105D (60-0498) of the 149th TFS, seen here visiting Greater Pittsburgh IAP, Pennsylvania in July 1972, shows the markings that became standard during the unit's first few years of flying the Thud. Note the placement of the state's name on the tail and the squadron insignia on the forward fuselage. (Jerry Geer)

The minimal markings of the 149th TFS were enhanced when a yellow band bordered in white was painted on the tail. The improved look is illustrated in this view of an F-105D (61-0134) at Byrd Field in July 1974. (Jerry Geer)

A 149th TFS F-105D (62-4384) taxiing at Sheppard AFB, Texas during a transient stop on 7 September 1975. (Robert J. Mills, Jr. via James Geer)

Poised for another training mission, this 149th TFS F-105F (63-8315) awaits its crew at Byrd Field on 30 March 1976. Later that year, the unit gained experience in the NATO operational environment when it deployed to England with the 121st TFS from Andrews AFB, Maryland under the code name Coronet Fife. (Jerry Geer Collection)

As seen on this F-105D (61-0164) at Byrd Field on 29 July 1978, the 149th TFS later revised its tail markings to include a shield style ANG badge and a black lightning bolt within the yellow band. (Stephen H. Miller via Paul Minert)

A pair of 149th TFS Thuds (62-4411 and 60-0498) holds formation over the snow covered Virginia terrain during a training sortie on 14 February 1980. (Katsuhiko Tokunaga via Jerry Geer)

Pictured at Byrd Field in September 1981, this F-105D (61-0086) of the 149th TFS featured a *KEEP'em FLYING* motif under the left intake to reflect the squadron's view of the Thud's imminent retirement from service. (Don Spering via Paul Minert)

Appendix 1: Glossary

AAA	Anti-aircraft Artillery
AB	Air Base
ABCCC	Airborne Battlefield Command and Control Center
ACCS	Airborne Command and Control Squadron
AD	Air Division
ADS	Air Demonstration Squadron
AF	Air Force
AFB	Air Force Base
AFRES	Air Force Reserve
AGM	Air-to-Ground Missile
AIM	Air-Intercept Missile
AIRCENT	Allied Air Force, Central Europe
ANG	Air National Guard
ANGB	Air National Guard Base
AP	Airport
ARDC	Air Research and Development Command
ARM	Anti-Radiation Missile
ARN	Airborne Radio Navigation
ATC	Air Training Command
ca	circa
CBU	Cluster Bomb Unit
CCTG	Combat Crew Training Group
CCTS	Combat Crew Training Squadron
CCTW	Combat Crew Training Wing
CFB	Canadian Forces Base
DACT	Dissimilar Air Combat Training
Det	Detachment
ECM	Electronic Countermeasures
EWO	Electronic Warfare Officer
FWIC	Fighter Weapons Instructor Course
FWS	Fighter Weapons Squadron
FWW	Fighter Weapons Wing
GCI	Ground Control Intercept
IAP	International Airport
IOC	Initial Operating Capability
IRAN	Inspect and Repair As Necessary
LORAN	Long Range Aid to Navigation
MAP	Military Assistance Program or Municipal Airport
MASDC	Military Aircraft Storage and Disposition Center
MATS	Military Air Transport Service
MIA	Missing in Action
MiGCAP	MiG Combat Air Patrol
Mk	Mark
mm	millimeter
MOAMA	Mobile Air Material Area
mph	miles per hour
NAS	Naval Air Station
NATO	North Atlantic Treaty Organization
NVAF	North Vietnamese Air Force
ORI	Operational Readiness Inspection
OT&E	Operational Training and Evaluation
PACAF	Pacific Air Forces
PCS	Permanent Change of Station
POL	Petroleum, Oil, and Lubricants
POW	Prisoner of War
QRC	Quick Reaction Capability
RAAFB	Royal Australian Air Force Base
RAF	Royal Air Force
RE	Republic
ResCAP	Rescue Combat Air Patrol
RHAW	Radar Homing and Warning

RS	Reconnaissance Squadron	TFS	Tactical Fighter Squadron
RTAFB	Royal Thai Air Force Base	TFTG	Tactical Fighter Training Group
RTU	Replacement Training Unit	TFTS	Tactical Fighter Training Squadron
SAC	Strategic Air Command	TFTW	Tactical Fighter Training Wing
SAM	Surface-to-Air Missile	TFW	Tactical Fighter Wing
SEA	Southeast Asia	TFWC	Tactical Fighter Weapons Center
SIOP	Single Integrated Operational Plan	TR&D	Test, Research, and Development
SOS	Special Operations Squadron	TRS	Tactical Reconnaissance Squadron
SVN	South Vietnam	TRW	Tactical Reconnaissance Wing
TAC	Tactical Air Command	TUSLOG	The United States Logistics Group
TAWC	Tactical Air Warfare Center	USAF	United States Air Force
TDY	Temporary Duty	USAFE	United States Air Forces in Europe
TEWS	Tactical Electronic Warfare Squadron	USS	United States Ship
TFG	Tactical Fighter Group	VHF	Very High Frequency
TFRS	Tactical Fighter Replacement Squadron	WWS	Wild Weasel Squadron

Appendix 2: Code Names

Air Boon Choo: Multinational peacetime training exercise held at Korat RTAFB, Thailand from 20-30 April 1964

Barrel Roll: Interdiction missions flown in Laos beginning on 14 December 1964; limited to northern Laos when southern area was preempted by Steel Tiger on 3 April 1965

Big Lift: Large-scale transoceanic Army-USAF deployment to Europe from 22-25 October 1963

Bolo: Anti-MiG sweep conducted over North Vietnam on 2 January 1967

Combat Fox: 4537th FWS, 4525th FWW deployment of six EF-105Fs to Osan AB, Korea from January to May 1968 under Coronet Wasp

Combat Lancer: Combat evaluation of the F-111A by the 474th TFW at Takhli RTAFB, Thailand from 17 March to 22 November 1968

Combat Martin: F-105Fs modified to block communications between North Vietnamese MiGs and their GCI centers

Combat Skyspot: All-weather bombing missions controlled by ground-based MSQ-77 radars

Combat Thunder: F-105D Thunderstick II operational test and evaluation program conducted by the TAWC at Eglin AFB, Florida in early 1970

Commando Club: All-weather bombing missions in North Vietnam controlled by TPQ-81 and TACAN radar site in northern Laos

Commando Hunt: Supply interdiction campaign against Communist infiltration routes in the Laotian panhandle beginning in November 1968

Commando Nail: Night, all-weather bombing missions in Southeast Asia by tactical aircraft using self-contained radar systems

Commando Nail Papa: Pathfinder missions flown by Commando Nail aircraft for all-weather strikes

Commando Scrimmage: USAF war exercises in Southeast Asia during 1974-75

Constant Guard: Build-up of tactical aircraft forces in Southeast Asia beginning in April 1972

Coronet Big Horn I: Redeployment of the 355th TFW from Southeast Asia to McConnell AFB, Kansas in October 1970

Coronet Bolo IV: Redeployment of Detachment 1, 561st TFS from Southeast Asia to George AFB, California in September 1973

Coronet Crane: 466th TFS, 508th TFG deployment to NAS Barbers Point, Hawaii in January 1978

Coronet Exxon: Redeployment of the 17th WWS from Southeast Asia to George AFB, California in October 1974; unit reorganized as the 562nd TFS, 35th TFW

Coronet Fife: Joint 149th TFS, 192nd TFG and 121st TFS, 113th TFW deployment to Europe from 23 October to 6 November 1976

Coronet Intake: 466th TFS, 508th TFG deployment to NAS Barbers Point, Hawaii in January 1979

Coronet Rudder: 466th TFS, 508th TFG deployment to Denmark in August 1981

Coronet Wasp: Deployment of aircraft and personnel to Korea in response to the *Pueblo* Incident in January 1968

Coulee Crest: Joint Army-USAF simulated war exercise held at the Yakima Firing Range, Washington from 30 April to 20 May 1963

Desert Strike: Joint Army-USAF simulated war exercise held in the Mojave Desert from 5-29 May 1964

Fact Sheet: Psychological warfare program involving the dropping of some four million leaflets weekly over North Vietnam during 1965

Fast Wind: USAF world record speed attempt in the F-105B for the 100-kilometer course at Edwards AFB, California in December 1959

Firefly: Build-up of air power in Korea due to the *Pueblo* Incident

Flying Fish: Deployment of F-105 to PACAF to equip the 8th and 18th TFW

Fox Able 147: 334th TFS, 4th TFW deployment to Europe from 1 April to 13 August 1963 for rotational alert duty

Fraction Cross Alpha: Series of "protective reaction" strikes in North Vietnam below the 20th parallel from 21-22 March 1971

Freedom Porch Bravo: Series of strikes in North Vietnam above the 20th parallel in April 1972

Freedom Train: Air operations in North Vietnam below the 20th parallel from 6 April to 7 May 1972; replaced by Linebacker I

Gate Guard: Supply interdiction campaign in southern North Vietnam during the summer of 1966

Goldfire I: Joint Army-USAF training exercise held at Fort Leonard Wood, Missouri from 29 October to 11 November 1964

Gunsmoke: USAF worldwide fighter gunnery meet held biennially at Nellis AFB, Nevada since 1981

High Flight: F-105 ferry flights between USAF bases in Germany and MOAMA in the U.S. for modifications under Look-Alike

Hot Wheels: Series of joint services training exercises held at Buckley ANGB, Colorado during 1974

Igloo White: Surveillance system used on Ho Chi Minh Trail comprised basically of sensors, relay aircraft, and an infiltration surveillance center

Iron Hand: Mission of seeking and destroying SAM and radar-controlled AAA sites

Linebacker I: Air operations in North Vietnam from 9 May to 22 October 1972

Linebacker II: Eleven day war against Hanoi-Haiphong region from 18-29 December 1972

Look-Alike: F-105D repair and modification program from June 1962 to June 1964

Louisville Slugger: Series of "protective reaction" strikes in the Ben Karai Pass area of North Vietnam in February 1971

Northscope: Modification program of EF-105Fs to carry out night, all-weather radar bombing missions

One Buck Nine: 561st TFS, 23rd TFW deployment to the Far East/ Southeast Asia from 6 March to 10 July 1965 for rotational back-up/combat duty

One Buck 10: 354th TFS, 355th TFW deployment to the Far East/ Southeast Asia from 6 March to 18 June 1965 for rotational back-up/combat duty

Optimize: F-105B repair and modification program from late 1959 to early 1960

Pacific Concord I: Multinational peacetime training exercise held at RAAFB Williamtown, Australia from 4-17 October 1965

Pocket Money: Aerial mining of North Vietnamese harbors and ports by the Navy on 9 May 1972

Polar Siege: Joint USAF-Army simulated war exercise held in Alaska from 24 January to 21 February 1964

Proud Deep Alpha: Series of "protective reaction" strikes in North Vietnam below the 20th parallel from 26-30 December 1971

Queen Bee: USAF communications reconnaissance missions over the Gulf of Tonkin beginning in 1964

Rattler: Dissimilar air combat and air-to-ground training exercises held at Hill AFB, Utah beginning in the fall of 1978

Ready Alpha: Relocation of the 355th TFW from McConnell AFB, Kansas to Takhli RTAFB, Thailand in late 1965

Red Flag: Series of simulated war exercises held regularly at Nellis AFB, Nevada since November 1975

Rolling Thunder: Air offensive against North Vietnam from 2 March 1965 to 1 November 1968

Sand Dune: Refined plan developed by the 4520th CCTW to establish the TFWC at Nellis AFB, Nevada

Sky Soldier IV: Multinational peacetime training exercise for the defense of Taiwan in October 1963

Steel Tiger: Interdiction missions in southern Laos beginning on 3 April 1965

Thundereast: 4th TFW deployment to Ramstein AB, Germany in July 1961

Thunderwest: 4th TFW deployment to Kadena AB, Okinawa in August 1961

Tropic Lightning: Joint Army-USAF training exercise held at Hickam AFB, Hawaii in the spring of 1964

Two Buck Nine: 562nd TFS, 23rd TFW deployment to Southeast Asia from 13 August to 6 December 1965 for rotational combat duty

Two Buck 13: 335th TFS, 4th TFW deployment to the Far East/ Southeast Asia from 3 July to 15 December 1965 for rotational back-up/combat duty

Two Buck 18: 334th TFS, 4th TFW deployment to Southeast Asia from 28 August 1965 to 5 February 1966 for rotational combat duty

Two Buck Charlie: 563rd TFS, 23rd TFW deployment to Southeast Asia from 8 April to 15 August 1965 for rotational combat duty

Vampyrus: Combat evaluation of the ECM pod by the 355th TFW at Takhli RTAFB, Thailand from 26 September to 8 October 1966

Whip Lash: F-105s on strip alert at Thailand bases for close air support and rapid response strikes in Laos beginning in July 1965

Wild Weasel: Tactical aircraft fitted with RHAW and anti-radiation missiles for operations against SAM sites

Yankee Team: Tactical air reconnaissance missions in Laos beginning on 19 May 1964

Appendix 3: Squadron Summary

Squadron or Det	Organizational Action[1]	Assignment	Base	Period[2]	Variant(s) and Period(s) of Operation
TAC, USAFE, PACAF					
7 TFS		49 TFW	Spangdahlem AB, Germany	10/61-02/67ca	F-105D (51-67), F-105F (64-67)
8 TFS		49 TFW	Spangdahlem AB, Germany	ca12/61-02/67ca	F-105D (51-67), F-105F (64-67)
9 TFS		49 TFW	Spangdahlem AB, Germany	ca02/62-02/67ca	F-105D (52-67), F-105F (64-67)
12 TFS		18 TFW	Kadena AB, Okinawa	10/62-05/72	F-105D (52-72), F-105F (64-72), EF-105F (68-70)
12 TFS Det 1		18 TFW	Korat RTAFB, Thailand	09/70-11/70	EF-105F (70), F-105G (70)
13 TFS	Attached[3]	388 TFW	Kadena AB, Okinawa	05/66-06/66	F-105D (56)
	Moved	388 TFW	Korat RTAFB, Thailand	06/66-10/67	F-105D (56-67), EF-105F (66-67), F-105F Commando Nail (67)
17 WWS		388 TFW	Korat RTAFB, Thailand	12/71-10/74	F-105G (71-74)
22 TFS		36 TFW	Bitburg AB, Germany	05/61-05/66	F-105D (61-66), F-105F (64-66)
23 TFS		36 TFW	Bitburg AB, Germany	06/61-06/66	F-105D (61-66), F-105F (64-66)
34 TFS	Attached[4]	388 TFW	Yokota AB, Japan	05/66-06/66	F-105D (56)
	Moved	388 TFW	Korat RTAFB, Thailand	06/66-05/69	F-105D (66-69)
35 TFS		8 TFW	Itazuke AB, Japan	ca04/63-06/64	F-105D (63-64), F-105F (64)
	Reassigned, moved	41 AD	Yokota AB, Japan	06/64-04/65	F-105D/F (64-65)
	Reassigned	6441 TFW	Yokota AB, Japan	04/65-11/66	F-105D/F (65-66)
	Reassigned	41 AD	Yokota AB, Japan	11/66-05/67ca	F-105D/F (66-67)
36 TFS		8 TFW	Itazuke AB, Japan	ca04/63-06/64	F-105D (63-64), F-105F (64)
	Reassigned, moved	41 AD	Yokota AB, Japan	06/64-04/65	F-105D/F (64-65)
	Reassigned	6441 TFW	Yokota AB, Japan	04/65-05/66	F-105D/F (65-66)
39 TFTS		35 TFW	George AFB, CA	07/77-10/78ca	F-105G (77-78)
44 TFS		18 TFW	Kadena AB, Okinawa	11/62-12/66[5]	F-105D (62-66), F-105F (64-66)
	Reassigned, moved	388 TFW	Korat RTAFB, Thailand	04/67-10/69	F-105D (67-69), EF-105F (67-69), F-105F Commando Nail (67-68), F-105F Combat Martin (68-69)
	Reassigned, moved	355 TFW	Takhli RTAFB, Thailand	10/69-12/70	F-105D (69-70), F-105F Combat Martin (69-70), EF-105F (69-70), F-105G (69-70)
53 TFS		36 TFW	Bitburg AB, Germany	08/61-06/66	F-105D (61-66), F-105F (64-66)
66 FWS		57 FWW	Nellis AFB, NV	10/69-07/75	F-105D/F/G (69-75), EF-105F (69-70)
67 TFS		18 TFW	Kadena AB, Okinawa	10/62-11/67	F-105D (62-67), F-105F (64-67)
80 TFS		8 TFW	Itazuke AB, Japan	ca04/63-06/64	F-105D (63-64), F-105F (64)
	Reassigned, moved	41 AD	Yokota AB, Japan	06/64-04/65	F-105D/F (64-65)
	Reassigned	6441 TFW	Yokota AB, Japan	04/65-11/66	F-105D/F (65-66)
	Reassigned	41 AD	Yokota AB, Japan	11/66-01/68	F-105D/F (66-68)
	Reassigned	347 TFW	Yokota AB, Japan	01/68-02/68	F-105D/F (68)
333 TFS		4 TFW	Seymour Johnson AFB, NC	12/60-12/65	F-105D (60-65), F-105F (64-65)
	Reassigned, moved	355 TFW	Takhli RTAFB, Thailand	12/65-11/70	F-105D (65-70), EF-105F (67-70), F-105F Combat Martin (68-70), F-105G (69-70)
334 TFS		4 TFW	Seymour Johnson AFB, NC	06/59-11/66	F-105B (59-64), F-105D/F (64-66)
335 TFS[6]		4 TFW	Eglin AFB, FL	05/58-11/61	F-105B (58-60), F-105D (60-61)
	Moved	4 TFW	Seymour Johnson AFB, NC	11/61-11/66	F-105D (61-66), F-105F (63-66)
336 TFS		4 TFW	Seymour Johnson AFB, NC	ca08/59-11/66	F-105B (59-64), F-105D/F (64-66)
354 TFS		355 TFW	George AFB, CA	09/62-10/64	F-105D (62-64), F-105F (64)
	Moved	355 TFW	McConnell AFB, KS	10/64-11/65	F-105D/F (64-65)
	Reassigned	835 AD	McConnell AFB, KS	11/65	F-105D/F (65)
	Reassigned, moved	355 TFW	Takhli RTAFB, Thailand	11/65-12/70	F-105D (65-70), EF-105F (66-70), F-105G (69-70)
357 TFS		355 TFW	George AFB, CA	09/62-07/64	F-105D (62-64), F-105F (64)
	Moved	355 TFW	McConnell AFB, KS	07/64-11/65	F-105D/F (64-65)
	Reassigned[7]	835 AD	McConnell AFB, KS	11/65-01/66	F-105D/F (65-66)
	Reassigned, moved	355 TFW	Takhli RTAFB, Thailand	01/66-12/70	F-105D (66-70), EF-105F (67-70), F-105F Combat Martin (68-70), F-105G (69-70)

Squadron or Det	Organizational Action[1]	Assignment	Base	Period[2]	Variant(s) and Period(s) of Operation
419 TFTS		23 TFW	McConnell AFB, KS	10/69-05/71	F-105B/D/F (69-71), F-105D T-Stick II (70)
421 TFS		355 TFW	George AFB, CA	03/63-07/64	F-105D (63-64), F-105F (64)
	Moved	355 TFW	McConnell AFB, KS	07/64-11/65	F-105D/F (64-65)
	Reassigned	835 AD	McConnell AFB, KS	11/65	F-105D/F (65)
	Reassigned, moved	6234 TFW	Korat RTAFB, Thailand	11/65-04/66	F-105D (65-66)
	Reassigned	388 TFW	Korat RTAFB, Thailand	04/66-04/67	F-105D (66-67)
469 TFS		355 TFW	McConnell AFB, KS	07/64-11/65	F-105D/F (64-65)
	Reassigned, moved	6234 TFW	Korat RTAFB, Thailand	11/65-04/66	F-105D (65-66)
	Reassigned	388 TFW	Korat RTAFB, Thailand	04/66-11/68	F-105D (66-68)
560 TFS		388 TFW	McConnell AFB, KS	07/63-02/64	F-105D (63-64)
	Reassigned	23 TFW	McConnell AFB, KS	02/64-06/68	F-105D/F (64-68), F-105B (66-68)
561 TFS		388 TFW	McConnell AFB, KS	07/63-02/64	F-105D (63-64)
	Reassigned	23 TFW	McConnell AFB, KS	02/64-06/72	F-105D/F (64-72), F-105B (66-69), EF-105F (69), F-105G (70-72), F-105F Combat Martin (71)
	Reassigned	832 AD	McConnell AFB, KS	07/72-07/73	F-105G/F (72-73)
	Reassigned, moved	35 TFW	George AFB, CA	07/73-10/79ca	F-105G/F (73-79)
561 TFS Det 1	Attached	388 TFW	Korat RTAFB, Thailand	04/72-09/73	F-105G (72-73)
562 TFS		388 TFW	McConnell AFB, KS	07/63-02/64	F-105D (63-64)
	Reassigned	23 TFW	McConnell AFB, KS	02/64-06/72	F-105D/F (64-72), F-105B (66-69),
	Reassigned	832 AD	McConnell AFB, KS	07/72	F-105D/F (72)
	Reassigned, moved	35 TFW	George AFB, CA	10/74-07/80	F-105G/F (73-80)
563 TFS		388 TFW	McConnell AFB, KS	07/63-02/64	F-105D (63-64)
	Reassigned	23 TFW	McConnell AFB, KS	02/64-06/72[8]	F-105D (64-70) F-105F (64-72), F-105B (66-69), F-105D T-Stick II (70-72)
	Reassigned	832 AD	McConnell AFB, KS	07/72	F-105D T-Stick II (72), F-105F (72)
563 TFTS	Reassigned, moved	35 TFW	George AFB, CA	07/75-07/77	F-105G/F (75-77)
4519 CCTS		23 TFW	McConnell AFB, KS	01/68-10/69	F-105B/D/F (68-69), EF-105F (69)
4520 ADS		4520 CCTW	Nellis AFB, NV	12/63-05/64	F-105B (63-64)
4523 CCTS		4520 CCTG	Nellis AFB, NV	10/62-08/63	F-105B/D (61-63)
	Reassigned	4520 CCTW	Nellis AFB, NV	08/63-02/67ca	F-105B/D/F (63-67)
4525 Student Sqn		4520 CCTG	Nellis AFB, NV	ca03/62-08/63	F-105D (62-63)
	Reassigned	4520 CCTW	Nellis AFB, NV	08/63-02/64	F-105D (63-64)
	Attached	TAWC	Nellis AFB, NV	02/64-12/65	F-105D (64-65)
4526 CCTS		4520 CCTG	Nellis AFB, NV	08/60-05/61	F-105B/D (60-61)
	Reassigned	4520 CCTW	Nellis AFB, NV	05/61-10/61	F-105B/D (61)
	Reassigned	4520 CCTG	Nellis AFB, NV	10/61-08/63	F-105B/D (61-63)
	Reassigned	4520 CCTW	Nellis AFB, NV	08/63-01/68	F-105B/D/F (63-68)
4537 FWS		4525 FWW	Nellis AFB, NV	09/66-10/69	F-105D/F (66-69), EF-105F (66-69), F-105F Commando Nail (67-68), F-105G (68-69)
6010 WWS		388 TFW	Korat RTAFB, Thailand	11/70-12/71	EF-105F (70-71), F-105G (70-71)
TR&D Div	Attached	Ftr Wpns Sch	Nellis AFB, NV	ca03/62-08/66	F-105D (62-66), EF-105F (66)
Ftr Wpns Sch	Attached	4520 CCTW	Nellis AFB, NV	01/66-08/66	F-105D (66), EF-105F (66)
Wild Weasel Det		388 TFW	Korat RTAFB, Thailand	05/66-06/66	EF-105F (66)
AIR FORCE RESERVE					
457 TFS		506 TFG	Carswell AFB, TX	07/72-03/73	F-105D T-Stick II (72-73), F-105F (72-73)
	Reassigned	301 TFW	Carswell AFB, TX	03/73-01/82	F-105D T-Stick II (73-82), F-105F (73-82), F-105D (81-82)
465 TFS		507 TFG	Tinker AFB, OK	05/72-03/73	F-105D/F (72-73)
	Reassigned	301 TFW	Tinker AFB, OK	03/73-10/75	F-105D/F (73-75)
	Reassigned	507 TFG	Tinker AFB, OK	10/75-11/80	F-105D/F (75-80)
466 TFS		508 TFG	Hill AFB, UT	01/73-03/73	F-105B (73)
	Reassigned	301 TFW	Hill AFB, UT	03/73-10/75	F-105B (73-75)
	Reassigned	508 TFG	Hill AFB, UT	10/75-09/82	F-105B (75-81), F-105D/F (80-82)
	Reassigned	419 TFW	Hill AFB, UT	10/82-02/84	F-105D/F (82-84)

Squadron or Det	Organizational Action[1]	Assignment	Base	Period[2]	Variant(s) and Period(s) of Operation
AIR NATIONAL GUARD					
119 TFS		177 TFG	Atlantic City IAP, NJ	06/70-01/73	F-105B (70-73)
121 TFS		113 TFG	Andrews AFB, MD	02/71-12/74	F-105D/F (71-74)
	Reassigned	113 TFW	Andrews AFB, MD	12/74-01/82	F-105D/F (74-82)
127 TFTS		184 TFTG	McConnell AFB, KS	01/71-12/79ca	F-105D/F (71-79)
128 TFS		116 TFW	Dobbins AFB, GA	09/78-05/83	F-105G/F (78-83)
141 TFS		108 TFG	McGuire AFB, NJ	04/64-12/74	F-105B (64-74)
	Reassigned	108 TFW	McGuire AFB, NJ	12/74-04/81	F-105B (74-81)
149 TFS		192 TFG	Byrd Field, VA	02/71-01/82ca	F-105D/F (71-82)

Notes:
1) Temporary detachments from parent units are not included.
2) Months noted are for the arrival of the first aircraft, departure of the last aircraft, or when the unit was activated or inactivated.
3) The 13th TFS was detached from the 18th TFW.
4) The 34th TFS was detached from the 41st AD from May 1966 to January 1968 and the 347th TFW from January 1968 to March 1971.
5) The 44th TFS was maintained at minimum operating status from May 1966 to December 1966.
6) The 335th TFS established Detachment 1 at Eglin in May 1958 to conduct F-105B Category II flight tests while under the control of the ARDC. The squadron gradually phased-out the F-100C/F at Seymour Johnson as Detachment 1 grew in size and was fully in place at Eglin by May 1960.
7) The 357th TFS was attached to the 23rd TFW during the entire period it was assigned to the 835th AD.
8) The 563rd TFS was non-operational from mid-August 1966 to early November 1966 due to aircraft unavailability.

Appendix 4: Souteast Asia Combat Squadron Summary

Squadron or Det	Organizational Action	Date	Upper Echelon	Base	Remarks
12 TFS	Portion of unit deployed, attached	10-Jan-65ca	2 AD	Da Nang AB, SVN	Supported Det 2, 18 TFW
	Remainder of unit deployed	01-Feb-65	2 AD	Da Nang AB, SVN	
	Portion of unit moved	08-Feb-65	2 AD	Korat RTAFB, Thailand	
	Remainder of unit moved	19-Feb-65	2 AD	Korat RTAFB, Thailand	
	Returned (attachment ends)	15-Mar-65	18 TFW	Kadena AB, Okinawa	
	Deployed, attached	15-Jun-65	6234 TFW	Korat RTAFB, Thailand	
	Returned (attachment ends)	25-Aug-65	18 TFW	Kadena AB, Okinawa	
	Augmented combat units	26-Aug-65	-	-	Periodically rotated aircraft and aircrew to Thailand through May-66; supplied aircrew to combat units from mid-1966 through 1967
	Augmentation ends	31-Dec-67ca	-	-	
	Augmented 44 TFS, 388 TFW	15-Jun-68ca	-	Korat RTAFB, Thailand	Supported Wild Weasel operations
	Augmentation ends	15-Aug-68ca	-	-	
	Augmented 6010 WWS, 388 TFW	01-Nov-70	-	Korat RTAFB, Thailand	Supported Wild Weasel operations
	Augmentation ends	01-Dec-71	-	-	
	Augmented 17 WWS, 388 TFW	15-Jan-72ca	-	Korat RTAFB, Thailand	Supported Wild Weasel operations
	Augmentation ends	31-Mar-72ca	-	-	
12 TFS Det 1	Organized, attached	24-Sep-70	388 TFW	Korat RTAFB, Thailand	Wild Weasel mission
	Discontinued	01-Nov-70	-	-	Redesignated 6010 WWS
13 TFS	Activated, organized, attached	15-May-66	388 TFW	Kadena AB, Okinawa	Formed from assets of 44 TFS; Strike and Wild Weasel mission
	Moved	15-Jun-66ca	-	Korat RTAFB, Thailand	
	Ceased operations	18-Oct-67	388 TFW	Korat RTAFB, Thailand	Absorbed by 44 TFS

Squadron or Det	Organizational Action	Date	Upper Echelon	Base	Remarks
17 WWS	Activated, organized, assigned	01-Dec-71	388 TFW	Korat RTAFB, Thailand	Replaced 6010 WWS; Wild Weasel mission
	Ceased operations	29-Oct-74	388 TFW	Korat RTAFB, Thailand	
	Inactivated	15-Nov-74	-	-	
34 TFS	Activated, organized, attached	15-May-66	388 TFW	Yokota AB, Japan	Formed from assets of 36 TFS
	Moved	15-June-66ca	-	Korat RTAFB, Thailand	
	Moved	01-Feb-69	-	Takhli RTAFB, Thailand	Temporarily moved due to runway repairs at Korat
	Moved	27-Feb-69	-	Korat RTAFB, Thailand	
	Re-equipped with F-4E	15-May-69ca	388 TFW	Korat RTAFB, Thailand	
35 TFS	Deployed, attached	24-Sep-64	2 AD	Korat RTAFB, Thailand	
	Returned	20-Nov-64	41 AD	Yokota AB, Japan	
	Deployed, attached	04-May-65	6235 TFW	Takhli RTAFB, Thailand	
	Returned (attachment ends)	26-Jun-65	6441 TFW	Yokota AB, Japan	
	Deployed, attached	19-Oct-65	6235 TFW	Takhli RTAFB, Thailand	
	Attached	08-Nov-65	355 TFW	Takhli RTAFB, Thailand	
	Returned (attachment ends)	15-Nov-65	6441 TFW	Yokota AB, Japan	
	Augmented combat units	16-Nov-65	-	-	Periodically rotated aircraft and aircrew to Thailand through May-66; supplied aircrew to combat units from mid-1966 through May-67
	Reassigned (augmentation continues)	15-Nov-66	41 AD	Yokota AB, Japan	
	Ceased operations	31-May-67ca	41 AD	Yokota AB, Japan	
36 TFS	Deployed, attached	09-Aug-64	2 AD	Korat RTAFB, Thailand	First F-105 combat deployment to Korat
	Returned (attachment ends)	05-Oct-64	41 AD	Yokota AB, Japan	
	Deployed, attached	06-Mar-65	2 AD	Takhli RTAFB, Thailand	First F-105 combat deployment to Takhli
	Attached	10-Apr-65	6235 TFW	Takhli RTAFB, Thailand	
	Returned (attachment ends)	04-May-65	6441 TFW	Yokota AB, Japan	
	Deployed, attached	26-Aug-65	6235 TFW	Takhli RTAFB, Thailand	
	Returned (attachment ends)	28-Oct-65	6441 TFW	Yokota AB, Japan	
	Augmented combat units	29-Oct-65	-	-	Periodically deployed aircraft and aircrew to Thailand
	Augmentation ends	15-May-66	-	-	Assets formed 34 TFS
44 TFS	Deployed, attached	18-Dec-64	2 AD	Da Nang AB, SVN	Established Det 2, 18 TFW
	Portion of unit moved	01-Jan-65ca	2 AD	Korat RTAFB, Thailand	
	Remainder of unit moved	31-Jan-65ca	2 AD	Korat RTAFB, Thailand	
	Returned (attachment ends)	25-Feb-65	18 TFW	Kadena AB, Okinawa	
	Deployed, attached	21-Apr-65	6234 TFW	Korat RTAFB, Thailand	
	Returned (attachment ends)	23-Jun-65	18 TFW	Kadena AB, Okinawa	
	Augmented combat units	24-Jul-65ca	-	-	Periodically deployed aircraft and aircrew to Thailand through May-66
	Deployed	10-Oct-65	-	Korat RTAFB, Thailand	
	Attached	19-Oct-65	6234 TFW	Korat RTAFB, Thailand	
	Returned (attachment ends, augmentation continues)	29-Oct-65	18 TFW	Kadena AB, Okinawa	
	Assumed minimum operational status	15-May-66	18 TFW	Kadena AB, Okinawa	Assets formed 13 TFS
	Ceased operations	31-Dec-66	18 TFW	Kadena AB, Okinawa	
	Reassigned, moved, gained operating status	25-Apr-67	388 TFW	Korat RTAFB, Thailand	Replaced 421 TFS; Wild Weasel mission from 18-Oct-67
	Moved	01-Feb-69	-	Takhli RTAFB, Thailand	Temporarily moved due to runway repairs at Korat
	Moved	27-Feb-69	-	Korat RTAFB, Thailand	
	Reassigned, moved	15-Oct-69	355 TFW	Takhli RTAFB, Thailand	Strike and Wild Weasel mission
	Reassigned (non-operational)	10-Dec-70	13 AF	Takhli RTAFB, Thailand	
67 TFS	Portion of unit deployed	02-Jan-65ca	-	Da Nang AB, SVN	Supported Det 2, 18 TFW
	Returned	31-Jan-65ca	18 TFW	Kadena AB, Okinawa	
	Deployed, attached	18-Feb-65	2 AD	Korat RTAFB, Thailand	
	Attached	05-Apr-65	6234 TFW	Korat RTAFB, Thailand	
	Returned (attachment ends)	26-Apr-65	18 TFW	Kadena AB, Okinawa	
	Augmented combat units	27-Apr-65ca	-	-	
	Deployed, attached	16-Aug-65	6234 TFW	Korat RTAFB, Thailand	
	Returned (attachment ends, augmentation continues)	23-Oct-65	18 TFW	Kadena AB, Okinawa	Periodically rotated aircraft and aircrew to Thailand through May-66; supplied aircrew to combat units from mid-1966 through the fall of 1967
	Augmentation ends	30-Nov-67ca	-	-	
80 TFS	Deployed, attached	30-Oct-64	2 AD	Korat RTAFB, Thailand	

Squadron or Det	Organizational Action	Date	Upper Echelon	Base	Remarks
80 TFS cont.	Returned (attachment ends)	29-Dec-64	41 AD	Yokota AB, Japan	
	Deployed, attached	27-Jun-65	6235 TFW	Takhli RTAFB, Thailand	
	Returned (attachment ends)	26-Aug-65	6441 TFW	Yokota AB, Japan	
	Augmented combat units	27-Aug-65	-	-	Periodically rotated aircraft and aircrew to Thailand through May-66; supplied aircrew to combat units from mid-1966 through 1967
	Reassigned (augmentation continues)	15-Nov-66	41 AD	Yokota AB, Japan	
	Reassigned (augmentation ends)	15-Jan-68	347 TFW	Yokota AB, Japan	
333 TFS	Moved, reassigned	08-Dec-65	355 TFW	Takhli RTAFB, Thailand	Strike mission (65-70); Wild Weasel mission (66-70)
	Reassigned, moved (non-operational)	15-Oct-70	23 TFW	McConnell AFB, KS	
334 TFS	Deployed, attached	02-Sep-65	6235 TFW	Takhli RTAFB, Thailand	Operation Two Buck 18
	Attached	08-Nov-65	355 TFW	Takhli RTAFB, Thailand	
	Returned (attachment ends)	05-Feb-66	4 TFW	Seymour Johnson AFB, NC	
335 TFS	Deployed, attached	03-Jul-65	6441 TFW	Yokota AB, Japan	Operation Two Buck 13; back-up duty for 6441 TFW mission requirement before rotating to Thailand
	Moved, attached	03-Nov-65	6235 TFW	Takhli RTAFB, Thailand	
	Attached	08-Nov-65	355 TFW	Takhli RTAFB, Thailand	
	Returned (attachment ends)	15-Dec-65	4 TFW	Seymour Johnson AFB, NC	
354 TFS	Deployed, attached	03-Mar-65	313 AD	Kadena AB, Okinawa	Operation Two Buck 10; back-up duty for 18 TFW mission requirement before rotating to Thailand
	Portion of unit moved	13-Mar-65	-	Korat RTAFB, Thailand	
	Remainder of unit moved, attached	05-Apr-65ca	6234 TFW	Korat RTAFB, Thailand	
	Returned (attachment ends)	12-Jun-65	355 TFW	McConnell AFB, KS	
	Reassigned	08-Nov-65	835 AD	McConnell AFB, KS	
	Reassigned, moved	27-Nov-65	355 TFW	Takhli RTAFB, Thailand	Strike mission (65-70); Wild Weasel mission (66-70)
	Reassigned (non-operational)	14-Dec-70	13 AF	Takhli RTAFB, Thailand	
357 TFS	Deployed, attached	09-Aug-64	41 AD	Yokota AB, Japan	Back-up duty for 41 AD mission requirement
	Returned (attachment ends)	12-Dec-64	355 TFW	McConnell AFB, KS	
	Deployed, attached	12-Jun-65	6234 TFW	Korat RTAFB, Thailand	
	Portion of unit moved	20-Aug-65ca	-	Kadena AB, Okinawa	Back-up duty for 18 TFW mission requirement
	Portion of unit returned, reassigned (attachment ends)	08-Nov-65	835 AD	McConnell AFB, KS	
	Attached	08-Nov-65	23 TFW	McConnell AFB, KS	
	Remainder of unit returned	21-Nov-65ca	-	McConnell AFB, KS	
	Reassigned, moved (attachment ends)	29-Jan-66	355 TFW	Takhli RTAFB, Thailand	Strike and Wild Weasel mission (66-70)
	Inactivated	10-Dec-70	-	-	
421 TFS	Deployed, attached	07-Apr-65	313 AD	Kadena AB, Okinawa	Operation Two Buck Three; back-up duty for 18 TFW mission requirement; rotated aircrew to Thailand to support combat operations being conducted by sister squadrons
	Augmented 354 TFS, 355 TFW	15-Apr-65ca	-	Korat RTAFB, Thailand	
	Augmented 357 TFS, 355 TFW	12-Jun-65	-	Korat RTAFB, Thailand	
	Returned (attachment ands)	20-Aug-65	355 TFW	McConnell AFB, KS	
	Reassigned	08-Nov-65	835 AD	McConnell AFB, KS	
	Reassigned, moved	20-Nov-65	6234 TFW	Korat RTAFB, Thailand	
	Reassigned	08-Apr-66	388 TFW	Korat RTAFB, Thailand	
	Reassigned, moved, assumed F-4D operations	25-Apr-67	15 TFW	MacDill AFB, FL	Replaced by 44 TFS
469 TFS	Deployed, attached	30-Nov-64	41 AD	Yokota AB, Japan	Back-up duty for 41 AD mission requirement
	Portion of unit moved, attached	15-Dec-64ca	313 AD	Kadena AB, Okinawa	Back-up duty for 18 TFW mission requirement
	Portion of unit moved	05-Jan-65	-	Korat RTAFB, Thailand	Rotated aircraft and aircrew to Thailand for combat duty
	Remainder of unit moved from Yokota	07-Jan-65	-	Kadena AB, Okinawa	
	Returned (attachment ends)	13-Mar-65	355 TFW	McConnell AFB, KS	
	Reassigned	08-Nov-65	6234 TFW	Korat RTAFB, Thailand	
	Moved	15-Nov-65	-	Korat RTAFB, Thailand	
	Reassigned	08-Apr-66	388 TFW	Korat RTAFB, Thailand	
	Re-equipped with F-4E	17-Nov-68	388 TFW	Korat RTAFB, Thailand	
561 TFS	Deployed, attached	06-Mar-65	41 AD	Yokota AB, Japan	Operation One Buck Nine; back-up duty for 41 AD/6441 TFW mission requirement
	Augmented combat units	06-Apr-65	-	Takhli RTAFB, Thailand	
	Returned (attachment ends)	10-Jul-65	23 TFW	McConnell AFB, KS	
561 TFS Det 1	Organized	06-Apr-72	23 TFW	McConnell AFB, KS	

Squadron or Det	Organizational Action	Date	Upper Echelon	Base	Remarks
561 TFS Det 1	Deployed, attached	07-Apr-72	388 TFW	Korat RTAFB, Thailand	Operation Constant Guard I; Wild Weasel mission
	Returned (attachment ends)	05-Sep-73	35 TFW	George AFB, CA	
562 TFS	Deployed, attached	13-Aug-65	6235 TFW	Takhli RTAFB, Thailand	Operation Two Buck Nine
	Attached	08-Nov-65	355 TFW	Takhli RTAFB, Thailand	
	Returned (attachment ends)	06-Dec-65	23 TFW	McConnell AFB, KS	
563 TFS	Deployed, attached	08-Apr-65	2 AD	Takhli RTAFB, Thailand	Operation Two Buck Charlie
	Attached	10-Apr-65	6235 TFW	Takhli RTAFB, Thailand	
	Returned (attachment ends)	15-Aug-65	23 TFW	McConnell AFB, KS	
6010 WWS	Activated, organized, assigned	01-Nov-70	388 TFW	Korat RTAFB, Thailand	Replaced Det 1, 12 TFS; Wild Weasel mission
	Inactivated	01-Dec-71	-	-	Replaced by 17 WWS
Wild Weasel Det	Accepted first EF-105F	28-May-66	388 TFW	Korat RTAFB, Thailand	Established during Nov-65 with F-100F Wild Weasel
	Discontinued	15-Jun-66ca	-	-	Absorbed by 13 TFS

Appendix 5: F-105 Aerial Victories Over Southeast Asia (Chronological Order)

Date	Aircrew Personnel	Crew Position	USAF Aircraft	Squadron	Assignment	Radio Call Sign	Enemy Aircraft	Official Credit	Weapon
29-Jun-66	Maj Fred L. Tracy	Pilot	F-105D	421 TFS	388 TFW	Unknown 02	MiG-17	1.0	20mm
18-Aug-66	Maj Kenneth T. Blank	Pilot	F-105D	34 TFS	388 TFW	Honda 02	MiG-17	1.0	20mm
21-Sep-66	1Lt Karl W. Richter	Pilot	F-105D	421 TFS	388 TFW	Ford 03	MiG-17	1.0	20mm
21-Sep-66	1Lt Fred A. Wilson, Jr.	Pilot	F-105D	333 TFS	355 TFW	Vegas 02	MiG-17	1.0	20mm
04-Dec-66	Maj Roy S. Dickey	Pilot	F-105D	469 TFS	388 TFW	Eglin 04	MiG-17	1.0	20mm
10-Mar-67	Cpt Max C. Brestel	Pilot	F-105D	354 TFS	355 TFW	Kangaroo 03	MiG-17	1.0	20mm
10-Mar-67	Cpt Max C. Brestel	Pilot	F-105D	354 TFS	355 TFW	Kangaroo 03	MiG-17	1.0	20mm
26-Mar-67	Col. Robert R. Scott	Pilot	F-105D	333 TFS	355 TFW	Leech 01	MiG-17	1.0	20mm
19-Apr-67	Maj Leo K. Thorsness	Pilot	EF-105F	357 TFS	355 TFW	Kingfish 01	MiG-17	1.0	20mm
	Cpt Harold E. Johnson	EWO						1.0	
19-Apr-67	Maj Frederick G. Tolman	Pilot	F-105D	354 TFS	355 TFW	Nitro 03	MiG-17	1.0	20mm
19-Apr-67	Maj Jack W. Hunt	Pilot	F-105D	354 TFS	355 TFW	Nitro 01	MiG-17	1.0	20mm
19-Apr-67	Cpt William E. Eskew	Pilot	F-105D	354 TFS	355 TFW	Panda 01	MiG-17	1.0	20mm
28-Apr-67	Maj Harry E. Higgins	Pilot	F-105D	357 TFS	355 TFW	Spitfire 01	MiG-17	1.0	20mm
28-Apr-67	LtC Arthur F. Dennis	Pilot	F-105D	357 TFS	355 TFW	Atlanta 01	MiG-17	1.0	20mm
30-Apr-67	Cpt Thomas C. Lesan	Pilot	F-105D	333 TFS	355 TFW	Rattler 01	MiG-17	1.0	20mm
12-May-67	Cpt Jacques A. Suzanne	Pilot	F-105D	333 TFS	355 TFW	Crossbow 01	MiG-17	1.0	20mm
13-May-67	LtC Philip C. Gast	Pilot	F-105D	354 TFS	355 TFW	Chevrolet 01	MiG-17	1.0	20mm
13-May-67	Cpt Charles W. Couch	Pilot	F-105D	354 TFS	355 TFW	Chevrolet 03	MiG-17	1.0	20mm
13-May-67	Maj Robert G. Rilling	Pilot	F-105D	333 TFS	355 TFW	Random 01	MiG-17	1.0	AIM-9
13-May-67	Maj Carl D. Osborne	Pilot	F-105D	333 TFS	355 TFW	Random 03	MiG-17	1.0	AIM-9
13-May-67	Maj Maurice E. Seaver, Jr.	Pilot	F-105D	44 TFS	388 TFW	Kimona 02	MiG-17	1.0	20mm
03-Jun-67	Cpt Larry D. Wiggins	Pilot	F-105D	469 TFS	388 TFW	Hambone 03	MiG-17	1.0	AIM-9/20mm
03-Jun-67	Maj Ralph L. Kuster, Jr.	Pilot	F-105D	13 TFS	388 TFW	Hambone 02	MiG-17	1.0	20mm
23-Aug-67	1Lt David B. Waldrop III	Pilot	F-105D	34 TFS	388 TFW	Crossbow 03	MiG-17	1.0	20mm
18-Oct-67	Maj Donald M. Russell	Pilot	F-105D	333 TFS	355 TFW	Wildcat 04	MiG-17	1.0	20mm
27-Oct-67	Cpt Gene I. Basel	Pilot	F-105D	354 TFS	355 TFW	Bison 02	MiG-17	1.0	20mm
19-Dec-67	Cpt Philip M. Drew	Pilot	EF-105F	357 TFS	355 TFW	Otter 03	MiG-17	1.0	20mm
	Maj William H. Wheeler	EWO						1.0	
19-Dec-67	Maj William M. Dalton	Pilot	EF-105F	333 TFS	355 TFW	Otter 02	MiG-17	0.5[1]	20mm
	Maj James L. Graham	EWO						0.5[1]	

Note:
1) Shared kill with Maj Joseph D. Moore (AC) and 1Lt George H. McKinney, Jr. (P) flying an F-4D from the 435th TFS, 8th TFW.

Appendix 6: Color Artwork

Illustrations by Robert Robinson

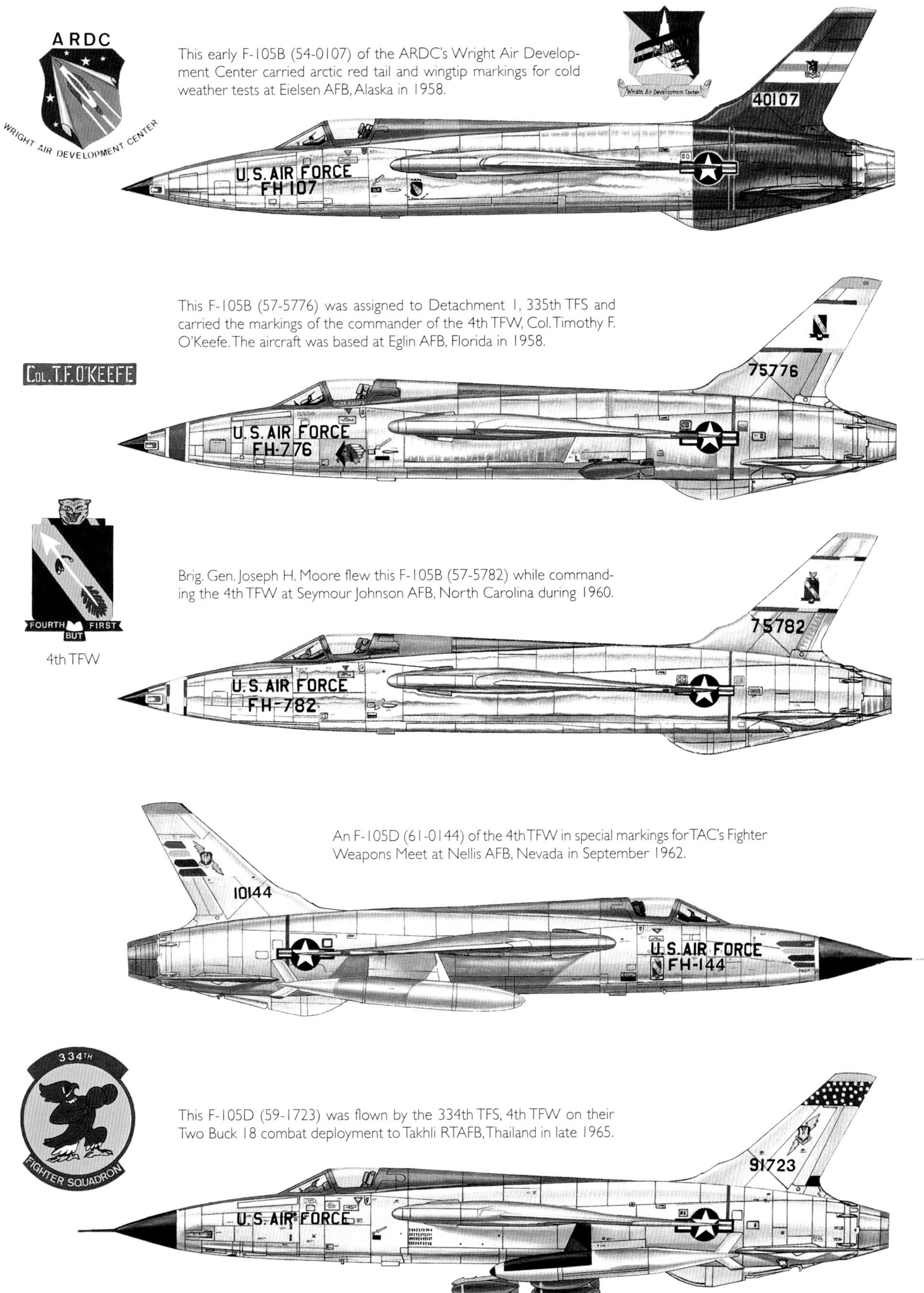

This early F-105B (54-0107) of the ARDC's Wright Air Development Center carried arctic red tail and wingtip markings for cold weather tests at Eielsen AFB, Alaska in 1958.

This F-105B (57-5776) was assigned to Detachment 1, 335th TFS and carried the markings of the commander of the 4th TFW, Col. Timothy F. O'Keefe. The aircraft was based at Eglin AFB, Florida in 1958.

Brig. Gen. Joseph H. Moore flew this F-105B (57-5782) while commanding the 4th TFW at Seymour Johnson AFB, North Carolina during 1960.

An F-105D (61-0144) of the 4th TFW in special markings for TAC's Fighter Weapons Meet at Nellis AFB, Nevada in September 1962.

This F-105D (59-1723) was flown by the 334th TFS, 4th TFW on their Two Buck 18 combat deployment to Takhli RTAFB, Thailand in late 1965.

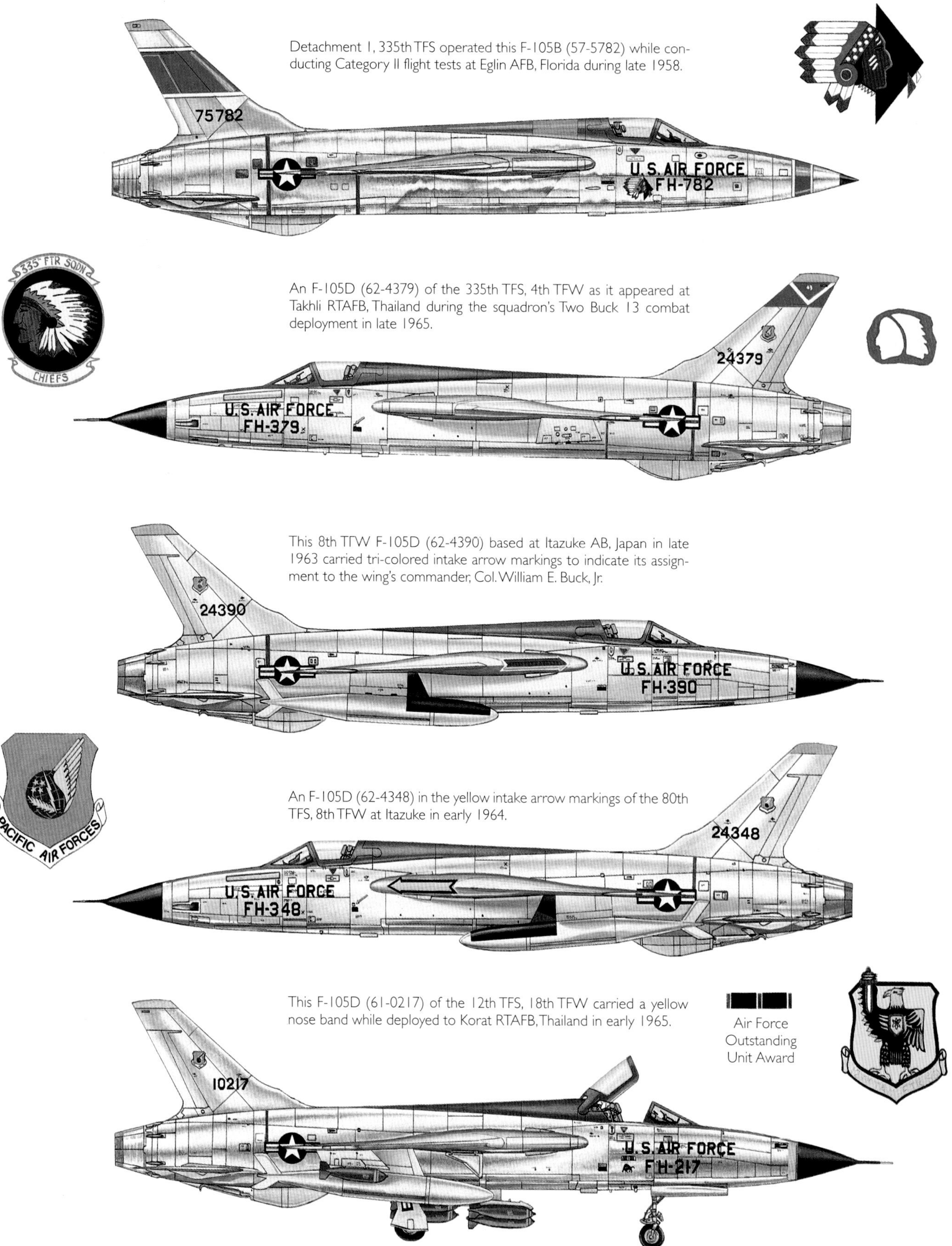

Detachment 1, 335th TFS operated this F-105B (57-5782) while conducting Category II flight tests at Eglin AFB, Florida during late 1958.

An F-105D (62-4379) of the 335th TFS, 4th TFW as it appeared at Takhli RTAFB, Thailand during the squadron's Two Buck 13 combat deployment in late 1965.

This 8th TFW F-105D (62-4390) based at Itazuke AB, Japan in late 1963 carried tri-colored intake arrow markings to indicate its assignment to the wing's commander, Col. William E. Buck, Jr.

An F-105D (62-4348) in the yellow intake arrow markings of the 80th TFS, 8th TFW at Itazuke in early 1964.

This F-105D (61-0217) of the 12th TFS, 18th TFW carried a yellow nose band while deployed to Korat RTAFB, Thailand in early 1965.

Air Force Outstanding Unit Award

An F-105D (62-4284) of the 12th TFS on combat duty at Korat displays the yellow "wing" tail band adopted by the 18th TFW in mid-1965. A yellow name block on the canopy serves as the only squadron identifier.

This ZA-coded EF-105F (63-8302) was assigned to the 12th TFS, 18th TFW at Kadena AB, Okinawa during 1971.

An F-105D (61-0181) in the blue nose band markings of the 44th TFS, 18th TFW at Kadena during 1964.

An F-105D (62-4246) of the 67th TFS, 18th TFW as it appeared in the spring of 1965 during the squadron's deployment to Korat RTAFB, Thailand.

This F-105D (60-0527) carried the MG tail code of the 419th TFTS, 23rd TFW at McConnell AFB, Kansas during 1970. The 419th was formerly designated the 4519th CCTS.

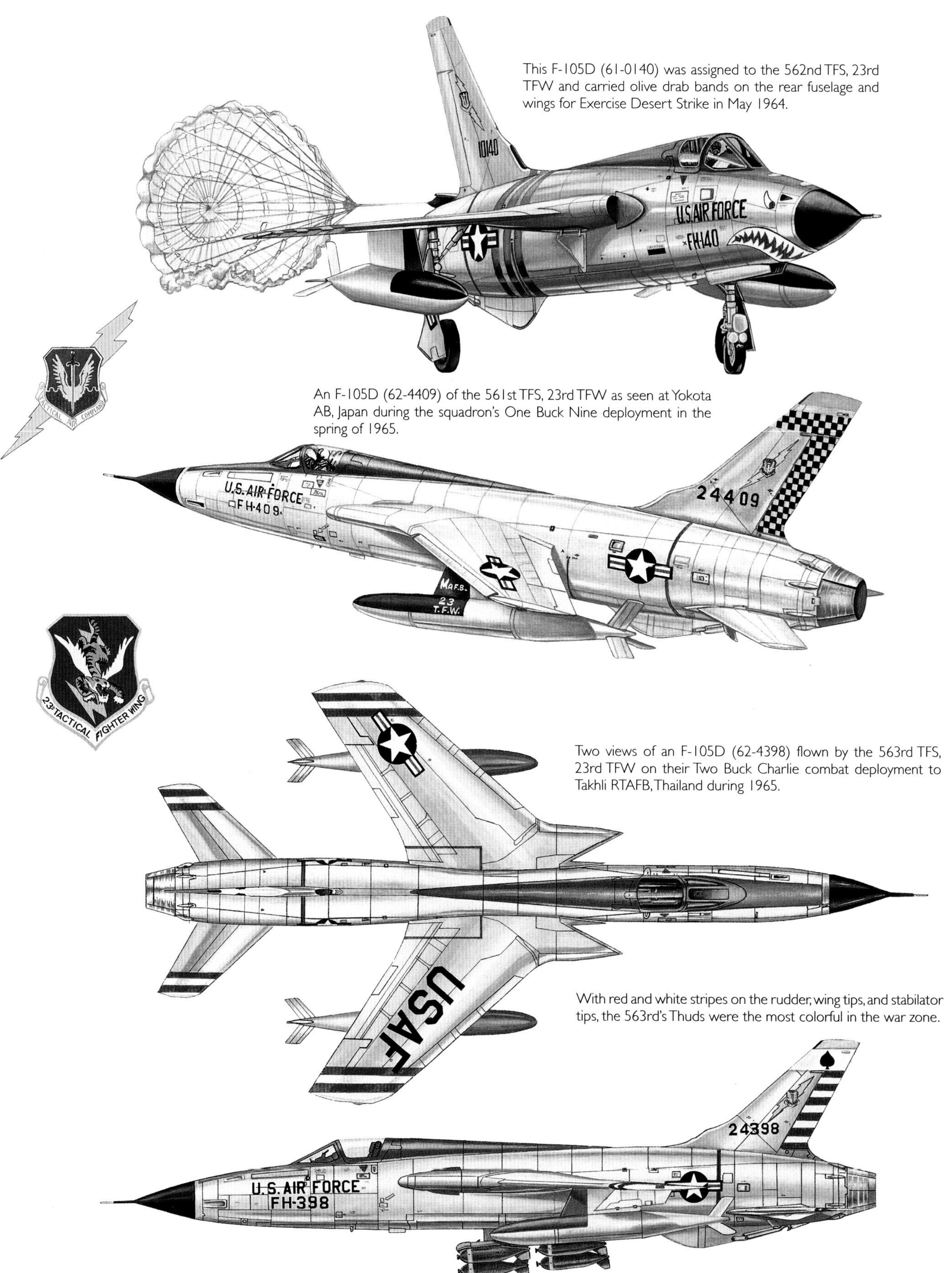

This F-105D (61-0140) was assigned to the 562nd TFS, 23rd TFW and carried olive drab bands on the rear fuselage and wings for Exercise Desert Strike in May 1964.

An F-105D (62-4409) of the 561st TFS, 23rd TFW as seen at Yokota AB, Japan during the squadron's One Buck Nine deployment in the spring of 1965.

Two views of an F-105D (62-4398) flown by the 563rd TFS, 23rd TFW on their Two Buck Charlie combat deployment to Takhli RTAFB, Thailand during 1965.

With red and white stripes on the rudder, wing tips, and stabilator tips, the 563rd's Thuds were the most colorful in the war zone.

An F-105D (60-0452) in the markings of the 560th TFS, 23rd TFW based at McConnell AFB, Kansas during 1968.

This MD-coded F-105F (63-8362) of the 561st TFS, 23rd TFW had a reverse camouflage scheme while operating out of McConnell during 1970.

An F-105D (62-4406) of the 562nd TFS, 23rd TFW carrying the markings used by the squadron during their Two Buck Nine deployment to Takhli RTAFB, Thailand during 1965.

This Thunderstick II modified F-105D (61-0063) wears the MF tail code of the 563rd TFS, 23rd TFW at McConnell during 1972.

This F-105F (63-8315) carried the MG tail code of the 4519th CCTS, 23rd TFW at McConnell during 1969.

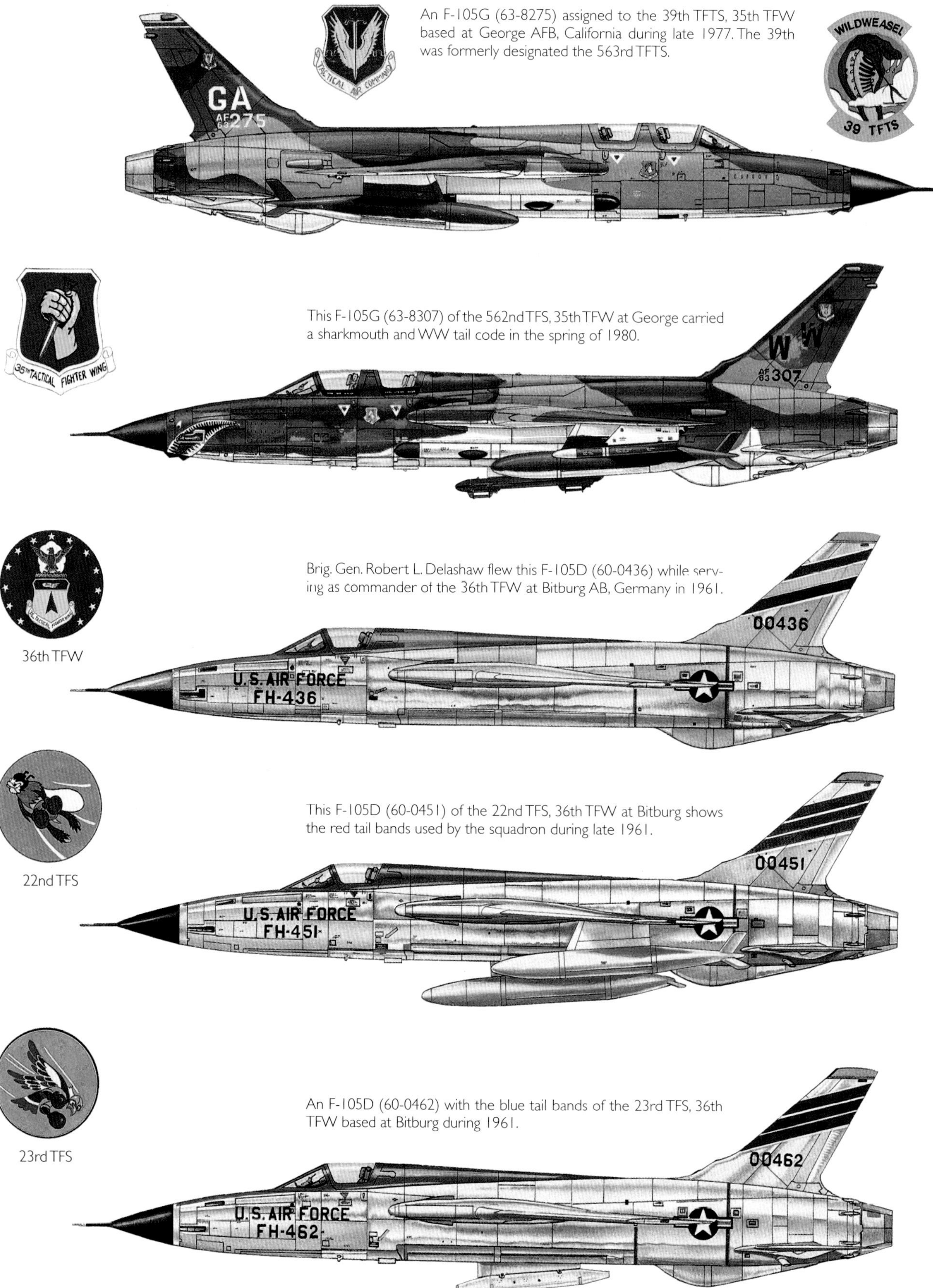

An F-105G (63-8275) assigned to the 39th TFTS, 35th TFW based at George AFB, California during late 1977. The 39th was formerly designated the 563rd TFTS.

This F-105G (63-8307) of the 562nd TFS, 35th TFW at George carried a sharkmouth and WW tail code in the spring of 1980.

Brig. Gen. Robert L. Delashaw flew this F-105D (60-0436) while serving as commander of the 36th TFW at Bitburg AB, Germany in 1961.

This F-105D (60-0451) of the 22nd TFS, 36th TFW at Bitburg shows the red tail bands used by the squadron during late 1961.

An F-105D (60-0462) with the blue tail bands of the 23rd TFS, 36th TFW based at Bitburg during 1961.

This F-105D (60-0436) carried the standard tri-colored tail markings of the 36th TFW at Bitburg in 1963. The blue triangle below the cockpit indicates that the aircraft was assigned to the 23rd TFS.

53rd TFS

Yellow tail bands identify this F-105D (60-0527) as belonging to the 53rd TFS, 36th TFW at Bitburg in early 1962.

6441st TFW

This F-105D (62-4375) was flown by Col. Chester "John Black" L. Van Etten while he commanded the 6441st TFW at Yokota AB, Japan in 1965.

41st AD

An F-105D (62-4388) with the blue intake arrow markings of the 35th TFS, 41st AD at Yokota in late 1964.

This F-105D (62-4330) was one of several 35th TFS, 6441st TFW aircraft that briefly carried experimental blue tail markings during mid-1965.

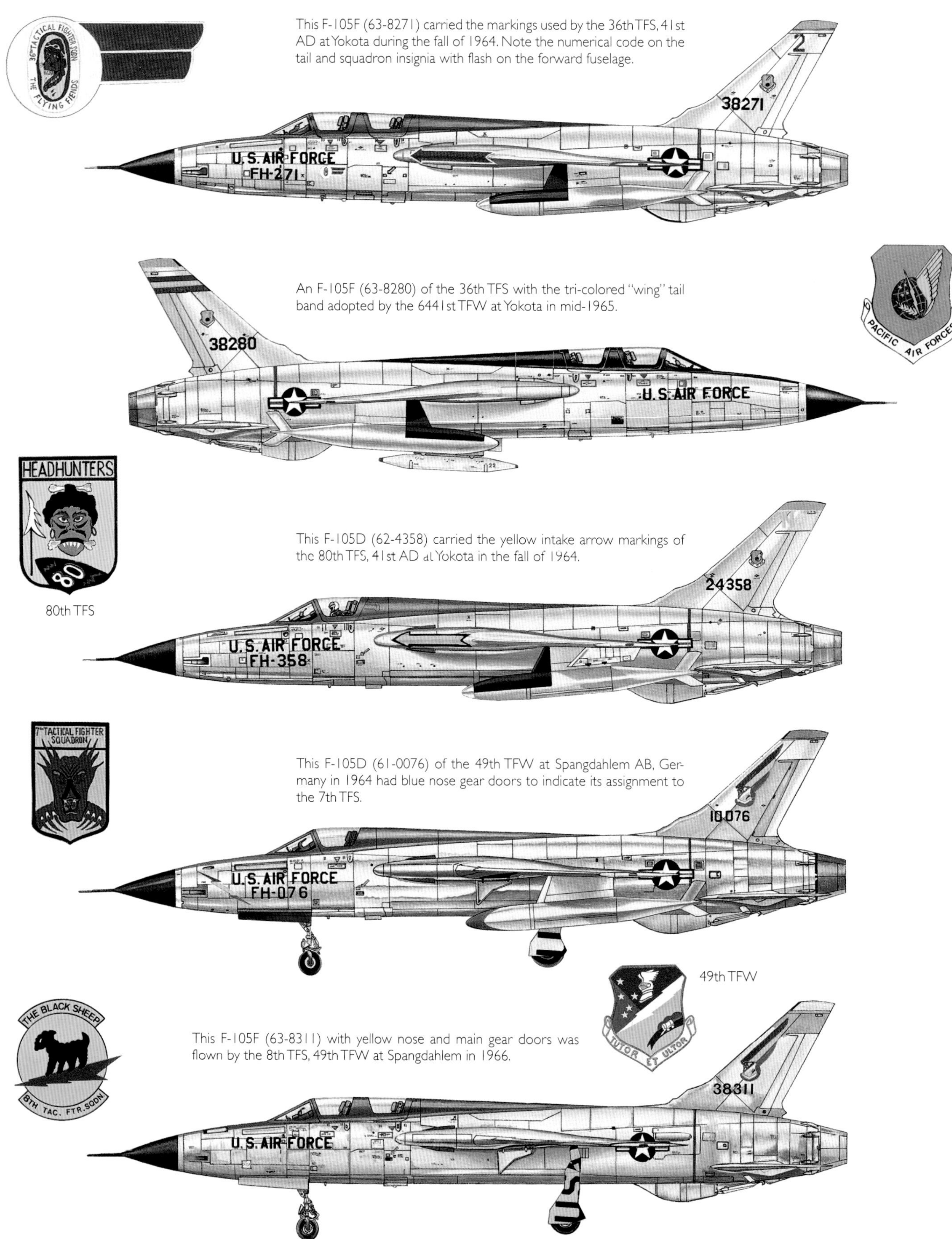

This F-105F (63-8271) carried the markings used by the 36th TFS, 41st AD at Yokota during the fall of 1964. Note the numerical code on the tail and squadron insignia with flash on the forward fuselage.

An F-105F (63-8280) of the 36th TFS with the tri-colored "wing" tail band adopted by the 6441st TFW at Yokota in mid-1965.

This F-105D (62-4358) carried the yellow intake arrow markings of the 80th TFS, 41st AD at Yokota in the fall of 1964.

This F-105D (61-0076) of the 49th TFW at Spangdahlem AB, Germany in 1964 had blue nose gear doors to indicate its assignment to the 7th TFS.

This F-105F (63-8311) with yellow nose and main gear doors was flown by the 8th TFS, 49th TFW at Spangdahlem in 1966.

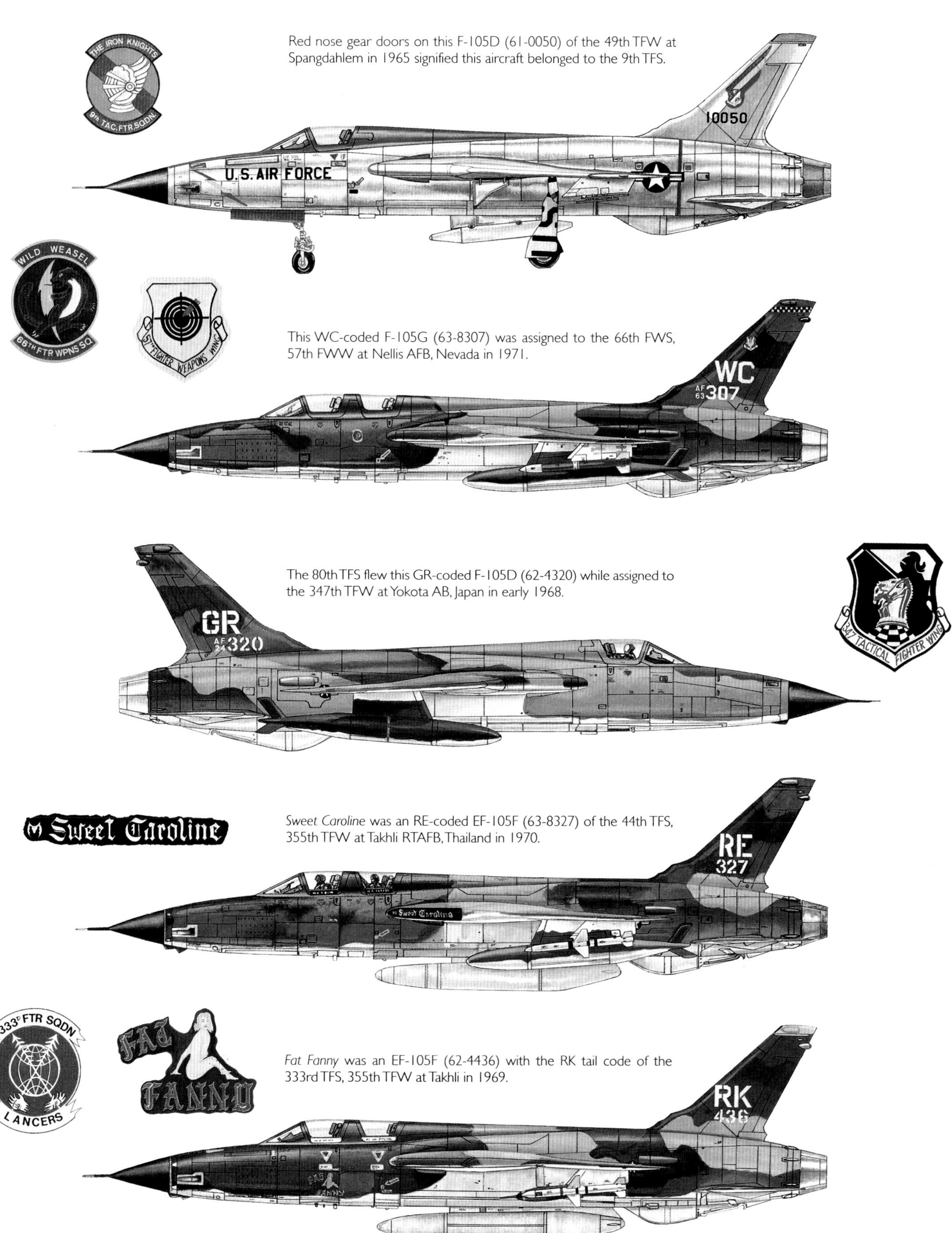

Red nose gear doors on this F-105D (61-0050) of the 49th TFW at Spangdahlem in 1965 signified this aircraft belonged to the 9th TFS.

This WC-coded F-105G (63-8307) was assigned to the 66th FWS, 57th FWW at Nellis AFB, Nevada in 1971.

The 80th TFS flew this GR-coded F-105D (62-4320) while assigned to the 347th TFW at Yokota AB, Japan in early 1968.

Sweet Caroline was an RE-coded EF-105F (63-8327) of the 44th TFS, 355th TFW at Takhli RTAFB, Thailand in 1970.

Fat Fanny was an EF-105F (62-4436) with the RK tail code of the 333rd TFS, 355th TFW at Takhli in 1969.

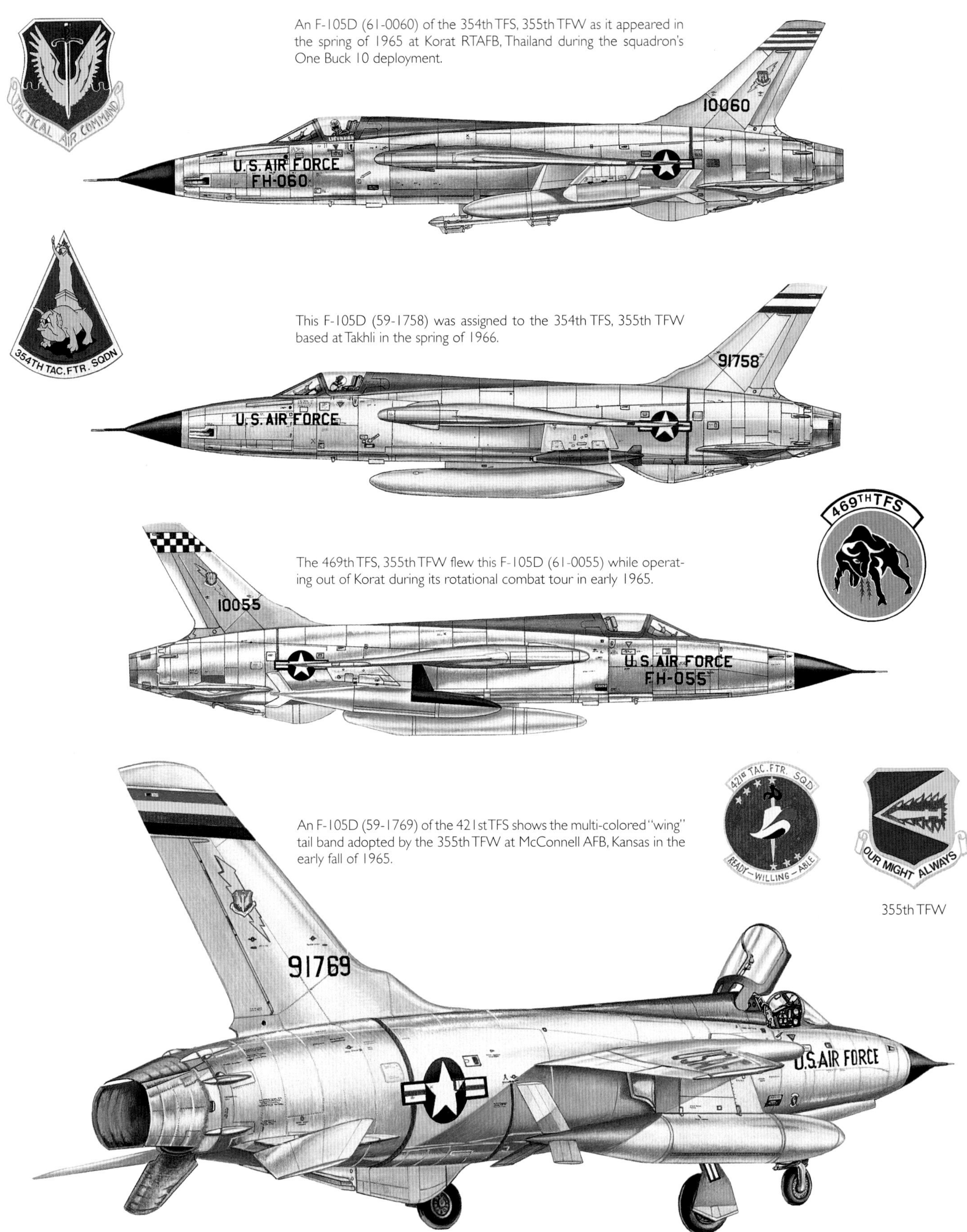

An F-105D (61-0060) of the 354th TFS, 355th TFW as it appeared in the spring of 1965 at Korat RTAFB, Thailand during the squadron's One Buck 10 deployment.

This F-105D (59-1758) was assigned to the 354th TFS, 355th TFW based at Takhli in the spring of 1966.

The 469th TFS, 355th TFW flew this F-105D (61-0055) while operating out of Korat during its rotational combat tour in early 1965.

An F-105D (59-1769) of the 421st TFS shows the multi-colored "wing" tail band adopted by the 355th TFW at McConnell AFB, Kansas in the early fall of 1965.

355th TFW

COMMIE STOMPER was an RM-coded F-105D (61-0071) of the 354th TFS, 355th TFW at Takhli in 1970.

Carolina Thunder was an F-105D (60-0455) that carried the RU tail code of the 357th TFS, 355th TFW at Takhli during 1970.

MISS MOLLY was an EF-105F (63-8356) assigned to the 13th TFS, 388th TFW at Korat RTAFB, Thailand during 1967.

This Commando Nail F-105F (63-8312) of the 13th TFS, 388th TFW at Korat in mid-1967 had tan and olive green undersurfaces for night bombing operations.

ZERO was an F-105G (62-4440) with the JB tail code of the 17th WWS, 388th TFW at Korat during 1973.

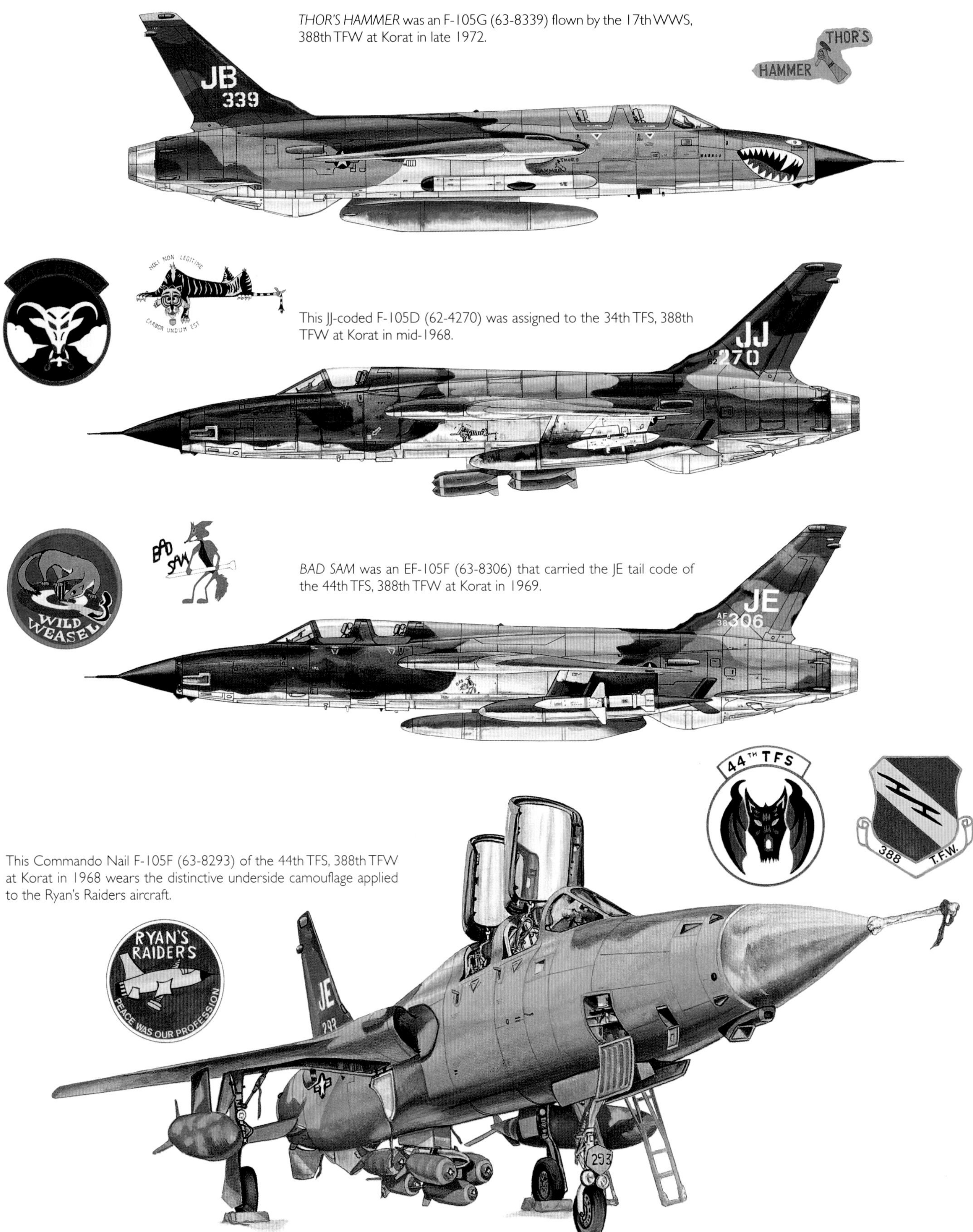

THOR'S HAMMER was an F-105G (63-8339) flown by the 17th WWS, 388th TFW at Korat in late 1972.

This JJ-coded F-105D (62-4270) was assigned to the 34th TFS, 388th TFW at Korat in mid-1968.

BAD SAM was an EF-105F (63-8306) that carried the JE tail code of the 44th TFS, 388th TFW at Korat in 1969.

This Commando Nail F-105F (63-8293) of the 44th TFS, 388th TFW at Korat in 1968 wears the distinctive underside camouflage applied to the Ryan's Raiders aircraft.

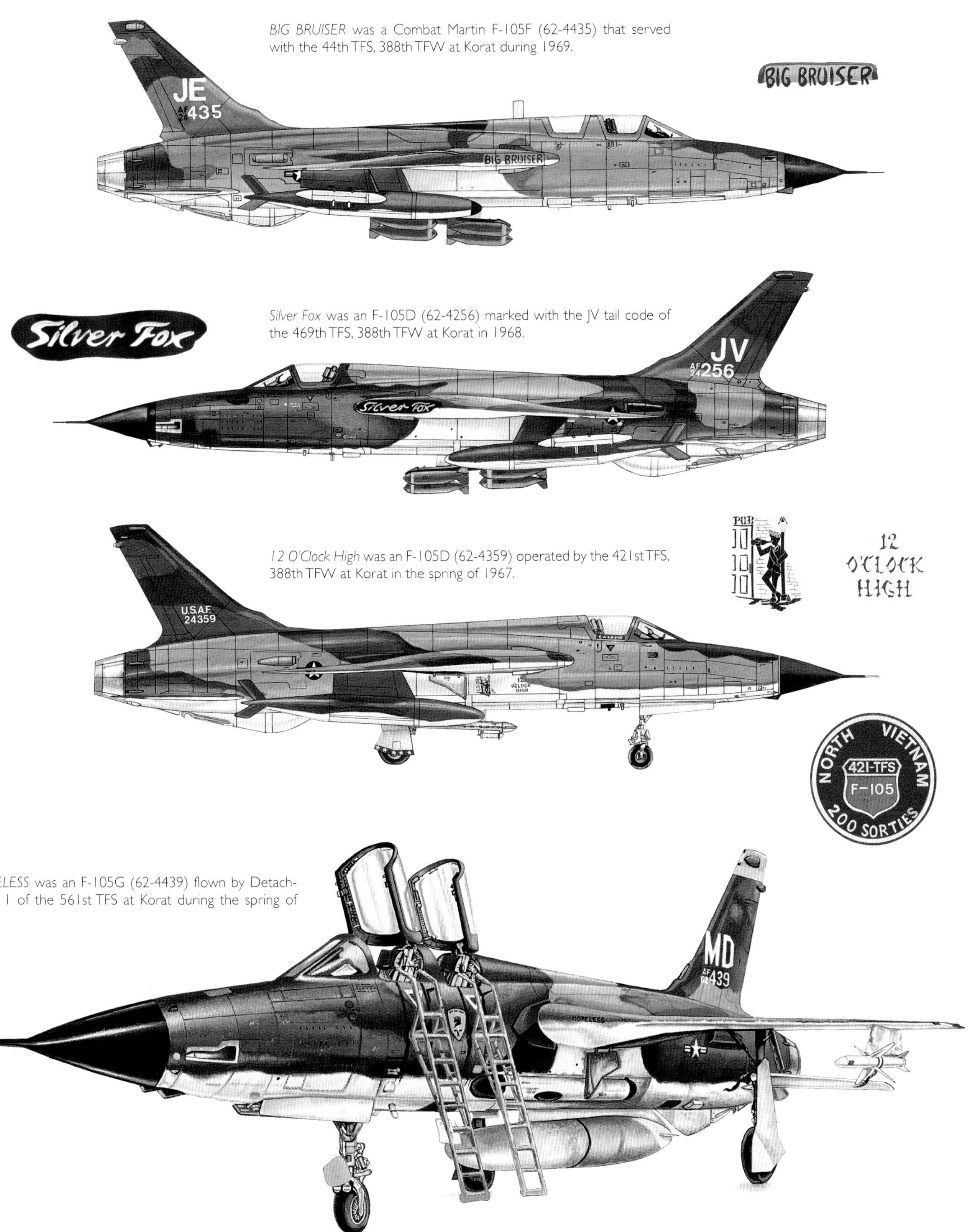

BIG BRUISER was a Combat Martin F-105F (62-4435) that served with the 44th TFS, 388th TFW at Korat during 1969.

Silver Fox was an F-105D (62-4256) marked with the JV tail code of the 469th TFS, 388th TFW at Korat in 1968.

12 O'Clock High was an F-105D (62-4359) operated by the 421st TFS, 388th TFW at Korat in the spring of 1967.

HOPELESS was an F-105G (62-4439) flown by Detachment 1 of the 561st TFS at Korat during the spring of 1972.

TDY TOO was a WW-coded F-105G (63-8351) assigned to Detachment 1 of the 561st TFS at Korat in early 1973.

This F-105G (62-4425) carried the ZB tail code of the 6010th WWS, 388th TFW at Korat in 1971.

This F-105D (60-0525) served with the Test, Research, and Development Division within the USAF Fighter Weapons School at Nellis AFB, Nevada in 1962.

This EF-105F (62-4438) with a reverse camouflage scheme carried the WC tail code of the 4537th FWS, 4525th FWW at Nellis during 1968.

An F-105D (61-0062) operated by the 469th TFS, 6234th TFW at Korat in late 1965. The multi-colored tail band was carried over from the aircraft's previous assignment with the 355th TFW.

This Thunderstick II modified F-105D (60-0465) wears the TH tail code of the 457th TFS, 301st TFW at Carswell AFB, Texas in 1973.

An F-105D (62-4242) of the 465th TFS, 507th TFG based at Tinker AFB, Oklahoma during 1979. Note the claimed MiG-17 kill from its service in the Vietnam War.

This HI-coded F-105D (62-4328) of the 466th TFS, 419th TFW at Hill AFB, Utah had a wraparound camouflage scheme during 1983.

This F-105D (62-4299) was assigned to the Kansas Air Guard's 127th TFTS, 184th TFTG at McConnell AFB in 1978.

An F-105G (62-4444) flown by the 128th TFS, 116th TFW, Georgia ANG, based at Dobbins AFB during 1981.

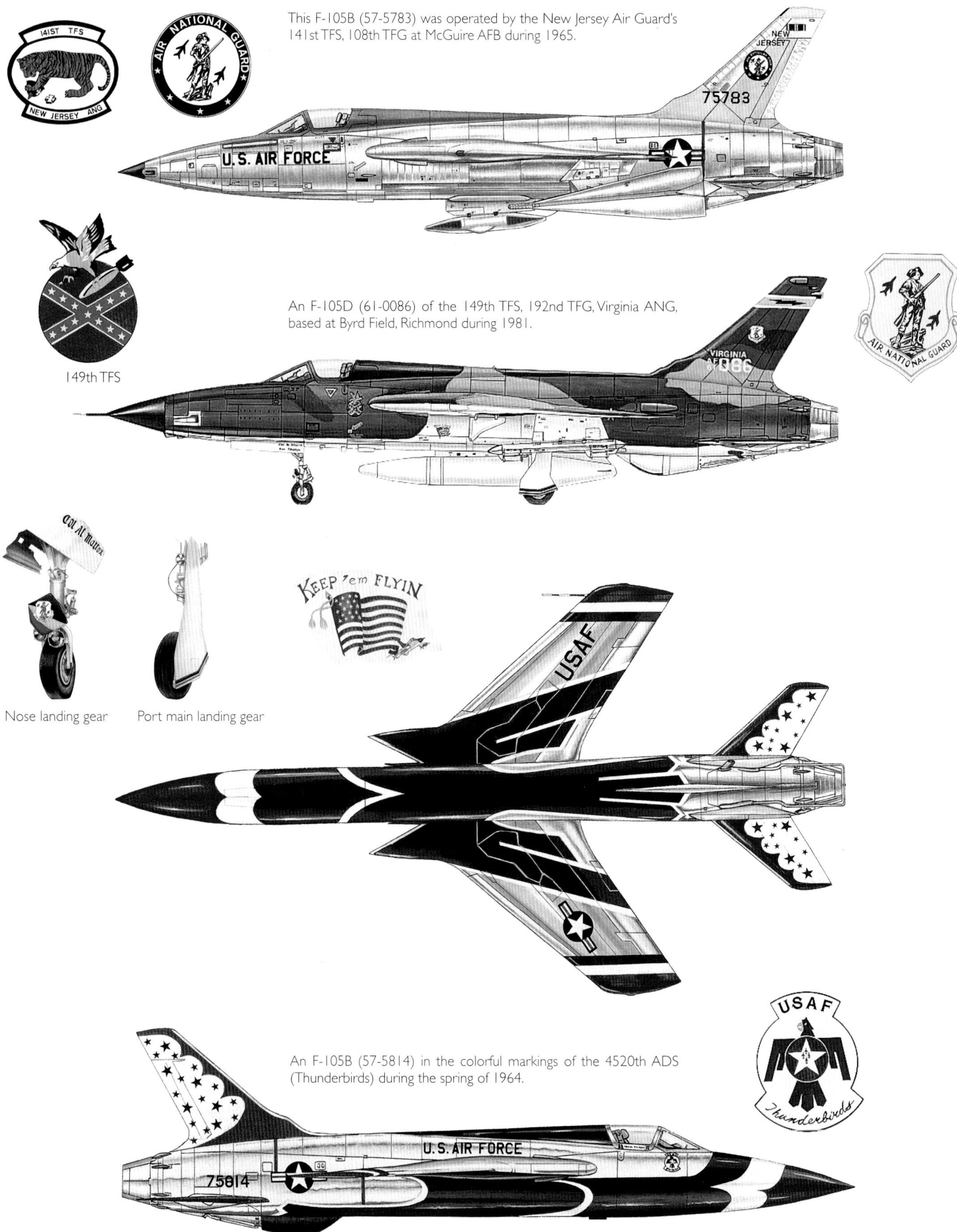

This F-105B (57-5783) was operated by the New Jersey Air Guard's 141st TFS, 108th TFG at McGuire AFB during 1965.

An F-105D (61-0086) of the 149th TFS, 192nd TFG, Virginia ANG, based at Byrd Field, Richmond during 1981.

149th TFS

Nose landing gear

Port main landing gear

An F-105B (57-5814) in the colorful markings of the 4520th ADS (Thunderbirds) during the spring of 1964.

Bibliography

The records kept by the USAF were the major source materials for this book. In particular, valuable operations information was gained from individual wing and squadron unit histories and the records maintained at the Air Force Historical Research Agency at Maxwell AFB, Alabama. Other useful sources included a series of reports conducted under the Contemporary Historical Evaluation of Combat Operations (CHECO) project and the still picture documentation records on file at the National Archives.

Governmental Sources

Books and Printed Studies

Berger, Carl, ed. *The United States Air Force in Southeast Asia: An Illustrated Account.* Revised ed. Washington, D.C.: Office of Air Force History, 1984.

Burbage, Maj. Paul, et al. *USAF Southeast Asia Monograph Series, Vol. 1, The Battle for the Skies over North Vietnam.* Washington, D.C.: Office of Air Force History, 1976.

Commando Hunt. San Francisco, California: Headquarters Seventh Air Force, May 20, 1969.

Corum, Col. Delbert, et al. *USAF Southeast Asia Monograph Series, Vol. 1, The Tale of Two Bridges.* Washington, D.C.: Office of Air Force History, 1976.

Doglione, Col. John A., et al. *USAF Southeast Asia Monograph Series, Vol. 2, Airpower and the 1972 Spring Invasion.* Washington, D.C.: Office of Air Force History, 1976.

Drew, Col. Dennis M. *Rolling Thunder 1965: Anatomy of a Failure.* Maxwell AFB, Alabama: Air University Press, 1986.

Futrell, Robert F. *The United States Air Force in Southeast Asia: The Advisory Years To 1965.* Washington, D.C.: U.S. Office of Air Force History, 1981.

Futrell, Robert F., et al. *Aces and Aerial Victories: The United States Air Force in Southeast Asia, 1965-1973.* Washington, D.C.: Office of Air Force History, 1976.

Michael, Maj. Albert L. *Ryan's Raiders: A Special Report.* Maxwell AFB, Alabama: Project Corona Harvest, January 1970.

Mueller, Robert. *Air Force Bases, Volume 1: Active Air Force Bases within the United States of America on 17 September 1982.* Washington, D.C.: Office of Air Force History, 1989.

Ravenstein, Charles A. *Air Force Combat Wings: Lineage and Honors Histories, 1947-1977.* Washington, D.C.: Office of Air Force History, 1984.

Thompson, Wayne. *To Hanoi and Back.* Washington, D.C.: Smithsonian Institution Press, 2000.

Van Nederveen, Capt. Gilles. *Sparks Over Vietnam, The EB-66 and the Early Struggle for Tactical Electronic Warfare.* Maxwell AFB, Alabama: Air Research Institute, 2000.

Van Staaveren, Jacob. *The Air Campaign Against North Vietnam, 1966.* Washington, D.C.: Office of Air Force History, 1968.

—. *Interdiction in Southern Laos, 1960-68.* Washington, D.C.: Office of Air Force History, 1993.

Project CHECO Reports

Bonetti, Lee. *The War in Vietnam, January-June 1967.* 1968.

Bonetti, Lee, et al. *The War in Vietnam, July-December 1967.* 1968.

Heffron, Charles H., Jr. *Air-to-Air Encounters Over North Vietnam, 1 January-30 June 1967.* 1967.

Helmka, MSgt. Robert T., and Hale, TSgt. Beverly. *USAF Operations from Thailand, 1964-65.* August 10, 1966.

Johnson, Maj. Calvin R. *Linebacker Operations, September-December 1972.* 1973.

Lofgren, Maj. William W., and Sexton, Maj. Richard R. *Air War in Northern Laos, 1 April-30 November 1971.* June 22, 1973.

MacNaugton, 1st Lt Robert L. *Barrel Roll 7.* July 3, 1965.
—. Yan*kee Team.* March 8, 1966.
Melyan, Wesley R.C., and Bonetti, Lee. *Rolling Thunder, July 1965-December 1966.* 1967.
Nicholson, Charles A. *The USAF Response to the Spring 1972 North Vietnamese Offensive.* 1972.
Overton, Maj. James B. *Rolling Thunder, January 1967-November 1968.* 1969.
Paterson, L.E. *Evolution of the Rules of Engagement for Southeast Asia, 1960-65.* September 30, 1966.
Porter, Melvin F. *Linebacker: Overview of the First 120 Days.* September 27, 1973.
Project CHECO Team. *Rolling Thunder, March-June 1965.* March 28, 1966.
Sams, Kenneth, et al. *Air Operations in Northern Laos, 1 November 1969-1 April 1970.* May 5, 1970.
—. The *Air War in Vietnam, 1968-1969.* 1970.
Thompson, Maj. A.W., and Thorndale, C. William. *Air Response to the Tet Offensive, 30 January-29 February 1968.* 1968.
Valentiny, Capt. Edward. *USAF Operations from Thailand, 1 January 1967-1 July 1968.* 1969.
Vining, Robert L. *Rolling Thunder.* November 17, 1967.
Weaver, Robert B. *Air-to-Air Encounters Over North Vietnam, 1 July 1967-31 December 1968.* 1969.

Articles

"44th, 'Thuds' Have Rich History. *Sawadee Flyer* October 4, 1969.
"Air Force Pilots Transition in 562 TFS." *Contrails* April 21, 1974: 4.
Allen, Msgt. K.A. "He Believed." *The Airman* 1967.
Blair, Ed. "A Man Doing His Job." *The Airman* 1969.
Carson, Capt. Don. "F-105s Join USAF Reserve Forces." *Air Force Magazine* 1974.
—. "Flying the Thud." *Air Force Magazine* 1974.
—. "Trolling for SAMs." *Air Force Magazine* 1974.
Everett, Capt. Robert P. "Destroy Doumer Bridge!" *The Airman* 1968.
—. "The Thud is No Dud." *The Airman* 1968.
"First Group of 355th TFW F-105s Arrives Today." *Contrails* October 23, 1970: 1, 4-5.
Guimond, Capt. Gary A. "Mission Accomplished." *The Airman* 1971.
Harris, Hap. "Lots of Mach 2 Moxie." *The Airman* 1965.
Kasler, Col. James H. "The Hanoi POL Strike." *Air University Review* November-December 1974: 19-28.
"Last T-Stick II Arrives." *Contrails* 13 August 1971: 1.
"Local Guard Gets First Thuds." *Contrails* 22 January 1971: 1.
"Long Ride Home." *Contrails* 30 October 1970: 4-5.
"MOAMA Looks Ahead." *The Airman* 1963.
Moore, Brig. Gen J. H. "4 Points for the Fourth." *Flying Safety* 1960.
Morrison, Blake C. "Requiem for a Heavyweight." *Aerospace Safety* 1980.
Nasuti, Capt. Nick. "War Comes to Smoky Hill." *The Airman* 1968.
Piowaty, John. "Reflections of a Thud Driver." *Air University Review* January-February 1983: 52-53.
Roth, Rusty. "Thunderchief." *Flying Safety* 1959.
Scott, Col. Robert R. "Mission Improbable." *The Airman* 1969.
Sturn, Ted R. "Battle at the Bridge." *The Airman* 1969.
—. "We Are Ready Now." *The Airman* 1975.
Ternamian, Capt. Brian T. "Thunderchiefs for the Warriors." *The Airman* 1973.

Non-Governmental Sources

Books

Anderton, David. *Republic F-105 Thunderchief.* London, England: Osprey Publishing Limited, 1983.
Archer, Robert D. *The Republic F-105.* Fallbrook, California: Aero Publishers, Inc., 1969.
Basel, G.I. *Pak Six.* La Mesa, California: Associated Creative Writers, 1982.
Bishop, Chris, and Dorr, Robert F. *Vietnam Air War Debrief.* Westport, Connecticut: Airtime Publishing, Inc., 1996.
Broughton, Jack. *Going Downtown: The War Against Hanoi and Washington.* New York: Orion Books/Crown Publishers, Inc., 1988.
—. *Thud Ridge.* New York: Bantam Books, 1985.
Davis, Larry. *Wild Weasel: The SAM Suppression Story.* Carrollton, Texas: Squadron/Signal Publications, Inc., 1986.
Davis, Larry and Menard, David. *Republic F-105 Thunderchief. Warbird Tech Series, Vol. 18.* North Branch, Minnesota: Specialty Press Publishers and Wholesalers, 1998.
Donald, David. ed. *U.S. Air Force Air Power Directory.* Westport, Connecticut: Airtime Publishing, Inc., 1992.
Dorr, Robert F. *Air War Hanoi.* London, England: Blanford Press, 1988.
Drendel, Lou. *Air War Over Southeast Asia, Vol. 1.* Carrollton, Texas: Squadron/Signal Publications, Inc., 1982.
—. *Air War Over Southeast Asia, Vol. 2.* Carrollton, Texas: Squadron/Signal Publications, Inc., 1983.
—. *Air War Over Southeast Asia, Vol. 3.* Carrollton, Texas: Squadron/Signal Publications, Inc., 1984.
—. *...And Kill Migs: Air to Air Combat in the Vietnam War.* Carrollton, Texas: Squadron/Signal Publications, Inc., 1984.
—. *F-105 Thunderchief in Action.* Carrollton, Texas: Squadron/Signal Publications, Inc., 1974.

—. *Thud.* Carrollton, Texas: Squadron/Signal Publications, Inc., 1986.

Francillon, Rene J. *The United States Air National Guard.* Westport, Connecticut: Airtime Publishing, Inc., 1993.

—. *Vietnam: The War in the Air.* New York: Crown Publishers, Inc., 1987.

Guarino, Larry. *A POW's Story: 2801 Days in Hanoi.* New York: Ivy Books, 1990.

Harvey, Frank. *Air War: Vietnam.* New York: Bantam Books, 1967.

Herring, George C. *America's Longest War: The United States and Vietnam, 1950-1975.* New York: Newbery Awards Records, Inc., 1986.

Imai, Kesaharu. ed. *Republic F-105 Thunderchief. Famous Airplanes of the World, No. 4.* Tokyo, Japan: Bunrindo Co., Ltd., 1987.

Lake, Jon. ed. *McDonnell F-4 Phantom: Spirit in the Skies.* Westport, Connecticut: Airtime Publishing, Inc., 1992.

Llinares, Rick, and Lloyd, Chuck. *Warfighters: The Story of the USAF Weapons School and the 57th Wing.* Atglen, Pennsylvania: Schiffer Publishing Ltd., 1996.

Logan, Don. *The 388th Tactical Fighter Wing at Korat Royal Thai Air Force Base 1972.* Atglen, Pennsylvania: Schiffer Publishing Ltd., 1995.

Martin, Patrick. *Tail Code: The Complete Guide of USAF Tactical Aircraft Tail Code Markings.* Atglen, Pennsylvania: Schiffer Publishing Ltd., 1994.

Menard, David. *Colors & Markings of the F-100 Super Sabre, Vol. 14.* Blue Ridge Summit, Pennsylvania: Tab Books, 1990.

—. *Colors & Markings of the F-100 Super Sabre, Vol. 21.* Waukesha, Wisconsin: Kalmbach Publishing Company, 1993.

Menard, David, and Robinson, Robert. *F-100 Super Sabre in Color.* Carrollton, Texas: Squadron/Signal Publications, Inc., 1992.

Mormillo, Frank B. and Thornborough, Tony. *Wild Weasels: Elite Radar-Killers of the USAF.* London, England: Osprey Publishing Limited, 1992.

Peacock, Lindsay. *North American F-100 Super Sabre. Warpaint Series, No. 4.* Bedfordshire, England: Hall Parks Books Ltd., 1996.

Red River Valley Fighter Pilots of Vietnam. 2 vols. Paducah, Kentucky: Turner Publishing Company, 1989-93.

Richardson, Doug. *Republic F-105 Thunderchief.* New York: Smithmark Publishers, Inc., 1992.

Risner, Robinson. *The Passing of the Night: My Seven Years as a Prisoner of the North Vietnamese.* New York: Ballantine Books, 1973.

Scutts, Jerry. *Wolfpack: Hunting MiGs Over Vietnam.* Shrewsbury, England: Airlife Publishing Ltd., 1988.

—. *Wrecking Crew: The 388th Tactical Fighter Wing.* New York: Warner, 1990.

Takeda, Masahiko. ed. *U.S. Forces Japan & Fifth Air Force 1945-88. Koku-Fan Illustrated, No. 41.* Tokyo, Japan: Bunrindo Co., Ltd., 1988.

Toperczer, Istvan. *MiG-17 and MiG-19 Units of the Vietnam War.* Oxford, England: Osprey Publishing Limited, 2001.

Articles

"100-Plane Flights Blamed for Loss of Big Bombers." *New York Daily News* December 21, 1972.

"2 McConnell Units to Shift to Reserves." *The Wichita Eagle and Beacon* March 30, 1972.

"355th and 388th Tactical Fighter Wings Surpass 100,000 Combat Flying Hours." *Thunderchief: Worldwide Report on Republic's F-105 Fighter-Bomber* 3.9 (1968): 1.

"355th Tactical Fighter Wing Receives Presidential Unit Citation." *Thunderchief: Worldwide Report on Republic's F-105 Fighter-Bomber* 3.10 (1968): 4.

"355th TFW Wins Presidential Unit Citation for Daring Doumer Bridge Raid." *Thunderchief: Worldwide Report on Republic's F-105 Fighter-Bomber* 5.5 (1970): 1-2.

"355th TFW Wins Third Presidential Unit Citation for SEA Action." *Thunderchief: Worldwide Report on Republic's F-105 Fighter-Bomber* 5.11 (1970): 1-2.

"561st Returning to McConnell." *The Wichita Eagle and Beacon* August 31, 1972.

"562nd Squadron Is First to Earn Ready Rating for Tactical Fighters." *The Wichita Eagle and Beacon* December 16, 1970.

"563rd TFS Nears End of Training Role." *Thunderchief: Worldwide Report on Republic's F-105 Fighter-Bomber* 5.12 (1970): 1.

"Air Force Receives First T-Stick Aircraft; 'Combat Thunder' Underway." *Thunderchief: Worldwide Report on Republic's F-105 Fighter Bomber* 5.7 (1970): 1-2.

Brownlow, Cecil. "F-105 Modified for Vietnam Role." *Aviation Week and Space Technology* 1967.

—. "F-105D's Limited-War Capability Boosted." *Aviation Week and Space Technology* 1963.

—. "USAF Conducts Tactical Training in Libya." *Aviation Week and Space Technology* 1961.

—. "USAF to Strengthen F-105 Survivability." *Aviation Week and Space Technology* 1968.

Buza, Zoltan. "MiG-17 Over Vietnam." *Wings of Fame 8* (1997): 100-117.

"Departure of 561st and Last F-105s Leaves McConnell an All-SAC Base." *The Wichita Eagle and Beacon* July 4, 1973.

Davis, Larry. "Thuds and Weasels: The F-105 Thunderchief in Southeast Asia, 1964-1974." *Wings of Fame 18* (2000): 16-37.

Dorr, Robert F. "Huns over Vietnam." *Wings of Fame 3* (1996): 4-25.

Duncan, Capt. Scott. "The Combat History of the F-105." *Aerospace Historian* 1975.

"F-105 Bombers About to Retire." *The Topeka Capital-Journal* January 28, 1984.

"F-105Bs to Guard Unit." *Thunderchief: Worldwide Report on Republic's F-105 Fighter-Bomber* 5.11 (1970): 3.

"Final Mission." *Thunderchief: Worldwide Report on Republic's F-105 Fighter-Bomber* 6.1 (1970): 1-4.

Francillon, Rene J. "Lockheed Constellation Military Variants." *Wings of Fame 20* (2000): 112-139.

Guiver, Peter F. "The 'Thuds' at Lakenheath." *Airfix Magazine* 1977.

Halvorsen, Dick. "Nightmare at Thai Nguyen." *Saga* 1969.

Harvey, Frank. "Thunderchiefs Under Wraps." *Argosy* 1967.

Hoehn, Jean-Pierre, and Kuklok, David L. "Wheelus Air Base." *Air Fan International* 2.1 (1996): 42-53.

"Homecoming." *Thunderchief: Worldwide Report on Republic's F-105 Fighter-Bomber* 6.2 (1971): 1.

Jacquet, Chris. "Thud-Part 1." *Air Fan International* 1.3 (1996): 38-46.

—. "Thud-Part 2." *Air Fan International* 1.4 (1996): 46-55.

"Jets, MiGs Tangle in Fight Near Hanoi." *The Topeka Sunday Capital-Journal* October 9, 1966.

Jordan, Bob. "Guard Starts Training of F-105 Pilots." *The Wichita Eagle and Beacon* August 21, 1971.

—. "Thud Drivers Weasel Past North Viet SAMs." *The Wichita Eagle and Beacon* September 25, 1971.

"Kansas Air Guard Becomes First In Country to Receive F-105 Jets." *The Wichita Eagle and Beacon* January 21, 1971.

Knotts, Capt. James. "The Wild Weasels." *Air Combat* 1977.

"Last of F-105s Leave Thailand After 10 Years of Heavy Duty." *Fairchild World* 1975.

MacKnight, Nigel. "F-105s over Southeast Asia." *Air Pictorial* 1977.

Mancus, Peter. "Sam Slayer: Flying the F-105...The Brick with Fins!" *Airpower* 14.1 (1984): 24-37, 53-54.

"McConnell Will Become SAC Base in Transfer Ceremonies Friday." *The Wichita Eagle and Beacon* June 29, 1972.

"Mig Bases Blasted Again." *The Topeka Daily Capital-Journal* April 25, 1967.

Miller, Barry. "F-105 Modified for Blind Bombing Role." *Aviation Week & Space Technology* 1969.

Peacock, Lindsay. "F-105 Phase-out: The Final Chapter." *Aviation News* 12.19 (1984): 806-819.

"Pilot's Luck." *RAF Flying Review* 18.9 (1962): 32-33.

Piowaty, John. "Dropping Doumer Bridge." *Vietnam* 6.3 (1993): 34-40.

Plunkett, Lt. Col. W. Howard. "562nd TFS - TAC's Strong Right Arm." *Friends Journal* 1994.

Reed, William S. "TAC Trains Pilots for F-105D Missions." *Aviation Week* 1961.

"Republic Thunderchief-Equipped 388th TFW Wins Presidential Unit Citation and AFOUA." *Thunderchief: Worldwide Report on Republic's F-105 Fighter-Bomber 4.9* (1968): 1.

"Rolling Thunder with the Thunderchiefs in Vietnam." *Thunderchief: Worldwide Report on Republic's F-105 Fighter-Bomber* 3.9 (1968): 2.

"Rolling Thunder with the Thunderchiefs in Vietnam." *Thunderchief: Worldwide Report on Republic's F-105 Fighter-Bomber* 3.10 (1968): 4.

Soldeus, Lars G. "Thunderchiefs on the Rhine." *AAHS Journal* 8.1 (1973): 34-36.

Spering, Don. "Goodbye Thunderchief!" *Aviation News* 1983.

Stanfield, Robert I. "F-105 Spearheads TAC Fighter Forces." *Aviation Week* 1959.

"Standard ARM is Tested on F-4D, F-105." *Aviation Week & Space Technology* 1969.

Stevens, Rick. "The 'Earth Pig'." *World Air Power Journal* 14 (1993): 42-101.

"Surface-to-Air Missile Site Strike Mission Described by Thunderchief Pilot." *Thunderchief: Worldwide Report on Republic's F-105 Fighter-Bomber* 1.4 (1965): 2-3.

"TAC Completes Service at McConnell AFB." *The Wichita Eagle and Beacon* July 3, 1973.

"The Thud: Republic's Last Fighter." *Air International* 1986.

"U.S. Fighters in Dogfight with New Red-Built MiG-21s." *The Topeka Daily Capital-Journal* April 25, 1966.

"U.S. Planes Bomb Missile Site; F-105 Lost." *The Wichita Eagle* October 10, 1967.

"U.S. Planes Set Sorties Record for North Viet." *The Wichita Eagle* March 9, 1966.

Warren, Jim. "The Bombs Fall First in Kansas." *Midway* August 21, 1966.

"Wichita F-105s Ordered to War." *The Topeka Daily Capital-Journal* April 7, 1972.

"With the Thunderchiefs in Vietnam." *Thunderchief: Worldwide Report on Republic's F-105 Fighter-Bomber* 1.4 (1965): 1.

REPUBLIC
F-105
Thunderchief
DANGER

The U-2 Spyplane - Toward the Unknown: A New History of the Early Years. *Chris Pocock.* The full story of the development and early use of the U-2 has never been properly told – until now. This book describes in vivid detail how the high-flying spyplane was conceived, designed, built, and deployed in record time. Will appeal to students of aviation and intelligence history, and to anyone wishing to learn more about a key episode in the Cold War.
Size: 6" x 9" • over 110 b/w and color photographs, line drawings • 288 pp.
ISBN: 0-7643-1113-1 • hard cover • $29.95

Republic F-84: Thunderjet, Thunderstreak, & Thunderflash - A Photo Chronicle. *David R. McLaren.* The F-84 performed its unheralded role in a true yeoman fashion. It, and its pilots and groundcrews, fought the ait-to-mud role as a fighter bomber in Korea. It served as an interceptor, and in photo reconnaissance. It was the first jet fighter to be operationally capable of air refueling, and it was the first to be able to deliver a nuclear weapon. 4,300 of the straight-wing fighters were built, along with 2,713 of the swept-wing F-84Fs, and 715 of the reconnaissance RF-84Fs.
Size: 8 1/2" x 11" • over 450 b/w and color photos • 208 pp.
ISBN: 0-7643-0444-5 • soft cover • $29.95

Lockheed F-94 Starfire: A Photo Chronicle. *David R. McLaren & Marty Isham.* The first U.S. night/all-weather fighter aircraft is chronicled, as is its use by Air Defense Command, Continental Air Command, Alaska and others.
Size: 8 1/2" x 11" • over 220 b/w and color photos • 128 pp.
ISBN: 0-88740-451-0 • soft cover • $19.95

The 4th Fighter Wing in the Korean War. *Larry Davis.* This book covers the history of the 4th Fighter Wing, from re-activation in 1946, through the end of the "short TDY" to Korea in 1957. Photo coverage includes most of the aces and their aircraft, maintenance, and airfield scenes. A complete list of every victory, and all the losses, is also contained. Interviews with pilots, crew chiefs, and factory tech reps tell the complete story of the "Fourth But First" before, during, and after the Korean War.
Size: 8 1/2"x11" • over 390 color and b/w photos • 200 pp.
ISBN: 0-7643-1315-0 • hard cover • $45.00

Convair F-102 Delta Dagger. *Wayne Mutza.* With vivid detail and many exclusive photographs, Wayne Mutza chronicles the Convair F-102 Delta Dagger's unsteady course through history, from its inception to present-day survivors. Presented for the first time are the fascinating details surrounding the F-102 in the air defense role, special projects, its unconventional use during the war in Southeast Asia, service with foreign air arms, the Air National Guard and its extensive involvement with the drone program. Includes a detailed listing of each aircraft's assignment history and many of the insignia associated with the F-102.
Size: 8 1/2" x 11" • over 530 b/w and color photos • 192 pp. •
ISBN: 0-7643-1062-3 • soft cover • $29.95

Phantom in Combat. *Walter J. Boyne. Phantom in Combat* puts you in the cockpit with the missile-age aces as they fight for their lives in the skies of Vietnam and the Middle East. Leading USAF ace Steve Ritchie speaks more in sorrow than anger of the politically inspired rules that so frustrated him and his comrades in Vietnam. Here is the human face of modern air warfare, described by the commanders and crews who earned for the Phantom its reputation as the world's finest fighting aircraft.
Size: 8 1/2" x 11" • over 300 b/w and color photos • 192 pp.
ISBN: 0-88740-599-1 • hard cover • $35.00

Tomcat! The Grumman F-14 Story. *Paul T. Gillcrist.* Told in an anecdotal format, this new book is richly marbled with the salt air of fleet experience. Perhaps the F-14 program's greatest success is its overwhelming acceptance by the youngsters in the fleet. Anecdotes about the Tomcat legend abound...especially in the chapters devoted to its employment by the fleet in the oceans of the world. This is not a garden variety history about an airplane. It is a sometimes heart-stopping story of how a controversial airplane finally made it into the hearts and minds of the fleet...after stumbling at the starting gates of an outmoded defense acquisition system.
Size: 8 1/2" x 11" • over 150 color & b/w photographs • 208 pp.
ISBN: 0-88740-664-5 • hard cover • $39.95

Convair B-36 Peacemaker: A Photo Chronicle. *Meyers K. Jacobsen.* Explores the history of the Strategic Air Command's biggest bomber that helped keep the peace during the early years of the Cold War. This book will give the reader a concise overview of the story of the Peacemaker in the 1940s-1950s. A serial number listing is included, as well as a list of all ten B-36 bomb wings.
Size: 11" x 8 1/2" • over 130 b/w photographs • 96 pp.
ISBN: 0-7643-0974-9 • soft cover • 9.95

Martin B-57 Canberra: The Complete Record. *Robert C. Mikesh.* No story about one type of aircraft could be more complete than this coverage about the B-57 Canberra. A brief history of its British inception sets the stage for the conversion that took place to American standards for production in the United States. The Canberra was needed to fill the night intruder role in the USAF that was identified during the Korean War and later Vietnam. The B-57 did that, and far more.
Size: 8 1/2" x 11" • over 420 color and b/w photos • 208 pp.
ISBN: 0-88740-661-0 • hard cover • $45.00

North American XB-70 Valkyrie: A Photo Chronicle. *John M. Campbell & Garry R. Pape.* The North American XB-70 is one of the most unusual looking aircraft in aviation history, and only two were constructed. It was originally designed as a Mach 3 high-altitude bomber, but was later used as a research aircraft. This book gives a short, detailed history of the XB-70, including production, flight tests, and the fatal crash of Aircraft #2 in 1965.
Size: 11" x 8 1/4" • 100+ b/w photos and line schemes • 48 pp.
ISBN: 0-88740-906-7 • soft cover • $9.95

81161